HIRED DAUGHTERS

HIRED DAUGHTERS

*Domestic Workers among
Ordinary Moroccans*

Mary Montgomery

INDIANA UNIVERSITY PRESS

This book is a publication of

Indiana University Press
Office of Scholarly Publishing
Herman B Wells Library 350
1320 East 10th Street
Bloomington, Indiana 47405 USA

iupress.indiana.edu

© 2019 by Mary Montgomery

All rights reserved
No part of this book may be reproduced or utilized in any form or by any means, electronic or mechanical, including photocopying and recording, or by any information storage and retrieval system, without permission in writing from the publisher. The paper used in this publication meets the minimum requirements of the American National Standard for Information Sciences—Permanence of Paper for Printed Library Materials, ANSI Z39.48-1992.

Manufactured in the United States of America

Cataloging information is available from the Library of Congress.

ISBN 978-0-253-04100-5 (hdbk.)
ISBN 978-0-253-04101-2 (pbk.)
ISBN 978-0-253-04104-3 (web PDF)

1 2 3 4 5   24 23 22 21 20 19

To Fatima

Domestic work is work. Domestic workers are,
like other workers, entitled to decent work.

ILO CONVENTION 189

These last worked only one hour, and you have made them equal to us
who have borne the burden of the day and the scorching heat.

MATTHEW 20:12

CONTENTS

Dramatis Personae   xi

Preface   xv

Acknowledgments   xxv

Note on Transliteration   xxix

Part I The Social Relations of Domestic Service

  1 A City Quarter and the "Popular" Ideal   3

  2 Mothers and Daughters   33

  3 A Civilizing Mission: Charity, Reward, and Gratitude   59

  4 Serving Neighbors, Serving Strangers: Markets and Marketplaces   90

Part II Domestic Workers in the Wider World

  5 Domestic Workers in the City   121

  6 Domestic Workers at Home   149

  7 Domestic Workers and the Law   176

     Conclusion   202

References Cited   213

Index   237

DRAMATIS PERSONAE

Interlocutors referred to multiple times are listed here. All names and some biographic details have been fictionalized.

The Sebbaris

Mui Latifa	great-grandmother, head of the Sebbari household, widow
Hamza	Latifa's late husband
Jihane	Latifa's daughter, unmarried, lives with Latifa
Raja	Latifa's daughter, married, lives elsewhere in l'Océan
Salima	Latifa's daughter, married, lives in Casablanca
Nadia	Latifa's daughter, married, lives in the Sebbari building
Zahra	Nadia's daughter
Ḥajja Jamila	Latifa's oldest neighbor, lives in the Sebbari building

Workers Connected with the Sebbaris

Imane	former domestic of house across the street
Khadija Hinde	brought up and married off by Latifa
Najat Rachida	
Mui Fatiha	Rachida's mother-in-law, herself a domestic worker
Wi'am	brought up by Latifa's sister
Loubna	stayed with Latifa as teenager, returned to work briefly at Nadia's
Soraya	worked during her summer holiday for Latifa, fourteen years old
Badia	worked briefly for Latifa, married with children
Mina	worked briefly at Latifa's and Nadia's
Huriya	worked at Nadia's
Malika	worked briefly at Nadia's
Ikram	Malika's younger sister, worked briefly for Nadia's sister Salima
Hanane	former long-term worker at Nadia's, left to marry

xi

xii | *Dramatis Personae*

Other Employers

Touria	my host mother in l'Océan, retired teacher, formerly/occasionally employed Salma and Mbarka
Hassan	my host father
Bouchra	L'Océan resident
Souad	L'Océan resident
Nejlae	L'Océan resident
Asmae	nurse and activist, *medīna* resident
Hayat	government office employee, employed Rahma, then Zineb, in city center
L-Ḥajja	employed Hafida, city center

Workers Living in l'Océan

Fatima	lives out, married, my "agony aunt"
Salma	once worked for Touria, married with children
Mbarka	Salma's mother-in-law

Women from Ba Karim and Awlad Ahmed Villages (Gharb Region)

Miriam	worked briefly in l'Océan
Safae	Miriam's younger sister
Hafida	Miriam's older friend, divorced
Aziza	Hafida's younger sister
Dawiya	Hafida's brother's wife, not working
Ilham	Hafida's friend
Rouqia	Ilham's friend and relative
Nawar	Hafida's paternal cousin, divorced
Yousra	Nawar's sister, no longer working
Hala	Hafida's maternal cousin, not working

Other Workers

Zineb	met at *mūqef* (labour market), worked at Hayat's, lives out in l'Océan
Sharifa	Zineb's sister
Hakima	young woman at mūqef
Nabila	older woman at mūqef
Nafisa	neighbor who interfered at the mūqef

Brokers and Agents

Mehdi	office in l'Océan, closed down
Naima	office in l'Océan
Fouzia	office in Salé
Soumiya	office in center of Rabat
Warda	*samsāra* in suburb of Rabat

PREFACE

"But no Moroccan women work as domestics anymore!" A preeminent Moroccan sociologist was trying to persuade me to drop my "ridiculous" idea of an ethnographic study of domestic service in Rabat when who should walk into her living room with the tea but a plainly Moroccan domestic? The sociologist did not introduce this woman, who, after depositing her tray, disappeared once more into a back region of the apartment. I was surprised that my host enthused about the phenomenon of Filipina domestics, employed by relatively few elite Moroccans, as a worthy subject of study but was uninterested in matters of class among her own compatriots and under her own roof. It is hoped that this book demonstrates that what goes on between women locally does matter, in Morocco and elsewhere.

Denial seems an appropriate word. The elite feel that "progress" has been made; their friends run "projects" for poor women somewhere, so why would anyone have to work as a domestic nowadays? It was perhaps a similar blind optimism that prompted American sociologist Lewis Coser to predict that servants would soon be obsolete. That was in 1973, and domestic workers are still not out of work. Many women in Morocco are indeed working as domestics today, and not only in wealthy households but also among ordinary folk of modest means, those known locally as sha'bī Moroccans. It is now commonplace to argue that service does not die but simply takes another form (*The Economist* 2011, 80). The present ethnography captures a moment at which, not for the first time, service among ordinary Moroccans is changing. The new form of interest here is not (as the Moroccan sociologist would have it) that local women are leaving this insalubrious work to transnational migrants but instead a subtler shift with a deeper history. Domestic work, once performed by kin, neighbors, or the children of clients brought up charitably as "daughters of the house" until marriage, is increasingly done by easy-come-easy-go strangers who are paid a wage.

Of course change in domestic work is not wholesale; older forms of service exist alongside emerging forms, just as slavery existed alongside free labor. "A fine set of gradations marked the continuum running from one to the other," argued Mohammed Ennaji, writing on nineteenth-century

Morocco (1999, 89). Elsewhere slavery has been described as "a combination of elements, which if differently combined—an ingredient added here or subtracted there—might become adoption, marriage, parentage, obligations to kinsmen, clientship, and so forth" (Miers and Kopytoff 1977, 66).[1] In Morocco these coexisting "spheres of exchange" (Piot 1991) forge and maintain different kinds of relationships, reflecting, among other things, the varying importance of connectedness and how open people are to strangers. But the issue is more complicated and challenges the assumptions of narratives of modernity and gendered inequality. While employers pay domestics, they still invoke the language of kinship so that a paradox emerges: workers are hired to be daughters. Traditional ways of talking about domestics as "daughters of the house" are applied to quite different persons, like pasting an old label on a jar of newly made jam.

There are plenty of labels for domestic workers. *Kheddāma* is a feminine active participle and simply means "worker" but, unqualified, always refers to a domestic (just as *khādim/a* in standard Arabic means "servant"). *Sekhkhāra*, from the verb *sekhkher*, "to run errands," functions in the same way but is more pejorative and conjures up the hurried steps of a child who will be in trouble if she does not do the job quickly. The French term for maid, *bonne* (or *petite bonne* in the case of a minor), is commonly used in Morocco, thrown into otherwise Arabic sentences by women whose ease with the language of the protectorate reflects a certain level of education. Meanwhile, official discourse has moved from *bonne* to *domestique* and now alternates between the more politically correct (for the time being) terms *employée de maison, travailleuse domestique*, and *travailleuse de maison* or, in standard Arabic, *musā'ida manzilīya* (literally "house helper"). But a rose by other names does not in fact smell as sweet; many *mulīn d-diyūr* (household heads) insist that their domestics are not *kheddāmāt* or any of these other things but their "daughters." Relations of kinship, which imply sharing "without reckoning" (Fortes [1969] 2004) over the long term, are used to describe arrangements where a wage is indeed "reckoned," on the basis of work done in a shorter time frame.

I unpack the "one of the family" rhetoric by asking not only why it is so irreplaceable but also what it means to be a daughter in Morocco in the first place. Notions of daughters as recipients of care as well as givers of service play into expectations from both sides and explain an emphasis on payment in kind as a sign of care. "Maternalism" (Katzman 1978) and its attendant "gift giving" are well-documented features of domestic service around the world, but in Morocco this trait owes its particular flavor to the Islamic ethics of charity and religious merit as well as the legacy of the colonial *mission civilisatrice*, through which country girls who "don't know how to brush their hair" are transformed by the lady of the house (*mulat d-dār*) into "human beings." Living with a Moroccan family, I too was embedded in a civilizing narrative. My host mother would proudly tell visitors, "When she came to me, she did not even know how to peel a tomato!" I resisted the temptation to add that I did not know a tomato *needed* to be peeled. In this context, the untimely departures of domestic workers who are accused of "following the money" are seen as marks of ingratitude, a poor return for the motherly attention shown them.

Many hired daughters are children as young as seven or eight years old, and this despite the Moroccan government's ratification in 1993 of the International Labour Organization's (ILO) convention on the Rights of the Child.[2] The working and living conditions of child domestics vary, but arrangements are often thought to be beneficial to rural girls, removing them from the poverty of their families and the harsh realities of life in the countryside. In recent years the press and human rights groups have highlighted the exploitation and abuse of children placed by brokers with strangers who prevent them from attending school and rob them of their childhood. While abuse is a real and tragic problem, Western notions of childhood overlook the fact that the labor of girls in urban households forms a continuation of life in the village, where all children work from a young age and school is an unlikely undertaking (Crawford 2010a, 142).[3] Most writing on domestic service in Morocco centers on these child domestics while less attention has been paid to adult workers who are often treated like children. These women, many of whom began work as girls, are the focus of this book, along with the women who employ them. When seen from both sides, their labor relations emerge not as those of violator over victim but as a struggle between women who seek divergent rewards—rewards that go beyond a clean apartment and some money to save or spend.

The present study documents the persistence of this moral economy even as domestic labor is increasingly commoditized, with households looking to the market for what community no longer provides. Community, to use Gudeman's terms, refers to "real, on-the-ground associations and to imagined solidarities that people experience" while market "designates anonymous short-term exchanges" (2001, 1). This reflects shifts in the way rich and poor, city and country are connected to each other. The city thrives on the cheap labor of rural Moroccans while migrants' families could not maintain their village lifestyles without remittances from the city. As Hafida, a domestic from the Gharb plain, explained, "We are just working in order to help ourselves and our household. The countryside is hard.... No, there's nothing there. If you don't bring something into it, you won't have anything."

Crawford (2008), who deals with the relationship of a Berber village to the global economy, and to whom, it will be seen, this book owes a great deal, calls these households "articulated": they have one foot in the countryside, the other in the city. What is changing is that the hinge points between the two worlds are becoming impersonal and atomized: workers move from one urban employer to another, and employers clutch at straws to hire someone they can trust. These ruptures go against the grain of a traditional, popular (shaʿbī) ideal, held by ordinary Moroccans, that privileges acquaintance. Ordinary Moroccans emphasize their reluctance to rely on marketplaces to source domestic labor; these are for people who lack contacts. Intermediaries, brokers, and day-labor markets are nonetheless a necessary part of domestic service, and their use points to the tensions and contradictions of a cultural ideal that relies on openhandedness and connection in the finitely resourced and private domestic domain.

Rural women ostensibly migrate to earn cash, often used to pay for the construction of a breeze block house in place of their family's adobe dwelling in the village, but the bright lights of the city have their lure here as elsewhere, making domestic service an attractive option despite low wages. There is also the desire to get away from a demanding mother and whining younger siblings. As a general servant in 1930s Britain recalled, "Before I left home I was at everyone's beck and call; 'do this, go there, do that, look after him'—you can imagine. I never had a life of me own.... When I got into service, I know you were restricted then, but you still hadn't got the kids around you and your mother" (Mullins and Griffiths 1986, 4). A life of one's own has been, since Woolf (1929) at least, a major objective of Western feminism; however, little is understood about how marriage, often viewed as a prefeminist issue, plays a major part in aspirations of autonomy. Marriage is the only obvious way for Moroccan domestic workers to set up their own homes. But with the disintegration of ties of loyalty and obligation comes the loss of the enduring protective relations that characterized the patron-"daughter" relationship, and workers now feel the job of finding a husband falls into their own hands. This is something for which many employers, including "modern women" who would in theory support freedom of choice in selecting a marriage partner, fail to allow their workers time.

The position of women became vital in the construction of "modern" identity in postcolonial Morocco, and Newcomb observes that "it sometimes seems that those concerned with defining Moroccan identity are obsessed with women: where they are, how they occupy space" (2009, 9–10).[4] Access to work is often used as a measure in global comparisons of women's status (Moghadam 1993, 29), and the high demand for domestics among ordinary Moroccans is attributed to the education of housewives who begin to be active outside the home (Kapchan 1996, 220; Ennaji and Sadiqi 2008, 75). But one woman's liberation from domesticity is facilitated by another woman's lack of options. Makdisi, a lecturer who employed a "housekeeper" in Lebanon in the 1970s, admits that this undermines the idea that a woman's entry into the labor market is a sign of her liberation from domesticity: "having help at home was made possible by the class divisions with which I felt deeply uncomfortable" (1999, 51). In Morocco, Nelly Forget listed various professions open to women in urban settings—"modern" (secretary, teacher, factory worker); "traditional" (embroideress, ḥammām[5] attendant, water carrier); and "ambivalent" (tradeswoman, entertainer, domestic)—and asked both women and men, "Is it good or bad for a woman to have this occupation?" (1962, 98–9). Domestic workers fell into the category of "widely disapproved of" (103), the potential for promiscuity being cited as a primary concern (105).[6] Those who did this kind of work explained that they were pushed into it by poverty. The status of domestic work is much the same today.

That domestic service everywhere brings together two women of different statuses is something mainstream feminism, always tunneling along lines of gender, does not address. While rank among men has been the subject of much ethnography, literature on female hierarchy within the moral unit of the household remains sparse. One exception is Belarbi's (1988) comparative study of Moroccan women, which showed that while those with high-level jobs were able to relax after work, those with intermediate-level jobs had relatives as household help whom they felt obliged to assist. These lower-middle-class employers have, in the face of screaming inequalities, been promoting a popular rhetoric that "we are all the same," but this now meets a new line of thought from international human rights discourse that attempts to equate domestic workers with all other kinds of workers. Extending rights such as time off and a minimum wage to domestics, together with increasing access for girls and women to education and employment, threatens to wreak havoc on the flimsy boundaries that distinguish one ordinary Moroccan woman from the next and the middle-class women who have for a little while now been enjoying some of these rights start to sound like the workers in the parabolic vineyard. Because this exchange between households rests on hierarchy within them, legal reform, which seeks to make atomized individuals equal, seems ill-equipped to mediate between those who share a living space or to determine who should do what about a dirty floor or a kitchen sink piled with dishes. At the same time, the price of "rights" means transparency to the state and with it the erosion of local forms of empowerment. This is salient wherever state intervention is gaining ground. Exploring this problem, the present study is more than a portrayal of Moroccan society through the lens of its serving class; it offers a way to think about the intersection of households with the wider world.

Writing on domestic workers worldwide can be divided into three roughly successive bodies of literature. First, researchers studied rural-urban migrants in developing countries, predominantly in Latin America, where peasant women migrate to serve urbanites.[7] Since the 1980s, study in other developing countries has continued, focusing on class and rural-urban differences between employer and domestic.[8] In the meantime, largely feminist researchers turned attention to "women of color" serving "whites" in South Africa (Whisson and Weil 1971; Cock 1980; Gaitskell et al. 1984) and the United States (Rollins 1985; Colen 1989; Palmer 1989; Romero 1992; Dill 1994), and they emphasized domestics' subordination on the triple axis of gender, class, and race. Most recently, researchers have examined domestics in an international labor market: migrants from the "poorer" global south to the "richer" north. Studies of Filipina and Indonesian migrants dominate (Constable 1997, 2003; Cheng 2003, 2004; Parreñas 2001, 2008; Ueno 2010). Others focus on migrant domestics in countries such as Taiwan (Lan 2003, 2006), Singapore (Huang and Yeoh 1998, 2000), Malaysia (Chin 1998), Britain (Cox 2006), Italy (Andall 2000), Canada (Bakan and Stasiulis 1997), and the United States (Hondagneu-Sotelo 2007).[9] In these studies race and gender are foregrounded, but the notion of class is problematic; there is often a contradiction for migrants between declining social status and improved economic status.[10]

Since most domestics in Morocco, unlike their counterparts in the Levant and the Persian Gulf, do not hail from another country but are themselves Moroccans, the present study revisits earlier research, drawing in particular on the rich historical work on European domestic service. The problem of status differentials in the home, discussed in household manuals, is also played out in fiction and theater, and these, as much as historical accounts, serve as reference points. In early twentieth-century Britain, for example, the lack of free time in service sent domestics in WWI running to work in munitions, which, though unhealthy and poorly paid, offered considerably greater freedom and was preferable to being at the beck and call of the lady of the house, who had a tendency to be morally overbearing.[11] For, as Mrs. Beeton advises in her *Book of Household Management*, "A lady should never allow herself to forget the important duty of watching over the moral and physical welfare of those beneath her roof. Without seeming unduly inquisitive she can always learn something of their acquaintances and holiday occupation, and should, when necessary, warn them against the dangers and evils of bad company" [(1861) 1907, 15].

Cranford's Miss Matty anticipated such advice by forbidding her maid to have "followers" (Gaskell [1851] 1977), but remember how the tables turned when the maid's eventual marriage provided a home not only for the young couple but also for the financially ruined Miss Matty. That single women everywhere, particularly poor ones, are to be incorporated into the households of others seems as much a moral as a financial imperative. In the Moroccan shaʻbī world, these concerns translate into the predominance of live-in arrangements as well as domestics not generally being allowed to spend their leisure time out and about unaccompanied.

This kind of intertextuality, which threads its way through the following chapters, does not imply that Morocco is behind Europe in a unilineal march to civilization but rather that these patterns persist into the present day in Europe and elsewhere. If readers find the intractability of Moroccan domestic service surprisingly familiar, this tells us something about ourselves that is potentially universal and speaks to growing concerns about new forms of servitude in the peer-to-peer exchange of the gig economy. More and more people in Britain are hiring cleaners and nannies (Churchill Home Insurers 2011), and the on-demand economy for domestic work is growing rapidly in both developed and developing countries (Hunt and Machingura 2016). Although these trends are observable in statistics, much of the sector is invisible. Au pairs, for instance, need not be registered as workers unless they receive above a certain amount of pocket money (UK Government 2014), and in Morocco no statistics whatsoever exist for numbers of domestic workers.

But invisibility is also a feature on the ground, as the opening vignette demonstrated. Moroccan women I visited at home would point to the floor or ceiling, insisting their neighbors in the apartments above or below either did or did not have domestics. Sometimes a knock on the door revealed the opposite to be true, but more often the door remained shut, and the presence of a worker behind it could be neither confirmed nor denied. While some people claimed "everyone here has a domestic," others would wave a hand over the same part of town, saying the habit of employing servants had long since fallen by the wayside. How, then, do you find out what is really happening inside people's homes? Ehrenreich's account of low-wage America was made possible by her taking a job as a cleaner, and the detail she describes of a world where one woman cleans the floor as another watches does not come across in statistics, only in ethnography:

> So here I am on my knees, working my way around the room like some fanatical penitent crawling through the stations of the cross, when I realize that Mrs. W. is staring at me fixedly—so fixedly that I am gripped for a moment by the wild possibility that I may have once given a lecture at her alma mater.... If I were recognized, would I be fired? Would she at least be inspired to offer me a drink of water? ... Not to worry, though. She's just watching that I don't leave out some stray square inch, and when I rise painfully to my feet again, blinking through the sweat, she says, "Could you just scrub the floor in the entryway while you're at it?" (2010, 84–85).

Although I was unable to persuade anyone in Morocco to hire me to scrub their floor, I spent time unofficially working (and not working) alongside domestics in a number of households. For twelve months, starting in June 2012, I based myself in Rabat, eventually accompanying workers back and forth on visits to their home villages; I followed up with a three-month return visit in the summer of 2016. In 2012, I chanced initially to rent an apartment from the Sebbari family, who drew me into their lives, often joking that I needed go no further to study domestic service: "It's all here!" Their network was a crisscrossing of old and new kinds of domestics, offering a close-up view of changing, overlapping, and conflicting practices. I had to work harder to make contacts outside, chatting with people in the street and at small grocery shops and knocking on doors, which led to a three-month home stay and a friendship with a network of domestics from two neighboring villages in the Gharb region. In the mornings, when I could not politely visit people at home (with the exception of the Sebbaris and, later, my host family), I often sat on the pavement with domestics at the day-labor market. Many women there were mature, lending a diachronic perspective that younger workers could less easily offer. While some contacts at the labor market brought me back full circle to the Sebbaris, others flung me further afield, for example to the apartment of a government employee who moved in quite a different sphere. Hayat wanted me to teach her children English at home, affording me the possibility both to regularly see my domestic worker friend Zineb in her workplace and to be a listening ear to Hayat's angst about her relationship with the working class.

As the white protagonist of *The Help* (Stockett 2010) found when collecting the life stories of her friends' black domestics in America's Deep South, loyalties were sometimes conflicting. Because my education and foreign identity meant employers expected me to spend time with them, I had to be tactful gaining access to the domestics' realm, namely the kitchen, for which my love of washing dishes proved a good excuse. While some researchers have avoided contact with both domestics and their employers, the messiness of human life rarely serves us up people on their own, and employers and workers in particular usually come in pairs. Cold-shouldering one while mining the other for material seemed as unethical an approach as any other, not to mention antisocial. Nor could I stop people from telling me what they wanted to tell me. While I did not relay to each what the other had said, I frequently offloaded to an older domestic worker, Fatima, who became a close friend and kind of agony aunt and gives voice to her feelings about many a situation in the following pages.

The book is divided into two parts. Part 1 is concerned with the social relations of domestic service, the nitty-gritty of getting someone to do your housework, as well as the underlying forces that drive the circulation of women from house to house. Part 2 locates domestic workers in the wider world of city, village, and nation. Chapter 1 describes l'Océan, the former Spanish quarter where I based myself, and the popular (shaʿbī) ideal that animates it as a neighborhood and influences the way residents think about whom they should be employing and how. I sketch a shaʿbī household, the Sebbaris, and the housework done there daily. The Sebbaris become life-size in chapter 2, where anthropological perspectives on kinship inform an analysis of domestic service as a kind of fosterage. Workers who were "brought up" by the Sebbaris until they were married contrast with workers of the next generation, who do not stay long.

Chapter 3 explores the moral economy to explain why it matters to people that domestics are "daughters," not workers, and why aspirations to pious care persist. The book's movement from the home to the outside world hinges around chapter 4, which looks at the relational aspect of different modes of recruitment to explore the intersection of the household with market economies and the alleged shift in domestic service from community to market-based exchange.

In part 2 we find ourselves beyond the confines of the domestic space. The question of whether commoditized labor goes hand in hand with greater individualization is addressed in chapter 5, which deals with the consumer practices and marriage aspirations of domestic workers through the lens of their activities on days off. Chapter 6 takes us out to the countryside, where workers are seen as members not of their employing families but of their birth families, and sheds light on what being a daughter means there as well as on rationales for labor migration and the impact of return. Chapter 7 sets up as oppositions the popular preference for personalized connectedness and the modern state's emphasis on regulatory legal codes to enforce the moral equality of individuals. The book concludes by revisiting timeworn anthropological themes of household, kinship, and gender.

Notes

1. I leave others to pursue this area of study. See, for example, Hamel (2013).
2. This prohibits the employment of children in work that is dangerous or will harm their development or interrupt their education.
3. On child domestics in Morocco, see also Pelham 2000; Sommerfelt 2001; Lahlou (n.d.). Child domestics have inspired works of fiction such as Bougdal's *La petite bonne de Casablanca* (2010) and Fihri's historical *Dada l'yakout* (2010), neither of which makes for comfortable reading.
4. Cf. Charrad (2001); Combs-Schilling (1999).
5. Public bathhouse.
6. Forget placed domestics in the ambivalent category because "in Moroccan households [the domestic] is integrated with the family, with all the advantages and restrictions flowing from this state of semi-adoption" (1962, 99). Davis (1978) similarly analyzes women's work in a Moroccan village, assessing women's income-generating options according to the increase or decrease in status they accord. Cf. Nieuwkerk (1995) on attitudes toward female entertainers in Egypt who have a status close to that of domestic workers.
7. See, for example, Nett (1966); Smith, M. (1973); Jelin (1977); Rubbo and Taussig (1983).
8. Including, for example, India (Tellis-Nayak 1983, Ray and Qayum 2009), Zambia (Hansen 1986), Bolivia (Gill 1994), Tanzania (Bujra 2000), Nepal (S. Shah 2000) and China (Yan 2008).
9. See also comparative studies such as Anderson, B. (2000) and Chang (2000).
10. See Parreñas (2001, 150) on the "contradictory mobility" of Filipina domestics.
11. By the middle of the war, around 750,000 women were employed in British munitions (Storey and Housego 2011, 38).

ACKNOWLEDGMENTS

Very great thanks are due to my Moroccan friends and hosts for their trust, hospitality, and willingness to engage in the research that resulted in this book. It is dedicated to Fatima, whose story, told among the pots and pans of her employers' kitchen over a decade ago, planted the seed from which the whole project grew. I am also much indebted to the El-Louisa family, whose house in Marrakech has long been a home away from home for me, and especially to Amal for teaching me Moroccan Arabic.

The book owes a great deal to my parents—and this on top of a personal debt: thank you for patiently reading multiple application forms, book proposals, and chapter drafts and for relentlessly encouraging me through every step of the process. Thank you for the many hours spent listening and praying over Skype and in person and for taking us children on holiday to Morocco all those years ago.

My anthropological heritage comes from Paul Dresch, whom I count it an immense privilege to know. I am so grateful for his thorough supervision, careful reading of drafts, and ability to get to the heart of the matter through my many words. My thanks also go to Judith Scheele for discussing ideas, reading my work, and inspiring me to study anthropology in the first place. Walter Armbrust had a hand in this too, and I still refer to his excellent reading list on the society and culture of the Middle East.

Writing can be a lonely business, but this was not my experience. I would like to thank the Magdalen College librarians for brightening my days and tirelessly ordering obscure books and Garance Auboyneau for her friendship and sense of humor in and out of the library. My thanks also go to Imogen Clark and other fellow students at ISCA for their solidarity and frank discussions, to Ammara Maqsood for treading the path ahead of me and passing on her wisdom, and to Ellie Reeve for the honest lunchtime conversations. I could not have weathered the ups and downs of academic life without steadfast friends like these.

"The field" is notoriously an even more solitary place than the library, but I am grateful that I did not find myself alone. Big thank-yous go to the Wallis family for welcoming me to Rabat and including me in their lives and to May Ngo, Eva Jakob, Eun-Jung An, and Caroline Kirby for their companionship and sharing of experiences in the field. I am equally grateful to my sister, Sarah, who visited me with a suitcase full of muesli and the rest of the time dispensed care and advice remotely, and to my brother Stephen, whose arrival on the scene turned a visa trip to Spain into a proper holiday. Stephen also edited my photos—thank you!

Thanks to Wafa for kindly helping me understand the legal texts, to Najat Sedki for clarifying some important details after I left the field, and to Suriyah Bi for making pertinent suggestions for reading. Alison Shaw and Zuzanna Olszewska read and commented helpfully on portions of my thesis, as did Morgan Clarke, Bob Parkin, and Judith Scheele for a paper written in preparation for the field. I am also grateful for the detailed attention Elizabeth Ewart and Carolyn Steedman paid to examining my thesis and for their suggestions for publication. At a later stage I learned a lot from Andrew Shryock's generous engagement with my work. Ideas suggested by anonymous reviewers of a journal article, as yet unpublished, have also found their way into this book.

I would like to thank my colleagues and students at the London School of Economics for being a memorable part of my anthropology story and for encouraging and inspiring me while I worked on this project. Particular thanks go to Catherine Allerton and Katy Gardner, who mentored me, and to Rita Astuti, whose office, alive with foliage, provided a peaceful writing space during my two years there. Alice Tilche, Ryan Davey, Anni Kajanus, and Geoffrey Hughes read portions of my work and helped shape ideas for the book.

I am very grateful to the two anonymous reviewers who read my manuscript and whose insightful comments and suggestions gave me renewed energy, drew out many interesting connections I had missed, and helped make the book more readable. I worked on these revisions during a summer at the University of Helsinki, and I am grateful to Phaedra Douzina-Bakalaki, Carl Rommel, Suvi Rautio, and Sarah Green for their support during that time.

The Senior Mackinnon Scholarship from Magdalen College funded the three years of doctoral research on which this book is based as well as my MSc, during which I began to read around the topic of domestic service. The Anthropology Department at the London School of Economics financially supported my three-month return visit to the field in the summer of 2016. The Centre Jacques Berque provided a workspace in Rabat and connected me with other researchers.

Beyond particular times and places, a number of incredible people gave me courage and much-needed perspective while I worked on the book: Frith Ellingham, Pip King, Trish Sullivan, Lois Fulton, Grace Le, Sarah Ong, Fiona Gliddon, Ollie Ogunlade, Sarah German, my brother Peter, "the other" Mary Montgomery, Lauren and James Melachrino, and Steve and Viv Bateman—thank you.

Finally, my sincere thanks go to Jennika Baines, Kate Schramm, David Miller, Julia Turner, and everyone at Indiana University Press who helped make this book a reality.

M. M.

NOTE ON TRANSLITERATION

There is no academic consensus on the way to transliterate Moroccan Arabic, locally termed *dārija*. I therefore follow the system used in the *Encyclopedia of Islam*, with some modifications. Consonantal pairs (e.g., <u>kh</u>, <u>sh</u>, <u>gh</u>) are underlined to clarify that each represents a single letter in Arabic (خ, ش, غ). Instead of capitalizing the emphatic letters ص, ض, ط and the aspirated ح, a subscript dot is used: ṣ, ḍ, ṭ, ḥ. The letter ع is represented with a superscript c (ʿ) and ء with an apostrophe (ʾ).

It should be noted that Moroccan Arabic confounds some of the consonants of standard Arabic, often using, for example, a hard *g* sound in place of *q*, so *qāl* (he said) is pronounced *gāl*, and *t* in place of <u>th</u> (*tiqa* instead of <u>th</u>*iqa*, trust). Variation exists across regions, but transliterations here reflect most common speech patterns in northwest Morocco. The transcription system for consonants is summarized in table 0.1.

As is conventional for Standard Arabic, short vowels are represented with the letters *a*, *i*, and *u* while long vowels have a macron: *ā*, *ī*, *ū*. A distinctive feature of Moroccan Arabic is, however, the collapse of short vowels and the shortening of long vowels, again with regional variation. These are therefore omitted or shortened in transliteration, reflecting speech in the fieldwork setting. When *a* is even shorter than in Standard Arabic, it is represented by *e*. The definite article is shortened to *l*, so *al-kitāb* (the book) becomes *l-kitāb* and, in the case of "sun letters" (which assimilate the *l*), is represented by the repetition of the initial consonant, as in *d-dār* (the house). Where this occurs at the beginning of a transliterated expression, it is omitted for simplification—for example, *s-salām ʿalikum* is rendered *salām ʿalikum*.

Place names, the fictionalized names of people, and Arabic words used frequently in English follow the most common spelling and are capitalized according to English conventions. Plurals are given only where relevant. Unless noted otherwise, translations from Arabic and French are mine. Translations of passages from the Qurʾān are based on Malik (2013).

Note on Transliteration

Table 0.1: Transcription system for Moroccan Arabic consonants

ب	ت	ث	ج	ح	خ	د	ذ	ر	ز	س	ش	ص	ض
b	t	th/t	j	ḥ	kh	d	dh	r	z	s	sh	ṣ	ḍ

ط	ظ	ع	غ	ف	ق	ك	ل	م	ن	ه	و	ي	ء
ṭ	ẓ	ʿ	gh	f	q/g	k	l	m	n	h	w	y	ʾ

HIRED DAUGHTERS

PART I
THE SOCIAL RELATIONS OF DOMESTIC SERVICE

1

A CITY QUARTER AND THE "POPULAR" IDEAL

"The first thing people ask when you visit them in Rabat is, 'When are you leaving?'" This was said by a Moroccan from a town six hours' drive south of Rabat, Ouarzazate, where the stereotype is that people in the capital are so busy making ends meet that they have little time for hospitality. Rabat's identity as an administrative city makes for a work-oriented way of life, supposedly different from that of Marrakech or Fes. If cuisine is any indication of the time people have, the processing of cucumbers and tomatoes for the most basic Moroccan salad is illustrative: chopped very finely in Marrakech, they are left chunky in Rabat. A *Ribāṭī*'s time is dear.[1]

This suggests one would find a demand for cheap labor to help maintain standards of domesticity in the homes of busy, double-income families. But space is also dear in Rabat. High real estate prices mean homes are smaller than those of people with similar incomes elsewhere in Morocco—a limiting factor in the employment of live-in domestic workers if not of casual help. A mother of two who had grown up with a live-in domestic in a large house in Casablanca thus swept her hand around her Rabat apartment, saying, "I'm sorry, but if I want to employ [*jīb*, literally bring] a worker, where is she going to sleep? There's my room, there's the children's room, there's the salon. I'm not the kind who makes them sleep in the kitchen." Accommodating a domestic worker in the kitchen was not uncommon in less wealthy families in the past (Khelladi 1938, 266), and some workers I met had memories of struggling to sleep with the noise of the refrigerator. Even today, proximity to the kitchen is deemed appropriate, and modern apartments in the affluent Hay Riad area have small *chambres de bonne* (maids' rooms) off the kitchen.[2]

But compared with a large Hay Riad property, much less labor is needed to keep one of *quartier de l'Océan*'s typically small apartments clean. Indeed, some women affirmed that their homes were so small there was little to do. Nonetheless, other families employed live-in domestic workers despite lack of room, indicating that to have a <u>kh</u>eddāma (paid worker or servant) outweighed for them the inconvenience of an extra body in a small house. My fieldwork took me to this kind of employer: hardworking lower-middle-class families living in small apartments with domestics whom they called their daughters. While government statistics are unavailable and numbers are difficult to establish without access to every home, about one in ten households on my street had a live-in worker; many more had casual help.

In this chapter I describe the neighborhood of l'Océan, where I based myself for fieldwork, outlining the historical background and examining the implications of l'Océan's demography. The chapter concludes with an introduction to the Océani branch of the Sebbari family (a fictionalized patronym) who constitute a case study, to be developed more fully in later chapters, of fairly ordinary Moroccans learning on the job what it means to employ paid workers.[3]

Le Quartier de L'Océan

Rabat's quartier de l'Océan (Arabic *ḥay l-muḥīṭ*) lies, as its name suggests, next to the Atlantic.[4] At its northeastern end the quarter's spread is curbed by a cemetery and the *medīna* (the old, walled city) from Bab l-'Alu to Bab l-Hed. To the southeast, the main road from Bab l-Hed, along which the brand-new tram runs, marks l'Océan's boundary with the neighboring quarter of Diour Jamaa, while the *cité universitaire* and the disused military hospital separate it from the Akkari quarter to the southwest.

L'Océan's streets are named after cities and countries around the world: rue Tokyo, rue Canada, and so on. At some point after independence in 1956, street names like rue Emile Zola and rue Lamartine were replaced along these lines, as if to rid the quarter of the memory of a bookish French presence. But l'Océan had never been particularly French. At its heart, the white building of the Spanish San José church, now the Complexe Culturel Mehdi Ben Barka but still colloquially known as "the church," serves as a reminder of l'Océan's original inhabitants, who were largely manual workers, many of whom came from Cadiz and Malaga during the protectorate period—1912 to 1956 (Findlay, Findlay, and Paddison 1984, 42). Smaller numbers came from Italy and Gibraltar (J. Abu-Lughod 1980, 172). As well as the church

A City Quarter and the "Popular" Ideal | 5

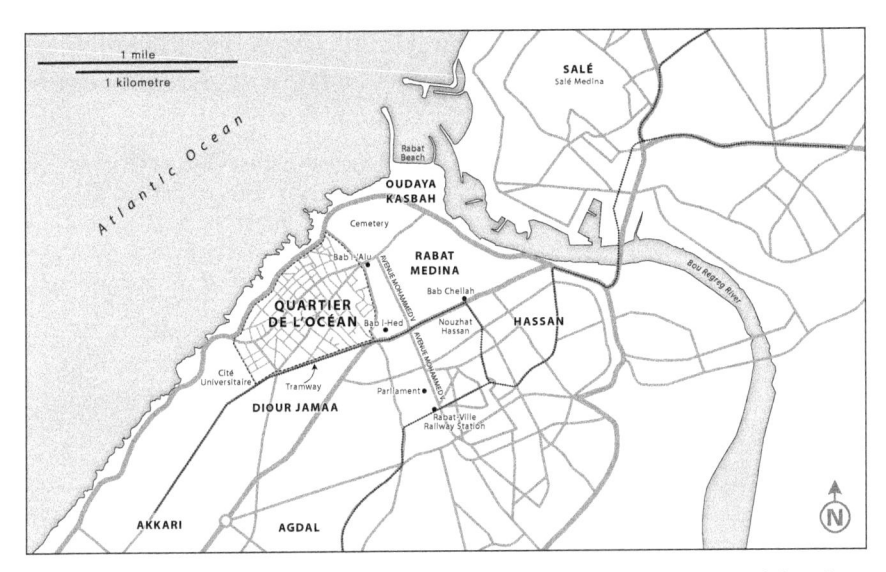

Fig. 1.1 Map of Rabat showing the Quartier de l'Océan. Cartography by Martin Lubikowski.

and a Catholic mission, there was a Spanish school near rue Leningrad, a basketball team at the Joso stadium, and Saturday evening entertainment at the Casa de España on rue Dakar. One resident recalls a certain Señora Escobar's ice cream shop, which "brought the whole of Rabat together . . . her *horchata* was unequalled."⁵ I was told that the Spanish came to Rabat to escape Franco's regime. Whether for economic or political reasons, their community became well established.

This ghettoization of l'Océan was not unique in protectorate Rabat. The city was and still is characterized by sharp demographic contrasts between different quarters—a textbook example of colonial town planning; indeed, French North Africa is widely used as such (Eickelman 1981; Findlay, Findlay, and Paddison 1984; Studer 2014). Rabat was recommended as the administrative center of the French protectorate in Morocco by Maréchal Lyautey, who governed Morocco from the protectorate's establishment in 1912 until 1925. He argued that to remain in Fes, where the Moroccan government (the *makhzen*) was, would "slow and impede any administrative action" (Lyautey 1953, 147–48, cited in Abu-Lughod, J. 1980, 139).

Throughout the country Lyautey was keen, in the fashion of a museum curator, to "conserve" existing Moroccan architecture and ways of life while planning European-style cities to accommodate the colonial enterprise. These *villes nouvelles* (new cities), he argued, should be outside the

Moroccan cities because, drawing on what he saw as the failure of town planning in Algeria, the styles of European and native homes and ways of life were incompatible:

> You know how jealous the Muslim is of the integrity of his private life; you are familiar with the narrow streets, the facades without opening behind which hides the whole of life, the terraces upon which the life of the family spreads out and which must therefore remain sheltered from indiscreet looks. But the European house, with its superimposed stories, the modern skyscraper which reaches ever higher, is the death of the terrace.... Little by little, the European city chases the native out; but without thereby achieving the conditions indispensable to our modern life.... In the end it is always necessary [for the European] *to leave the indigenous town* and, in haste, create new quarters (Lyautey 1927, 452, translated in J. Abu-Lughod 1980, 143, emphasis hers).

Besides aesthetic and cultural considerations, separation of the European and Moroccan communities was intended to prevent conflict and to make control of Moroccans more straightforward. Lyautey's chief of municipalities, de la Casinière, argued that this scheme "avoided direct contact of the European population with the indigenous elements of the lower class, whose physiological misery and filthiness would be important factors in the spread of epidemics" (Casinière 1924, 88, cited in J. Abu-Lughod 1980, 144).

Preprotectorate Rabat consisted of the medīna and the Oudaya Kasbah—a fortified citadel built by the Almohads in the twelfth century.[6] The European ville nouvelle appended to the existing city was designed by Henri Prost, who allocated all the land surrounding Rabat's medīna, an area ten times larger than the medīna itself, to accommodate a European population that would never account for more than a third of Rabat's inhabitants (J. Abu-Lughod 1980, 160). The European quarters thus effectively barricaded the Moroccan city, leaving nowhere officially sanctioned by the city for the expansion of its population.

In the early 1920s large numbers of laborers were required on the construction sites building European-style boulevards and homes for French administrators. There was also a steady recruitment of Moroccan *petits fonctionnaires* (low-ranking civil servants) and domestics (Montagne 1952, 132). Urban demands for labor coincided with famines striking rural areas in 1913, 1921, 1928, and 1937 (13) and with French expropriation of the best farming land so that many subsistence farmers and transhumants, no longer able to live off agriculture, migrated to the coastal cities "for bread alone."[7] Available space in the medīna soon reached capacity, and poorer Moroccans constructed *bidonvilles* (shantytowns) at the periphery or on areas that were thought unsuitable for European construction (Montagne 1952, 138; J. Abu-Lughod 1980, 161–62). Initially the most prevalent form of rural-urban movement was "temporary masculine emigration"—a man would leave his family to work in the city for a period and on his return to the village would be replaced in his city occupation by a kinsman (Adam 1973, 327). These lone migrants lived as bachelors, called *ruwwāsa* (Montagne 1952, 234; Adam 1973, 334), and the role of the *garsūna* (from the French *garçon*) originated: "This woman, usually widowed or divorced, kept house for several *ruwwasa*, and satisfied their other needs" (Adam 1973, 334–35).[8] Later whole families migrated, as illustrated by J. Etienne's (1951) insightful account of a rural family who moved to Casablanca during the 1920s and Nouvel's (1938) study of paid jobs for children in the shantytowns.

The topography of Rabat served to reinforce socioeconomic and ethnic distinctions. The land rises steeply from the medīna, the coast, and the Bou Regreg river valley, providing an area of high ground that enjoys a cooling breeze in summer, far from the humidity of the coastline. The high ground was chosen for the central sector allotted to administration, commerce, and housing for Europeans and is to this day the preserve of the wealthiest inhabitants. L'Océan's less desirable climate, with sea mist making it cold and damp in winter as well as uncomfortable in summer, explains why it was inhabited not by French administrators or businessmen but by working-class southern Europeans whose status, though above that of most Moroccans, was moderate (Findlay, Findlay, and Paddison 1984; J. Abu-Lughod 1980, 309). Although it was not illegal for Moroccans who could afford it (which construction and domestic workers could not) to settle in European quarters, laws and regulations governing property ownership and registration of land titles made it difficult, thus creating an "urban apartheid" (J. Abu-Lughod 1980, 147).

In the 1920s, domestic servants who were accommodated with employers in European quarters and a small number of "assimilated" Moroccan aristocrats were the only exceptions to the rule of separate residence. By the late 1940s, however, l'Océan had witnessed an "infiltration" by better-off Moroccans.[9] Villème observed that in l'Océan, in contrast to other areas, "the intermixture of the two societies is an accomplished fact. There, from repurchase of land and houses, and above all from construction in the open spaces, are houses and shops for the Moroccans.... The infiltration has followed the major streets: the avenue of Temara has been transformed into a Moroccan street by extremely recent constructions" (Villème 1952,

89). These new Moroccan houses in l'Océan, "villas with elevated walls and windows protected from sight" (89), contrasted with existing Spanish architecture.

After independence in 1956, the French and Spanish left Morocco slowly—unlike the precipitate departure of *colons* from Algeria. The church of San José was given to the governor of Rabat and Salé in 1972, an indication that most of its congregation had left by that date, but residents who reminisce about flamenco dancing in the streets recall that some Spanish families remained until Spain joined the European Community in 1986. Older Moroccans who had grown up in l'Océan spoke proudly of the history of their quarter and their intermingling with Spaniards. One woman told me: "There was space between the houses. The Spanish people would sit out in cafés in the evening. It was very nice and clean and people lived in harmony. We all lived together: Jews, Spanish, French, Moroccans."

The variation in type and quality of the housing constructed in l'Océan during the protectorate meant that as the Spanish left, a void opened up in the quarter's housing market. While some Moroccan houses were extended, many of the larger Spanish houses were divided to create smaller, cheaper homes. In l'Océan, argue Findlay, Findlay, and Paddison, "the deteriorating housing stock has been occupied by a population from a wider variety of socio-economic groups than would be true of practically any other district of Rabat" (1984, 49).

A significant number of households in l'Océan, 12.5 percent of Findlay's sample, had moved there from the medīna, which was relatively cheap compared with the other adjacent areas vacated by Europeans of a higher status. I came across several such households in l'Océan—branches of expanding "original Ribāṭī" families who had outgrown their *riyāḍ*.[10] Other branches of these families still occupied the riyāḍs, so a link with the medīna was maintained. They were people of a certain standing—the fact that they were urbanized before 1912 set them apart from peasants who migrated to the city during the protectorate—but had comparatively modest incomes (wealthier Ribāṭīs moved into zones previously inhabited by the French).

Although the Spanish have all but disappeared from l'Océan, the heterogeneity that characterized the quarter from the later years of the protectorate onward still distinguishes it from other quarters of Rabat. Most other areas are more clearly inhabited by either the employing classes or the working classes. Although wealthy and poor neighborhoods are sometimes juxtaposed, a stark contrast existing between the housing on one side of a main road and that on the other, the two neighborhoods will both have their markets or commercial centers and will bear distinct names, separating the two groups of residents from each other both physically and symbolically. Visitors to l'Océan, however, are struck by the mixture of styles of housing, where the former homes of the Spanish and Moroccans are packed between newer apartment buildings.

Space, Class, and Country Neighbors

The Atlantic, associated by Moroccans in Rabat with damp and cold rather than picture-postcard views, remains a negative factor in the housing market. A sliding scale of status can thus be identified across l'Océan quarter: from the highest and most central point along the tramway where new apartment buildings are in the majority, down the gradient, which becomes increasingly steep, to the seafront, *l-taḥt* (literally the bottom, lowest point, physically and symbolically), where many older, smaller houses remain (see fig. 1.2 below). In practice, the pattern on the ground is jumbled rather than a straightforward gradation from high to low, but imagined differences smooth this over. This gradient also coincides with notions of safety and danger, and Moroccans were often concerned when I mentioned that I lived by the ocean ("not at the very bottom?!"), then relieved to learn I was not too close ("just halfway down"). In the past decade or so l'Océan has also received migrants from sub-Saharan Africa, further adding to its diversity so that the street names rue Bamako and rue Dakar no longer seem such a stretch. Many of these migrants have settled in the cheaper housing closer to the coast, which, due to racist attitudes, makes the seaward side seem still more undesirable and supposedly dangerous. Teachers, doctors, and low-ranking government office workers are typical Océanis, as are members of lower-income groups: car mechanics, bakers, butchers, electricians, decorators, tailors, shopkeepers, waiters, and domestics. The main roads run parallel to the coast and the smaller residential roads at right angles, thus running through middle-class neighborhoods at the top of the slope down to lower-class neighborhoods at the bottom, making it possible for both employers of domestic workers and workers themselves to be nearly neighbors.

Factors such as having the power to employ others, maintaining an extensive kin or fictive kin network, or doing things the traditional way stand as determinants of status that Moroccans can fall back on when money in the bank is lacking. So while *working* and *middle class* as customary or

Marxist-derived terms do not align well with local conceptions of status that go beyond education, occupation, and property (see Cohen, S. 2004, McMurray 2013), these terms are freely used in Rabat to differentiate people living in l'Océan. Here middle- and working-class people rub shoulders buying vegetables in the daily market and waiting for their children outside school. My host mother, Touria, was a teacher, and her husband, Hassan, like many others in l'Océan, made a living from "buying and selling." They owned their home, which they had inherited from Hassan's father, and were university educated, as were their children. Touria first met her former domestic worker because their sons were classmates. This residential mix of workers and employers is not found in other quarters of Rabat such as Hassan or Agdal, where house prices exclude people with low incomes, so that live-out domestics who work there must commute from elsewhere in the city.[11]

Doorkeeper or concierge (caretaker) families whose housing comes with the job are an exception. As people of working-class and often rural origins who live in middle-class buildings, they suffer social exclusion (Ozyegin 2001, 5–12, 55–58). The wife of a concierge in an apartment building near my host family's house was the only woman in the building not to be invited to the wedding of one of the residents' daughters. It was to take place in a five-star hotel, and my host mother commented, "Well, you don't invite the concierge to a hotel. That's just how it is. Moroccans confuse the _khedma_ [job] with the _shakhṣīya_ [person]. [To them,] the concierge is only a concierge." Incidentally, when the concierge's own daughter got married, his wife invited everyone in the building except this family, who then complained that they had been excluded.

In buildings without a concierge, each household pays a small monthly sum for someone to clean the communal staircase; 30dh to 40dh was the going rate during my fieldwork. Women who clean the stairs of apartment buildings in l'Océan are not outsiders; they might live opposite or next to the buildings they clean. Many have been in l'Océan a good deal longer than most of the residents. One woman who lived in a long-established squatter settlement near the sea could point to many buildings and tell me when they were built, how long the new apartments had stayed empty, how large they were, and who had cleaned the apartments, who the stairs, and so on.

It was this socioeconomic variation across a small space and the lively movement of people through the market, together with a tip-off from a Moroccan student that l'Océan was where the "classe moyenne moyenne [middle middle class]" could be found, that led me to select it as a primary field site. It seemed the kind of place one could easily meet new people. Indeed, many people in l'Océan hailed from elsewhere, mostly from rural Morocco, and the difference between country and city ways was often pointed out to me. L'Océan, in these many respects, was a *ḥay shaʿbī*, a *quartier populaire*.

The cohabitation of socioeconomic classes in l'Océan did not go unremarked. The woman who spoke about the harmony that reigned while Moroccans and Spaniards were neighbors complained that the houses the Spanish left were now rented room by room to migrants from the countryside. Blaming their lack of education and a surplus of freedom (presumably a reference to underemployment), she complained that the migrants "don't clean the streets in front of their houses as we do."

In a similar spirit someone had spray-painted on the wall of an old house at the ocean end of one street, "ICI, C'EST PARIS"—THIS IS PARIS. Against the backdrop of run-down buildings and the stench of refuse overflowing the municipal bins on the coastal road just below, it can only have been intended ironically, and a few days later an addition was made next to it: "Les aigles ne volent pas avec les pigeons"—eagles don't fly with pigeons. Differences between people in l'Océan often came down, in local discourse, to a distinction between country and city folk. Domestic workers on return visits to the countryside make a point of saying "in the capital . . ." when referring to their life in Rabat, aligning themselves with the "original" inhabitants of Rabat, who, along with those of Salé, Meknes, and Marrakech but especially Fes, lay claim to a particular urban way of living originating in the precolonial past (Ossman 1994, 23). But Paris, even more than Rabat, is the symbolic opposite of the Moroccan countryside. One often hears the phrase *arūbīya f Bārīs*, "a country bumpkin in Paris," to index rural women with their striped bags of oranges or onions on the train, or those afraid to ride on the escalator leading out of the Rabat-Ville train station. The masculine form is *arūbī*, and both are used as an insult for someone who is "uncivilized" (Newcomb 2009, 41). Ossman (1994, 24) explains, "Originally ʿrubi referred to people from a region just east and south of Casablanca, but it has come to include unworldly or uncultured behavior or persons in general." The message of the graffiti was clear—this might not be Paris, but country folk do not belong here either. While people from the countryside were the scapegoats on which blame could be laid for the rubbish in l'Océan's streets and for giving the lower end of the quarter a reputation for being dangerous, they

Fig. 1.2 "Ici, c'est Paris," reads graffiti sprayed on the wall of a traditional house while newer apartment buildings tower behind. A two-minute walk downhill from here brings you to the Atlantic Ocean. Photograph by author.

could also conveniently be employed, because close at hand, as domestic workers or to clean the staircases of apartment buildings. Elsewhere in the city these socioeconomic divisions are more clearly spatialized.

"Classes [*ṭabaqāt*], that's what makes Rabat what it is," said Fatima, a domestic worker in her forties who lived in l'Océan and worked in Agdal, a more prosperous district half an hour's walk away. She continued:

"There's the *ṭabaqa l-kādiḥa* [toiling class]. . . ."

"Who is that?" I asked.

"Us."

"What does it mean? *Nās ʿādīyīn* [ordinary people]?"

"No, less than ordinary. Ordinary people have money in the bank; they have their own house. The ṭabaqa l-kādiḥa, we don't have money in the bank. If we haven't worked we won't eat that day. We don't have a house, and the rent is more expensive than the money we bring from work. It isn't enough. What do you do? You borrow from people and you tell them you will give it back. But when you have to give it back, you don't have it. You don't have it!"

Fatima's voice was almost hysterical as she realized she described herself. She had borrowed 400dh from me and was not going to return it—it's impossible if one can never scrape together savings.[12]

Moroccans from the countryside experience explicit class divisions in new ways in the city. Living in l'Océan possibly made the sense of difference more acute for Fatima than if she had lived in a quarter like Takkadoum, where the residents are more uniformly working class. In l'Océan, people of other classes were her neighbors but did not function as neighbors in the way country people do or are supposed to. In Fatima's words, "There are no classes in the countryside. Someone could have a bigger house or more animals . . . but people help each other. If there is a party or some occasion, the girls from one house will help another. This doesn't happen in the city except in *aḥiyā' shaʿbīya* [quartiers populaires]."

Fatima did not consider l'Océan a *shaʿbī* (popular) quarter while most people who have lived all their lives in the city did. Rural households are not equal, but the point is that their exchanges are reciprocal; such exchange among rural households serves to swell temporarily the domestic labor available to the household either regularly or at peak times, and its significance will be explored in later chapters.

Fatima's vision of the city involved not groups with which she could exchange but groups from which she was excluded: "ordinary people" made up the *ṭabaqa mutawassiṭa* (middle class), above them were the people of the *ṭabaqa rāqīya* (the "elegant," "sophisticated" upper class), and finally there was the king—"he's in a class on his own." The separation of rich and poor is seen by Moroccans as a relatively new trait of urban life, changing the way people recruit labor. In the clan-based society of nineteenth-century Morocco, networks of patrons and clients, that is asymmetric dependency relations, linking countryside and city were important channels of supply and demand for domestic workers. Particularly in times of mass rural exodus, "elites had their choice in providing themselves with dependents of all sorts" (Ennaji 1999, 88).

A number of studies underline the continuing importance of patron-client relationships in twentieth-century North Africa (Cherifi 1983, Geertz, Geertz, and Rosen 1979, Rosen 1984, Smith, A. 2002). Maher argues for the historical importance in southern Morocco of patron-client relationships contracted within "a hierarchy of social categories, differentiated by ritual status" (1974, 24–25). At the top are s̲h̲urfa, held to be descendants of Mohammed, followed by Arabs, Berbers, and finally ḥarātīn (descendants of West African slaves), who were expected to serve the other estates.¹³

Membership in these groups is inherited patrilineally, as are patron-client relations between the groups. Patron-client relations are also often contracted between rich and poor kin (Maher 1976, 59). The cluster of households studied by Hildred Geertz in Sefrou contained a group of poverty-stricken, unemployed kin who, while sleeping elsewhere, ate their meals at their wealthy cousin's house and performed domestic chores for him and his wives (1979, 337). More recently, Newcomb observed "mini patron-client relationships" between the members of an extended Fassi family: "those who received the generosity of other family members went out of their way to help with domestic tasks and other nonmonetary exchanges" (2009, 114). This literature is echoed by oral accounts from residents of l'Océan who tell of a bygone (but much more recent than the nineteenth century) era when rich and poor were "neighborly" and cooperated in relationships like those Fatima recalls from her rural upbringing. A set of linked vignettes may bring the idea to life.

One telling conversation was between my host mother, Touria, and other guests at a sbūʿ (seventh day after the birth) party for her grandchild. My host mother had already thrown a party at our house in l'Océan. We had worked hard: Touria had cooked with the assistance of an elderly and long-time neighbor, Mbarka, the mother-in-law of her former domestic worker, Salma. Salma herself had come to help with preparations, clean the blood that spilled across the roof terrace from the customary sacrificial sheep, and do the washing up. These neighbors were given a small sum of money but for the most part were rewarded with leftover chicken, meat, and fruit and the satisfaction that they had helped a neighbor. They remained behind the scenes throughout the party while my host sister, her two cousins, and I served, running up and down stairs from the kitchen on the second floor to the two salons on the first and ground floor, where men and women were catered to separately.

But the family of the newborn's father also wanted to throw a party, which took place the following day, at their home in Hay al-Fatih, a newer and less s̲h̲aʿbī (French *populaire*) part of town than l'Océan. The work my host sister, her cousins, and I had been performing the previous day was here done by paid staff. A team of three cooks was employed, and Karima, a k̲h̲eddāma (servant, worker) who had been with the family for twenty years, supervised and served, which allowed the hostess to circulate. While the men were being entertained with music in the larger front salon, we women sat rather bored in the smaller back salon. The mother of our hardworking cousins had excused the girls from this second party, telling us that they were exhausted from the day before: "They are not used to serving like that, up and down the stairs." The conversation turned to how visiting and hosting used to be done differently. My host mother said, "Nowadays you have to phone your own sister before going round, and she'll tell you to come between four and six o'clock. And the reason? Because people feel they have to put on a whole spread. They tell you the time so they can be ready with all the food on the table for you. Previously, you could knock at any time on anyone's door—neighbors, not just family—and they would welcome you with whatever they had. They'd give you just a piece of bread, and you'd be laughing and having fun and dancing."

Other women chipped in:

"And if you were ill, your neighbors would come and wash up and cook for you. When someone had a baby, the neighbors would come—four, six, ten of them—and each one or two would cook something different."

"And if someone didn't have the strength to knead the dough, the women would take it in turns, and that's how the bread would come out!" The second speaker opened and closed her fists several times, a gesture used to express beauty, in this case signifying beautifully risen bread.

My host mother then told about an old lady, a neighbor of her mother in Fes, who used to call from her first-floor window, "Come and help me lift a mattress." This was a ruse to get Touria to come in. Touria would go into the woman's home and find a whole table laid out. The neighbor would say, "Sit down, drink your tea, and eat your breakfast so that you have the strength to look after your children." My host mother concluded, "There was *insijām* [harmony.]" She felt that l'Océan's neighbors had lived more cooperatively at that time than in the present.

Although it was not made explicit, the conversation served as a comment on two sorts of hospitality. The first followed the old pattern of family members (cousins, aunts) working for free and needy neighbors working for little; the second involved hired labor supervised by a paid worker. Crawford also identifies a shift in the countryside from long-term reciprocity to short-term gain: "The decision by ever more local patriarchs to send their children to the cities for wage labor rather than loan them to relatives who need help, signals a newly significant articulation between the rural and urban sectors of Morocco" (2008, 6). My host father, Hassan, then in his late fifties, whose family came from the Sous valley to l'Océan after independence, often told me about this old way of working, which supposedly had been common in the city's past as well as in the countryside. He related this change to what he saw as the dwindling importance of neighbors, which he illustrated with a story: A man had thousands of "friends" on Facebook. When he was planning to move to a new house, the man messaged all his online friends asking for help, but on the day of the move, no one turned up. A neighbor saw the man struggling with his furniture and offered to lend a hand. "This neighbor wasn't friends with him on Facebook," said Hassan, "so the man hadn't told him he was moving that day, but he was happy to help. The Facebook friends weren't friends at all!"

The ideal of neighborliness was encoded for my host father in the architecture of the medīna. His view of the matter was quite the opposite of Lyautey's assumption that a "Muslim" quarter refuses sociality: "It was built for people to meet up with each other. The streets are narrow, with one door right in front of another so people meet when they come in and out. And the roofs were all on one level, so people could talk. One roof is next to another, to another, to another. We have a proverb: to have a neighbor is to have seventy neighbors. Because it just goes on and on."

What outsiders perceive as antisocial architecture is for insiders, who have access to the roof terraces (predominantly women's space), decidedly social. The distinction between inside and outside the house is an organizing feature of writing on Morocco. Self-conscious about their natural position on the outsides of houses, writers prized and wrote about access to insides. Celarié's *Behind Moroccan Walls* (1931) is a classic example; Peets's *Women of Marrakech* ([1983] 1988) and Hart's memoir, *Behind the Courtyard Door* (1994), follow suit. Fernea did not enjoy such intimacy with her Moroccan neighbors, although she met them on the roof terrace. Her *A Street in Marrakech* (1988) contains the recurrent motif of closed houses, echoing Boughali's claim that "the traditional Moroccan house hardly ever has openings that are visible to a visitor" (1974, 45). Kenneth Brown similarly described a house in Salé as a "closed off, private universe unto itself" (1976, 39).

Although l'Océan's architecture, with buildings spaced along relatively wide streets, differed from the dense network of houses and narrow alleyways in Rabat's medīna, in my host father's memories of growing up, the street in l'Océan was also a space for interaction between neighbors. They acted as brothers, sisters, fathers, and mothers to each other, so children playing in the street could be called in to take their tea with any one of the eight families in the cluster of houses where he lived. This recalls Eickelman's description of the *darb* (small street or alleyway) of a typical Arab medīna: "Component households in a *darb* should be able to assume a certain moral unity so that in some respects social space in their *darb* can be regarded as an extension of their own household" (1974, 283). This common life is unattainable in today's l'Océan, where, to quote my host father, "No one knows who is who."

L'Océan may never have been quite like the medina, but in local discourse it is increasingly characteristic of the ville nouvelle in which the street, as argued by Chekroun and Boudoudou (1986, 105), is a common space not for sociability but for transit—for the movement of traffic, pedestrian or otherwise. This, they suggest, has the effect of making Moroccan families turn in on themselves, having to fulfill alone the functions that previously were shared by others on the street. Rather than managing alone, it seems that people regularly traverse the city for help from long-standing acquaintances, passing over neighbors as though they are not there. "We don't have neighbors" was how one woman justified the twenty-minute taxi ride she took to reach a woman from whom she borrowed an electric whisk—a common appliance that could doubtless be found closer to home.

While Moroccans talk about the neighborly interaction they miss today as part of what it means to be sha'bī, evocations of a past community where one knew and interacted with all one's neighbors are not unique to Morocco. Dresch (2006, 206) provides examples from the Persian Gulf where "almost everywhere . . . an image recurs of an older world where everyone knew everyone else." Nostalgia for neighbors, while presented as novel, also plays into longstanding notions of privacy and prestige in Arab domesticity (M. Montgomery 2019).

The Popular Ideal

Being sha'bī is an ideal that is seen as having been more prevalent in the past than it is today and more prevalent in the countryside or in *aḥīyā' sha'bīya* (quartiers populaires) of the city than in middle- or upper-class urban settings. It is thus often equated with an attachment to tradition, to doing things the way they have been done for a long time. Sha'bī Moroccans "still" sit outside in the evenings. They still go in and out of one another's houses. They still say "salām ʿalīkum" (peace be upon you) when they meet in the street.

Shaʿbī, the adjective of shaʿb ("a people" in the sense of ethnos, a populace), is often translated as "folk" in English or "populaire" in French, as in *al-bank ash-shaʿbī*, Banque Populaire du Maroc, whose advertisement campaign (2012–13) on television, radio, and billboards featured Moroccan stars saying how shaʿbī or populaire they are. In the advertisements, a series of signed photos of celebrated artists bore the caption "anā shaʿbīya" or "je suis populaire," (I am populaire) thus projecting the qualities of these public figures onto the target audience and onto the bank itself, which boasts a closeness to and knowledge of the needs of "ordinary people." An extract from the radio will serve to convey the sense of the advertisement:

[*In Moroccan Arabic*] "Welcome to your program: 'Talking with Stars.' Si Boustawi, the audience loves you a lot. What is the secret of shaʿbīytik [your shaʿbīya—in this case, your popularity]?"

"Well, my shaʿbīya comes from my audience, who are always with me, like my bank."

[*Switch to standard Arabic voiceover*] "Yes, you [plural] are distinguished for ḥisin shaʿbī (shaʿbī feeling), and we are like you. We work in shaʿbī feelings. Banque Populaire, a bank for you."

[*In Moroccan Arabic*] "Mouna Fettou, you have lots of fans. How do you live this shaʿbīya?"

"I live it with pride. And when you are shaʿbī, you always have to take an interest in every person, just as my bank does."

[*Switch to standard Arabic*] "Yes, you [plural] are distinguished for shaʿbī feeling, and we are like you."

While being shaʿbī is portrayed here as a positive quality, it is viewed negatively in other contexts. Some residents of l'Océan complain the area is too shaʿbī for comfort. Such people are keen to distinguish themselves from those who are, in their opinion, too working class or common, or not affluent enough or refined enough, to make easy neighbors.[14] But attempts to locate the term shaʿbī within a simple economic framework are misguided. The Banque Populaire would fail in its publicity campaign if it appealed only to those who identified as working-class; the advertisements are geared toward a middle-class clientele. Fatima, who considers herself shaʿbīya and working class, has no bank account, and this is not uncommon.

Thinking about sha'bī in terms of an identification with the past is more helpful than mapping it onto a scale of income brackets. "Traditional" might be a suitable translation in certain contexts, such as when talking about sha'bī music or dance, but also when referring to certain forms of life and ways of relating to others. Sha'bī parallels in these respects the Egyptian identity concept of *ibn al-balad* (literally "son of the *balad*," the meaning of which varies according to the context; *balad* can refer to a town, place, region, or country). The feminine form, *bint al-balad* (daughter of the *balad*) is equally common. The upper class in Egypt had, prior to the 1952 revolution, assimilated to Western lifestyles and "uprooted itself completely from its past, that is, [from] the *awlād al-balad* [plural of *ibn al-balad*] identity" while the masses, on the other hand, "became isolated within that identity" (Messiri 1978, 104). Thus an ibn al-balad values what is local over what is foreign as well as what is traditional over what is new while treating powerful foreigners and their local acolytes in class terms. Drawing on Messiri's essay, Early (1993, 85) defines *baladī* through a series of *baladī* versus *afrangī* (traditional versus modern or foreign) oppositions: "There are *baladī* ways and there are *afrangī* ways to earn a living, practice religion, celebrate a wedding, cure a disease, talk to a friend, or solve a problem." In the same way, there are sha'bī and non-sha'bī ways to do things in Morocco, including ways to get someone to do your housework for you.[15]

In Armbrust's discussion of the Egyptian television serial *White Flag*, ibn al-balad is "a real Egyptian, a regular guy; sometimes the salt of the earth, in other contexts a rough diamond" (1996, 25). Similarly, sha'bī Moroccans consider themselves ordinary Moroccans who do not "put on airs." The significance of this for domestic work is that sha'bī employers point out that they do not differentiate between their own children and their domestic workers. When employers state that a live-in domestic eats with them or sleeps in the same room as their children—"*beḥel beḥel*," they are the same—this is often followed with "we are sha'bī" by way of explanation. My conversations with security guards and chauffeurs outside villas in the decidedly less sha'bī Souissi and Bir Qasim residential areas suggested this rhetoric is absent there. Talking about l'Océan, one security guard said, "Yes, but that's a ḥay sha'bī [a popular quarter]. The people are *muwaẓẓafīn* [office workers], teachers, people working in government offices. . . . Here they are the ministers themselves and the CEOs and principals of private schools. This is not sha'bī. There's no 'my son,' 'my daughter' here. They don't want you to be that to them."

While sha'bī behavior is not normally associated with the upper class—in fact, the upper class often provides a rhetorical contrast to sha'bī in Morocco—wealth does not in itself preclude people from identifying themselves as sha'bī. One of Messiri's interviewees in Cairo commented that "it is not so much the *amount* of wealth that one possesses as what one does with it which identifies one as an *ibn al-balad*" (1978, 42). Wealth in the Moroccan sha'bī ideal is associated with generosity, particularly as far as food is concerned, and allows inequality a moral form. Several domestic workers and employers noted the difference between sha'bī employers and those who "count Danones." Danone is the prevailing brand of and therefore the generic term for yogurt. Its portion-size pots, costing around 2dh each, are inexpensive but easily counted and therefore often a trivial subject of contention between employers and workers. A worker named Safae talked of a household where she had been happy: "They had yogurts all right," she said simply, as though this summarized the whole situation: a time of plenty. In nineteenth-century England a similar trope describes "the real gentlefolk" (Mullins and Griffiths 1986, 15) as distinct from people of "new money." A fictional example is found in Surtees's *Mr Sponge's Sporting Tour*, in which Sponge asks a servant about the profligate Sir Harry Swift and is told, "*He was a real gentleman now, if you like—free, open-handed gentleman—none of your close shavin', cheese-parin' sort of gentlemen, or imitation gentlemen, as I calls them, but a man who knew what was due to servants and gave them it. We had good wages, and all the 'reglars'*" [(1853) 1981, 74].

Asmae, a Moroccan employer explained to me, "Well-off people [*nās lā bās 'alīhum*] keep food locked away. They count it. But we sha'bī people, we can't count food. It is *khayr* [goodness, blessing, a gift] from God. We say, 'Just take it!'" One could do this whether rich or poor.

The meanings of sha'bī are so contextualized that a case-by-case understanding is more helpful than a wholesale translation. Nonetheless, a group of Moroccan students enrolled in a master's program in *thaqāfa sha'bīya* (popular culture), when asked about the meaning of sha'bī in the context of Banque Populaire's advertising, came up with a single factor. They responded that sha'bī involved openness to people. This is why sha'bī people say hello in the street or sit outside their houses in the evening (although l'Océan is said to be not quite, or rather no longer, sha'bī enough for this). But more so than with the artists of Banque Populaire's advertisements, in the context of a community such as l'Océan or the neighborly past described by my host father, sha'bī is specifically a *safe* openness—an openness to people who are "known." As soon as there is an influx of foreigners whom the older residents have no wish to meet, or the apartment buildings become too large, concentrating more people in one street than the inhabitants can possibly know, people will stop saying hello to one another.[16] Eickelman argues similarly that for ties of "closeness" or kinship within a darb, "there is an optimal range, above and below which such ties become untenable" (1974, 287). This is what is happening in l'Océan and why someone can point to my street and say, "This half is still sha'bī, that half less so." The sha'bī half, nearer the coast, is lined with houses and smaller apartment buildings; the less sha'bī half has newer, taller apartment buildings that are not designed with neighborliness in mind—the emphasis is on privacy rather than on shared spaces. During my time there, those residents of l'Océan who distanced themselves from the sha'bī identity were keen to point out that they did not like to intrude on others, explaining that "it is shameful," while those who would have liked l'Océan to be more sha'bī complained that no one came to see them.

Different forms of neighborliness in country and city meant Moroccans arriving from the countryside in the last thirty years found l'Océan was not sha'bī enough. When those they met on the staircases of their buildings or in the street did not respond to their greetings, they felt it keenly. In the words of Fatima's sister, Selwa, "It's like you are a foreigner in your own country. Though you are in Morocco and everyone says they are Muslim, it's not the same. It's like another country. People don't say 'salām,' don't ask after you, don't knock on the door. You could die, and your neighbors wouldn't notice. Rabat is not nice. Casa, Marrakech—people there would ask after you. It's just Rabat that's like this."

For Selwa, greeting people in the street was both a Moroccan and a Muslim thing to do. When people failed to greet her, they were failing to affirm that she and they belonged to the same community or *umma*, so she felt alienated. Others stressed that greeting people was required of Muslims. Hafida, on a return visit to her home village in the Gharb, was greeted by everyone who passed. She commented: "Everyone knows me here, not like in the city. There, no one says 'salām'; no one knows you. Even the neighbors who live in the flat opposite me, they don't reply when I say 'salām 'alikum,' and that's something God asks for. '*Salām*' is for God, not for them, but they don't even reply. Everyone just thinks about himself in the city."

Hafida says she is greeted in the countryside because she is known. The size of her village partly accounts for this, but in urban contexts involving similarly small numbers of people, "knowing" others is not a given. I asked a *gardien* (a watchman) if he knew the residents in the complex of apartments he guarded in Mabella, a *ḥay rāqī* (upper-class quarter):

"'*Salām*' doesn't exist here. Some people won't even look at me. They are *shabʿān* [full—i.e., not hungry]. They are not going to die."

"We are all going to die."

"No, they are not going to die. They have 4x4s. Us, we have God."

In the watchman's view, the residents' illusion of self-sufficiency meant they felt no need to relate to him. He was also hinting at their comparative godlessness (*salām* being linked to a duty toward God) and their lack of concern for consequences in the hereafter: "They are not going to die." When I recounted this conversation to my host family, my host sister was unsurprised, commenting, "No, people are no longer shaʿbī."

Separated from the working-class community in the way European arrivals once were, newcomers to l'Océan—those who make the move for career reasons, who buy the new apartments in the tall buildings that make the quarter less shaʿbī, park their cars in the basement and, avoiding their neighbours, take the lift directly to their floor—would not know whose door to knock on if they needed help with spring cleaning, and their mothers are often too far away to babysit children.[17] These people, like residents of the Hassan or Agdal districts, tend to have higher incomes and think of themselves as having busy lives and thus little time for shaʿbī socializing with neighbours or for doing the housework. The imperative to have a domestic worker to maintain "proper" family life, then, outweighs a fear of strangers, so they are likely to employ someone unknown and see how it goes. To find a worker, they might have recourse to an agency, flick to the back of *Le Matin* for the classifieds, or search online.

Dār Sebbari: A Shaʿbī Household

Dār Sebbari (the house of Sebbari) is a family whom almost everyone could agree, are in some sense shaʿbī.[18] The Sebbaris are not, relatively speaking, newcomers to l'Océan. Latifa was born in the late 1930s, in the medīna of Rabat. She was orphaned and brought up in the house of her maternal grandfather, who, after the death of his first wife, married the daughter of a high-ranking official of Sultan Hassan I (r. 1878–94). This stepgrandmother, who did not have any daughters of her own, was good to Latifa: "better than a mother." This may have been the inspiration for Latifa's own career as a foster mother of sorts. Historical demographic studies (e.g., Laslett 1965) demonstrate the importance of such foster arrangements in a context in which it was rare for people over a certain age to have both parents living.[19]

The family in which Latifa grew up was reasonably well off, owning farmland outside Rabat, which they sold to the state to make way for the *autoroute* completed in 1987. *Mui* (mother) Latifa, as most young people now call her, told me that her grandparents did not let her do housework. They had two *dada*s (female slaves assigned to the care of the children) and a male slave "from the Sahara" who bought the household's daily provisions at the market and did the cooking. Retainers of the kind who were once slaves (in particular dadas) are hard to assess but were a fixed part of the household.[20] Latifa was still at school when her grandfather decided to marry her to Hamza Sebbari: "I cried and cried, but my 'mother' would not go against my grandfather," so Latifa left school and went to live with her husband's family. It was there that she learned to cook, under the watchful eye of her mother-in-law.

In the 1980s Latifa, Hamza, and their six children moved out of the medīna and bought a *bildī* house (a traditional house with a courtyard) in l'Océan; they occupied the downstairs and rented the upstairs to another family. In the 1990s they demolished the old house and constructed an apartment building on its site. Latifa's late husband designated the spacious ground-floor flat, with its private courtyard, for their own use, and the family with whom they had shared the bildī house took one of the first-floor apartments. *Ḥajja* Jamila, the mother of this family, now lives there alone, all her children having moved out.[21] "She's my oldest neighbor—like family," Mui Latifa told me. The two elderly women drink coffee together every evening. The remaining apartments in the building were taken by ordinary families of moderate income. One of Mui Latifa's daughters, Nadia, married the son of the family who occupied the other first-floor apartment, thus solidifying ties between the households on the lower floors of the Sebbari building; he, like my host father, was in "buying and selling."

Although some researchers assert that coresiding extended families are no longer the norm in North Africa (Kapchan 1996, Guerraoui 1996), Holmes-Eber's study of women's kin networks in Tunis demonstrates that many families are nuclear only in appearance: "socially and psychologically they still live with their extended family" (2003, 74). She argues that "the extended household has simply 'gone up' or 'out', becoming instead the 'extended street' or 'extended apartment complex'" (70). *Dār Sebbari* denotes at once the building, the Sebbaris who live in it, and the Sebbaris who live elsewhere. It also sometimes includes those who are not (or not always) family but who live and work with them. This ambiguity is one the present study seeks to unpack.

Nadia's door was often left open, usually revealing a domestic worker in the kitchen. The door of Ḥajja Jamila's apartment, though closed, was never locked, allowing people from Nadia's and Mui Latifa's households to come and go without knocking. Nadia's eighteen-year-old daughter, Zahra, in particular treated the neighbor's apartment as an extension of her home, not least because, having no bedroom of her own, she slept there, along with Nadia's domestic worker, usually a young woman from the Moroccan countryside. Turnover for this post was high; I was reminded of the kitchen maid in Proust's *Swann's Way*, which Fortes (1987, 252) cites in his discussion of personhood: "The kitchen-maid was an abstract personality [French *une personne morale*], a permanent institution to which an invariable set of attributes assured a sort of fixity and continuity and identity throughout the long series of transitory human shapes in which that personality was incarnate; for we never found the same girl there two years running" [Proust (1922) 1973, 54].

Nadia's household would often ask Ḥajja Jamila to join them for lunch, and there was much to-ing and fro-ing of cups of olive oil, spices, or preserved lemons when whoever was cooking found herself short, or to fetch someone to speak on the landline the two households shared. This coming and going among households is stereotypical of sha'bī Moroccans.

Mui Latifa's only son also took an apartment on the second floor, although, since his divorce, he ate most of his meals with his mother and unmarried sister downstairs, and his mother's domestic worker would come up to his apartment to tidy and clean. As well as leaving Latifa largely responsible for the burden of her son's domestic work, the divorce had deprived her of a daughter-in-law to serve her. When the son went to stay with one of his sisters for the summer, he put his apartment up for a short-term sublet, which suited my needs on arrival in Rabat. The *samsār*, or broker, told me, "It's a family building. It will be like you're living with the family. It's shameful to live alone anyway. This is better for you." When the son returned at the end of the summer, I moved to a host family one street away and eventually to my own place close by but continued to visit Latifa's, Nadia's, and Jamila's households regularly until I left the field. This allowed me to follow the daily and seasonal rhythms of housework and the comings and goings of domestic workers old and new.

Excepting the son's apartment, each household carried out their daily domestic work more or less independently but shared labor in times of need. Ḥajja Jamila employed a woman who lived in l'Océan but further "down" (i.e., in the less desirable housing nearer the coast) to do the cleaning a couple of times a week; she was related to an ex-domestic of Mui Latifa's and was introduced to me as being "from the family." When Jamila's domestic was not there, Nadia's worker would sometimes be asked to help with heavy or messy jobs. Mui Latifa employed her own domestic. Turnover was high, but typically the worker was from Yacoub El Mansour (a working-class quarter in southwest Rabat) or from a poor area of Salé and so commuted daily. When a domestic could not be persuaded to live at Latifa's, Latifa arranged with her daughter, Nadia, for a share of her live-in worker's time, namely at breakfast before her own worker arrived and at teatime after she had gone. Nadia's own domestic (always live-in) would then complain of having to do two jobs, a fact not reflected in her wage. Another woman was employed to clean the stairs two or three times a week. Sometimes this was a relative of one of the workers employed in Nadia's or Mui Latifa's household; usually she was a neighbor. In all, the extended Dār Sebbari controlled a good deal of domestic labor. What did all these workers do? While by no means average, a day in the life of Malika, Nadia's twenty-one-year-old live-in worker for a brief period in the summer of 2012, is illustrative.

Malika got up around half past seven. She would make a pot of sugary tea, a flask of fresh filter coffee, and another of hot milk. She and the family ate these with bread or pastries from the bakery a few streets away. When Nadia's daughter, Zahra, who was taking a year off before university and called the shots in the kitchen, told Malika they ought to start making bread at home, Malika responded that she did not know how. "I do know," Malika confided in me, "but it's too much work for me!" Malika had once made pancakes for an employer who was so pleased with them that from then on, she asked Malika to make them every day, and not only for herself but also for her mother and friends. "I got tired of it," she explained. "When that happens, workers ruin the pancakes so that the *mulat d-dār* says, 'Enough! You don't know how to make them anymore!'" But for Malika "food is a blessing from God," so rather than "ruin" a loaf to make a point to Zahra, she resorted to the lie that she did not know how to bake.

When the family got up, Malika folded and stored the blankets or sheets used the night before. Except couples, few sha'bī Moroccans sleep in designated beds but rather on the traditional *ferāsh* (couches) that are used for seating at other times. Malika had to turn the couch mattresses on their sides, brush the dust off them, put them back, and dust, plump, and straighten the numerous cushions that ran the length of the ferāsh. She did this twice daily. "It's like taking medicine: morning and evening!" Malika joked one day. She would then dust other surfaces and clean the rugs with a manual sweeper consisting of a plastic box into which rotating brushes flicked crumbs. The sweeper had no handle (some have a very short horizontal handle, as on a dustpan), and Malika always pushed it back and forth across the rug while bending from the hip rather than getting down on her hands and knees. This technique was consistent with all floor-based work in Morocco and something nineteenth-century Englishwoman Emily Keene, who married the *Sharīf* of Wazan, failed to understand: "As to scrubbing, I have never been able to get a slave or other woman to kneel in cleaning a floor, even with a mat provided for the purpose. Wooden floors, such as I have, were not in use generally at this period. Marble, stone, or brick ones were oftener to be found. These are cleaned by flooding, which is followed up by a palmetto broom with a very short handle" (1912, 157–58). Even outside Morocco, domestic workers are loath to take up such an undignified position, especially with employers looking on.

The floors of l'Océan's apartments, as everywhere in contemporary Morocco (both rural and urban), are cleaned daily, although "flooding" is generally reserved for bathrooms and courtyards where furniture is not at risk. Nadia liked her white tiled floor to be swept and mopped (sprinkled with water and bleach and then wiped with a cloth) several times a day. On returning from work, she would often remove her socks and walk slowly across the floor barefoot in order to detect dirt.[22] Malika sometimes ignored Nadia's requests for her to go over the floor a third or fourth time in one day: "I have to cheat. Cheating is bad, but this house pushes you to cheat and to lie. She wants me to clean the floor. It's already clean. . . . I'm not going to waste the water and bleach and my health. Everything is wasted." Nadia's bathroom was similarly cleaned, with diluted bleach flicked by hand over the porcelain, chrome, and tiles, wiped with a cloth, and rinsed with water. Malika then pushed a rubber squeegee over the tiles to encourage the water toward the drain in the slightly sloping floor. A dry cloth would finish things up if necessary.

At some point Zahra, who was not an early riser, would decide about lunch and send Malika with a trolley bag to get fresh produce from l'Océan's market. As is often the case in Moroccan households, sometimes Nadia's husband would go to the market instead, emphasizing his role as breadwinner and his ability to drive a hard bargain. Malika would scrub, peel, and chop the vegetables, herbs, and fruit, do the messy preparation of meat or fish, and then stand over the stove, stirring and waiting. Malika complained that Zahra would drop in and out of the kitchen, season the food, and take the credit for successful dishes (those her elder brother liked), as in the Moroccan saying "the slave woman makes the *trīd* and her mistress reaps the compliments."[23] After eating lunch with the family, Malika would clear away and wash the dishes and wipe the kitchen stove, surfaces, and floor.

The afternoon might be spent doing less regular (i.e., not quite daily) tasks such as cleaning windows, which became misted with salt from the nearby Atlantic; washing laundry and hanging it out on the roof to dry in the sea breeze (Nadia had a machine, but insisted on some items being washed by hand, including her voluminous white net curtains); and taking cushions, mattresses, and carpets up to the roof terrace to air in the sun. Cushion and mattress covers were changed every so often. This was harder than it sounds, since Nadia's cushions were well stuffed (a sign of quality), and it was a struggle to get the tight-fitting covers on and zipped up. The long, heavy mattresses needed to be lifted one end at a time to get the covers over them. This is really a two-person job, but domestics often do it alone.

Occasional kitchen work might include shining the aluminum pans with *jīkz ū ṣābūn* (wire wool and traditional soap), cleaning out and tidying cupboards, shelling peas, chopping a quantity of fresh herbs to be frozen, or sifting painstakingly through sesame seeds spread out on a tray to look for stones. Sometimes Malika could watch television or, if left alone, talk on her mobile phone while she went about her work. She rarely napped, although many Moroccans do take a siesta.

Once businesses were open again in the late afternoon, Malika might run an errand to the pharmacist or dry cleaner (ironing, particularly of traditional Moroccan garments like Nadia's *jellāba*, was generally outsourced) or ask to go to the *ḥammām* (public bathhouse). *Casse-croûte*, a light meal taken in the early evening, needed to be prepared much like breakfast—with tea or coffee and some pancakes, bread, or similar, bought or homemade. Around this time Malika might be called downstairs to help at Mui Latifa's. Soon after casse-croûte, preparations would start for supper—generally a lighter meal than lunch but for which Malika sometimes had to cater to several different requests. It was not uncommon for her to make two kinds of soup, one in which the vegetables were blended with cream and one where they floated around in chunks.

With supper over and the dishes washed up, the housework was generally done for the day. By this time it could be midnight or later, and Zahra might still expect some companionship until she felt like sleeping. I marveled at them all—Malika for how hard she worked and her employers for finding so many things for her to do. With the exception of the washing machine, water heater, and food processor, labor-saving devices are not much in evidence in this kind of household. Labor is to be used, not saved.

Nadia, Mui Latifa, and Ḥajja Jamila were the only households in the building who employed regular domestics. The other tenants—shopkeepers, secretaries, and teachers, living in one- or two-bedroom apartments—were amused by my asking them if they had domestic workers. There was not much to do, and what there was they did themselves; as for live-in workers, there was no space, and they were not used to having domestics anyway. Life without paid help was plainly possible.

Ḥajja Jamila's age, ill health, and poor eyesight prevented her from doing housework easily herself, but in Nadia's household this was not the case. Although Nadia worked full time, Zahra was able-bodied and had time on her hands. Yet the housework did not fall to her. In this respect Nadia's household, despite occupying the same number of square meters as her neighbors, was a cut above them. Accustomed to employing a domestic, they coped poorly when a worker left and they had to go without until they found a replacement.

Mui Latifa's apartment, the largest in the patronymic group, was the social center of the Sebbari family. On Fridays, the whole family and their dependents were invited there for the weekly couscous meal. This is a stew of meat or chicken with vegetables on a bed of couscous, traditionally served in a large, round earthenware dish from which everyone would eat. If several guests were expected, Nadia's household (specifically the domestic worker, under Zahra's instructions) might also cook a quantity of the couscous grains to be added to the communal dish downstairs. These meals were useful for mapping how people were related to the house and their hierarchical status relative to those around them.[24] Before the main dish was filled and brought to the salon table, a number of smaller dishes would be made up in the kitchen, and Mui Latifa would direct the domestic worker as she ladled out portions—more meat here, less there. These would then be kept back for family members not present or taken to various people in the neighborhood. One medium dish would be taken to the people who rented the basement of the apartment building as an office and another smaller dish across the street to Imane. Originally from rural Morocco, Imane was the former servant of a large household who had remained living in the *dawīra* (literally "little house")—a tiny kitchen where the meals for the house were traditionally prepared, with stairs up to a sleeping area above. Her room, next to the front door, was windowless, and there was space for two or three people to sit down on stools between the sink and the stove. Imane no longer worked for the owner of her house, who had gone abroad but allowed Imane to stay on rent-free in the dawīra while the main house was rented. Mui Latifa saw Imane as her responsibility, and, aside from providing her with couscous on Fridays, paid at the end of every week for the milk Imane took daily from the grocer's across the street.

Although a small dish of Dār Sebbari couscous was always sent to Imane, she was not invited to eat with the household. Those who ate in the house either had a higher social status than Imane or were current or former domestics with closer relationships to Dār Sebbari. And, although everyone ate from one dish in the sha'bī fashion demanded for most meals and especially for couscous, the seating arrangements indicated who was who. Older male guests, such as Latifa's brother, were often given their food separately, prior to the main gathering. Non-servile guests were always encouraged to sit on the couch at the back of the room, facing the door, together with older family members as well as Mui Latifa, her sister, and Ḥajja Jamila. These seats had to be filled first and vacated last, as the people on the couches on either side of the table blocked the way through, so those seated at the back were least expected or able to get up and take dishes out or fetch things. Mui Latifa's unmarried daughter, Jihane, might sit on one of the side couches, as would Nadia, if she came home from work for lunch. Zahra might take one of these places too.

The side of the table near the door had no couch, but the domestics would pull up various chairs and stools for themselves. They remained ready to go to the kitchen whenever anything was wanted, and when everyone had finished, they carried the heavy couscous dish back to the kitchen, brought a cloth to wipe the table, and began making tea and washing up. The women who took these places at the table were not just the domestics currently employed by Mui Latifa and Nadia but also those whom the family had brought up and who came to visit often. Many of them Mui Latifa referred to routinely as her "daughters."

Conclusion

During my time in l'Océan, while few people could still get a neighbor to do their housework, neighborly cooperation remained an ideal that influenced the way people thought about who they should be employing: emphatically, not a complete stranger. We see that a sha'bī household, illustrated by the Sebbaris, is one with open doors; its members spill over into the homes of neighbors, and its wealth (in this case, in the form of milk money and couscous) finds its way across the street. Hierarchies within and beyond the household are expressed through naming practices—*Mui* and *Ḥajja*, for instance, are general respectful terms of address for one's elders; through who is invited, who sits where, and who is expected to help in the kitchen; and through food—who is assigned more meat and who receives the chef's compliments. So although everyone is connected "like family," not everyone is really "beḥel beḥel." Known domestic workers are easily brought inside the boundaries of the household and slotted into a ready-made subordinate "daughter" rung. When workers known through kinship or vicinage are not available, the most sha'bī of Moroccans might go without employing a domestic. In many sha'bī settings, though, a daughter-shaped space awaits an outsider.

Notes

1. A person from Rabat is called a Ribāṭī. It has been argued that Moroccan domestic techniques are labor intensive to combat boredom: "Townswomen especially, are often more concerned about how to spend time and effort than how to save them" (Maher 1974, 104). There is also an argument that time-consuming housework serves to keep women out of "mischief." See Hirschon (1978) on "prostitute's food" among Greeks in Asia Minor and Rivière (1984, 11, 89) on Amazonian women pounding manioc for longer than necessary to make it edible. Female ethnographers of Amazonia insist, however, that Rivière's portrayal of women effectively "chained to the hearth" is the misconception of a male anthropologist who has not participated in this work, which is experienced by women as convivial and vitalizing (Nahum-Claudel 2017). I could not say the same for women's work in Morocco, although at times boredom in the field made even shelling peas seem fun.

2. In one Hay Riad apartment I noticed the kitchen light switch was inconveniently on the far side of the room, next to the chambre de bonne, which was being used as a store; they had no maid. Clearly the domestic worker imagined by the architect was to be first awake and last asleep.

3. Some branches of the family remained in the old city of Rabat while others are in other Moroccan cities, and some of the younger generation have moved to Europe.

4. It is rare to hear the quarter referred to by its Arabic name (the French is the original name, the Arabic a translation), although it does appear on the fronts of buses to that quarter.

5. Anonymous blogger, VIP blog (n.d.). Horchata is a traditional Spanish drink, originally made from tigernuts.

6. Rabat came into prominence under the Almohads as a fortress for launching attacks on Iberia. The name of the Oudaya dates from a later arrangement between the Alouite sultan Yacoub al-Mansour and the Arab Oudaya tribe whom he hired to defend the city, which he refortified with further ramparts to the west (Terrasse 1952).

7. This is the title of volume 1 of Choukri's (1993) autobiography, which recounts his family's migration from their village in the Rif Mountains during a famine in the 1930s.

8. See Rivet (1999, 319) on *garsūnāt*.

9. In wealthier quarters Moroccan aristocrats who were integrated with the French-run economy had also moved into villas originally built for Europeans (Villème 1952, 89, cited in J. Abu-Lughod 1980, 212).

10. A traditional house that, technically speaking, contains an inner garden.

11. See Saaf (1999) on communities of regulars on buses from the poorer quarters of Rabat.

12. See Ehrenreich (2010) on low-wage workers in America and the difficulty of escaping the poverty trap.

13. The Arab-Berber distinction is more imagined than real; Moroccans often say "every Arab has a Berber grandfather" (Maher 1974, 25). On Berber identity, see Crawford and Hoffman (2000) and Hoffman and Miller (2010). Cf. Ensel (1999) on estates of "saints" and "servants" in southern Morocco.

14. Ossman (1994) describes Casablanca's Aïn Chok as "populaire" in the sense of working class.

15. Janet Abu-Lughod (1971) distinguishes "traditional urban" from rural and modern or "industrial" urban. Messiri follows her observation that in Cairo "traditional urbanism," or "the community of *ibn al-balad*" is most strongly linked to the physical spaces in the city that are the oldest inhabited—i.e., in which traditional activities survive despite the mobility of populations (1978, 58). See also Singerman (1995, 11–13). Sha'bī and *baladī* coexist as distinct terms in Egypt. Moroccans use *bildī* (i.e., *baladī*) to refer to authentic Moroccan produce—for example, *z-zīt l-bildī*, or olive oil. On urban Moroccan notions of bildī as "proper food," see Graf (2016).

16. Community features as an exception in writing on globalizing Arab cities. To take an example from the Persian Gulf, Al-Za'ab, named after its inhabitants, *Za'abīs*, who arrived as a group in Abu Dhabi in the 1960s, is "the one predominantly 'national' area on Abu Dhabi island where one sees people outside their houses in the evening talking to neighbors" (Dresch 2006, 207).

17. For middle-class Bengalis in Kolkata, the difficulty of hiring servants was a deterrent to moving into new residential areas. Apartments designed for nuclear families where young mothers would have to bring up children without the help of the extended family were to be avoided (Donner 2013).

18. The convention is to name houses after the male household head. See Munson's (1984) *House of Si Abd Allah*. The word *dār* denotes both the physical building and the members of the household. If a man asks his friend 'how is the house?' he is politely enquiring after the friend's wife and children. See Bourqia (1996: 23).

19. The idea is taken up in Willa Cather's American novels describing the years around 1900. See, for example, her *My Antonia* [(1918) 1994].

20. See Goichon (1929, 18). My host father was nursed as a child by a Saharan dada whom his family brought with them when they moved to l'Océan from Agadir. The dada eventually married and set up her own household in l'Océan, but even after her death, her son's wife regularly paid visits to my host mother.

21. The title *Ḥajja* denotes a woman who has performed the *Ḥajj* (pilgrimage to Mecca) and is used as a term of respect for the elderly more generally.

22. Tom McDonald (2011) examines relationships between people and floors in China and, inspired by Ingold's "barefoot" approach (2004), suggests much is to be gained if anthropologists attend to the ground beneath their feet.

23. *Trīd* is a time-consuming dish that involves first making layered *ghayf* (pancakes) then tearing them into tiny pieces over which a spiced stew is poured.

24. For a discussion of food as it relates to social status see Appadurai (1981) on "gastropolitics" in Hindu South Asia.

2

MOTHERS AND DAUGHTERS

It is common to hear Moroccans say that so-and-so took in a girl "to help with the housework" and treated her "like a daughter." This familial model of domesticity harks back to the widespread long-term placement in wealthier households of the daughters of poor families, often from the countryside. Mernissi stated in the 1980s that "the domestic who is paid a wage is a new phenomenon; traditionally domestics lived in and were supported, but received no actual wage" (1982, 31). Writing on Algeria, Jansen similarly attested to a rise in the importance of market relations over patronage relations by the 1980s: "There is an increased tendency to pay [women workers] with money, rather than gifts and fictive kinship" (1987, 241). Of interest, then, is the continued use of idiomatic kinship for shorter-term waged employment, which in many respects follows the logic of the market rather than the family. In this sense Moroccan households resemble Lévi-Strauss's concept of houses in *sociétés maison* where economic interests "borrow the language of kinship, though it is foreign to them, for none other is available" (1983, 186–87).[1] Lévi-Strauss argued that kinship terms naturalize differences of rank in the transition between kin and class-based society. The theme runs throughout this book.

The Logic of Kinship

The use of idiomatic or "practical" kinship is not restricted to domestic work in Morocco but applies to waged service around the globe.[2] Writing on South African domestic service, Cock argues that fictive kinship blurs the boundaries between paid and unpaid labor, but "in no case was there the sharing of power and resources that authentic family membership might be thought to involve" (1980, 132). This, of course, is a naive idea of family equality. Ray and Qayum, meanwhile, argue that in Kolkata, India, the "one of the family" rhetoric indexes both the hierarchical structure of family in which the servant stands "on the lowest rung" and the characteristics of love, loyalty, and generosity that family members (and servants) are expected to manifest (2009, 96). Of Tanzanian domestic service, Bujra writes, "the intimacy between family members is brought into uncomfortable liaison with the distance required between class unequals" (2000, 87). An obvious solution is to employ an "unequal" family member. The tendency to "foster" rather than simply employ, familiar from English literature and history, is a way to mediate the tension.

This idea led, in the Bertram household of Austen's ([1814] 2003) *Mansfield Park*, to "a reliance on the lower-class stationary niece," Fanny, who was "useful" for running errands, "as defence against the dangers of 'encroaching' employees" (Sutherland 2003, xxx). But if someone is not kin, calling them kin might be the next best thing. Lethbridge argues that when "lady-helps" came into vogue in early twentieth-century Britain, they looked "something like the older form of [female] dependant that one might have found in the seventeenth-century English household: the relative, widowed perhaps or unmarried, who occupied a place in the house" (Lethbridge 2013, 170–71). Significantly, the first agency offering this kind of help in Britain (established in 1921) used a kinship term in their name: Universal Aunts (175–76); Country Cousins was another agency that specialized in placing "well-born ladies with no money" (283).

If *daughter* is the kinship term most commonly used by Moroccan employers to refer to their domestic workers, let us consider what it means to be a daughter in Morocco. My own experience echoes that of other fieldworkers—the longer we stayed, the more "like a daughter" we became, and the more our hosts assigned to us household tasks. Lila Abu-Lughod describes this progression in her fieldwork among Egyptian Bedouin: "Although I never completely lost my status as a guest in their household, my role as daughter gradually superseded it. . . . I became part of the backstage when we had company, found myself contributing more to household work than I wished, and had my own chores" (1986, 15). The mediator who introduced me to a Marrakechi family I stayed with in 2006 said that because I was paying, I was not expected to contribute to housework. I thought nothing of this at the time and, often out of boredom, did help with housework, although my help was not solicited. My host parents always said that I was like a daughter to them. *Not exactly*, I thought, *since I pay you rent and you never tell me to clean the floor.* But as I continued to visit over the years, more as a friend or pseudo-daughter than a lodger, my host mother began to ask me to do more, particularly when she had guests. She would instruct me to heat water and wash dishes or *sekhkher*—to run errands, go to the shop or "street oven,"[3] jobs usually given to prepubescent girls—so that she need not put on her headscarf. Just before I started my doctoral work, my host mother, bemused by my sudden interest in domesticity, seemed more conscious of my (tiny) contribution. She began to give me tasks with a twinkle in her eye: "Come on. So you can tell your mother *sekhkhertī* [you worked] for us!"[4]

That being a daughter is associated with service was made explicit when I spent the afternoon in l'Océan with a neighbor whom I called *khāltī* (aunty) because she was about my mother's age. As she was kneading the dough for *ghayf* (pancakes), she asked me to take a frying pan out of the cupboard, saying, "*Kankheddemik* [I'm making you work]! *Ṣāfī* [that's it], you've become my daughter!" But there is another dimension to being a daughter. My neighbor wanted to give me some pancakes to take home with me. I told her not to trouble herself, but she responded, "You're our daughter," which involved not only giving but also receiving care. Because Moroccan daughters are expected to work, it makes sense that those who work are classified as daughters even if they are not biological relatives. And because Moroccan daughters receive care (food, shelter, clothing, love), it also makes sense that a young woman living in the home of an employer and receiving some or all of these things should be classified as a daughter.

When employers call their workers "my daughter," they invoke the logic of a patriarchal economy based on an intergenerational contract where gift and return gift link one generation with another.[5] Mauss (1925) used the term *don et contre-don* to point to the logic of reciprocal exchange between groups. In Morocco daughters owe their labor to men and older women and will receive their recompense, such as being served in turn by younger women, only later in life (Crawford 2008, 50). But while a mother effectively says to her biological daughter, "Work for me now, and when you are a mother, your daughter will work for you," domestic workers, as eternal "daughters," rarely come to be recompensed in this way.[6] The unequal long-term exchange of the old model in which domestics are "brought up" by patrons who profit from their social sterility, as it were, is replaced in the market economy by a short-term exchange of work for monthly pay. A Moroccan domestic worker can now walk out with her payment in hand. Thus a "daughter" may suddenly leave for a more lucrative post or one with better conditions, calling into question the permanence of relatedness.

As Bloch argues, for the Merina and more generally, long-term relationships are characterized by a high degree of morality: "balance is not sought in the short-term because the relationship is assumed to endure" (1973, 76).[7] He stops just short of stating that kinship is the moral relationship par excellence. Elsewhere Bloch, together with Parry (1989), argues that short-term exchange cycles belong with individual acquisitive activity while long-term exchanges occur to reproduce the social order. If workers are not staying long-term, however, the relationship can be assumed to have a low moral content, and kinship terms are misnomers—unconditional terms for a conditional relationship of pay for work. The cash payment is an important change, as it is a way to seek balance in the short term. As Caplan argued for Nepal, "transactions in the market place are market exchanges, meaning short-lived, 'self-liquidating' relationships involving almost exclusively a cash medium" (1971, 271). Caplan found that cash was unsuitable for bribing officials since "in its 'untamed' state, [it] demands an immediate and equivalent return, ignores status differentials between the parties to the transaction and is therefore not, like kind, a suitable medium for transforming simplex into multiplex ties" (276). Paying domestic workers in cash means fewer "ties that bind." Without such a payment, arrangements often look something like fosterage.

Fosterage

Increasing the number of hands available for work by taking in a dependent, often a child or teenager, is common in many societies. Meillassoux points to the transfer of children in rural Africa as a means of correcting the discrepancy between natural reproduction and the exigencies of material production in family units (1975, 76), but children are also transferred to help with "unproductive" housework—work that does not produce goods for subsistence or trade.[8] In Morocco we might call such arrangements fosterage, although the term covers a range of meanings (Maher 1974, 5) and, if used indiscriminately, hides more than it reveals.

Fosterage overlaps adoption in many respects, but while the former tends, in comparative work, to denote temporary arrangements in which children maintain their initial status, the latter is often used for arrangements where a child is given the name of his or her adopting parents and stands to inherit from them.[9] Those, like J. Goody (1969), who adhere to this distinction point out that while caring for an orphan is meritorious in Islamic teaching, adoption (*tabannī*, "to make one a son") is forbidden. Muhammad himself was orphaned and cared for by kin (Qur'ān 93:6). The Qur'ān commands believers to do good to orphans (2:177, 4:36), spend their wealth on them (2:215), feed them (76:7–10), and not to appropriate their property (4:2, 4:6, 4:10, 6:15). Just treatment of orphans is also a subject in *ḥadīth* (Hamid 2003, 29). The prohibition of tabannī, meanwhile, is based on Qur'ān 33:4–5: "nor has He made your adopted sons your sons." Family law in Muslim states follows this prohibition, with the exception of Tunisia (Borrmans 1977; Charrad 2001, 227), but culturally sanctioned forms of social parenting are found across the region. Sonbol's (1995) historical overview of adoption in Islamic societies shows how practice and law diverge. Similarly, studying "new kinship" in Muslim communities in Lebanon, Clarke gleaned from conversations with lawyers and orphanage staff that "fostering arrangements often shade into adoption in fuller senses" (2008, 164).

The separation of adoption and fosterage does not go uncontested in comparative literature. Brady (1976) observes a continuum between the two in Oceania, noting that arrangements are sometimes "inclusive" and sometimes "exclusive" in regard to inheritance, authority, and incest prohibitions. Bargach argues against a "legally oriented Eurocentric definition of adoption" that "denies, in general, the Muslim world its share and contribution to this phenomenon because of a religious prohibition" (2002, 7). Pointing out that the absence of the *legal* category of adoption does not preclude the practice of *culturally* sanctioned forms (27), she describes three forms of social parenting in Morocco: *trebbī* (family or customary adoption, literally bringing up), which is not formalized and looks from the outside something like "an interminable visit"; extralegal, secret adoption (tabannī), where parents pass off as their own the biological child of another (27–29); and *kafāla* (guardianship without filiation), which was legalized in Morocco in 1993. The term *kafāla* is applied across the Arab states to a wide variety of arrangements, including, in the Persian Gulf, a means of controlling foreigners (Dresch 2005; Mahdavi 2016).

A central concern in the literature on adoption and fosterage is whether it fills a need in the foster family, what Barraud (2011, 9) calls "kafāla utilitaire"— for instance, by providing an heir (Waltner 1990)—or is for the benefit of the child, often orphaned or poverty-stricken (Goody, J. 1969, 57–58, 65; Etienne, M. 1979, 79).[10] Fosterage seems most likely to occur where the child, the birth family, *and* the fostering family benefit, but where mutual gain is not automatic, labor is a way of settling the balance.[11] This was the case when the fictional Anne of Green Gables was nearly adopted by Mrs. Blewett, who intoned, "I'll expect you to earn your keep, and no mistake about that" (L. M. Montgomery [1908] 1994, 55).

The line between earning your keep and exploitation is a thin one, and this concern, more recently addressed as a human rights issue, has long existed in Morocco as part of a religious debate. The proper balance between charity and gain was invoked by the sultan in 1883, when he brought to order a *qā'id* (rural headman) who had taken in the daughter of a free man during a famine and effectively enslaved her to his household. In response to the father's plea, the sultan ordered the qā'id to return the girl: "One does not appropriate free people for one's personal use. Even if you did acquire her during a famine, and fed her *for the love of God*, do not render useless your good work" (Ennaji 1999, 87, emphasis mine). This was an echo of Qur'ān 2:177: "it is righteousness . . . to spend of your substance, 'alā ḥubbihi [out of love for him—i.e., God], for your kin, for orphans, for the needy." Ennaji explains that during nineteenth-century famines, it was common for a child to be "given away for a bit of bread, or 'confided to the care' of a third party, while waiting for better times to come" (Ennaji 1999, 80). Only those with extended families managed to protect themselves against hard times, and marginals had no option but to seek protection with patrons (88).[12]

A number of characteristics of Moroccan society sustain the incorporation of dependents into the domestic labor force of wealthier households. Not least, social parenting is practiced widely among relatives; girls in particular are frequently fostered by uterine kin (S. Davis 1983, 164–65; Maher 1974, 132), and I met several women in the countryside and in a *shaʿbī* (ordinary) urban context who were bringing up their granddaughters or nieces for indefinite periods.[13] When I asked the reason, people sometimes referred to previous arrangements that were now being reciprocated. Rachida's explanation of why she was looking after her niece, Ghita, is typical: "Ghita's mother, my sister, brought up our little sister anyway, and I was brought up by Dār Sebbari, and I brought up the daughter of my brother, and my other sister's daughter stayed with me for six months, and another one for four months. . . ." Hardly anyone in Rachida's family had spent all of their childhood with their biological parents. There was a sense in which women within this kin group took turns in bringing up the group's children. In a rural community one reason given was that the child had "got used to being with us. When her mother took her away to sleep with her, she didn't like it and cried, so now she stays with us, and we bring her up." There was no criticism of the child's biological mother in this statement. It was just that the child preferred staying at her grandmother's.

It is only a step further from these arrangements between close family members to send a child to more distant kin. Childlessness is often a reason at the receiving end. Tahara, whom I met in Salé, was brought up in l'Océan by the daughter of her paternal aunt, who had had several miscarriages. Tahara explained, "It was poverty that let my mother [give me away]." She called her foster mother *māmā lī rbbātnī* (mother who brought me up), or just *māmā*; she called her biological mother *māmā f l-blād*, or mother in the countryside. Tahara was strongly attached to the family who had brought her up but disagreed with the practice in general. When a relative had asked her to give away one of her own girls, she had refused: "A mother has to bring up [her child]. Yes, a mother has to give birth, but a mother also has to bring up." Tahara maintained that she herself had not been fostered to help with housework. But she had not gone to school, and when she was twelve she began to take responsibility for things in the house. Later in life Tahara cut short her time working as a domestic in a Bahraini palace (organized through Mehdi's agency in l'Océan, see chap. 4) in order to stay at home and care for her ailing foster mother so that the biological son and daughter, born after Tahara was fostered, could pursue their careers.

The link between fosterage and domestic work is well documented in literature on Morocco. Maher argues that, although there are many motivations for fosterage (death, divorce, sterility, maintenance of kinship bonds, schooling), it occurs most often in the interest of the adults involved (1974, 133). Not without exaggeration, I suspect, she states that "foster-children are essentially servants" (136). A quarter of the households in her small-town sample contained foster children, "generally maids-of-all-work," many of them kin of their foster parents (71). Significantly, fostering enabled childless couples to enact norms of status and seclusion, as the wife could "send her small minion on missions to the outside world" (133). She might also equip the child to deal with the world and thus discharge a carer's duty.

The institution of *mutaʿallima* (literally learner; plural *mutaʿallimāt*), noted by Davis in her Moroccan village study, closely resembles fosterage: "Often their families live in the country and can barely support all the children, and so are relieved to send one off to a wealthier branch of the family. Neither she, nor her family, receives any remuneration, but she is fed and clothed *like a member of the family*. . . . Girls from 7 to 8 years old may work as *mtaʿllmat* [sic]; until they are married" (1983, 78, emphasis mine).

By putting the stress on the girl's role as a learner—a kind of domestic apprenticeship—the shame of working for another household could be muted. This also relieves employers of the responsibility to pay a wage.[14] Salahdine documents how during the 1980s, a Moroccan woman who was "training" a thirteen-year-old apprentice stated that she paid her nothing but gave her parents 200 or 300dh when they visited three or four times a year. She stressed that this was not remuneration for housework performed by the girl, claiming that the burden of keeping her (the cost of her training, broken plates, food, clothing) outweighed the gain from any work she did: "It's she who ought to pay me, not the other way round" (Salahdine 1988, 108).

As with apprenticeship, the reclassification of unequal relationships as "fosterage" (trebbī) reduced the implication of shame. In her Algerian study, Jansen found that "women without men," who had to work, preferred to serve Algerians rather than the French, so the relationship could be seen as fosterage and was therefore less dishonorable (1987, 204). While the girl's status as a daughter saved her from the stigma of working as a servant, "she had no right to any pay" (204). As a daughter the girl could expect her foster family to arrange her marriage and provide her with a dowry, but the employer might see "her maintenance through the years as sufficient pay for her services, and the arranging of the marriage as an extra" (204). Where families did arrange and finance the marriages of their foster daughters, they were "quick to point this out to others in order to get full credit" (205). Alternatively, to avoid long-term responsibility for a foster daughter, "it was sometimes easier to pay them a small wage and send them away when they reached puberty" (205).

Goichon points to similar arrangements in Fes during the 1920s. As the use of domestic slaves declined, the bourgeoisie sought orphans or poor children as "*petites bonnes, mutaʿllemāt* [sic]" (Goichon 1929, 43). Most families treated these children somewhat like the children of the house, occupying them "according to their capabilities, to wash the *zellīj*, a bit of laundry, to help in the kitchen, bring the table and the dishes for meals" (44).[15] They were allowed to play with the other children: "even though the latter were not completely fraternal with them" (44). The longer a domestic stayed, the more she was treated as a member of the family, but always with "a nuance of inferiority" (48). The role of the *maîtresse* vis-à-vis her *bonne* extended beyond the latter's marriage and departure from the household—she was maternal but not intimate: "she gives them presents from time to time" (47). Not all girls were treated as "one of the family"; Goichon found some overworked, beaten, and covered in burn marks.[16] A sick domestic, unlike the slave whom she had replaced, could be dismissed at no loss, and another could be procured at no cost (45).

Writing much later, Bargach argues that "adoption" replaces indentured service in Morocco: "Given the difficulty of finding domestic workers . . . a number of people have resorted to 'adopting' older girls from orphanages in order to employ them as maids" (2002, 98).[17] During my fieldwork, I came across many domestic workers who were being or had been "brought up" by the households they served until they were married. At Dār Sebbari in l'Océan, I got to know several such "daughters of the house" who had been raised by Mui Latifa. Though they lived elsewhere, their ongoing membership in the familial group required continual work from both sides—work in the sense of housework as well as the symbolic work of acting as family. They were certainly not slaves, but neither could one call them free.

Milk Teeth and Photographs: Mui Latifa's "Daughters"

"Do you know how many *bnāt* [girls, daughters] I've brought up [*rbbīt*] and married off?" boasted Mui Latifa, holding up ten fingers.[18] "They came to me very young. They lost their milk teeth with me!" This was my introduction to Khadija, who had come with her three-year-old son to visit. It was the first time I had met one of the "daughters" Latifa had "brought up," as opposed to her biological daughters.

Khadija, originally from Ouezzane, had been brought to Dār Sebbari at the age of seven by her father, who wanted to remove her from household disputes—there were often fights. She saw her own family once a year but claims she did not miss home because the Sebbari house was always so full of people. That Khadija stayed at Dār Sebbari until she was married was in accordance with custom, except that she married late: "I stayed [*gālsa*] with them thirty-three years."[19]

The word *gālsa* (remaining, sitting) conceals a large contribution to the work of the house: cleaning, errands, cooking, and laundry. But Mui Latifa insists that Khadija is not a <u>kh</u>*eddāma* (a servant, a paid worker): "Khadija is *bintī* [my daughter]. Haven't you seen the photo of her son on the chest of drawers?" Indeed, the little boy who sat next to Khadija on the settee also smiled, sailor-suited, from a golden picture frame next to the television—proof of an authentic line of descent. I noticed too that Khadija had the same mannerisms as Mui Latifa's own daughters, particularly the way she tightened then loosened the muscles around her mouth at the end of a sentence and patted my arm for emphasis as she talked. The words of one of Mui Latifa's biological daughters to her domestic worker came to mind: "I'll knead you like dough in my hands." Mui Latifa had shaped Khadija to the form of her own daughters. Only her slightly darker skin and curlier hair suggested she was not a blood relation. The Sebbaris had the sought-after pale coloring typical of northern Moroccans; darker skin is seen as a marker of someone forced to spend time working in the sun or of slave origins.[20]

Mui Latifa was known for taking girls in; everyone talked about it. But what I did not discover for many months was that she sent one of her own daughters, Jihane, to be brought up in her uncle's household, where she stayed until she completed her studies. Jihane showed me photographs of herself with *bnāt ʿammhā* (the daughters of her father's brother), wearing fashionable dresses in front of fountains and monuments in Paris, at Versailles. These people clearly had money to travel and were of a different class from their cousins in l'Océan. Jihane, now in her sixties, never married, and I wondered if being brought up between two worlds had something to do with this. Potential suitors of her own class might have seemed unpromising in comparison with the kind of men her cousins were destined to marry, but, like Austen's Fanny Price, Jihane was probably not considered her cousins' social equal. Fanny Price's uncle was concerned she should know her place: "'There will be some difficulty in our way, Mrs. Norris,' observed Sir Thomas, 'as to the distinction proper to be made between the girls as they grow up: how to preserve in the minds of my *daughters* the consciousness of what they are, without making them think too lowly of their cousin; and how, without depressing her spirits too far, to make her remember that she is not a *Miss Bertram*'" (Austen [1814] 2003, 12).

One of the photos from Jihane's time with her cousins showed a man-servant pouring tea. His job was also to guard the family's villa in the upper-class Soussi area. Because the servants did everything at her cousins' house, Jihane never learned to cook or clean. When she moved back to her mother's house in l'Océan and began working as a secretary in a government ministry, "Jihane didn't know how to do anything in the house except shout instructions," recalled Rachida, another former domestic. "She wasn't brought up that way. Her cousins are shīkī [posh, from the French word *chic*]. At Mui Latifa's they are much more shaʿbī."

Mui Latifa's household had no manservant, just little girls like Khadija and others who appeared in family photos with Jihane's sisters, the same height but with darker skin. "Who is that?" I would ask, and Jihane would respond, "Just a girl who was staying [gālsa] with us." She did not recall all their names. Jihane's sisters were taught housework alongside these girls, as is common in sha'bī households. "We had a woman who did the housework, but my father told me to help so that I would learn from her," said one l'Océan resident. Another related how the domestic worker would say to her, "Do you want to go out? Then go and clean downstairs." She acknowledged, "I benefited from it. If it hadn't been for her, I wouldn't know how to do anything."

These remarks present a challenge to the notion, held by many white-collar workers, of domestic labor as unskilled. The skills required to keep a house in order are not innate but learned through watching, doing, correction, and doing again. This patient process is a labor of love on the part of the teacher as well as the learner and helps make sense of Latifa's pride in what she did for the girls she brought up.

Jihane alone was fostered out from Dār Sebbari, but Khadija was one of many who were fostered in. One evening I dropped in at Mui Latifa's when three of her bnāt had gathered there for evening coffee: Khadija, Hinde, and Rachida. "We were Mui Latifa's *équipe* [team]," joked Hinde. "Rachida brought me up. She used to smack me!" she added with a swipe of a tea towel in Rachida's direction, revealing their difference in age and the hierarchical relationships that had maintained order in the kitchen. In contrast to Mui Latifa's biological daughters, who had attended school, these girls had been educated at home: "I taught them to cook well and to make ḥelwa [sweets]," Latifa explained with pride. These were skills that prepared them for their current occupations: Khadija cooks in a *snack* (small café), Hinde sells her homemade ḥelwa, and Rachida takes jobs, off and on, as a domestic worker or cook.

Even in their absence, the traces left by these women at Dār Sebbari show the extent to which they remain associated with their former role. Mui Latifa would make offhand remarks like "there's the carpet that Khadija washed when she was here yesterday" or "taste these ḥelwa that Hinde came to make for me!" And when I was invited to Mui Latifa's to share Friday couscous, it was often Rachida I found in the kitchen: "They are crazy about my cooking. They've got used to it. The other day I made them trīd and they ate it all, and their hands too!" The image was akin to the notion of licking the plate clean; sha'bī Moroccans eat trīd with their hands.

Rachida had come to Dār Sebbari from Azilal in 1975. She was eight years old and had already lost her milk teeth, she is sure of it. The qā'id in her region of the countryside was from Bani Mellal, where one of Mui Latifa's own daughters was living at the time, and it was through him that the arrangement was made. Rachida stayed until she was married to a carpenter who came often to fix Mui Latifa's shelves and cupboards and whose mother worked as the domestic of a Moroccan ambassador. Rachida, a domestic, married the son of a domestic. There was no sense that being brought up in Dār Sebbari gave Rachida access to people of the Sebbaris' class, who were educated for white collar, albeit relatively low-ranking, jobs. Her fosterage did, however, probably mean the difference between marrying in the city and marrying in the countryside.

One afternoon Rachida's mother-in-law, Mui Fatiha, showed me her photo albums. The pictures had captured the mixing of two classes at shared rites of passage throughout her forty years of service. Along with photos of Mui Fatiha ironing or standing next to a long table covered in silver dishes, there were passport photos of the ambassador's sons at various ages. "Can I have one too?" she must have asked every time they came back from the photographer's. There was a photo of Mui Fatiha next to a boy riding a bicycle down a European street, another with her arms round the shoulders of well-dressed adolescents in a Moroccan embassy somewhere. In another the ambassador's wife was smiling while her domestic's grandson (Rachida's son) blew out the candles on his birthday cake. Rachida's daughter was later named after this lady, memorializing the intersection of the two families' trajectories. Similar photos of the servants are discussed in Light's (2007, 73) book about those who worked for Virginia Woolf and others in the Bloomsbury group:

> Sophie sent [the photographs] to Virginia. She wrote that she remembered her photograph being taken: 'One day your beloved mother found me in the kitchen shelling peas & said that's what I like to see you doing wait until I fetch Miss Stella to take a snap of you. Then came Mr Gerald [who] said I like to see you stirring with a big spoon. So hear [sic] they are.' She asked for the photographs back, then later changed her mind and wanted 'dear Miss Genia' to keep them . . . Like others trained in self-sacrifice she felt more comfortable giving away what she had. "I can always see myself in the glass," she wrote. It was more important to be reflected in Virginia's life.

Which photographs ended up in whose album was also important here. Mui Fatiha went on to show me pictures of Rachida's wedding, which clearly took place in Mui Latifa's house—the one in the medīna, before they moved to l'Océan. Surprisingly, though, Mui Latifa appeared only in the corner of one or two pictures, seen from behind, or with half her face cut out of the frame. It was only later that Jihane showed me her photographs, which told the other side of the story. Of the photos from Rachida's wedding, Jihane had kept those that showed herself, Mui Latifa, and the other biological Sebbari daughters alongside the bride. The photos in Mui Fatiha's album, which featured the groom's side of the family and in which Mui Latifa was cut out of the picture, were simply the ones the Sebbaris did not want.

The wedding photographs raised the question: who is Rachida's mother? Her biological mother, still living in the *blād*, who must have been present at the decisive moment when Rachida lost her milk teeth? Or Mui Latifa, who "brought her up"? Or Mui Fatiha, her mother-in-law, with whom she and her children live today, although Rachida's husband (Fatiha's son) lives elsewhere with a second wife? How are these mother-daughter relationships forged, broken off, or continued? Just as Mui Latifa's photo of Khadija's sailor-suited son served to include him in her genealogy, the photos in Mui Fatiha's album framed Rachida with her in-laws, leaving Mui Latifa, a rival mother, out. Contrary to the story told by her mother-in-law's album, Rachida has not cut Mui Latifa off but works hard to maintain the relationship with her, as well as with her other two mothers.[21]

When Rachida's husband took a second wife, Rachida went to work as a domestic for various employers, many of whom were foreigners who came and went. Whenever Mui Latifa heard Rachida was *gālsa* (sitting, implying she was at home without work), she called her to come and help at Dār Sebbari: "I can't say no. She's like my mother," Rachida explained. Rachida often managed and assisted the work of the current paid domestic in Mui Latifa's or Nadia's apartment, thus saving the family from having to oversee things.[22] Two other biological daughters of Latifa, and a now grown-up granddaughter whom Rachida had nursed as a child, also call Rachida for help with *l-ʿawāshīr* (thorough cleaning before feast days). On these occasions her identification with the house comes across clearly in contrast to the paid domestic's attitude, as illustrated by her criticisms of Mina's cleaning while doing l-ʿawāshīr at Nadia's:

MINA: "It's so dusty!"
RACHIDA: "You're the one who is here all the time."
MINA: "Well, dust comes every day."
RACHIDA: "That's not daily dust; that's the dust of a year."

Mui Latifa asked Mina to help her current paid worker, Jamila, to roll up a carpet that had been cleaned and left to dry. The carpet was still damp, and Mina pointed this out, but Jamila's response was "that's her problem, not our problem." They rolled up the damp carpet. I remember thinking that had Rachida been present, she would not have allowed this; for Rachida, Mui Latifa's problems were also hers.

Joseph argues for the existence in Arab societies of a specifically patriarchal connectivity ("relationships in which a person's boundaries are relatively fluid so that persons feel a part of significant others"), in which the production of selves is organized to "privilege the initiative of males and elders in directing the lives of others" (1999, 12–13). The literature is less vocal about matriarchy, which tends to be obscured under the rubric of kinship in which interest in relationships between mother-in-law and daughter-in-law eclipses mother-daughter relationships.[23] The fluidity of boundaries, to use Joseph's terms, between Rachida and the Sebbaris throughout her childhood and adolescence made her willing even twenty years on to undertake free labor for them: "When I work there, I feel as though I'm in my house.... There are no other families like them, who let you go wherever you want in the house, who get you to eat at the table with them. They never made any difference between us." Rachida was not, however, ignorant of the difference between herself and Latifa's biological daughters. When Mui Latifa was seriously ill for a while, Rachida went to visit her and relayed to me what Latifa said: that *l-bnāt lī rbbāthum* (the girls she brought up) are very dear to her; that first are her brothers and sisters, second her own children, then come the girls she brought up; that she had asked *l-bnāt diyālhā* (her own daughters) to take care of l-bnāt lī rbbāthum after she is gone. Rachida was delighted: "So we come third in all the world for her!" Rather than dwelling on boundaries that excluded her from the inner circles of the Sebbari family, she congratulated herself on being included in the group of loved ones Mui Latifa had delimited. A daughter "brought up" by *kafāla*, informally or formally, does not legally inherit. But Mui Latifa hinted that her biological daughters would inherit her role of "patron" to Rachida as a "client" and the responsibilities that come with that, like helping Rachida pay for medical expenses.[24] This configuration of concentric boundary lines around the family meant Rachida played the role of daughter toward Mui Latifa in the sense that she could not say no to her demands for labor, but not in the sense that she will receive an inheritance equivalent to that of Mui Latifa's biological daughters. The boundary line between "family" and "not family" is therefore a floating one. It can include a domestic worker as a *bint d-dār* (daughter of the house) for certain functions and exclude her for others.

I made several attempts to represent the temporary inclusions and exclusions created through fosterage and service at Dār Sebbari on a "kinship diagram," but the result was a mass of dotted lines and overlapping circles that became indecipherable. Writing on "the meaning of family ties" in Morocco, Hildred Geertz makes the point that the personal links forged through temporary or long-term fosterage "escape the crude techniques" of kinship charts "to which we anthropologists cling mainly because we know how to make them" (1979, 330). She rightly calls our attention to a broader range of personal ties, but the argument that "social ties of friendship and patronage intergrade with family, and many of the same norms apply to any of them" (377) avoids analysis of the norms that are not shared across the various types of connection.

In the absence of a legal framework for domestic work in Morocco, workers and employers impose limits on the connection between them according to their relative positions of power. An increase in the proportion of girls in education and a focus in the media over the last two decades on the abuse of child workers mean that domestic service has become less a matter of *petites bonnes* (child domestics) than of adult workers who are capable of refusing the manipulative and infantilizing aspects of fictive kinship while profiting, on a temporary basis, from other aspects of such a relationship.[25] I found that employers and workers together negotiate the limits and meanings of "mother-daughter" relationships, which are often ended abruptly by the departure of the worker.

"I'm Not Their Daughter"

Dār Sebbari illustrated the legacy of fosterage for domestic work, the traces of the past in the present, but most of the time when employers said of their current domestic workers "this is my daughter," it was code for "we take care of her":

> We don't make a difference between her and us. We are *kīf kīf* [the same]. If something hurts me, it hurts her; if it hurts her, it hurts me. This is my daughter.
>
> HAFIDA: "So you've just got two daughters?"
>
> HAYAT: "I've got three daughters! One very old [pointing to her domestic worker] and the others very young. There's a big [age] gap between them!"

HAFIDA: "*Allāh ykhlīhum lik* [God keep them for you]. God keep them for you, the three of them."

TOURIA: "It's hard for me to say kheddāma. She was my daughter. Hiba was very beautiful. When we went out or if she went to the market, I would tell Hiba to comb her hair and put on nice clothes. She looked lovely."

She narrated how they had taken Hiba to hospital to have her eye treated, and on their way home a neighbor saw them and said, "Hey, hey, it looks like you're the kheddāma and Hiba is the *mulat d-dār* [lady of the house]." Touria had replied, "Good. I'm glad you think that. It means there's no difference between me and her. She's my daughter. I don't want her to look like a kheddāma."

The use of the term *daughter* in these examples did not signify fosterage to anything like the extent that was common practice when Goichon was writing in the 1920s or even when Rachida was brought up in the 1970s. It was simply the conventional shaʻbī way of talking about one's domestic. Significantly, most workers did not call the mulat d-dār "māmā", although "khāltī (aunty)" was possible. Although some workers rejected employers' attempts to affiliate them, others resented the way employers paid lip service to this model, using the vocabulary of a mother-daughter relationship without acting that way. To quote Safae, "What upsets me the most is that they say, 'You're like our daughter!' And it's not like that. They say, 'You are like [name of daughter] and [name of daughter],' but I am not." Similarly, the neighbor who wanted me to help her make and eat pancakes, on the grounds of my being her "daughter," argued:

There are few that treat them like daughters. It's just from their mouths [i.e., it's just words]. If she is their daughter, they have to give her money for the *ḥammām* [public bathhouse] and take her out once a week and dress her and give her presents at *ʻīd* [a feast day]. Their daughter goes to school and comes home and puts her things down, and the kheddāma has to pick those things up and give her food and wash her clothes. She is not the same as a daughter. People who say that are *munāfiqīn* [hypocrites]. They say one thing and do another thing. And a worker who says [of her employers], "These are like my parents, I treat them like my mother and father," she is only saying this so she can cheat them and steal from them.

For the worker, indeed, the question is not always "how can I be included in the family?" but sometimes "how can I distance myself?" Writing about domestic workers in Britain, Todd argues that in view of servants' readiness to leave their positions when other economic sectors were expanding in the first half of the twentieth century, servants' relationships with their employers were characterized by "detachment." This, she suggests, is a more useful concept for social historians than deciding between "deference" and "defiance," which had been a preoccupation of academic writers between the 1960s and 1980s (Todd 2009, 183). Without using the term *detachment*, Steedman argues for a similar attitude among (fictional and nonfictional) servants in late eighteenth-century Yorkshire. Their "disaligned, disconnected stoicism" in the face of employers' idiosyncrasies showed that "they are not mothers, daughters, sisters, wives but domestic servants, hired hands" (2007, 213) who worked primarily to put aside some savings. In a discussion of Emily Brontë's ([1847] 2003) *Wuthering Heights*, Steedman contrasts the figure of Joseph, "a very old servant, and a very old servant-type," who has lived and worked sixty years at the Heights, with that of younger Nelly Dean, who, despite being brought up as a kind of foster sister in the Earnshaw household, "is the modern type, flitting over the hills from one hiring to another, calculating her wages with a very nice reckoning of what she will and will not do, and when and whom she'll love" (2007, 215). This kind of detachment rings true for many domestics in Morocco and contradicts Borrmans's rose-tinted vision of domestics in Algeria in the 1950s: "the Muslim woman, traditionally family orientated, has just one wish, to be allowed to take part in the family life of her employers" (Borrmans 1955, cited in Brac de la Perrière 1987, 123).

Just as the servant types of Joseph and Nelly overlapped at the Heights, two modes of serving were evidenced under the same roof at Dār Sebbari, where women like Rachida contrasted with a newer kind of worker for whom Dār Sebbari represented only a short stage in her career. One floor above Mui Latifa's apartment lives her daughter Nadia, a clerk in one of the government ministries and mother of three adult children. Far from enjoying thirty-three years of service, as her mother had, it is difficult for Nadia to get a domestic to stay more than three months. When I first moved into the building, I met Malika (twenty-one years old), who was introduced to me as "the friend" of Nadia's eighteen-year-old daughter, Zahra. Malika, who grew up in a squatter settlement outside Fes, left Nadia's after six weeks. She complained that they wanted her to be "like a daughter": "There should be *ḥudūd* [boundaries] between the employers and the kheddāma, but they have taken away all the boundaries."[26] Her words made me think of what Zahra had said about a former domestic: "Hanane was my sister. We were the same age. We slept in the same bed, and she would hold me in her arms." This embrace would have horrified Malika: "I'm *not* their daughter," she told me. "I work in their house, and that is all."[27] In contrast to Hanane, Malika did not like it when Nadia greeted her with a kiss; did not want to listen to Zahra talk about boyfriends ("I don't give her the chance!"); did not want to take photos of Zahra in numerous outfits, which she demanded at eleven o'clock at night; and did not want to sleep in the same room as Zahra.

The smallness of Nadia's apartment—comprising one salon and two bedrooms (one for the parents, the other for the two sons)—meant that Zahra and Malika slept in a spare room in Ḥajja Jamila's apartment (the neighbor on the same floor who had shared the bildī house with the Sebbaris when they first moved to l'Océan). Malika repeatedly told me how other employers had given her the run of entire floors of their villas. It is therefore not surprising that she felt herself too much in proximity with Zahra. When at home on the outskirts of Fes, Malika sleeps with her five siblings in one room about the same size as Ḥajja Jamila's spare room, but sleeping in the company of others clearly sat ill with her idea of a workplace. Her strict code of dress and behavior (Malika wears the *ḥijāb* and avoids contact with men) also presented challenges in this small apartment, where three unrelated men came and went, and she did not have anywhere private to change her clothes.[28]

For Malika, being "their daughter" signified being available twenty-four hours a day, seven days a week. She did not have fixed working hours and had to say she was feeling ill in order to go to bed before Zahra. For her part, Zahra slept in each morning during the summer holiday period, which coincided with Ramadan, but Malika had to get up to do the housework; she was the bint d-dār to work at all hours but not to rest during the morning in Ramadan. In fact, Malika did not have any days off: "The weekend is the worst because the employers are there the whole day to pester me." Although the Moroccan *code de travail* stipulates a maximum of forty-four hours of work and at least a day of leave each week, it does not include domestics, and the law specific to domestic workers, still in draft, does not stipulate working hours.

For the majority of domestic workers, therefore, the hours they are expected to work are revealed bit by bit on the job and are subject to sudden modifications. Rouqia, for example, with whom I regularly spent Sunday afternoon, was often faced with the news that her day off was cut short. When an employer telephoned to tell her to come back and look after the children earlier than usual so she could go out herself, Rouqia complained:

"It's my day off. She should give me space. *Kayfūtū ḥudūdhum* [they overstep their boundaries]."

"*Their* boundaries?"

"Yes, it's they who set the conditions because it's their house, and we live at theirs. *Mktūb* [it is written]."

Rouqia was referring to divine predestination rather than to a written contract.

The question of limits and boundaries is particularly pertinent for those who work *b l-embāta* (literally "with staying the night"—i.e., live-in workers). Fatima explained, "No one wants to work b l-embāta. They double your work. Like *Itiṣālāt*![29] You never finish. It's as though your entire person belongs to them. You need ḥudūd to live your own life."

Just as some workers prefer to live away from their employers' homes so as to maintain boundaries around their personal lives, some employers prefer to employ live-out domestics for the same reason. Usually they have had a bad experience with one or more workers. One employer spoke of a series of thefts and concluded, "I prefer to employ someone who comes and has her hours to work and then leaves rather than someone who is always there. Then everyone knows her boundaries. She won't go through your stuff, for example." Some women who employed live-in workers operate a policy of changing them often, "otherwise they start to take advantage of you," one employer told me. This approach is, of course, open to both sides.

Temporary Daughters

Nadia's house was the tenth house in which Malika had worked in three years.[30] Malika was replaced at Nadia's by Loubna, who barely stayed a month. Mui Latifa, too, seemed to have lost her hold on people. In the twelve months I knew the family, I saw four successive domestic workers come and go in her apartment. Malika explained, from the worker's side, this strategy of short-term work: "At the beginning, she [the employer] treats you well; she greets you, she says, 'Welcome, you will be our daughter.' For a while, she respects your working hours, allows you to rest. But after a month, she tries to exploit you. Then you leave, and you find another household."[31]

I told Malika's story to Rouqia, who suggested it was an extreme case: "It's khayb [bad, literally ugly] like that. You really need to stay a bit longer in a household." Nonetheless, Rouqia agreed that employers' behavior often changed after a honeymoon period: "Yes, at the beginning they are very nice. 'Do you need anything?' . . . But they soon cease to *yḥssū bik* [be sensitive toward you, literally feel for you]. And when you live with someone, there are always things you argue over. So you leave. It's also true that you get bored; you leave for a change of scene."

That workers show themselves to be choosy is no doubt the cumulative effect of having worked for several households; they are equipped with knowledge of work elsewhere and are able to make comparisons. Malika, having worked in ten households, made numerous comparisons of Dār Sebbari with other *ménages*, starting with the size of the apartment and the lack of space assigned for her own use and moving on to household management and décor: "They don't know how to live!" was her conclusion. A major criticism was that the Sebbaris were "not clean." We encountered Nadia's fastidiousness regarding her white-tiled floor in chapter 1, but Malika pronounced, "If she wants to be clean, she should have a *système*," as in other households for whom she had worked, whereby indoor sandals were left at the front door to be worn by anyone who came in. The floor would then not need a second or third mopping each day.

Malika further criticized Nadia's failure to separate different garments for washing: "Underwear should be washed separately, in a separate bucket that isn't used for anything else." This indictment was brought on by Nadia placing on the kitchen countertop a towel she had used to wash herself. "The kitchen side! I wasn't going to touch it. It stayed there for hours. Then I picked it up with a plastic bag and poured bleach everywhere." Dirt, which Douglas ([1966] 2002) defined as "matter out of place," was probably categorized differently in each of the ten houses where Malika had worked. She had absorbed each household's theory of dirt to the extent that almost everything was dangerously dirty to her, and her hands were suffering from the use of so much bleach. At home in Fes, her mother, sisters, and aunts accused Malika of *l-weswās* (neurosis, whispers in the head): "You weren't like that before you started working in houses!"

By drawing on outstanding practices from each of her ex-employers, Malika was able to make unfavorable comparisons with her current ones, thus fueling a claim of superiority over them. This possibly served to counter her more general feeling of inferiority. The complement of this is that women who have employed many workers can also make comparisons between them, as Nadia did: "Soraya didn't complain when we asked her to scrub all the pans with *jīkz ū ṣābūn* [wire wool and traditional soap], and she's a lot younger than you!"

Discussing the high turnover of workers at Dār Sebbari, Rachida commented, "They want someone to stay always, just as we stayed. But they won't find anyone like that these days." Rachida, Khadija, Hinde, and others who not only had stayed a long time but, once married, had stayed in touch, served as points of reference for comparisons with current workers at Dār Sebbari. Employers like Nadia complained that the flightiness of "nomadic"[32] domestics is disruptive of family life (Salahdine 1988, 113n1) and one woman suggested a parallel with the divorce rate, which she believed to be increasing: "Half of my friends who married are now divorced. People have realized they have options now. Divorce is an option. People say, 'Okay, I'll divorce then.' Because all relationships require work. You have to work to maintain your relationships in the workplace, with your boss, with your family, with your maid even. . . . This high turnover, it [didn't used] to be like that. I remember we had a driver who stayed with us ten years."

Rachida did not offer an explanation for why long-term workers like herself are not to be found these days, but in another conversation, "girls all want to go to school now" was suggested as a reason, indicating that it was largely child domestics who had stayed a long time in one household. Others maintain that this mobility is motivated by a new desire to "follow the money." This expression seems to be a newer form of "following the bread," in which bread, an essential part of almost every meal in Morocco, stands symbolically for the bare minimum needed to survive. When patron-client relationships were no longer profitable for clients, they might say "my bread has dried up here." "Following the bread" thus emphasizes the necessity of working for a living; "following the money," by contrast, implies greed.

A fairer assessment than saying workers simply "follow the money" would be that workers will move jobs to better their overall conditions, a nexus that includes money but is usually not solely determined by it. According to domestics, a good salary (*temen*) and good treatment (*muʿāmela*) do not always go hand in hand. A third element is the volume of work (*temmāra*— hard, daily work). In making decisions about taking or leaving jobs, some workers prioritized one of these three factors, others another. The difference between Malika and her younger sister Ikram illustrates the point. Malika reminisced: "I was thinking about the people with whom I spent Ramadan last year. They were nice. They treated me like a daughter—they only had sons. They took me on outings, bought me things. . . . Whenever we walked around the neighborhood, people who knew the sons asked them who I was, and they replied that I was their sister. The people would say, 'I didn't know you had a sister,' and the sons would say, 'Well, now we do.'"

Malika related how when a boy had hassled her in the street, one of the sons had defended her, shouting, "Don't hassle my sister!" The two boys fought, and Malika ran inside to alert the mother, who, on learning the reason for the fight, said, "Good. Let them fight."

For Malika, both the willingness of this son to defend her and the mother's approval of his action were signs of the sincerity of family feeling toward her. Given this, I wanted to know why she had left them. "The salary was low," she replied.[33] In this household Malika had not rejected the mother-daughter relationship, nor the brother-sister relationship, in the same way that she rejected it at Nadia's, where she associated it with exploitation and a violation of her private life, her modesty even. She did not, however—to the great disappointment of this daughterless mother, I imagine—see herself as a "daughter" to the extent that she would stay with them when a position with a higher salary presented itself. Although they treated her well, temen took precedence over muʿāmela.

Malika's younger sister Ikram (eighteen years old) evaluated things differently. She too had worked in numerous households. On a single journey into the city, she pointed out four houses where she had worked, naming the monthly wages like a price tag attached to each. After leaving Nadia's sister in Casablanca, Ikram had gone to Asilah. The wage was low, but Ikram was *mertāḫa* (at ease, comfortable): "They were *mhallīyīn fiyā* [taking care of me]. They would take me out with them. . . . She [the lady of the house] would have lunch with me." But Malika persuaded Ikram to leave this position and replace her in another Casablancan family, saying they would pay more. It was common for older sisters to dictate to younger sisters where they should work, almost acting as brokers for them. Ikram told her employer that her mother was ill ("God forgive me. But it's true—she's been ill for two years!") and packed her bags. Concerned, the employer instructed her chauffeur to take Ikram all the way to the door of her house. They arrived in Fes at one o'clock in the morning, and the chauffeur turned around to make the return journey. "I felt sorry for him," said Ikram, who took the train to Casablanca the following morning. The next Sunday I met up with her, and she deeply regretted her move: "They don't have much temmāra [hard work], but there's no muʿāmela [(good) treatment] either. They don't take care of me like the family in Asilah."

Ḥajja Jamila's family, as employers, posited a similar contrast between their own offer of lower wages coupled with familial care and a situation with high wages coupled with neglect. They told the following story, which must have taken place some forty years ago and thus reflects an older pattern of service: Jamila's husband looked after the girl they had hired, buying sweets for her the way he did for his own children. He would check she was covered with a blanket at night, so she wouldn't catch cold. Once a year the girl's father came up from near Marrakech and was given 300dh for every month. One time he asked for more. They said, 'No, because she is fed, housed, clothed, and looked after." He took her to another house, where she slept in the kitchen and hung her things in a bag from a hook on the back of the kitchen door. The girl ran away from that house and came back to Ḥajja Jamila's family.

Today, it is less common for a father to collect his daughter's pay (except with young girls), but during a time when it was normal, this worker's flight from an uncaring household was understood less as an expression of agency on her part than as an illustration of the strong pull of care emanating from Ḥajja Jamila's family. "Taking care" of workers is specific to the sha'bī context. This became clear in a conversation between Hafida, a worker from the Gharb, and Hayat, an employer, about recommending Hafida's younger sister to some friends who were looking for a worker. Hafida voiced the concern of her parents: "The main thing is that they are a good family, reasonable, who will *ythallāw fihā* [take care of her]." "How?" asked Hayat. "In what way would they take care of her?" Hafida looked confused. This ythallāw fihā was a formulaic way of eliciting a guarantee of reasonable treatment from employers—at the very least assurance that there would be no physical abuse, that the worker would receive food and be allowed to rest enough. But Hayat's friends were not sha'bī employers and thus were not looking for a "daughter" to take care of. The job in question was in Les Ambassades, an affluent part of the city rather like Souissi or Bir Qasim, where the security guards I spoke to had noted a lack of family feeling toward workers. Hayat explained to Hafida that the position would be more like working in a hotel than for a family; there would be a hierarchical team of staff, and the mulat d-dār would not "interfere"; in other words, she would have little contact with the worker herself.

Conclusion

Most Moroccans, even sha'bī ones, do not behave as though domestics really are their daughters, for in the words of a worker's sister, "It's impossible. Think how they gave birth to their daughter, and they brought her up all these years, and they love her, and then you come, and they say you'll be the same as her to them. You can't be." However, the rhetoric is indispensable. Because sha'bī Moroccans extend kinship to those with whom they interact, to *not* speak about a worker as a daughter leaves a silence that suggests mistreatment and inequality. Given the stories of abuse that make the news almost weekly, everyone is alert to potential exploitation. But this is more than a one-sided argument. The boundary lines between family and worker are negotiated through words and actions on both sides. Inclusion as family requires constant work: showing photographs and telling stories about milk teeth to claim maternity; cleaning carpets and cooking couscous to keep filiation up to date.

Anthropological approaches to kinship as a process see relatedness as neither simply biological nor permanent (Carsten 2000), but the focus has been on activities that make people into kin. Howell (2003), for example, discusses the efforts of Norwegian couples to incorporate transnational adoptees into the family, a process she calls kinning. Less attention has been paid to the work that goes into *not* being kin or, having once been kin, de-kinning. Domestic service among ordinary Moroccans involves a double process of switching between relatedness and unrelatedness. Workers can invoke an identity as daughters in the sense of members of the household who have a right to "care" (gifts, outings) and reject this identity when it comes to responsibilities (remaining "faithful") or exploitation (working without time off) or when it no longer suits them (leaving for a higher salary). Employers can include workers as daughters to get them to pack suitcases late into the night before the family goes on vacation but exclude them from actually going along too. What jars with both employers and workers is seeing that the two sides of this fictive filiation—helping to make the pancakes and helping to eat them—are not in fact inextricable but instead, like oil and vinegar, separate as soon as you stop stirring.

Notes

1. See Carsten and Hugh-Jones (1995, 10).
2. See, for example, Childress (1956); Drummond (1978); Colen (1989); Bakan and Stasiulis (1997); Anderson, B. (2000); Búriková and Miller (2010).
3. Street ovens are privately run enterprises where local residents take their homemade food (bread, biscuits, sometimes even stews) to be baked for a small fee, thus saving them from having to light the oven at home. They are more commonly found in sha'bī neighborhoods.

4. *Sekhkhāra* (literally errand runner) is equivalent to <u>kh</u>eddāma (worker) in some contexts, particularly further south, but is more pejorative.

5. See Aboderin (2006) and Alber et al. (2008) on the "generational contract" in Africa. This sort of language becomes plausible only when paying someone else to care for one's relatives becomes an option and one is not dependent on parental support.

6. This was not the case for "life-cycle service" in pre-1800 England, which usually involved servants who were social equals to their employers but simply younger. Most offspring left the home for a period of service any time after the age of twelve (Laslett 1965; Mayhew 1991). When they grew older these women employed servants of their own (Wall 2004, 21).

7. Combs-Schilling's (1985) study of merchants in Imi-n-Tanout, southern Morocco, supports Bloch's theory.

8. In colonized Zambia many households "kept" young relatives who did household work without pay (Hansen 1986, 18).

9. Africanists have analyzed the circulation of women and children in various descent groups (E. Goody and J. Goody 1967). See J. Goody (1969) for a comparative survey of the literature on adoption in Hindu, Chinese, Greek, and Roman societies. Lallemand (1988, 1993) discusses the circulation of children in terms of alliance (like marriage). Despite these studies, the literature on adoption and fosterage is smaller than it might be due to a genealogical bias (Etienne, M. 1979, 66).

10. Waltner is writing on late Imperial China. Generally, little is said anywhere of the adoption of females, which must obey a different logic as far as property transfer is concerned.

11. This is often the case with "schooling fosterage" (E. Goody 1982; Alber 2010). Cf. Apt (2005) on the link between fosterage and domestic work in Ghana.

12. S. Shah (2000) records a similar pattern of "fosterage" in contemporary Nepal: marginal households place children to work in the home of a patron as surety or interest on a loan.

13. See Channa (1996, 21–35) on a Moroccan child who was "given" to her aunt.

14. For working children in Cairo, Farag observes that "frequently, their work is not conceived as labor at all, but disguised as some form of apprenticeship or training" (1995, 239).

15. *Zellīj* is tile work made from enameled terra-cotta.

16. If gold jewelry is the essential trope of the Moroccan rags-to-riches tale of a foster girl being accepted as "one of the family," burn marks are the sine qua non of abuse narratives. Stories of girls whose treatment falls between these poles tend to go untold, reinforcing "the almost mythic quality that the character of the maid is acquiring in Moroccan female society" (Kapchan 1996, 223).

17. See also Barraud (2011, 11).

18. Moroccan Arabic, like French, uses one word for both girl and daughter (*bint*, plural *bnāt*).

19. On guardians marrying off those in their care, see Maher (1974, 134). This is not restricted to Morocco; Jacquemin notes that domestics recruited as "*petites nièces*" in Côte d'Ivoire are given trousseaux (2002, 310).

20. On the disproportionate amount of earnings working-class Moroccan women spent on skin lightening products and sunscreen, see Cheikh (2011a, 177–78).

21. Not all fostered girls maintained relationships with their birth families, particularly in the case of a deceased birth mother.

22. In wealthy Victorian households, a large staff allowed some servants to perform this protective function since "those who were closest to defiling and arduous activities were, whenever possible, to be kept out of sight" (Davidoff 1995, 26).

23. More generally, for the Middle East, we have literature on kinship and gender but less on households, perhaps because fieldwork is largely done by young people without long-term constraints (Dresch 2000, 125).

24. Rachida's contribution to the housework for Dār Sebbari was otherwise unpaid.

25. For examples of media reporting on abuse of child domestics, see, Grotti (2004); Ksikes (2004); Azizi (2005); Deback (2010); *Le Parisien* (2011); Zerrour (2011); *Au fait* (2013).

26. The problem of boundaries between workers and employers is a common complaint. For instance, Cheikh's study of women sharing accommodation in Casablanca records a conversation between Atéka, a live-out domestic worker, and a potential employer whose probing questions provoked the comment "but you know these people do not know their limits, they only stop once they've properly hurt you" (Cheikh 2011a, 180).

27. A Japanese domestic who left service for factory work described, in the diary she published in 1912, a similar rejection of the daughter role as she refused her employers' offer of adoption (Nagata 2004, 224).

28. In Shi'a Muslim households in Iran, the sharing of the household space with servants was simplified by temporary marriage contracts (Khatib-Chahidi 1981). Servants, both male and female, were contracted in temporary marriages with relatives of the household head, usually infant sons or daughters, thus making the servant a son- or daughter-in-law. They were then subject to the sexual and marital prohibitions of unconsummated marriages so that women did not have to veil. Historically, another solution (open only to the wealthiest) was confining women to a *ḥarīm* guarded by eunuchs.

29. A humorous reference to a Maroc Telecom (*Itiṣālāt l-Maghrib*) promotion that doubled the value of prepaid telephone credit.

30. On workers who moved frequently in early twentieth-century Britain, see Scadden (2013, 124). One Welsh worker claimed to have had forty-three jobs in one year. On high turnover in England and France in the nineteenth century, see McBride (1976, chap. 4), who links it to both upward and downward social mobility.

31. Brac de la Perrière (1987, 103) records similar approaches in Algeria.

32. Borrmans' (1955) Algiers study opposes domestics who stay long-term, *sédentaires*, with *nomades* who change jobs frequently (cited in Brac de la Perrière 1987, 92).

33. Ilham made the same evaluation in one of her jobs: "I might change because of the pay. There's no hard work, and the treatment is good, but the pay is low." Ilham was paid 1,600dh a month.

3

A CIVILIZING MISSION

Charity, Reward, and Gratitude

THE "DAUGHTER" RHETORIC IS PART OF A BROADER moral framework through which workers and employers negotiate their relations and make sense of the vicissitudes of domestic service: the inequalities of give and take, patient endurance, or betrayal and reversals of affection. Just as Moroccan employers compare flighty workers who "follow the money" to those who serve faithfully, much discursive work also goes into defining domestic employment as caring or exploitative. Words of moral endorsement from social equals and gratitude from inferiors mark relationships as charitable, as does a bundle of very specific tropes about fictive daughterhood—what I call "signs of care." While these signs of care may be interpreted as controlling, alarm bells sound when they are missing. As convenient recipients of charity, domestic workers have been instrumental in defining the pious wealthy, and this is one of the points where a new discourse of workers' rights poses problems.

The making of persons through domestic service echoes the colonial *mission civilisatrice*—a rationale for colonization that used the expansion of civilization as a pretext for intervention. In this chapter a discussion of the civilizing mission of employers, which often takes on the language of family, is followed by an exploration of what happens when the process breaks down to reveal the "oil and vinegar" at the heart of these relationships. "Family" is clearly at odds with the market, but this problem is most likely older than the narratives of recent moral decline imply. I explore the enduring importance of charity (*khayr*), religious merit (*ajr*), and gratitude, which, hand in hand with the "daughter" rhetoric, obey a particular spatial and temporal logic. Geared to play out among neighbors (or at least among well-known clients) over the course of a lifetime, these ethics are disrupted by the easy-come-easy-go of the modern stranger-domestic. If employers earn ajr through the pious care of "kinning" their workers, workers do so through long-term patience and forgiveness. Those who abscond for short-term gain are meanwhile labeled thieves, a way of de-kinning that serves to emphasize differentials of wealth and morality.

"Kind" Payments: Signs of Care and Khayr

Whilst fosterage provides a clear opportunity to do khayr (good works, charity), employing a domestic worker is less obviously charitable, but by rewarding her labor at least partly in kind, and particularly in ways that represent maternal care, the lady of the house can still "do good." When talking about the *muʿāmela* (treatment) of domestics, both workers themselves and employers frequently point to formulaic signs of care that demonstrate how a given worker is "like a daughter." These often featured in narratives like the one told by Ḥajja Jamila's family in the previous chapter. In a similar fashion my host mother narrated how her neighbor, an older woman living alone, had a girl brought from the countryside to help her with housework. The woman treated the girl "like her own daughter," took her to the hairdresser's ("she didn't even know how to brush her hair!"), bought her clothes and gold jewelry, and eventually married her off.[1] Gifts of gold, associated with femininity and feminine power (Kapchan 1996, 225), equated workers symbolically with beloved daughters.[2] More often mentioned, however, was that workers ate with the family and were bought the same treats (biscuits, yogurt, etc.) that the children of the family were bought. Another common sign involved paying for the worker to go to the ḥammām each week (costing 10 or 12dh) and buying the necessary toiletries, particularly soap and shampoo (another couple of dirham).[3] Gifts of clothing were also much discussed. The "religious" imperative of new clothing at *ʿīd ṣ-ṣaghīr*, the feast which marks the end of Ramadan, meant some workers saw this as a kind of right and expected employers to provide it.[4] Soraya, a fourteen-year-old girl who was working at Dār Sebbari during her summer vacation "to earn money for school books," almost cried when she recounted how, although Latifa's Belgium-based daughter had given her a brand-new outfit, neither Latifa herself nor Jihane, the unmarried daughter who still lived with her mother, had given her anything: "Not a thread to floss my teeth with!" The Sebbaris probably considered the clothes from Belgium to suffice as a gift from the family as a whole, but Soraya would have been more satisfied with cheaper clothing as a sign of care from her own employer than with this relatively expensive outfit from another woman.

These things often took on an importance disproportionate to their monetary value. For Safae, whether shampoo was provided as part of the job was a deciding factor in choosing to stay or move on, and my suggestion that she calculate whether the amount she spent in buying these things for herself was more than the difference in salary between the two jobs in question fell on deaf ears. It was a matter of principle: "They have to pay for our shampoo, our ḥammām money, everything. We're living with them." For Algerian domestics in the 1950s, Borrmans noted that "to be the object of attention, to receive gifts, was more important than the salary they earned through work" (cited in Brac de la Perrière 1987, 123). But in the contemporary Moroccan context of my fieldwork, this was not the case for everyone. Others did make calculations or scorned employers' attempts to substitute for a decent wage the promise of provision in kind. When Sukaina's employer offered her very low pay but said, "I'll buy you clothes and things," Sukaina's friend objected and wanted to talk to the employer. "She can't do that—pay her little and then make up for it by buying the cheapest clothes she can find! No, Sukaina should have money to buy what she wants herself." Not only did the promised provision of clothing turn out to be very basic, but the arrangement also threatened the independence of this thirty-something worker. For Atéka, a former domestic who features in Cheikh's study of women living in shared apartments, independence of choice in clothing was a primary advantage of having left her live-in position: "Atéka manages to buy her own clothes and dress the way she wants, no one is there to give them to her out of charity or to tell her they are too figure-hugging. . . . Her clothes are not very beautiful but at least she chooses them herself" (2011b, 174). In fact, workers' clothing is often a point of contention. Giving "gifts" of clothing means employers feel not only that they can pay lower wages but also that they can control to some extent the appearance of the worker by making choices for her, as a parent would for a young child. As the literature on domestics worldwide suggests, female employers prefer workers to dress unattractively, not only out of fear that their husbands will be "tempted" (Kapchan 1996, 226; Constable 1997) but also to appear more attractive themselves by contrast.

In-kind payments of clothing or other items are reminders of the days when domestics and slaves were not paid at all but rather supported—a fact that protected them from sudden variations in the cost of living, such as the price of grain (Sarasúa 2004, 518). A general argument about modernization in Europe is that eighteenth-century economic rationalization eroded the "moral economy" (Thompson 1971) in which landowners were obliged to provide for laborers, so that labor became commoditized and payments monetized, although this has been criticized as an overly simplified view of the period (see, for example, Meldrum 2000, 194), and being paid at least partly in kind (usually food and lodging, and often clothing) has continued to be a feature of live-in work globally.[5] In eighteenth-century Spain, payment in kind accounted for about three-quarters of remuneration (Sarasúa 2004, 452–55; cf. McBride 1976, 240). The draft labor law for domestics in Morocco, which we will discuss in chapter 7, stipulates that workers should receive 100 percent of the minimum wage if they live out and 60 percent if they live in. It is unclear how equivalences in kind of the remaining 40 percent are to be ensured, given huge disparities in, for instance, the quality and quantity of food provided in different households.

More than a monetary reward, such payments, as in Britain, "favoured paternal social control because they appeared simultaneously as economic and as social relations, as relations between persons not as payments for services or things" (Thompson 1974, 384). From the Moroccan employer's point of view, payment in kind, which could easily be labeled gifts, meant she was doing *l-khayr* (good).

Charity Begins at Home

The notion of "doing good" to workers seems to contradict the "daughter" label applied to them. Mandeville ruled out the possibility of doing good toward kin in his "Essay on Charity": "When a Man acts in behalf of Nephews or Nieces, and says they are my Brother's Children, I do it out of Charity; he deceives you: for if he is capable, it is expected from him, and he does it partly for his own Sake: If he values the Esteem of the World, and is nice as to Honour and Reputation, he is obliged to have a greater Regard to them than for Strangers, or else he must suffer in his Character" ([1732] 1988, 286).

In the context of caring for kin in India, Bornstein writes that "such obligations are not announced and they are understood as duty; they are only marked if unfulfilled" (2012, 150).[6] It is significant that what employers do for domestics is announced; they are treating as kin someone who is not kin—someone whose very inequality makes charity possible.

The Qur'ān and sunna assign priority for charitable giving to those closest to the believer, not only to relieve social tension between rich and poor neighbors but also because of community knowledge of poverty, which allows people to differentiate between the deserving and the undeserving poor, between real and exaggerated need. Bringing someone into one's own home seems a highly legitimate form of giving, and in the context of weak neighborly ties between rich and poor, servants often bear the brunt of receiving from the wealthy. They provide an immediate answer to any practicing Muslim who knows she must give but is not sure to whom. For as Caillé, writing on the gift in general, points out, "In the framework of a small, symbolically solid society where roles and statuses are clearly distributed . . . the question is fairly easily resolved. As soon as the identity of this small society crumbles, the question of possible recipients of a gift explodes" (1994, 272).

The same appears to have been the case in early modern Europe. Jutte notes that in seventeenth-century Sienna, gifts to servants had overtaken all other charitable giving to the poor: "For testators their servants were in a sense the most respectable of all the needy" (1994, 93). It has been observed that in general people prefer to give to a cause where they can see the ongoing beneficial effect, as with schemes in which donors stay in touch, via letters and photographs, with a child they "sponsor." Giving to servants is a way of giving to one's own. This is problematic for Kuran, who argues, "The rich could offer assistance to their own servants or to the beggars in their own neighborhoods and, without giving any thought to the challenges of overcoming the causes of need, consider their *zakāt* duty fulfilled" (2003, 283). Ṣadaqa, as voluntary alms, stand in opposition to the obligatory zakāt (a kind of tax to be paid yearly, thus purifying the remaining wealth), although in Morocco zakāt are not organized or collected by the state but left to private conscience. Moroccans did not usually talk about gifts to their servants as zakāt or ṣadaqa but as generally "doing l-khayr." The prevailing approach seemed to be that specific duties regarding zakāt were generalized into doing good where one encountered need rather than donating a calculated portion of one's wealth to a distant cause.[7] But employers who engaged in this face-to-face, personal kind of giving that involved empathizing with workers were vulnerable to disappointment and emotional pain, as Bouchra's story illustrates. Bouchra suspected her new worker of lying about her need for financial help:

> She always says, "Give me, give me, give me . . . ." I said, "Enough!" Thirty-three thousand riyal [1,650dh] she took from me in less than a month. That's on top of her wage. . . . I can't live with a liar. Because if someone is lying to you, what can you do with them? It's hard when you give from your heart and

then you find that they were lying. She came to me crying, and I cried with her. Now I want someone older, who will come and respect the hours of work, and I'll pay her, and she'll go home.

Notice that the money Bouchra *gave* was retrospectively defined as having been *taken*.

When I mentioned that other women had argued for *ḥudūd* (boundaries) between employers and workers, Bouchra's response was, "But you can't. You can't live under the same roof with someone who is in need and not help them." As suggested by Light in her book about Virginia Woolf and her servants in early twentieth-century Britain, "Philanthropy had made sense of being a mistress. It was a way of managing the differences, the emotional housekeeping, which kept the tensions between rich and poor women under control" (2007, 83). Bouchra's "impulse to give" (cf. Bornstein 2012, 47) was a desire to lessen the difference between her material situation and that of her worker as the latter portrayed it. But if the worker was exaggerating her need, Bouchra was giving charity to someone more on a par with her than she had thought; she was being taken for a ride.

Had Bouchra known the worker as a neighbor or member of a family network, lies or the suspicion of them might not have featured so prominently. She would have felt more confident about the worker's situation because it would have been an established social fact. The term *maʿrūf* (known) figured in the jurist Shafiʻi's rulings on entitlement for zakāt, which prioritized giving to local people before strangers: "Shafi'i implies that the requirement to give charity to those to whom one is closest—in a locational or familial sense—is simply the most efficient and effective way to take care of the poor. A rich person should give first to those who live closest to him and to relatives in the area because no one else is in a better position to know that the people are needy. . . . This will save the needy from having to beg, because their neighbors and relatives who know them will take care of them" (Mattson 2003, 40).

The concern with identifying who is closest is all the more pressing when people are mobile and proximity becomes a matter of ascertaining how people are related. In Mark Cohen's study of the disbursement of alms in medieval Egypt, "knowing the person, or at least obtaining the testimony of someone who knew him or her, was an important key in the verification 'system', employed in both public and private charity" (2003, 61). Strangers arriving in the Jewish community of Fustat in eleventh- and twelfth-century Egypt carried letters with multiple signatures "vouching for their neediness in anticipation that communities or individuals might be reluctant to support unknown persons from distant locales" (55), and in lists of alms claimants foreigners were entered as *ma'rifat X*, "the person known by X," so their deservedness (*istiḥqāq*) could be personally verified (61). This finds its echo in the claims by the Moroccan brokers and intermediaries we shall meet in the next chapter, that a given domestic worker is "known." The implication is that she is known to be needy as much as known to be trustworthy. The greater the need, the more good an employer can do, and the more appreciative the worker ought to be.

(Un)Gratefully Civilized

Workers are expected to show gratitude to employers through faithful service, but their ingratitude often serves as the bitter conclusion to narratives that, brimming with signs of care, circulate among friends, neighbors, and family members. Hayat, a government employee, talked about her worker Zineb: "I took her to the dermatologist, but it's as though. . . . [She shrugged her shoulders.] Gratitude is everything. . . . You can't imagine what I wouldn't do for someone. I would give my eyes, on one condition: that people would give back to me—that they would be grateful."

Another employer echoed this: "They are . . . [long pause here] . . . ingrates. You take her to the club with you, you take her to visit other towns when you travel, you fill the fridge for her to help herself, you buy her things, heaps of clothes—to satisfy her. But in the end, she will leave you as though you've done nothing for her."

Such comments, which sound like a mother complaining that her child's waywardness is a poor return for the labor she spent in childbearing and rearing ("I did all this for you, and what do I get in return?"), attempt to place the working relationship squarely in the realm of the familial. Notions of giving and gaining are particularly ingrained when it comes to children. In Morocco, children are called *khayr min Allāh* (goodness, a blessing, or gift from God) but are expected to "do l-khayr" toward parents by taking care of them in their old age. The untimely departure of a domestic worker contradicts the image of a daughter's faithful dependency and is taken as a mark of ingratitude for the employer's care.

The role of charity and gifts given by employers to domestic workers has been documented in the literature on domestic service worldwide, and Katzman (1978, 153) introduced the term "maternalism" to characterize the "benevolent role which some employers assumed toward their servants."[8]

Since Mauss's (1925) "Essai sur le don," it has become commonplace in anthropology that gifts often do as much for the donor as the recipient: to give is to show one's superiority, particularly if the receiver cannot reciprocate. Domestics receiving unwanted gifts (often used items) from their employers are expected to show gratitude. A black woman working in the home of white employers in Boston during the 1980s was given castoffs and acknowledged, "I didn't want most of that junk. But you have to take it. It's part of the job, makes them feel like they're being so kind to you. And you have to *appear* grateful. That makes them feel good too" (Rollins 1985, 190). By pretending to welcome employers' charity, the domestic plays the role expected of her, "someone who will accept others' devalued goods" (193)—a pretense that helps to create the powerful benevolent person of the employer.

Here, I follow Graeber, who observes that "it is sometimes said that the central notion of modernism is that human beings are projects of self-creation. . . . [W]e are indeed processes of creation, but . . . most of the creation is normally carried out by others" (2006, 75). Graeber illustrates his point with the example of mourning: "Often political figures, as ancestors, martyrs, founders of institutions, can be far more important after their death than when they were alive" (74). He points to Bloch's (1982) conception of self-negating mourning practices as creating dramatic contrasts between the transitory and the transcendental, thus creating the person of the deceased. Significantly, the burden of this people-making falls on subordinates, particularly women.

So too with domestic service: the person of the employer is made by "lower" others. Domestic service, like mourning, is a labor of people-making in which having someone *act* inferior creates the illusion of the employer's superiority. By employing poor women from the countryside whose "hair is a mess" (Kapchan 1996, 216), wealthy and well-groomed women in Moroccan cities can enjoy a sense of superiority. If the domestic happens to have beautiful hair, this can be remedied. Miriam described having her waist-long hair cut by her employer on her first day of work as a young girl. Domestics in Morocco historically had their heads shaved (Mernissi 1982, 5; Bin Ashu 2013, 7).[9] Unflattering clothing can be bought for workers, or controls can be imposed in other ways. Like most Moroccan women, workers wear pajamas as daywear in the house but would usually change into street clothes to go out. Ikram, who was natty with clothing and, when given a chance, could pull off a very chic look, complained that her employer, Salima, never allowed her time to change when she went out but would insist she accompanied her, even to a distant and upmarket shopping mall, in her pajamas. Onlookers would have no doubt that the young, pajama-clad woman was Salima's domestic. The same logic meant domestics in nineteenth-century Britain appeared in church in regulation bonnets—so that staff would not be mistaken for one of the family (Lethbridge 2013, 43).[10] Clothing presented as gifts thus gives control a generous guise.

The argument that domestics help to create the person of the employer is not new. Rollins writes of the "self-enhancing satisfactions that emanate from having the presence of an inferior" (1985, 156), and Anderson, following Hegel's conception of the interdependency of master and slave, argues that "[the domestic's] presence emphasises and reinforces her employer's identity" (2000, 19–20). Their focus, however, is on the commodification of the domestic's *person* rather than her *performance*, and that performance I define as labor. To take an example from theater, Sartre argues in his introduction to Genet's play *Les Bonnes*, "In the presence of the Masters, the truth of a domestic is to be a fake domestic and to mask the man he is under the guise of servility" (1982, 20).

The domestic is not alone in this role-playing; it applies more generally to the category of "the poor." Simmel points to the poor person as a "personality" who performs a specific role, but he plays this role only "when society—the totality or particular individuals—reacts towards him with assistance. . . . The poor, as a sociological category, are not those who suffer specific deficiencies and deprivations, but those who receive assistance" [(1908) 1965, 138]. Simmel's poverty is, meanwhile, relative: "He is poor whose means are not sufficient to attain his ends" (136), and people's "ends" differ according to what is considered necessary or normal in their social group.

It was a belief in the relative poverty of North Africa that provided justification for French domination and "assistance" on the grand scale of the colonial mission civilisatrice. Speaking in Chamber in 1925, French socialist Léon Blum intoned, "We acknowledge the right and even the duty of superior races to attract those who have not arrived at the same degree of culture and to call them to the progress realised thanks to the efforts of sciences and industry. . . . We have too much love for our country to disavow the expansion of its thought, of the French civilisation" (translated by and cited in Katz 2001, 145).

This expansion was crucial to the definition of the Third Republic as a modern and, ironically, democratic nation (Conklin 1997; Costantini 2008), with love for France rather than for Morocco being a motivating force. Analyzing narratives surrounding the murder in 1907 of French doctor Emile Mauchamp in Marrakech, Katz (2001) notes that such medical missions were characterized by the same preoccupation with personal and national honor that circulated among French *bonne bourgeoisie* at home and should therefore be understood as an extension of metropolitan concerns.[11] He writes, "The middle and upper classes that sought to impose their values on the lowest levels and more backward corners of their own nations naturally extended their field of operation overseas when the opportunity presented itself. It comes as no surprise that Mauchamp should inveigh with equal ardour against the superstitions of the Bretons as he does against the customs of Morocco's Arabs and Jews" (Katz 2001, 145).

Nor does it come as a surprise, then, that Moroccans should operate their own civilizing missions toward their putative inferiors. For domestic workers, who are "poor" among the "rich," the relativity of poverty takes on particular significance. Hayat taking her domestic Zineb to the dermatologist is an example. Although Zineb's skin had always reacted strongly to the sun, giving her freckles, she had never seen this as a problem until she started working for Hayat. Zineb then became someone who could not afford to treat her own malady ("poor Zineb") and the recipient of financial support for medical treatment ("lucky Zineb"). Hayat, for her part, became the donor of charity ("Hayat does good works") but Zineb's apparent lack of gratitude left Hayat unaffirmed in her role as do-gooder. This medical mission was as much about Hayat's honor as Zineb's face.

Rather as in Eliza Haywood's (1743) classic *Present for a Servant-Maid*, a manual for conduct that boasted to be "*The Sure Means of Gaining Love and Esteem*," Hayat's gifts to Zineb sometimes came in the form of instruction for her betterment.[12] Zineb was talking on the phone to her family in the *blād* (countryside) while watching over a pot of steaming couscous on Hayat's terrace. From inside the kitchen, Hayat whispered, signaling with her hand, "Speak quietly, Zineb. The neighbors!" Zineb looked up but carried on talking without lowering her voice. When she hung up, Hayat said, "Zineb, it's good to talk quietly so that other people can't hear you or know what you are talking about." Zineb said nothing.

Hayat asked gently, "You didn't like it when I made that observation?"

"No, no . . ." Zineb mumbled. Even if you tell me, I . . ." She didn't finish, but it was as though she was trying to say, "It's not going to make me change my ways. That's just how I am; I speak loudly."

Hayat said, half to me, half to Zineb, "It's good to be in accordance with your surroundings. In the countryside you speak loudly—everyone does. It's true, they speak loudly; it's their custom. I too speak loudly when I'm in the country. And the houses are big, so if you want to talk to someone far away, you need to shout. But in the city, you speak quietly. Everyone is nearby."

Zineb still said nothing. The term workers use to describe this kind of intervention by employers is *qmaʿ* (to tame, curb, subdue). They generally acknowledge that although employers probably see their own input as kindness, it makes workers feel inferior. The maternalism of employers coincides here with a broader civilizing project in which differences between urban and rural Moroccans are accentuated as markers of progress in a self-consciously modernizing nation. Thus, taking in an *ʿarūbīya* (country girl) involves transforming her into a *bnī ādam*, a human being (Moujoud and Pourette 2005, 1099).

Eager to find ways to effect this "rags to riches" transformation, employers often misjudge the level of need of their workers, giving gifts that are offensive. Malika, who worked for Latifa's daughter in Dār Sebbari, noted, "Mostly employers give you old things. They think we are poor and are happy to wear old clothes." When Malika left Dār Sebbari, Nadia begged her to stay "so that I can give you one of my *jelālib* [plural of *jellāba*, traditional hooded over-garment] for your mother at the ʿīd." Malika was offended: "ʿīd doesn't require someone else's old clothing. It requires new clothing. My mother has already had her new ʿīd jellāba made."

Similarly, a French woman living in Morocco related how someone had given the parking attendant in their street some money "to buy shoes for your children." The man had replied, "That will be difficult. They're in the United States for their studies." Such attempts to clothe supposedly poorly dressed workers despite their ability to clothe themselves are infantilizing, and workers might identify with the sentiment expressed by King Mohammed V: "When France took Morocco under her tutelage, Morocco was a child, and France gave him clothes and institutions suitable to his size. Today the child has grown up, but the clothes and institutions are still the same" (n.d., cited in Granger 1987, 133). Many workers now in their twenties and thirties went into domestic service when they were children and feel they are still treated as such.

Workers have to pretend to be receptive to and grateful for this generosity on the part of employers, whether material, medical, or educational, even if they are not. Only those who are unconcerned with preserving a working relationship overtly question the value of employers' gifts or the motivation behind their beneficence. Salima, Latifa's Casablanca-based daughter, gave Malika's younger sister Ikram some clothing during the few weeks that she worked for her. But when Salima, on a visit to the Océani branch of the family, announced that she had done this, Malika was disapproving: "In front of everyone! God sees the khayr you do to people. You don't have to tell everyone."[13] When Ikram left Salima's employ, she came to spend the night with Malika, who was still working for Nadia in the Sebbari building. Salima phoned to direct Ikram to leave the clothes she had given her with Latifa. Ikram was outraged: "She gave me the clothes—they are mine now! She can't ask for them back!" But Malika saw the opportunity for moral high ground, instructing her sister, "Fine. Leave her clothes here! You don't need them. You have things to wear." To Salima, on the other end of the phone, Ikram said, "Fine. I'm going to leave your rubbish here!" To which Malika added with sarcasm, snatching the phone from Ikram, "So you can do l-khayr again, and help someone else!" Malika was playing with the idea that if one wanted "brownie points" for being charitable, recycling a gift was a way of earning double points.

Doing Ajr through Her

Muslim Moroccans believe that because, as Malika pointed out, God sees when they do khayr, it is a way of earning ajr, a word that paradoxically enough has connotations of work for wages. The terms can be used interchangeably in some contexts. In Modern Standard Arabic, al-ajr (plural ujūr) means "wages, pay, honorarium . . . price, rate, fee" (Cowan 1994, 6). But when Moroccan workers and employers used the term colloquially, they were not talking about payment in dirham for physical work but rather religious merit for charitable work, credited to them by God in the hereafter. Although ajr is from God, Moroccans talk about "doing" l-ajr in the same way they talk about "doing" l-khayr, and the word cropped up repeatedly in conversations about domestic service.

Ajr is characterized by a break in reciprocity, which Parry, in the well-known Indian context, termed a "deferred" return (1986, 462): a return comes from God rather than the beneficiary. "The theory is—as Trautmann (1981: 279) puts it—a 'soteriology, not a sociology of reciprocity . . .'. The gift does indeed return to the donor, but it does so as the fruits of *karma*. It is this 'unseen fruit' ... which withers on the branch if any return is accrued in the here and now" (Parry 1986, 462).

Insofar as it must be given without expectation of return from the recipient, ajr resembles the Hindu gift *dāna* (Parry 1986; Laidlaw 2000; Bornstein 2012).[14] This can lead to surprising reactions. Nieuwkerk (2005, 131) describes a case where receiving a thank-you gift for charitable work destroyed all hope of ajr for a pious woman who believed merit to be gained *only* when earthly recompense was absent.

Ethnographic accounts of ajr are few. Westermarck's (1926) work on Moroccan Islam, which discusses the ajr gained through sacrificing various animals, is a first point of reference. The focus then shifts to women. In her study of Moroccan women in an Atlas town, Maher links ajr to folk Islam, which lays stress on "generosity and lavish hospitality, on devotion to parents" (1974, 99). Buitelaar's (1993) work on women's roles in feasting and fasting describes ways ajr can be gained during Ramadan in particular. She observes that younger believers were less concerned with ajr than older ones, and men, who may gain ajr through additional prayers, were less concerned than women, who are disadvantaged in praying by menstruation (Buitelaar 1993, 4).[15] Ensel's account of saintly ("Sharif") and servile ("Drawi") castes in southern Morocco, which describes how Drawa are not paid but claim they earn ajr by helping the Shurfa (plural of Sharif) "only out of goodness" (1999, 200–203), is an exception to the focus on women. His economic argument is supported by Jansen's (2004) article on midwives in Algeria during the 1980s. Jansen suggests ajr is part of women's economic subjugation because it enables certain types of work to be classified not as labor deserving wages but as "meritorious acts" for which reward is delayed until the hereafter. Nieuwkerk (2005) discusses changes in ways of collecting ajr among Moroccan women in the Netherlands, who, like my friends in Rabat, complain of a lack of connections with poor people in their community, which makes almsgiving difficult.[16]

Ajr, as merit accumulated on each person's *ḥisāb* (account) with God, appears in numerous Quranic passages and forms a basis of "practical ethics" (Schacht 2012).[17] A number of metaphors are used to illustrate this reckoning: books with good and bad deeds listed, weighing scales (Nieuwkerk 2005), and, in Lebanon, a money box (Deeb 2006, 195). According to these understandings, the more ajr one has, the more likely one will be admitted to paradise. Ajr involves *qurba*—coming closer to God (Hoexter 2003, 146–47)—and some thus believe that one's ajr account determines not only entry to paradise but also one's place there, nearer or further away from God. Others envisage extra comforts, such as a tree for shade (Buitelaar 1993, 122), or accommodation of various qualities. For instance, a fellow train passenger who attempted to convert me to Islam was told by another woman that her success would secure her a *bīt* (room) in paradise. "Janouba," a member of the "Yabiladi" online forum, regularly posts requests in this manner to help needy Moroccans she knows. She incites people to "buy a house in paradise, God willing, by helping these poor orphans." Blogging in French, she also uses the term *ajr* more generally to motivate people to donate: "n hesitez pas vous gagnerez alajr [sic]." Taking ajr into account influences people's decisions and turns evaluations of circumstances on their head. Giving means gaining. Bad weather while travelling to visit someone in hospital means extra ajr. News of a sick person in the family who needs care is met with "lucky you! You can do ajr through her." Ajr also comes into consideration when incorporating someone into the household.

In chapter 2 we touched on the idea of fosterage as a meritorious act. Forms of social parenting, in which the charitable and the utilitarian coincided, were commonly practiced throughout the last century and up to the present. When, in 1883, the sultan warned the *qā'id* that continuing to enslave the daughter of a freeman would "render useless" his good work (Ennaji 1999, 87), he must have meant that the ajr gained through the initial charitable act of providing for the girl during famine would be cancelled out by the wrong the qā'id was now doing.[18] Goichon observed that taking in and educating a girl in early twentieth-century Fes was seen as meritorious: "Ladies undertake the education of their *petite bonne* as a pious deed. If she is intelligent and good natured, they treat her like a child that they are responsible for training up to be a nice, domesticated woman, not with the intention of keeping her, but of marrying her to a good boy and founding an honest and happy family" (1929, 47).

During fieldwork I came across direct references to ajr as the motivation for or consequence of taking in a girl. In a stationery shop in the *medīna*, I overheard one woman suggest to another, "Let's take in a couple of girls and *ndīrū fīhum l-ajr* [do ajr through them]." But mindful of Schielke's (2009) observation that there is sometimes too much Islam in the anthropology of Islam, I should underline that the Moroccan women I knew were not pious members of mosque movements emphasizing "self-cultivation," as in Mahmood (2005) and Hirschkind's (2006) oft-cited Egyptian studies; some prayed, some rarely except in Ramadan, but most shared an idea that moral good equaled religious good and would have a bearing on one's lot after death. Not everyone talked about ajr (Hayat, for example, spoke only of gratitude), and many women would discuss doing <u>kh</u>ayr without explicitly referring to the fact that it earned one ajr. If pressed, however, they would say, "Yes, of course that gives her ajr." But for those who did talk about ajr, it was a way of reifying complex, changing, and ambiguous relationships as either good or bad, utilitarian or charitable. This was made possible by the fact that although spiritual, ajr was imagined in material terms—i.e., as something that could be present in lesser or greater quantities. While advice aimed at "urban global Muslims" (Faris 2016) suggests ways to earn double, triple, or a hundredfold ajr by performing acts in specific contexts—for example, on a certain night in Ramadan—Mittermaier (2013) problematizes the contradiction between calculation and unquantifiable blessing in Islamic charitable work in Egypt, and I heard only two quantities being talked about in Morocco: ajr and a lot of ajr.

Rachida, who lived with Latifa from the age of eight until she was married, told me that Latifa had "a lot of ajr with God" for bringing her up and arranging her marriage, and this was something Latifa herself believed. Fatima, a worker who lived out but who received extra financial support from her employers, considered that they would be awarded ajr for this: "They will have ajr because they took me to the doctor. And they paid for an operation. They paid 20,000dh and another 10,000dh for the aftercare, and they also paid for my mother to have her hip operation, say another 20,000dh. And now and then they give me 50dh or 100dh or 200dh. And then for the 'īd, they always buy the sheep, every single year. They get ajr for that too. And when I married they gave me 5,000dh." Note that Fatima's precisely remembered sums of money all translate into uncountable ajr.

It was, of course, possible to talk about a lack of ajr—i.e., doing such-and-such did not earn so-and-so any ajr. Huriya, who worked for Latifa's family during my fieldwork, had her doubts where Rachida's failed marriage to the carpenter (he now lives elsewhere with a second wife) was concerned: "Brought her up? Married her off? Ajr? What sort of marriage is that? No, Latifa didn't do any ajr through her." Huriya implicitly accused Latifa of not being careful enough selecting a husband for Rachida, rejecting the notion that Latifa's good intentions for her domestic's married life could be treated as meritorious. The marriage of Najat, another of Latifa's former foster daughters, was even more contentious. Najat was married to Latifa's biological daughter's husband's mother's sister's son, whose father was said to have been a wealthy man. This marriage is played as a trump card by supporters of the house whenever the question of whether Latifa fostered in a utilitarian or a charitable way comes up in conversation. But those, like Huriya, who consider such relationships exploitative suggest that the triumph of Najat's social climb is undermined by the fact that her husband is now chronically ill. The debate pursues the question of whether Latifa saw signs of this when she arranged Najat's marriage to him twenty years ago, which seems unlikely.

This kind of indeterminism is discussed by Lambek, who argues that ethical interpretations of events are not fixed: "The individual incident is located within the stream of particular lives and the narratives that are constituted from them, changing its valence in relation to the further unfolding of those lives and narratives and never fully determined or predictable" (2010, 4). Domestics and employers alike were subject to ongoing reassessments of morality, and their words, which are sometimes contradictory, can be understood as bargaining positions that have social effects as much as reflections of belief and doubt.

One of the social effects of talking about ajr is that it makes sense of class differences by stressing interdependency; in this sense it explains rather than alleviates inequality. At the foundation of this approach is the belief that God made rich and poor to be unequal. Hayat, the government employee we encountered earlier, explained, "God made those who have and those who don't have so he could see if we help each other." A villa's security guard in the wealthy Mabella district expressed a similar idea:

"God created us all, people who have and people who don't have, for one thing."
"What's that?"
"So that the rich can give ṣadaqa. If there were no poor people who come knocking and say, 'Give me ṣadaqa,' then how would the rich give alms on behalf of their parents?"

The guard explained that when parents or other relatives die, one gives money to a person in need, and God transfers the merit to the deceased in the form of *raḥma* (mercy).[19] "How else would they get raḥma, if there were no needy people?" he asked rhetorically. In a similar way, a domestic day worker saw inequality as necessary for balance in the labor market: "God has made rich and poor to help each other. If we were all rich, there would be no one to work for the rich." The worker makes a good point; the industry depends on the existence of relative poverty. Significantly, ajr in Morocco is not done "for" (*li*) but "through" or "in" (*fi*) the poor so that helping them is a means to an end for the better off. The existence of the poor allows the rich to be tested in their generosity and given an opportunity to gain reward in the hereafter, as was observed by Freya Stark on her travels:

> The beggar in Asia, if the West has not yet touched him, comes up with no whine or servility ... his hand is held out in a gesture of giving almost more than receiving; and when you have handed your coin, he refers you to Allah: 'Allah will repay,' as a young woman buying a hat might tell them to send the bill to her husband.
> This is all a result of the acknowledged certainty that, whatever the beggar's own moralities may be, he is the cause of virtue in others (Stark [1948] 2013, 94).

Likewise, Mittermaier notes that volunteers in a communal kitchen in Egypt made sure they took equal turns to hand meals to the poor and gain *thawāb* (points), thus giving each other "the gift of giving" and "ironically backgrounding the very act of giving to 'the poor,'" who are configured as a "gate to paradise" (2013, 283).[20] This is not unique to Islam but seems common to "ethicised salvation religions" in which "rewards are contingent on conduct" (Parry 1986, 467). As Silber (2000) observes, however, the anthropological literature on religious giving has focused disproportionately on Buddhist and Hindu traditions of India and southeast Asia. In medieval Christendom, alms giving was seen as a way of redeeming sins, thus making the poor appear part of God's plan for salvation (Troeltsch 1931; Geremek 1994, 18, 20). Simmel points out that at times "the poor disappear completely as legitimate subjects and central foci of the interests involved.... When Jesus told the wealthy young man, 'Give your riches to the poor,' what apparently mattered to him were not the poor, but rather the soul of the wealthy man" (Simmel [1908] 1965, 121). For a secular version of the problem, see George Bernard Shaw's *Man and Superman*, in which Tanner accuses Octavius of "regarding the world as a moral gymnasium built expressly to strengthen your character" ([1903] 2004, 68).

Waiting for Justice

Domestic service plainly provides employers with weights to tone their moral muscles, but what of workers? I was interested to see how workers—generally thought of as receivers rather than givers of charity—might themselves do ajr through their employers. I asked Ilham if she would gain ajr for her work:

"Yes, if I do it *min qalbī* [from my heart]."

"And if you don't do it from your heart? You don't get ajr, you just get your wages here, and that's it?"

"Exactly."

Doing work "from the heart" seems to be a paraphrase of the Quranic concept of *niyya* (intention). I heard the term used in this context when Nawar was praised by her uncle for working "with her niyya" as opposed to those who "just clean where it shows" and watch television while the employer is out. Related to this is the fact that strictly speaking niyya must be declared before pious acts are undertaken in order to earn ajr. This may explain the prevalence of what often sounds like self-seeking calculation or immodest boasting as people announce their intention to do ajr. Malika, although she did not mention ajr, also expressed the importance of working conscientiously even when Nadia was not there to see. Despite complaining about not having time off, she said, "But I want to work well so that I can say that I'm worthy of this wage, that I really worked." Working well was a moral rather than economic matter: it would not change her pay, but it might make her feel better about herself. Malika once remarked to me that Zahra was friendly with her when no one else was around, but whenever a friend of Zahra's was there, Malika felt ignored. "I'm like a stone. You can leave me on the shelf, pick me up, put me back, throw me against the wall. I'm just a stone to her."

Ajr was to be gained not only through working well but as a kind of compensation for poor conditions. This seems a general principle in Islamic ethics; in the case of voluntary almsgiving, Weir (2012) observes that "not even affirmative action is required, for a Muslim whose property is stolen is credited with having given it as *ṣadaḳa* [voluntary alms]." Fatima claimed she would receive ajr from God to make up for what her employers (who, as already noted, gave her money for medical bills, wedding expenses, etc.) *failed* to give her:

> Because they haven't done my papers even though I have worked for them for thirteen, fourteen years and brought their children up and everything.[21] They should have paid into my national security account. When I leave, if they don't open an account and put money in it for me to live off as retirement, and I forgive them, then I will see that returned to me in the *ākhira* [the afterlife].

Because that is *min ḥaqqī* [my right], but I forgave them. Everything you do, God sees. He will *ḥsb lik dak shī* [take that into account for you].

So both Fatima and her employers are to be recompensed in the afterlife: they for giving above and beyond in certain areas, and she for not receiving enough in other areas and not holding this against them. Unlike the sultan's view of the qā'id's wrongdoing, Fatima did not see her employers' failure to respect her "rights" as cancelling out the ajr they earned through generosity to her on other fronts. In this sense ajr is a pliable concept that helps people make sense in different ways of the imbalances of give and take that are beyond their control.

Workers reminded each other of ajr as a comfort and motivation for putting up with poor conditions. Over and over I heard workers tell one another to "ṣabrī ū ṣāfī [just be patient]." The same is said to daughters-in-law suffering the demands of their mothers-in-law to whom, according to the traditional virilocal model, they owe labor (S. Davis 1983). The Qur'ān suggests believers will receive later recompense for patient endurance in this life (Qur'ān 23:111), exhortations to patience often being accompanied by reminders of paradise or the final "home" (Qur'ān 13:24). Demonstrating *ṣabr* or patience in the hope of delayed gratification is seen as a specific female quality (Buitelaar 1993, 129–33, 178). Qureshi, writing about ṣabr among Pakistani women in Britain, emphasizes the transformative role of ṣabr, "a show of inner strength that is directed towards God as well as a capacity that is granted by God" (2013, 121), to add an ethical dimension to forbearance in the face of illness and laborious kinship obligations. Paradoxically, although these women stress that ṣabr involves silent suffering, its narration "amid a flow of interpersonal relationships and tensions" (135) also gives it force. When a woman in the Berber village of Crawford's study was bitten by a snake on her way to the fields, continued stoically on to work, and then died on her return, she was talked about as a "great woman" for her display of endurance (Crawford 2010b, 214). Similarly, as Moroccan domestic workers encouraged each other in "words as gifts" (Anderson, P. 2011, 5) to be patient, they implicitly acknowledged suffering and the potential for reward, thus defining workers rather than employers as the ones "doing good."

As well as talking about ajr directly, Moroccans' comments indicated a belief that God gives people what they deserve and repays what they give, if not in this life then in the next. This takes on significance in the context of the modern domestic-labor market, where people are in practice unknown, and both workers and employers take a leap in the dark with new arrangements. When citing the risk of "falling on" bad employers, workers often said, "Because you are good, God will bring you to good people." This logic of divine justice was generally invoked by those who had not met with trouble. Others called on God to bring justice to situations where they had been the loser, with phrases such as "[May] God give to you according to your niyya [intention], and to me according to my niyya." In the same way, people were adamant that thieves will not prosper. Safae thus explained, "Flūs l-ḥarām [illicit money] does not last. For example, she steals 200dh from the employer's handbag. . . . But that 200dh, what will she do with it? She'll fritter it away, and it's like nothing. It just goes." Similarly a domestic day laborer reassured others that "when a woman works for nsārā [Christians] and steals from their house, this worker will go down to hell with the unbelieving people of the house." An employer who complained that workers do not take responsibility ("They say, 'I'm sick' or 'I had to go to see my mother.' I know they are lying, but I always pay them for the full month") comforted herself by saying that "God sees."

Ideas about divine justice reflect a preoccupation with recompense that also figures in everyday ways of thanking and asking: "Allāh ykhelif [God compensate you]" is said to hosts after a meal. Requests may be accompanied by any one or a number of the following: Allāh yʿaṭik r-riḍā (God give you contentment), Allāh yrahamlik l-wālidīn (God have mercy on your parents for you), Allāh yʿaṭik s-stir (God give you protection), Allāh ynajjḥik (God make you succeed), and the list goes on.[22] These expressions all come down to the same thing: recompense later for your service now. Invoking a God who keeps account of all things can thus be used to encourage people to do a good deed but also to threaten them. When Latifa's daughter Salima refused to provide Ikram, whom she had just dismissed, with her train fare back to Fes, Malika, as Ikram's older sister-cum-agent, responded with "if you don't give it to her then you won't trebḥī f yawm l-qiyāma [profit on the day of Resurrection—i.e., you will be punished on judgment day]."

Workers who felt they had been unfairly treated did not always call down hellfire on their employers. A common way of ending a tale of injustice was to say, "Allāh yʿafū [God forgive]," as Nawar often said.[23] Nawar seemed deeply moved by the fact that her employer was suffering with cancer, but, at the same time, my initial meeting with her in the city center was the first occasion she had been allowed time off for a month. Nawar kept shaking her head: "God forgive, God forgive." She seemed to feel sorry both for the employer and for herself for having to work for her, but she would not leave the employer. One thinks of Gloucestershire-born Winifred Foley's (b. 1914) account of domestic service. Foley worked for an elderly woman who assigned her an insalubrious attic as a bedroom: "Because of her rheumatics I had to act as 'kneel in' for the old lady's prayers. I thought she had a fat chance of getting to heaven with that attic on her conscience and two spare bedrooms in the house! But she was old and pitiful, so just in case there was a God up there listening I put in a plea for her on the quiet" (Foley [1974] 1991, 133).

Some workers believed, along with Fatima, that the very act of being patient with employers and forgiving them for failing to give them "their rights" earned the worker ajr. Incidentally, forgiveness curiously figured on the wall at the Ministry of Employment in Rabat. Outside the *inspecteur du travail*'s office, a row of plastic chairs had been placed for people to sit on as they waited to have their complaints heard, and opposite the chairs a framed notice read in characteristically rhyming literary Arabic, "Daqā'iq al-intiẓār, imla'hā bi al-istighfār [minutes of waiting, erase them with asking forgiveness]."[24] In the moral economy of domestic service, asking God to forgive employers was one way in which workers felt they could score long-term gains.

It's Over

Waiting patiently for justice is a plan for delayed gratification, just as the "you're my daughter" rhetoric makes use of a long-term logic of give and return that moves in step with the generational cycle. By staying like dutiful daughters despite unfair conditions, workers could earn ajr in the hereafter, but in this life would never be served by the next generation as they would be if they really were family. By quitting, workers perhaps forfeited the chance to earn ajr for the afterlife but could make tangible gains here and now. Meanwhile, for employers who saw service as a sign of recognition for their care and gifts, leaving was an affront—a display of ingratitude. Viewing their action toward domestics as ajr, with its break in reciprocity, did not prevent employers from also expecting gratitude and a return service from the object of their charity. Receiving both ajr and gratitude seemed important for people like Latifa, who was keen to point out that the women she had taken in as girls thanked her when they came back to visit.

Their continued occasional help with the housework could be seen as homage to her as a patron, another sort of return for the k̲hayr she did for them (cf. Benthall 1999, 36).

Debt was not explicit but implicit in my interlocutors' comments about gratitude, but studies of bonded labor elsewhere shed light on the matter. For example, Brass's study of Peruvian peasants concludes: "Idioms of patriarchal authority, duty, obligation and reciprocity can be utilized to control a workforce of debt bonded labour composed of godchildren, parents and classificatory co-parents while at the same time disguising the class basis of this control" (1986, 63). For Moroccan employers who see themselves as charitable, workers owe it to them to stay or, if they have to leave, to stay in touch. Hayat, the government worker who took Zineb to the dermatologist, told me how Rahma, a worker she had made into her "daughter," left her after nine years:

> I told her: "even if you leave, we stay in touch." But it was always I who called her. I asked her, how come she never called to ask how I was or how the girls are? She said she never had credit on her phone, but you know, if you want to do something, you can. I'd say, "Just call and hang up so I can call you back. I'll pay for the call." But she never did. And that hurt me a lot. I spent three months completely alone, and also distraught. I always say that you should never "cut" someone [off]. A relationship is a tree; you should never cut it down.

English servant Winifred Foley's account tells the other side of such stories—the gratitude she never expressed to an employer who kindly sent her home when her younger sister was ill:

> "When your little sister is better, promise you'll come back and work for me."
> ... I promised her that I would. I would have promised anything without scruple, as long as I could get home to my little sister. But I had no intention of coming back.
> Kind Mrs Fox! She made up a parcel of warm vests and clothes from her children's plentiful store. I took all her kindness; and I'm ashamed to admit I never even wrote to her ([1974] 1991, 131).

Not all employers wished their former domestics would phone them to catch up; there were other ways of dealing with the loss of a "daughter." As convenient recipients of charity, workers are also scapegoats on which the disappearance of valuable items can be blamed—many departed workers are accused of theft. Both charity and theft thrive on a real or illusory denial of reciprocity or exchange, and neither term is appropriate within a circle of equals or kin who share "without reckoning" [Fortes (1969) 2004].[25]

A gift can easily be redefined as something stolen and vice versa, just as ajr does not require affirmative action—Fatima might gain from the moral failure of her employers in the same way that "a Muslim whose property is stolen is credited with having given it as ṣadaḵa" (Weir 2012). Bouchra, it will be remembered, had given a new worker several sums of money and was later outraged at how much the woman had "taken" from her. Another worker of some months went home for 'īd, apparently taking three sets of brand-new winter pajamas, two Italian blouses, and a watch with her. Bouchra recalls:

> I asked her, "Where are they?!" . . . She said, "I'll come and find them for you. They'll be hidden away somewhere or fallen down behind something." I thought, better that she doesn't come at all, as she would only put them back somewhere. I didn't want to see her again. I said, "No, don't come back!" She left a coat, and I told her, "I'm not going to give it back to you. I'm going to give it to charity so that you feel what it's like to have something taken from you!" She left some money, and I didn't give that back to her either because she had stolen more than that. She also left the clothes I had bought her to wear—really nice clothes. . . .

Here the meaning of items exchanged switched from lost to stolen, from donated to left behind to stolen back and redonated, as Bouchra reclassified her role from that of donor of charity to victim of theft, to arbiter of justice, to donor once again.

Similarly Malika—who, during her time working for Nadia, had been introduced to outsiders as "like a daughter"—was talked about as a thief for weeks after she left. Malika had told Nadia she would not be returning to work after 'īd and took her pay home to her family. A few weeks earlier, Malika had asked for some money to send to her sister, and Nadia had "given" it to her. Nadia claimed she intended it only as an advance but forgot to deduct this from Malika's pay when she left. Malika, having thought the money was a gift, did not see why she should give it back.

I had accompanied Malika to stay with her family for a few days, and the "theft" came to light while I was away. On my return, Nadia asked me, "How did you not fear they would steal from you while you were with them?" Nadia was acting as though Malika had stolen the money from her handbag. Soraya, the fourteen-year-old who worked for Latifa during the summer to earn money "for her schoolbooks," was also introduced as a "daughter of the house." She joined in vehemently with criticism of Malika as a _sheffāra_ (thief) but met the same fate when she herself left. Soraya had allegedly taken money from the top of Latifa's wardrobe; at least, the money was no longer there. The dramatic contrast between "daughter," recipient of gifts, and "thief," someone who simply takes, seems to be a way of detaching or disowning the "daughter" by suggesting "we never liked her anyway," but it also publicizes the presence of valuables in the house and so is as much about prestige as morality (M. Montgomery 2019).

That intimacy brings moral danger and sudden reversals of affection (one cannot be both a daughter and a thief at the same time) is in no way confined to Morocco. The recent trial in Britain of celebrity chef Nigella Lawson's personal assistants, Francesca and Elisabetta Grillo, prosecuted for unauthorized spending on company credit cards, showed how familial sharing stands at odds with the language of transactions and contract: "'It's like if you wake up one morning and your mother says I'm not your mother anymore, sorry, you have been with me all your life but I don't know you anymore,' Francesca said" (Dixon 2014). The assistants claimed there were no ground rules for their spending, and Elisabetta, who had worked for Nigella since 1999, was described by the latter as her "rock," and "like a member of the family" (Dixon 2014). In this familial atmosphere where boundaries between familial and company expenses were not clear cut, the accusation of theft plainly came as a shock to the Grillo sisters.

Styles's (1983) discussion of the shifting borderline between customary rights and illegal embezzlement in preindustrial England finds an echo here. Legal customs in medieval England also reflected this clash of family and business in the choice disputants had between proceeding by "love" to make peace out of court or by "law"—that is, formal pleading (Clanchy 2003). Clanchy describes "love" not in terms of sentiment but as "a bond of affection, established by public undertakings before witnesses and upheld by social pressure" (50). Such a bond linked a lord and vassal in medieval England. The downside of "love" for peasants was that it meant payments ("love boons" and "love silver") or service. In the fourteenth century, "on the estates of St Albans abbey to make love meant to do an extra piece of work for the lord" (48).

In Morocco family is to be held at all costs out of reach of law, which these days means the state. I discovered as much when a large sum of my cash disappeared from the room I shared with my Océani host family's daughter. Since the incident occurred during a party that filled the house with relatives and neighbors, there was no suspicion cast on the daughter or other members of the household, who could have taken the money at any time. But in order to make an insurance claim, I would need a police report, and the very mention of the police sent my host mother into a frenzy: "How can you say you will bring the police here when we have treated you like family? Will you bring the police to question your sister? Your brother? Your uncle?" (I called my host father ʿammī, my paternal uncle, out of respect). They privileged love over law, but our relationship never fully recovered from this faux pas, and I moved out at the end of the month. Workers and employers, assumed to relate to one another by "love," as mothers and daughters, are similarly shocked when this is betrayed. As in the Nigella Lawson case, the reversal is unintelligible and therefore bitter.

Writing on Latina domestic workers in the United States, Hondagneu-Sotelo argues that looking at how domestic jobs end "exposes the degree to which domestic labor is viewed as something other than 'real work'" (2003, 56). She observes that domestic arrangements "end more the way relationships do than the way jobs do: with white lies or alibis, designed to spare feelings or avoid conflict. Often, both parties know that the real reason an employee leaves is not a sick relative or a return to her home country" (55).

This is even more the case in Morocco. Although in practice periods of time are sometimes agreed upon, work for domestics is conceived of as a relationship to be altered only by marriage. Changing allegiance is not a problem in that case: one would then owe labor to one's husband or, particularly so in the past, his family. It is thus virtually impossible to leave an employer without causing offence. A son or daughter would not leave. This is why workers, particularly live-in workers, rarely give notice but often use the excuse of an ill relative, real or fictive, as Ikram did when she left the family in Asilah (cf. Foley [1974] 1991, 131).

An alternative is simply to leave without telling the employer. A common feature in exit plans is to "go _khafīfa_ [light]." A worker will gradually move most of her belongings from her employers' house, taking a little to a friend's each time she has a day off, so when she finally leaves she will need only a small bag, and her employers will not realize she is gone for good. One worker planned that if her employer saw her with some of this pre-exit luggage, she would say it was winter clothing she no longer needed. Another worker, Safae, went to the blād (her home region in the countryside) for five days' leave without telling her employer she had no intention of returning: "I couldn't tell her I was leaving, as she didn't treat me well." Safae changed her mobile number so the employer could not get in touch with her: "She treats me badly, I'll treat her badly." Hafida waited until her employer, *l-Ḥajja*, went on holiday; l-Ḥajja had sent her home until she should call her to return, but by that time Hafida planned to have found work elsewhere. She felt she could not leave her employer overtly but would use the fact that she could not have remained without work (the imposed holiday was unpaid) as an excuse when the employer called. Workers are not without scruple. Some, despite wanting to leave, wait until a certain period of time they have verbally agreed to work elapses, despite no written contract existing. Workers have also stated that it was particularly *hashūma* (shameful), or *khayb* (bad, ugly), to leave an employer in the lurch (*tsmāh fihā*) during Ramadan.[26]

Disappearing without a trace is all very well for live-out workers from the countryside, but workers based in l'Océan, like Salma, my host mother's former domestic, whose house was just two streets across and one street down toward the sea, could not easily avoid a former employer. The arrangement had ended because Salma no longer needed the money, but my host mother, Touria, would regularly ask Salma if she would still come and "help" her. Salma never seemed to want to but did not like "to face someone and say no," so she gave excuses such as having to look after her young nephew. To simply say she did not need the extra money would have seemed selfish in view of Touria's "need" for help. Other l'Océan-based workers were potentially trapped in poor jobs because if they left, they would still bump into their employers.

Of course the fragility of domestic arrangements worked both ways, and employers have their own stock alibis for dismissing domestics they have promised to treat as daughters: relocating, going on holiday, new school routine. . . . A lack of contract, which meant Rahma suddenly left Hayat after nine years, also meant Hayat could dismiss Zineb, her new worker, when Rahma suddenly came back. It was Zineb's turn to be hurt: "They were like my little sisters," said Zineb of Hayat's young daughters—for whom she had cared for two months. "It's like I've got a hole in my heart. . . . I never want to be *mrsma* in a house again." Zineb pulled her elbows in to convey a sense of being trapped. *Mrsma* comes from the root r-s-m, like *rasmī*, "official." Another worker explained, "Like when you have an official job, with a contract saying you will always work for them." The implication was that being mrsma meant not having the freedom to move on. But Zineb did not have a contract, so the lack of freedom she sensed came from an emotional tie, in this case to Hayat's children. By remaining unattached, working here and there for various clients, Zineb would avoid forming another such tie and would be the one in control. Otherwise, "people will just bring someone else in your place and, 'bye-bye to you!'"

Fatima, my Océani friend, commented on Zineb's dismissal: "She's not savvy, that one. She doesn't understand. She should say in the beginning, 'If you don't like me, give me a month's notice. Don't wait until you've found another girl and then employ her before telling me.'" This preemptive defense is more commonly used by older women with greater experience than workers of Zineb's age and is seen by many employers as a new and shocking development. One said, "Now it's they who impose conditions on us. They state their hours, refuse to do the ironing or to stay the night. 'If that doesn't suit you, *Allāh y'āwenik* [good-bye, literally God help you].'" Such stipulations, which remove workers from the unconditionally loving "daughter" role, sit ill with the patronizing view that they should be grateful to have work and are therefore suitable recipients of charity.

Conclusion

In Moroccan domestic service, modeled on quasi fosterage, the door is open to trust, affection, and generosity—qualities that supposedly characterize moral relations between members of a family. But it is also open to disloyalty, exploitation, and ingratitude, not unheard of in the family either.[27] Looking at the ethical values that shape relations between domestic workers and their employers tells us something about the reproduction of inequality. Just as workers are able to transform passive exploitation into active patience and forgiveness to form a basis for moral autonomy and religious merit, employers can redefine what they gave (or in some cases simply lost) as something taken so that they identify as wealthy targets of theft instead of indiscriminate donors of charity. These narratives of charity and theft are two sides of the same coin. Both deny reciprocity to define strangers in the home as unequal, so either will do to reproduce the hierarchical relationships that get housework done. But while charity sustains relatedness, keeping the oil and vinegar in suspension ("these poor people need us"), theft explains separation ("but it is impossible for us to live together").

In the context of an increasingly activist civil society around issues of workers' rights, talking about charity makes less sense, and employers complain of hearing fewer words of thanks and praise for their good deeds toward workers. It is little wonder, then, that narratives of theft abound. Although the impossibility of trusting workers "these days" is presented as a relatively new phenomenon, this may simply be a rhetorical framework through which workers and employers have for a long time negotiated their relations and explained the circulation of people from one house to another.

While the mercenary approach of workers who "follow the money" goes unremarked in other professional contexts, it is often criticized in the context of domesticity since it makes a civilizing mission untenable. As Carrier (1997, 18) suggests, "Criticisms are likely to be most articulate when areas of life hitherto outside the Market realm become incorporated within it." Carrier gives the example of reproductive technologies by which "natural impossibilities" become choices that can be purchased. Natural resources are another domain whose incorporation in the market excites controversy.[28] Domesticity in Morocco has always been a "family" thing, a charitable thing; the very act of making kin out of poor people constitutes a good work before God. Complaints about materialistic workers seem to mark a transitional phase in which their profession, in a half-baked way, is becoming part of the labor market. In other sectors, a contract and a stated wage delimit the working relationship, protecting the two parties so that neither is dependent on the potentially changeable khayr of the other: the kindness of providing and caring like a mother and the reciprocal kindness of staying and serving like a daughter. So while "staying put" is elsewhere a matter of fulfilling a contract rather than being grateful, Moroccan domestic workers are charity cases whose departures signal an unthankful rejection of the gift of maternal care.

We have discussed the controlling and infantilizing aspect of gift giving and signs of care. By paying the worker a lower wage and "making it up" in kind (clothing or unwanted items presented as gifts rather than payment), not only is ajr accumulated and the identity of the rich donor constructed through a contrast with the "poor" recipient but a sense of debt is also created. Historically this meant no contract was required to ensure workers stayed—they owed their patrons loyalty and depended on them for support. Today, increased mobility, connectivity with strangers, and awareness of the availability of jobs mean workers have other options and usually still no contract to bind them. Added to this is the fact that paying even live-in workers a monthly albeit derisory wage has become standard practice, which effectively gives them a regular chance to walk out with cash in hand. The availability of an exit option, made possible by the punctual liquidation of debt, is, Godbout argues, what characterizes the market model and makes it so attractive (2000b, 25). The very fact that workers are unknown to employers (even if they arrive by a chain of connections that enables them to be *ma'rūfa* [known] in name) means arrangements are disembedded: there has been no sharing of life, no multiplex ties to make leaving complicated. And because they often hail from elsewhere (l'Océan, as we saw, is something of an exception), workers who leave employers in the lurch will probably never have to face them again.

It is easy for both employers and workers to point the finger at bad practice, but the root of the conflict seems to be the incomplete transition of this sector into the market, which leaves arrangements to be regulated by contradictory sets of values. This may well be a longstanding state of affairs, but the purported novelty of the situation allows room for improvisation. Most people appear to be trying to do "the right thing" while also protecting their interests in a context where everyone feels as though they've been treated somewhat unfairly: employers because domestics *no longer* seem as faithful as they used to be and workers because they are *still not* treated like other kinds of workers.

Notes

1. An emphasis on personal hygiene is typical of employers of domestic workers. Gill found that urban Bolivian women lectured their young Aymara maids on washing regularly (1994, 115).

2. Kapchan records the story of a Moroccan family who gave their domestic a gold necklace—a sign of her treatment as one of the family: "She'd bought [it for her] because they were bringing her up. She treated her like her daughter" (1996, 223). But the domestic gave the necklace to a lover who refused to return it. She was criticized for failing to seek the mediation of the household head and allowing the gold to leave the family network (224).

3. On the provision of toiletries, see also Human Rights Watch (2012, 23–24).

4. Literally the small ʿīd, ʿīd ṣ-ṣaghīr, is also known as ʿīd l-fiṭr, the breaking of the fast. Moroccans celebrate with a special breakfast; men attend prayers at the mosque, and women undertake reciprocal visiting among family and, in shaʿbī contexts, neighbors. This is the arena in which new clothes are displayed and admired.

5. See Hill (1996, chap. 4) on the decline of nonmonetary payments for eighteenth-century English servants.

6. On gifts between family members, see also Godbout (2000a).

7. See Rorty (1998, 46) on justice as a larger loyalty: because abstract notions of justice are at odds with loyalty to a smaller group, we might contract our circle for the sake of loyalty or expand it for justice.

8. Hill (1996, 136) argues that "the training of children of the poor as servants was the main objective of much eighteenth century philanthropy." See also Horn (2004, chap. 5) on charitable institutions and private endeavors that trained poor girls as domestics. The religious nature of these efforts is underlined (Horn 2004, 130).

9. Cutting domestics' hair is not unique to Morocco. Constable recounts how, in Hong Kong, an employer drove her new domestic from the airport directly to a barber for a man's haircut (1997, 539). Ueno (2010, 86) describes how Indonesian domestics enter Singapore via training centers where their hair is cut short.

10. See Styles (2007) on eighteenth-century English working people, who dressed so well that foreign visitors confused them with their masters and mistresses.

11. It has been noted that European imperialism often took the guise of medicine (Vaughan 1991).

12. Haywood's instruction was organized under the following headings: "Observance. Avoiding sloth. Sluttishness. Staying on Errands. Telling Family Affairs. Secrets among Fellow-Servants. Entring into their Quarrels. Tale-Bearing. Being an Eye-Servant. Carelessness of Children. Of Fire, Candle, Thieves. New Acquaintance. Fortune-Tellers. Giving saucy Answers. Liquorishness. Apeing the Fashion. Dishonesty. The Market Penny. Delaying to give Change. Giving away Victuals. Bringing in Chair-Women" (Haywood 1743, front cover).

13. See Qur'ān 2:264: "O believers! Do not make your charity worthless by reminders of your generosity or by injury to the recipient's feelings, like those who spend their wealth to be seen by people and believe neither in Allah nor in the Last Day"; Qur'ān 2:271: "To give charity in public is good, but to give to the poor in private is better and will remove from you some of your sins. Allah is aware of your actions"; and Qur'ān 2:110: "Establish prayer and give zakāt, and whatever good you send ahead of you to the Hereafter for yourselves, you shall find it with Allah; surely Allah is watching all your actions."

14. As Dresch (1998, 130) points out, although Parry's argument aligns alms with deferred reciprocity, "Islamic tradition argues quite the opposite"; the Muslim donor must give expecting no return.

15. See also Jansen (2004, 3); Nieuwkerk (2005, 128).

16. On the relationship between poverty, charity, and religious and social ethics in Muslim societies more generally, see Bonner, Ener, and Singer 2003; Sinemillioğlu 2007, 2009; Benthall 2012.

17. See, for example, Qur'ān 3:336, 12:57, 16:41, 68:3.

18. The cancellation of good deeds by bad, termed *iḥbāt*, is a Muʿtazilī doctrine. See Weir (2012). The doctrine is frequently brought up during fasting, when people are concerned about not doing anything that would discount the merit of each day's fast (Buitelaar 1993).

19. The assertion that merit from ṣadaqa is transferable is contested by some jurists (Weir 2012) and, outside a traditional North African context, usually decried as *bidʿa* (innovation, heresy).

20. Atia (2012) also writes about this in the context of Islamic development.

21. It was never clear what these papers would be. Fatima did not know herself, except that they would involve a record of the length of time Fatima had worked for this employer, which would enable her to access some form of benefit after retirement.

22. See Piamenta (1983) on the Muslim conception of God and human welfare as reflected in everyday speech.

23. Workers often used this phrase and another, "God guide her/him/them," which suggests a person is doing wrong but does not know any better. Sometimes the phrase "God guide us all" is used, implying that no one is without blame. This often brings to a close a conversation about a person's wrongdoing.

24. An online search revealed that this is a catchphrase, reproduced for downloading in many graphic forms.

25. I am grateful to Judith Scheele for this point (personal communication). For an exploration of generosity, theft, and kinship, see Lambek (2011).

26. See Stringham's (2011) discussion of the importance of internal (moral) constraints in the absence of external constraints such as contract law, and Macauley's (1963) study of noncontractual relations in business.

27. Exploitation and inequality within family groups is well documented in the literature on household petty commodity production [e.g., Harris (1982); Brass (1986); Lem (1991); White (1994)]. See also England (1993) for a critique of the neoclassical assumption that individuals do not behave as self-interested actors in relation to their families.

28. See Duxbury (1996) for a criticism of arguments for restricting the scope of markets in such domains and Sandel (2012) on the moral limits of markets.

4

SERVING NEIGHBORS, SERVING STRANGERS

Markets and Marketplaces

IN CHAPTER 1, WE MADE A DISTINCTION BETWEEN the help used at two kinds of parties: in l'Océan neighbors and kin were called on, in Hay l-Fatiḥ a professional team. These are two extremes. At one end we have the village-like model, where everyone knows everyone, neighbors are "like family," and kinship disguises inequality in long-term relationships so that work is not always explicitly rewarded. At the other end, we have people hired for a short-term purpose and with whom, once they have been paid, no relationship need continue—the transaction is atomized (cf. Polanyi 1957; Plattner 1989). In this case the actors are, or may as well be, strangers, but this does not matter too much, as they stay only for the duration of the party. In between are the live-in workers, something of a cultural oxymoron, who in effect are hired to be daughters. This raises a series of problems, apparent in chapters 2 and 3. If they are not neighbors or kin, who are these hired workers, and where does one find them? And can they be trusted? The present chapter explores the significance, for *shaʿbī* (ordinary) Moroccans, of knowing people—or at least knowing people who know people, which is often something of a pretense—and how, in the absence of an everyday acquaintance between potential workers and employers, marketplaces where strangers can meet take on new importance. In the pages that follow, we visit different kinds of marketplaces and meet brokers and intermediaries who offer various solutions to the "servant problem."

From Community to Market

When talking about the *medīna* (old city) or l'Océan during the bygone neighborly era, people often denied the existence of *kheddāmāt* (servants): "We didn't need them." What they meant is not that there was little housework to do but that there were always people around who could "help." This sort of labor is invisible in official statistics. Neighbors were one resource; family members who were staying as quasi guests were another. I asked Souad, now in her sixties, about her childhood in the medīna: "Did you have servants?" She responded, "No, we didn't. We did everything ourselves. And there was always a cousin, an aunt, a widowed family member who came to live with us. They would do the kneading for bread and the washing. We didn't need a *bonne* [maid]."

The use for domestic labor of women who were dependents of the household (often through some form of kinship) seems to have been common in both town and country in Morocco, as it was in Britain.[1] Hayat remembers how they hired *garçons* for outdoor work on her father's farm in the Taza region but had no need to hire help for domestic tasks: "My mother did the housework with us—my sisters and me. Or we would have *les dames*, especially in the summer—the destitute, who came to stay with us. The house was always open, you see. They would come and stay a few months, or they would come in the day and then go home at night. And while they were there they would help us, especially with washing clothes, as we didn't have a washing machine, or with cleaning the grain."

Hayat always spoke to me in a mixture of French and Moroccan Arabic. I presume she used *dames* (ladies) rather than *femmes* (women) to imply they were not young women but women of age and dignity. If not kin, they would have been women known to the family. The autobiography of Emily Keene, *Shareefa of Wazan*, suggests this practice occurred in nineteenth-century Morocco: "My household consisted of an English maid I had brought from England, a Spanish cook, and two Moorish women for my personal service, *and as many more as I liked to requisition, for the house was full of women of all kinds*. To a Shareef's house, which is a Sanctuary, rich and poor flock to be assisted in their different troubles" (1912, 6, emphasis mine).

Houses like this one and, half a century later, those of Souad and Hayat's childhood, were havens for "floating widows," the term Holmes-Eber uses for Tunisian widows who "move from relative to relative so that the burden of their support is shared evenly among kin" (2003, 95–96). Susan Davis points to a similar arrangement in her Moroccan village study, where a widow or divorcée can subsist by staying with kin and doing housework "to justify her presence" (1978, 424). The women who helped in Hayat's household were not necessarily kin, but the principle is the same: they had access to food, company, and a roof over their heads, and in return they helped with domestic tasks. During my fieldwork I met several older women who had lived in this way. Koutouba, in her fifties, lived for a while with a friend: "She was a little bit well off and *dārt fiyā l-khayr bezāf* [was very good to me]. The lady worked in a hospital canteen and brought food home: bananas, apples, meat, fish. She didn't have to buy it. But what did I have [to offer]? I had my arms [she indicated her biceps]. I used to sweep the floor and do the washing and the cleaning."

Zineb was in a similar position. Originally from the countryside of the Gharb, she moved to live rent free with an acquaintance in l'Océan in order to find work. When I visited, it became clear that Zineb's host relied on her for nearly all the housework. A Moroccan commented, "People feel sorry for you: 'Let me give you somewhere to live and some food, but first, sweep the floor, clean this, fetch that. . . .' There's nothing free."

The principle of work to justify one's presence is central to these arrangements and adds complexities to the ideal of Moroccan hospitality noted by admiring travelers to the region. As elsewhere, visits between new friends tend to follow a pattern of declining levels of hospitality. For the first visit, gifts are brought (traditionally milk and sugar), and, after food, guests will be chided if they attempt to help carry dishes out to the kitchen. But on subsequent visits, gifts are superfluous, insulting even ("don't keep on bringing things! This is your house!"), and help is no longer rejected; indeed, not to help out would be an imposition. One domestic worker argued that "a woman has to work wherever she goes; even if she is a guest, she needs to *nuḍḍ* [get up] and clear away and do the washing up. Then they will invite her again, as she was not *taqīla* [heavy] on them."[2]

Historically, and within the sha'bī ideal, domestic work is assigned to people one knows, or at least whose family one knows.[3] For sha'bī Moroccans, domestic service is embedded in common life (Plattner 1989; Carrier 1997), so the needy receive care and give service, and it makes little sense to talk of a labor *market*. In Gudeman's words, "The market realm revolves about short-term material relationships that are undertaken *for the sake of* achieving a project or securing a good. In the communal realm, material goods are exchanged through relationships kept *for their own sake*" (2001, 10, emphasis his). The sha'bī ideal sees domestic work by poor acquaintances as a by-product of patrons' care, not the other way around. The importance for sha'bī quarters of Rabat of this familial or "cousin labor," as I would call it, is hinted at in Findlay, Findlay, and Paddison's (1984) demographic study.

Analyzing data from an unpublished 1977 employment survey, they found that "in the medina 26.8 per cent of households had relatives outwith the immediate family staying with them. This may be compared with only 14.0 per cent in the 'centre moderne'" (50).[4] The fact that "in the 'centre moderne' 16.8 per cent of households had a 'maid' who lived permanently with the household," compared with only 2 percent in the medīna (50), suggests that distant relatives staying in the household may have fulfilled the function of the "maids" in other quarters.

Moroccans maintain that it has become more difficult to get help on this "cousin labor" basis; wage labor occupies many urban women, and a greater proportion of girls are now in school. If people must now employ rather than simply care for those who do their domestic work, the ideal would still be to employ someone known instead of a stranger. But even this is no longer a given. The trajectory of Ilham, a worker from the Gharb, is illustrative of the shift from working for known employers to working for strangers. She told me about starting work at the age of fifteen or sixteen in 1996:

"I worked in Rabat, but I didn't know the city. But in those days, you didn't have *waʿī* [awareness]. I worked, but I didn't go out. If I had gone out, I would have got lost.... There were no mobile phones."

"But weren't you scared the first time you left home to work?" I asked.

"No, you went to people who were *maʿrūfīn* [known]."

"From the family?"

"No, not from the family, but ... the person who took you there was from the family. And the people of the house were *maʿrūfīn ʿandū* [known to him]. [You were] *maḍmūna* [guaranteed]."[5]

"Ah, so that was better than now?"

"No, now is better. You can change if you don't like it. You can find a job with more money.... You phone the *samsār* [broker]. He says, 'Okay, leave.' He phones someone else, and you have another job.... He makes it easy."

Although Ilham's move from employers whom her family knew toward strangers is, in part, a natural progression that came with age and increasing independence (she was now in her thirties), it coincides with a more general change. Note that her contact with the employment broker is facilitated by a mobile phone. While in the domestic domain the need to deal with strangers is seen as new and problematic, Maroc Telecom's sales slogan, "ālam jadīd yunādīkum [a new world calls you]," relies on the notion that dealing with strangers is new and exciting.[6]

Employers struggled to find people that they knew and therefore trusted to work for them because, it could be argued, the people they would have employed through distant family connections were now picking up their phones and shopping around. Many women in l'Océan during my fieldwork articulated a choice between employing a stranger and employing nobody. The old ties that linked them to poorer people seemed to have broken down, so they no longer *knew* anyone who was prepared to work for them. But the way l'Océan residents expressed this is that "l-<u>kh</u>eddāmāt mā baqāw<u>sh</u> [there are no workers anymore]," a complaint that is reminiscent of "the servant problem" of twentieth-century Britain. Celia Fremlin, an Oxford graduate who took jobs in British domestic service as a way to investigate class divisions in the 1930s, noted the difficulty of the working and employing classes meeting: "The present chaotic methods of bringing together employers and employees . . . not only discourage many girls from entering service, but also once again provide a bonus for the bad mistress and the incompetent maid. Neither mistress nor maid has any really effective method of finding out anything about each other except by the exhausting and wasteful method of trial and error" (1940, 168).

Several women on my street in l'Océan claimed to have employed domestic workers in the past but now found it impossible to allow strangers into their houses: "How can you know what she will be like? There's no trust anymore." Again, this was expressed in general terms and as a new phenomenon. Linguistically, trust is expressed as something that is *in* people: *fihū/fihā t-tiqa* (literally in him/her is trust). But practically it exists *between* people; it is a product of people knowing each other, so the apparent scarcity of trust stems from a lack of relationships rather than a national shortage of trustworthy people.

I would suggest that trust between strangers never has been particularly strong. Writing on Jordan, Shryock argues:

> If Balgawi hosts must 'fear' their guests, it is because hospitality creates a momentary overlap of the inner and outer dimensions of a 'house' (a *bayt* or *dar*). As both a name and a space, a *bayt* can be identified with a set of physical structures, the kin who inhabit them, and the persons and properties attaching to these. Throughout the Arab world, houses are marked by a strong desire to receive visitors and, at the same time, to safeguard their own interiority, which is often described as *hurma*, as 'sacredness' or 'inviolability'. . . . Because guests are not members of the house, they must be delicately received. . . .

Hospitality creates a moral space in which outsiders can be treated as provisional members of the house, as aspects of its *hurma* (2004, 36).

The Muslim institution of *ḍayf Allāh* (literally guest of God) that facilitated travel in a strange country has largely fallen out of use because people are afraid to host strangers. Significantly, the time frame in which damage could occur was limited to three days only.[7] If "the problem of how to deal with strangers" (Pitt-Rivers 1977, 94) is solved by hospitality, the problem of how to employ strangers requires a different sort of hazard protection. In local discourse it is a modern problem—in the past people employed those they knew. When the known people no longer want to do domestic work for people they know, or the people who work are no longer known, some shaʿbī households cease to employ—it's not worth the moral risk. Those ex-employers I met in l'Océan were now getting by on their own; either their children were grown and so did not need constant attention or grandmothers were present to take some of the load.[8] A woman could be called in every other week to help with the *grand ménage*, or what in nineteenth-century England was called "the rough": "the scrubbing, elbow grease and heavy work" (Lethbridge 2013; Light 2007). This could be someone whom they had employed on previous occasions or a stranger from the *mūqef*, the day-labor market (literally a stopping or standing place) who would come, do her work, and leave. While these markets come into play when knowledge of people runs out, a more general knowledge of going rates and acceptable hiring behaviors is required for anyone to be able to use them.

The Mūqef

My host father pointed out that these labor markets, instigated by the French to tidy idle locals into places where Europeans could conveniently hire them, are found only in newer "European" quarters of the city. The Moroccan *mulīn d-diyūr* (household heads) of the medīna, like those of the bygone l'Océan that he spoke of nostalgically, had no need of a marketplace for locating workers; they could simply call on a poorer neighbor. The need for grounding the labor market in a physical place is evidenced in the literature on the protectorate period, when the most common encounter between "Muslims" and "Europeans" was that which took place daily between a domestic and her female employer (Brac de la Perrière 1987, 14).

Academic literature uses the term "day-labor market," and attention is fixed on male day laborers.[9] The North African women's mūqef has not been the subject of serious ethnographic study, but something of its history is traceable through passing references and oral accounts. For example, French researchers in Douar Doum, one of the *bidonvilles* that sprang up around Rabat, reported female day labor in the 1930s (Baron and Baron 1936, 176). The predominance of laundry work (this has lessened in importance since washing machines entered middle-class homes) meant the women who hired themselves out by the day to work for Europeans were called "femmes ṣābūn" (soap women, from French *savon*; the Moroccan Arabic verb to launder is *ṣbbn*). In his study of domestic workers in Algiers during the 1950s, Borrmans wrote that, "on certain streets in Bab-el-Oued, there is a 'Fatma' market.[10] . . . A woman calls them or shouts for them from her second or third floor: 'come up, there's work today'" (cited in Brac de la Perrière 1987, 55). Thirty years later, Jansen noted that the mūqef in an Algerian town provided work for mature women who were not prepared to accept the conditions of a live-in maid while they waited for a better position (Jansen 1987, 208).[11]

While other domestic workers are hidden from sight in people's homes, mūqef workers are by necessity in public space. Because of the general separation of poorer neighborhoods from wealthier ones, people who know where these women live are people like them, not people who would employ them, so there is nothing to be gained from waiting at home for a knock at the door. Women must appear in the streets where potential employers pass by. The public aspect of their work brings them dangerously close, in local opinion, to prostitutes.

The locations of labor markets are known by all. The first passersby I approached on day one of my fieldwork were able to point me toward a mūqef in the city center where women sat along a wall on the perimeter of a public park. This was known as *l-Jarda* (the garden) and, as I later learned, was considered the mūqef most associated with "corruption" (*l-fesād*), in this context meaning prostitution.[12] Other labor markets were to be found in l'Océan, Agdal, Hassan, and Hay Salam (Salé), each with its own feel. The Agdal mūqef, located next to the general market, is one of the largest. As I approached, a woman standing in the middle of the road raised her right hand and moved it from side to side with her fist closed, a charade of scrubbing a wall, accompanied by the shout "<u>kh</u>eddāma [worker]?" Women sat or stood alone or in twos or threes along the road and, when cars approached, raced each other to the drivers' windows. I was told that the mūqef in Agdal never empties from morning to night. As with l-Jarda, a shift in the type of work offered is said to occur partway through the day, making some women avoid the place completely. In the words of a l'Océan mūqef worker, "They do two jobs. When you clean and you dust, you finish your work and you go out the door with your honor [*karāmtik*]. But if you clean and dust and then you go [i.e., sleep] with *mul d-dār* [the man of the house], you don't leave with your honor. If you have l-fesād [moral corruption] in you, you can become rich, but you can't have your honor." Some maintain, however, that at the Agdal mūqef, domestic workers to serve or wash up at an evening party can decently be hired later in the day.

By contrast, the women in l'Océan go home at the noon call to prayer if they have not been hired by then: "It's shameful to stay any longer," explained one. Their numbers are small, and they nearly always sit together in a tight row on one side of the road. They claim a special status for their mūqef because it is located where there used to be a *bīrū* (from *bureau de placement*, employment office), which sets it apart from those associated with "corruption" (l-fesād). One of the mūqef workers related that a young woman placed by the bīrū jumped from a high window; the bīrū was investigated and shut down, and rumor has it that the owner, a man named Mehdi, went to France. Despite the tragic circumstances of the bīrū's closure, the comparative respectability of a bīrū that existed in the past casts a shade of decency on the site today, and whenever anyone mentioned the shame ('ayb or *ḥashūma*) of sitting on the street, they were reminded that "there is no 'ayb because everyone knows there used to be a bīrū here, so this is where women sit for work and nothing else. It's *maʿrūf* [well known]." The mūqef in Hay Salam (Salé) is a middle ground between the l'Océan mūqef's respectability and close-knit community on the one hand and the volume of workers and employers that pass through the Agdal market on the other. A newspaper article claims the Hay Salam mūqef is twenty-five years old but gives no details about its origin (Amrani 2012).

Seasonal work is usually associated with the tourist trade and agriculture, but domestic work too has its seasons. We are familiar, after all, with the term *spring cleaning*. The l'Océan mūqef was empty on rainy days, only in part because the women do not want to get wet waiting for work; thorough cleaning involves taking mattresses, cushions, and carpets up to the roof terrace or balcony to air and rid them of mites, which is not practical on rainy days. But as well as being weather dependent, demand for domestic work ebbs and flows with cycles of the calendar. The extra outlay for the year's schoolbooks in September, for example, means many families cannot afford to hire a worker that month. On a weekly cycle, Fridays—a holy day when male attendance at mosque prayers is higher than other days—are low days for domestic work. Women are too intent on preparing the special Friday couscous meal to think about getting someone in for extra cleaning.[13]

A Moroccan equivalent of our term *spring cleaning* might be *l-ʿawāshīr*, which could be translated as "festivities." Before *ʿīd* (a feast day), Moroccans will usually do a thorough clean or *grand ménage*, a religiously meritorious act believed to earn *ajr* (religious merit) (Buitelaar 1993, 180), but they will sometimes call a big clean ʿawāshīr even if no feast day is coming. In the run-up to any feast day, hopes for work at the mūqef will be higher than at other times, but women who attend only during ʿawāshīr periods will not be looked on kindly by more regular workers. While there is more domestic work during this time, workers themselves need more cash because festivities mean extra expenses. Essentials become dearer, as traders know people will pay high prices; ʿīd is not a time to go without. A discussion just before the holiday celebrating the Prophet's birthday demonstrated that work at the labor market was considered a limited good (cf. Foster 1965, 1972). A worker complained:

This month is *ʿayān* [tired—i.e., there is little work]. People, even the
    muwaẓẓafīn [office workers], don't have enough to pay us."
"No, I'm sorry but [office workers] are not like us. They have some money,"
    another woman chimed in.
"The problem is that there are more washing machines than women. And we
    Moroccans have lots of children. *Qūwat l-bashar* [too many people]!"

The shortage of work meant that women ran into difficulties if they appeared to be working for the "clients" of others. Workers throughout the year at the l'Océan mūqef often talked about moving to a different mūqef where they supposed there would be more work. To my knowledge these plans were not carried out, probably because newcomers would be perceived as a threat to the women who habitually frequented the other market.

Usually a mūqef is not subject to any regulation but the women's own. Although policemen often patrolled the grocery part of l'Océan's marketplace, asking outsized stalls to tuck themselves in or move elsewhere, they did not approach the mūqef.[14] Sometimes clients came in search of a particular worker whom they had hired from the mūqef on previous occasions, but when new clients did not specify whom they wanted, the workers tried to refer the decision back to the client. For example, when a *mulat d-dār* (lady of the house) said to a worker, "You come, and bring one other," another of the workers told her, "Decide which one you want and take her." This saved workers from being accused by others of taking jobs out of turn but meant they had to endure being looked up and down by clients as they made their selections.

Although everyone had as much or as little right to be there as anyone else—"the street belongs to the *makhzen* [the government]"—young women were discouraged by other workers. This seemed to be done out of kindness as much as fear that they would take older women's work. One morning in Hay Salam, I noticed a woman much younger than the others. Someone nodded toward her, saying, "It's her first time here today. See, her face is still white, not like ours." The young woman, Hakima, related how she had often seen the others sitting there and, having recently lost her job in a factory, had decided to join them until she found something else. Hakima had worn her oldest *jellāba* and covered her dyed and styled hair with a scarf, but despite her best efforts, she did not look like a mūqef worker. When she arrived, the other women told her, "It won't suit you. You're still young, and the work is hard." Youthfulness did not equate in an employer's eyes with maximum work in minimum time. Indeed, when I had suggested that I could be a second person for a job as only one worker had attended the mūqef that day, the mulat d-dār had looked me up and down and said, "You're ṣaghīra [young, small]. You'd faint. It needs someone who has . . ." she patted her biceps. It was also important to dress as employers expected; nice clothes did not provoke generous payment, and employers faced with selecting workers from a number of women were more likely to choose needy-looking ones.

The pay on offer at l'Océan's mūqef ranged between 50dh and 200dh a day; the hours varied hugely, and it was not uncommon for work to begin only at noon. Employers sometimes refused to name a price until they had shown workers the property or even until the work was completed. They often downplayed the difficulty of the job. For example, the mulat d-dār who had turned her nose up at my biceps told another worker that the job was "dusting, washing the dishes." That worker declined the job, commenting, "There is no such thing as dusting! It will be *temmāra* [hard work]! . . . I'd be better off staying at home."

In l'Océan, elderly residents, probably not of an employing class but too frail to do the work themselves, tended to offer the lowest pay. When they came looking for help, Nafisa, who lived in one of the divided up Spanish houses on the mūqef street, often persuaded women to accept the work. Nafisa would sit with the women on her way to or from the market, but she never took a job herself, although she needed money. Nafisa often asked me to find her a "girl" like myself who could lodge with her to help her pay the rent. The time I had offered my own elbow grease and been turned down, the mulat d-dār asked Nafisa, who was sitting with us, if she would not be the second worker herself. Nafisa had replied, "There's no shame in it." The mulat d-dār had said, "No, there's no shame in it. These days, work is work, whether you write, or you work with your hands, or you work in houses, it's all the same." All this to say that it was out of the question for Nafisa to do this work; if she became that desperate for money she would go to a mūqef farther away from her house. But hanging around the mūqef as a long-standing sha'bī neighbor to these elderly residents, she upset the otherwise impersonal approach of the workers, who by definition were not neighbors, by persuading them to take on charity cases. When an elderly man wanted two workers to clean his house for 80dh each, Nafisa said to the two women present, "Well, go with him!" She shook her head and turned to me: "Otherwise they'll just sit here all morning!"

The workers did often sit there all morning. Some days there were eight women at the l'Océan mūqef, but rarely were more than two hired, and often not one. In fact, demand for workers seemed too low to justify the outlay for the journey—one or two bus rides at 4dh each (a journey that could take almost two hours) and the same back again. What motivated their attendance at the mūqef? And why the mūqef over regular work? Several women had work for regular clients in l'Océan one or two days a week but would still pass by the mūqef on the way to employers' houses. A well-documented fringe benefit of markets is the sharing of information (Crawford 2008, 110). Workers gave others the lowdown on clients who chanced to be walking by and shared advice on economizing: where to buy cheap food, work opportunities for their menfolk, and guidance on accumulating ajr for the hereafter. Mūqef workers would also borrow money from one another and most days receive gifts of charity (bread or coins) from local residents. Some of the workers performed charitable acts of their own toward neighborhood cats: "God commands us to look after them." And so the mornings passed productively whether or not anyone was hired.

I frequented only one mūqef regularly, opting for my local one in l'Océan. This was naive; workers never go to their nearest mūqef. In a complete reversal of the sha'bī ideal of helping one's neighbors, the public element of mūqef work propels many workers at least a bus journey away from their homes. Although being seen is vital for hiring, no one wants to be seen at a mūqef by those they know personally.[15] As one worker explained, "It's not nice to be seen in the mūqef. It is *ḥashūma* [shameful]."

One morning I spotted one of Mui Latifa's daughters, Raja, making her way along the stalls of secondhand clothes at the market end of the street. I instinctively did not want to be seen and leaned back behind Nabila, who noticed and asked me what was wrong. "I know that lady," I replied. "I don't want her to see me here." Nabila proceeded to give me an account of all her dealings with the Sebbari household. Everyone at the mūqef knew Dār Sebbari—they would hire a mūqef worker if a regular worker left them in the lurch and they could not get a former worker to cover. I was afraid Nabila would be offended at my not wishing to be seen in the mūqef; saying hello to Raja would raise the question of whether I should introduce Nabila and the others to her, though I knew she would not wish to appear to be on too friendly terms with such women.

That first time I saw Latifa's daughter Raja, she moved on without seeing me, but a second time she caught me sitting on the pavement with four workers.

"What are you doing here?"

"She's come to see me," Nabila was quick to respond.

"Yes, I've come to see my friends."

"These are your friends?" Raja's eyes were laughing.

Once she had moved on, another worker said to Nabila, "You saved her there, saying she'd come to see you!"

Nabila had wanted to make sure Raja did not think I was at the mūqef as a job seeker because of the shame they associated with this work. What I wanted to avoid, however, was the repetition of the story to Mui Latifa and her other daughters next time I visited Dār Sebbari. This is precisely what happened, and the usual warnings were issued: "Be careful, Mary! Not everyone is good; not everyone is like us. Don't trust everyone!" The mūqef women were not people of l'Océan, nor did they come with any wider family to recommend them. They were to be approached with all the risks associated with detached, unvouched for strangers. Because of the lack of trust people had in them, they usually worked under supervision, a precaution only practical for short periods of time. For *shaʿbī* Moroccans with their preference for personalized connectedness, hiring a stranger from the mūqef is a compromise; desperate times call for desperate measures.

Employment Agencies

Employment agencies, which have sprung up worldwide since the 1980s, offer the convenience of a mūqef as a go-to for workers and employers, with the addition of a matching service, however perfunctory this may be in practice. In contrast with the mūqef, agencies also deal in requests for long-term live-in workers rather than just day work. The transactions that occur here are modern in that they are atomized and disembedded—people otherwise unconnected to the agency staff can be recommended through it to people equally unconnected. Domestic work is the only point at which the parties relate to each other, but the worker will be coming into the employers' house repeatedly or semipermanently.

Academic studies have questioned the contribution agencies make to formalizing the industry (Blackett 2011, 27–28; Tsikata 2011), but Moroccans who run agencies were keen to stress to me how they differed from the "illegal" service offered by a broker or *samsār* (feminine *samsāra*). Nonetheless, the term *samsār* is sometimes still applied colloquially to people running agencies because they functioned as *samāsira* (plural of *samsār*) before they set up offices. Fouzia, whose office was in a low-income neighborhood in Salé, told me how she had been a *wasīṭa* (intermediary).[16] "I just did it for friends. . . . But there were always problems—girls would not be paid, or would quit, leaving children alone in the house." This led her to set up a *sharīka* (company) whose "legality," in her eyes, made all the difference to how the girls she placed behaved and were treated: "It's *qānūnī* [legal]. The girls must be paid. They must be fed; they must feel comfortable in the house. If these things are in place, of course, she will work well. The girls cannot just leave suddenly. If they have a problem, they telephone the agency, and the agency finds another worker for the mulat d-dār and another job for the girl. They work it out. But they don't just run away."

Naima, who had worked in this field for twenty years, made the comparison of conditions for live-in work between when she started and now: "They used to sleep in the kitchen, to be beaten, not given good food, eat on their own, to never take their aprons off the entire day, not be allowed to change into their [nonwork] clothes, no holiday. Now that doesn't happen. They are treated well. They have the weekend off and twenty days holiday a year. They used to earn just 800dh a month, now they earn 1,500, 2,000, 3,000, 4,000 even."

The transition from agent to agency for both Naima and Fouzia involved locating themselves in offices distinct from their homes and producing literature with a name, address, and description of services, or, at least, in Fouzia's case, a sign on the office door.[17] Fouzia's agency was called after the family name; Naima's had an anglicized name (along the lines of International High Class Service) that I never heard anyone use. Her office was simply referred to as ʿand Naima (at Naima's). The rest of Naima's publicity flier was in French:

NEW COMPANY FOR MADE-TO-MEASURE SERVICES!!!
Domestic workers, nannies, nurses, gardeners, cooks, chauffeurs, carers, security guards, are all professions that we handle.[18]

Cleanliness, discretion and confidentiality will be assured by our team and our made-to-measure contracts.

Her agency may be "new" but *Naima* had been a household name in Rabat for much longer. Her work used to be lucrative: "We were few. In the beginning there was just Soumiya, Mehdi [of the famous l'Océan bīrū turned mūqef], and me. Now there are so many agencies." Soumiya and her agency, *Allo ma bonne* (again, I never heard workers or employers refer to it as anything but ʿand Soumiya), feature in an online article (Amrani 2006). While others were chattier, Soumiya refused to grant me an interview, telling me I could find out everything about how her agency functioned directly from the government, "because we follow the laws of the Ministry of Work."

Fouzia's, Naima's, and Soumiya's agencies functioned by matching workers and employers and charging the employers. They had clients in all the big cities of Morocco. Naima explained that she charges employers 500dh, which covers the placement of up to three workers. If the employer does not get along with the first, they have the right to a second or a third, but only within three months of the initial fee. If the employer wants a fourth worker within three months or a new worker after three months, they pay another 500dh. Naima thought she might place twenty or forty girls a month or none at all: "It's not that there aren't workers or people wanting them. It's just that there might be no matches." While Fouzia claimed that workers come to her—"one will bring her friend, who will bring another"—Naima made biannual trips to the countryside to source workers, who then remained in the countryside until she telephoned to say work was available.[19] Those who lacked skills could also stay with Naima or her daughter while they were "trained." One worker, Sharifa, related that Naima had asked her what wage she expected—1,500dh a month and a day off on Sundays—and what she knew how to do: "Well, well, you're demanding a high wage [*temen*], and you don't know how to do things!" Sharifa had protested that she was a fast learner: "People just have to show me how to do something once, and I can do it." But Naima told Sharifa, "The girl has to know everything already."[20] She offered her neither work nor training. But to me Naima explained that some employers preferred unskilled workers whom they could train themselves: "Then they pay them a lower wage. Maybe they would pay someone 1,500dh, but a <u>kh</u>eddāma who knows nothing, they pay her 1,000dh and train her." This kind of live-in position is reminiscent of the "petty places" of nineteenth- and early twentieth-century servants in Britain, which were seen as "stepping-stones to better things" (Mullins and Griffiths 1986, 7).

Lengths of stay varied enormously and depended on how the employers treated the workers and how well the worker did her job. Naima explained that when she discovers that particular workers habitually leave employers, she refuses them further work; in the same way, she stops providing workers for clients with whom workers never stay long. This contrasts with the rumors about Mehdi's business—that he would create problems between workers and employers in order to earn more through further placements. This practice is reported in the press and ethnographic literature on samāsira (Salahdine 1988, 104) and is exactly what the "legal" agencies pride themselves on not doing. But "legal" (qānūnī) meant different things in different agencies. As I discuss in chapter 7, the Moroccan labor code does not cover domestic work (probably Soumiya was operating according to an idea of law copied from another employment sector), but Fouzia and Naima, when using the word *legal*, seemed to be referencing a partly shared idea of what was right and fair. For Fouzia, a "legal" amount of holiday was one month (August) each year and from Saturday afternoon until Sunday afternoon every week or two days every other week. Naima, meanwhile, talked about "the weekend" off and twenty days leave a year, to be taken when it suited the employer.

Neither Fouzia nor Naima mentioned the word *contract* (although it appears on Naima's flier), and I saw no papers on the desks in their offices, whereas Soumiya's office was a whirlwind of paperwork. While Soumiya did not want to be interviewed, I was able to build up an idea of how her agency worked from Nabila, who has worked for Soumiya's clients many times, taking live-in work on a weekly or monthly basis: "You sign a paper.... The paper says whether you are going to do the cooking or the cleaning or the children or everything, if the house is small. So if you were brought to do the cleaning and they say, 'Do the cooking,' then you can say, 'No, that's not on the paper. I wasn't brought to do the cooking.' You can phone Soumiya, and she sorts it out."

I personally knew no one who had employed a Moroccan worker through an agency. I had contact with a wealthy family in Souissi who had recently used an agency for the first time to employ a Filipina nanny and a Senegalese cleaner but found their Moroccan cook through their security guard (who had asked the security guard of a neighboring villa, who had asked his employers' domestic, who had suggested her sister). Dār Sebbari had a tenuous link to Naima, as she was related to a girl they had brought up. Yet the Sebbaris did not take workers from her agency despite frequently finding themselves short of domestic help: Naima, they said, did not "know" the girls she placed.

The workers I met in Rabat who had used these agencies had jobs in the affluent Hay Riad district. In mid-nineteenth-century England and France, a rise in the importance of agencies for placements correlated with an increase in urban migrants who needed middlemen to connect them to clients (McBride 1976, 77). I suspect that, as with newcomers in European cities, much of the demand for agencies in Rabat came from newer residential areas, where people are distinctly not sha'bī. Sha'bī people do not trust agencies.

Samāsira

Agencies seem always to have evolved from the work of samāsira (singular samsār/a, broker or agent). Samāsira are often more attractive than agencies for sha'bī employers, not only because they are generally more affordable but also because, being a person, not a company, the samsāra plays the role of a "friend" (whether she is or not is a separate matter).[21] Samāsira are not in the yellow pages, so referrals take place among acquaintances, thus realizing the sha'bī ideal's preference for personalized connection.

Samāsira generally have a bad name in the press, where they are associated with "trafficking" petites bonnes. Human Rights Watch (2012, 18) reports that ten out of twenty former child domestics they interviewed said an intermediary arranged at least one of their jobs.[22] The Moroccan press portrays samāsira as predators roaming weekly markets in the countryside to take advantage of the poverty of rural families (Kuuwirti 2013), and mentioning the word samsāra on the streets during my fieldwork made people switch to a whisper or warn me, "Don't go with them," "They are kh̲aybīn [nasty, literally ugly]," and "Don't trust them." A local shopkeeper gave me the phone number of a samsār, but only on the condition that I not tell the samsār who had given me his number: "Don't say my name, don't say 'the shopkeeper,' don't tell him this street, nothing." Similarly, when I told my host mother that I was going to the home of a samsāra and would probably stay the night, she was extremely concerned.

The samsāra in question, Warda, was introduced to me by a friend of a friend without the usual warnings. As we drank tea, Warda explained, "It's not an agency. This is just something I do for people. . . . People tell their friends." A steady stream of people called either at Warda's house or at her shop around the corner. "Warda is maʿrūfa [well known]," explained a young woman who came to the shop in search of domestic work. Warda lived in a suburb where housing is cheaper than in Rabat itself, with a high concentration of recent migrants from the countryside. She maintained a strong link with her village of origin, where her mother still lived. Warda's mother could phone with news of local women looking for work, and Warda would send for them when something came up. Warda asserted that she placed only girls whose families she knew—for example, sisters or friends of someone she has placed before—and outlined to me an oddly formal process of obtaining permission, transfer of responsibility, and a guarantee of good behavior: "I always go to the family. Not if they are far away—in that case I go to an uncle or aunt who lives here. I say to them, 'Are you sending this girl to work?' They say, 'Yes.' I say to them, 'Will she create problems, steal?' They say, 'No.' So I don't have to worry about placing her? No. Do you guarantee her? Yes. They always say yes."

Warda suggested that workers she places sometimes do steal from employers. When this happens, she removes them from that client and sends them to another. "Then I have to see if they do it again. I take their [national identity] card. They can't work if they don't have the card."

Warda also put workers up in her home so they could leave one employer and begin working for another without having to go back to the countryside in between, thus saving transport costs and saving face. But it also seemed convenient for Warda, who never had to pay for childcare and could come home to a cooked meal. While "hosting" the workers, Warda assessed their aptitude for domestic tasks, and although she did not emphasize "training" so much as "testing" workers while they stayed with her, she offered advice and encouraged them to take opportunities to learn. She had a cookbook they could flick through to get ideas from the pictures. Batul, a kind of voluntary assistant and friend of Warda's, was useful in showing transitory workers the ropes. Warda also claimed to send women who did not know how to do much in the house to people who employ multiple workers so that the others could show the new worker how to do things.

Wages for the women Warda placed varied between 1,500 and 2,000dh a month, the latter for a live-out position. She explained that many workers she placed had become like one of the family of their employers: "Most of them stay until they get married. The employers give her a wedding party, and she visits them later with her children." This seemed to be more of an ideal than a norm in practice, as Warda went on to say that "today people are *mādīyīn* [materialistic]. They follow the money. They might find better paid work in a café. The employer will come home and find that suddenly there is no one to take care of her baby or cook dinner."

Each client pays Warda between 300 and 500dh, and she might place five or six workers a week. This could easily mean taking 6,000dh a month in fees, but Warda seemed to have little idea of her income from placing workers compared with her shop business, or how much she spent in overhead expenses such as transport or phone calls. In addition she made *ghayf* (pancakes) to sell to friends and neighbors and managed rental properties. All contacts, whatever they were interested in, were given Warda's business card, which mentioned only the shop. Outside the shop, a sign pointed people to the "agency" with a picture of a key, suggesting the real estate line of their business but not the domestic service side of things. Warda stressed the importance of this diversification: "You can't just do one thing. It's not possible. What if there are no domestic workers one day and you have to pay the rent?"

Warda's husband, meanwhile, as well as being involved in the shop, ran a further line of business, hiring out construction vehicles and buying and selling used cars. Much like the waiting domestics, who could be used to do odd jobs, the cars awaiting sale could be used to drive Warda and her workers to new clients.

Warda kept a notebook beside the phone; in the notebook, her thirteen-year-old son, Adam, when not at school, would write down the number of anyone who called (Warda is illiterate). Adam once showed me the notebook with pride: "Look how many people we've got!" Warda and Idriss worked in contacts; that was their business. The more people they knew, the more houses they could rent, the more domestic workers they could place, and the more cars and pancakes they could sell. Just as Carrier argues that from the Western capitalist viewpoint "the Market appears to exist only if it is a sphere of life rather than the whole of life" (1997, 45), Warda's transactions were embedded in her social life rather than being a separate sphere and her knowledge of people set her apart from other brokers.

Just as the agency women, Naima and Fouzia, were keen to stress the difference between their business and that of "illegal" samāsira, Warda wanted to show me what she was not. We took a shared taxi to a busy transport hub in her district, a suburb south of Rabat. "Sūq n-najāḥ [the market of success]!" joked one of the other passengers. Warda explained, "If anyone doesn't know where to go [for work], they can come here." She led me to a cluster of shelters (barārik) next to the roundabout and asked where "Halima" was. We were directed inside a blue tarpaulin shelter where about a dozen women, young and old, sat on makeshift benches, staring back at us. Halima explained that she placed them for domestic work on a first-come, first-served basis, charging employers 200dh for each placement. Halima told us that she does not take fees from the workers, just from the employers, but once we were out of earshot Warda asserted that Halima takes money from workers too: "A worker who gives Halima 100dh will be placed first. It's maʿrūf [known]." We then walked back across the roundabout, and Warda indicated a man sitting on a bench with two women next to him. She explained that he was maʿrūf as a samsār who also offers girls as prostitutes: "He places anyone with anyone. He doesn't know the women; he doesn't know their families. . . . He doesn't know the employers. . . ."

Warda stressed how different this was from her own way of working with known people. Halima and this bench-based samsār were "well known" in the community in the sense that people knew what they offered and where to find them. To meet Warda, people came to her home or shop, which was much less accessible than this public roundabout unless one had a personal acquaintance with someone who knew her. But when my friend Zineb asked me to ask Warda for work for her sister, I found that one need not know someone personally in order to stand as their guarantor. This particularly regretful tale in which, in typical shaʿbī fashion, I overstated my knowledge of Zineb's sister to help her out and return a favor, is recorded elsewhere (M. Montgomery 2019).[23] When things did not turn out well, one worker's mother, surprised by my naive trust in Warda's business, commented, "Of course the samsāra doesn't know people. She can't possibly know them. She only knows money."

The monetary market dovetailed with a moral economy of "doing good" in that samāsira could cash in on favor accrued along chains of connections. Gudeman (2001, 19) points out that "goods may pass through phases to serve as both commodities and gifts, shifting along a continuum from market exchange to reciprocity." Warda's friendly persona and informal way of talking about the work made the transition between connections exchanged for moral credit into connections for cash payment almost imperceptible.[24] Others were less successful. A newspaper reports that a sixtysomething samsār in Hattane (Khouribga region) "insists that it was never his *niyya* [intention] to trade in girls, but he was doing it '*min ajl fa'l l-khayr*' [in order to do good]." He was intermediary for some twenty girls, charging their employers 1,000 to 1,500dh per placement and receiving gifts including old furniture and worn clothes (Mshat 2013, 8). In many ways samāsira are the lifeblood of sha'bī domestic service, but because the monetary side of their transactions, even when obscured by a language of friendship and favors, stands at odds with the ideal of personalized connectedness, they must be consulted with caution and collectively maligned.

Nonprofessional Intermediaries

When I asked workers and employers who found their jobs or their domestics for them, the answer was often a long chain of connections: so-and-so asked so-and-so, who asked so-and-so. . . . While I met workers who used samāsira or even agencies, the majority of connections, particularly among sha'bī Moroccans, were made by acquaintances who put people in touch without payment. A preference for sourcing workers through acquaintances is not unique to sha'bī Moroccans. In her nineteenth-century *Book of Household Management*, Mrs. Beeton advised that "there are some respectable registry-offices, where good servants may sometimes be hired; but the plan rather to be recommended is, for the mistress to make inquiry amongst her circle of friends and acquaintances, and her tradespeople. The latter generally know those in their neighborhood, who are wanting situations, and will communicate with them, when a personal interview with some of them will enable the mistress to form some idea of the characters of the applicants, and to suit herself accordingly" ([1861] 1907, 14).

Writing on Nepal, Saubhagya Shah describes how intermediaries who arranged domestic service were not paid directly by either party but accumulated favor from both sides, which could later be translated into connections, jobs, patronage, or other benefits (2000, 94). In the same way, finding a domestic worker or job for a friend, neighbor, or family member in Morocco is seen as khayr or ajr—that is, a deed earning credit in paradise. Some Moroccans also spoke of connecting employers and workers with one another as a *wājib* (duty).

It was in the spirit of doing khayr that Hayat contacted me to ask if I knew anyone who could work for some friends of hers. She expressed it in terms of obligation because of her attachment to them: "They are very dear to me and asked this thing of me." By extension, if Hayat were dear to me, I would help her to help her friends. Taking care this time not to make a recommendation to either party, I put her in touch with Hafida, whose younger sister, Aziza (twenty-three), I knew to be looking for work. Hayat and Hafida's discussion of the job involved very few details. Most strikingly, no one mentioned the working hours or the wage. Talk about money sits ill with an exchange couched in terms of kindness, of doing one another favors.

Domestic workers like Hafida, who provided a link to her younger sister, often function as gatekeepers to the supply side of the labor market. The importance of employee referrals has been noted for blue-collar workers in North America: "[they] usually provide good screening for employers who are satisfied with their present workforce. Present employees tend to refer people like themselves, and they may feel that their own reputation is affected by the quality of the referrals" (Rees 1966, 562).[25] Workers know how well other women in their village work, particularly sisters and cousins. Ilham's sister, for example, had worked with a relative, Rouqia, and reported to Ilham that "sūqhā khāwī [literally her market is empty—i.e., she is unproductive]." Ilham would not, therefore, consider asking Rouqia to join her on a two-worker job, although they happily spent their days off together. Recommendations work both ways—family members and friends of the worker may hope that having one member of the group working for a "good employer" will soon lead to similar placements for others. They are sometimes disappointed, as are employers, for workers do not always wish to make introductions.

Hafida's story, touched on above, presented an example of repeatedly connecting workers with an employer she knew to be "bad." Hafida had worked for the same employer for eight years, during which time she become acquainted with a mulat d-dār in the same apartment building: "She's like a friend." L-Ḥajja, as Hafida respectfully called this woman, had asked her to bring her a domestic worker from the blād (her home region in the countryside). One of Hafida's sisters knew a girl, Miriam, from school. Miriam had never worked as a domestic before, but her mother took one look at Hafida's fair coloring and ample figure and said, "Are you a kheddāma? Impossible! You don't look like one. Just by your face, I know you are maʿqūla [reasonable], and I'll let my daughter go with you." Hafida and Miriam would meet on the stairs or hanging out the washing on the roof. Hafida explained, "I looked out for her. I was older than her, and I had brought her and told her mother I would take care of her." Miriam stayed only one month, however. She recalled that it was Ramadan:

> [L-Ḥajja] kept saying, "Clean the windows, lift up the furniture, and clean the floor underneath." All day long, and we were fasting. And I said to her, "I'm going to spend ʿīd with my family." She said to me, "No, you have to spend ʿīd with me. You can't work Ramadan and not the ʿīd. I have guests coming. You need to be here to host them." I said to her, "No, I'm going. Give me my pay." She gave me just 200dh to travel back home. But Hafida halved her month's wage with me. She said to me, "You can't go back empty-handed." She gave me 500dh.

L-Ḥajja then asked Hafida to bring her another worker. Yousra, the daughter of Hafida's next-door neighbors in the village, was thirteen years old when Hafida asked her parents to let her work for l-Ḥajja. "They said I was still too young for work," recalled Yousra. But Hafida kept asking until Yousra's parents gave in. Yousra worked for two months and was paid only 500dh for each month. She complained, "Taqarfsū ʿalīyā [they mistreated me]." During my fieldwork, Hafida began to work for l-Ḥajja herself but later regretted it:

> "I should never have worked for her. I knew she was like this. I've brought thirteen girls to work for her, and none of them stayed."

"Thirteen?"

> "Yes, I brought the whole village! . . . I know she doesn't treat people well—only in the beginning. I didn't want to work here. She was the one who made me work [for her]."

While Hafida responded to pressure from l-Ḥajja to supply workers, others refused or made excuses when employers asked, and many workers recounted bad experiences of bringing friends and family members to work with employers' acquaintances. Samira had found work for a friend's sister, and the girl invited a man into the employer's house: "When something happens, then *you* feel responsible," Samira said. Another worker stated, "Now I don't do it. When people ask me, 'Do you know a girl who could come and work for me?' I just say, 'No, I don't know anyone. All the girls I know are already working.'"

Similarly, when my host mother, Touria, got to know Salma at the l'Océan school gates and asked her to find a girl to help her in the house, Salma politely refused. She explained to me, "I couldn't send Touria a girl without knowing her well. What if she should steal or do something bad? Then I would feel responsible and feel bad with Touria. I couldn't." So Touria asked Salma to come and work for her herself. At the time Salma was working for another employer, but Touria persuaded her to come to her house after finishing work each day. These opposing feelings—on the one hand a sense of obligation to help employers by finding workers; on the other hand, a desire to avoid a responsibility that might destroy relationships—were difficult to juggle. Salma and Hafida both ended up, through some sense of obligation, working in positions they did not want.

As well as asking current domestic workers to bring women they know, it is not uncommon for the descendants of rural families who have white-collar jobs in Rabat to remain attached to their blād, and announcements of return visits are often heralded with requests from city-based friends for young women from the countryside to employ as domestics: "shūfī liyā shī bint [look out a girl for me]." Employers have also asked villa watchmen (ḥurās, singular ḥāris, French *gardien*) or, in the case of l'Océan, the concierges of apartment buildings. "It's his job to know lots of people," said Nejlae, a mulat d-dār on my street who told me she always asks the building's concierge when she needs a new worker. He asks current workers in the building to ask their sisters, other family members, and neighbors or brings someone from his own blād. Local shopkeepers, the majority of whom in Rabat come from the Sous valley or other Amazigh areas, also source workers for customers from their home communities, which are seen as fertile domestic-worker territory.[26] One journalist uses the metaphor of a particular Amazigh region being a *mushtil* (plantation or nursery) for domestic workers (Kuuwirti 2013, 8).

Nejlae told me that she does not use an agency: "It's impossible for me to let someone I don't know into the house." An agency differs from a samsār or a concierge who brings workers as an unpaid "part of his job" because its shop-front visibility means that people who have no connection to the agent, who are not maʿrūf to anyone concerned, may drop in. Although Nejlae did not require a worker she herself knew, it was important that the concierge knew someone who knew someone, and so on. The number of links in the chain of connections did not seem to matter a great deal; moral responsibility was located at the end of it, however far away that might be. While Nejlae's concierge might "know" the worker only to the extent that a samsār "knows" the worker, the fact that he is not explicitly paid is significant. While the concierge participates in a moral economy of "doing good," the monetary element in a samsār's interactions removes the exchange from this sphere.

The necessity for "known" connections across class boundaries means many women from the countryside are dependent on someone else to find them placements. This puts them in a very different position from their male contemporaries, who, if they go to the cities, find work predominantly in cafés or on construction sites.[27] The difference is illustrated by a conversation between Safae, a domestic worker from the Gharb, and a male friend who had suggested they both find work in Agadir. Safae explained the difficulty: "Their work is *bayna* [obvious, visible from the outside]. Our work is not visible. I know no one in Agadir." She described how men only have to choose a city and call up some *awlād l-blād* (sons of the home country) with whom they can share rented accommodation when they arrive: "They'll then go and find a construction site and ask if there's work, and the foreman will say, 'Yes'. But we aren't going to rent. A girl needs someone to find the work for her. We need to go straight to the house."

Because it is in the public view, a construction site, like a mūqef or employment agency, is a place workers can access whether they know the employers or not. In this respect they are marketplaces where strangers can meet. But precisely because marketplaces are public, it is risky and shameful for young women or girls to seek work in this way. Safae's predicament, of being dependent on an intermediary to provide access to a private home rather than being able to walk onto a worksite, applies to most young female workers coming from the countryside. Some women with more experience in the city do rent shared apartments, often risking their reputations (Cheikh 2009); others lodge more respectably, with acquaintances who host them in exchange for housework. Having a base in the city allows these women to spend time seeking work autonomously—doing the rounds of security guards outside villas, door knocking, attending the mūqef, or registering at an employment agency.

Conclusion

Domestic labor in Morocco has historically been arranged between acquaintances, but ties between rich and poor appear to be breaking down. Or so the story goes. This narrative may have served for some time to explain the intractability of domestic service—why it is so difficult to get a worker to stay or to find one who will not steal. In this context, it is important for Moroccans to employ a domestic who is maʿrūfa, if not to them then to someone they know. Indeed, the modes of recruitment that source relatively known workers remain more prevalent than impersonal recruitment: 46 percent of two hundred workers interviewed by GIZ and the Ministry of Employment were recruited through familial networks and acquaintances.[28] Twenty-five percent were recruited through a samāsira, and 19 percent found their jobs by door knocking, whereas only 10 percent used an agency (Royaume du Maroc 2011). Because contacts with people of the "other" class are valuable, particularly in a climate where trust is a "rare pearl," connections are thus extracted from dependents (workers and concierges) and people, like myself, who are eager to please others. In these exchanges money and trust correlate negatively. When it's performed as a favor, people are unconcerned about the number of links in the chain of connections. But paying an agent or agency to share their connections to people of another class supplies the most "unknown" workers or employers. The possibility of employing such an unknown person seems open and necessary only to people who do not identify with the shaʿbī ideal.

While shaʿbī Moroccans could, and ideally still can, arrange domestic employment through "markets" in the broader sense of networks of embedded transactions that are not confined to a geographic location, Europeans in Rabat, and more recently connection-poor Moroccans, rely on "market *places*" (Plattner 1989, 171) where strangers from the supply and demand sides can meet. Simmel's [(1908) 1965] argument linking strangers with traders follows a similar logic; goods not available within a community have to be brought from outside, and this necessarily involves an outsider coming in.[29] We are familiar with metaphorical marketplaces, such as the classifieds in newspapers or online. The abundance of *petites annonces* concerning domestic work in *L'Echo du Maroc*, Rabat's daily newspaper during and after the protectorate period, suggests this was a recognized form of recruitment as early as 1914. Similar adverts appear in the classifieds today. These modes of recruitment, like physical marketplaces, do not rely on specific intermediaries who move between socioeconomic groups. Different uses of these markets reflect how open people are to strangers, how important trustworthiness is, how much responsibility they want to bear, and how much they want to ask of others and therefore owe them in return. From the workers' point of view, in choosing mūqef work, they trade off the security of having patrons to care for them for the relative freedom to work only when they want.[30] This is, however, a constrained freedom, given workers' daily needs and their weak position within the labor market. It is difficult to have the best of both worlds.

Notes

1. The marginal dependent relative who figures often in nineteenth-century English literature is typically female; their male counterparts were expected to join a profession such as the church or the military, according to their class.

2. Writing on women in rural Morocco, Maher maintained that "to recommend a girl highly, people say of her '*Ka-tnud*', or in Berber, '*da-tkerr*', 'she gets up', meaning that she is always submissive and ready to serve" (1974, 111).

3. Slavery constitutes an important exception, but we do not have space to discuss it here.

4. The *centre moderne* was the area originally assigned as the administrative and residential home for the French, including what is now Hassan, Residences, and Centre Ville.

5. Guarantors regulate both the treatment and conduct of workers. This custom is not limited to Morocco. In seventeenth-century Japan, it was encoded in law to crack down on theft. The guarantor was required to at least be from the same province as the servant or have personal connections to the servant or his family (Nagata 2004, 214). Cf. Graham (1988, 19) on domestics in Rio de Janeiro who were required to "name someone to guarantee their conduct."

6. Some of the employment brokers I met in Rabat had been operating for at least twenty years. Salahdine's (1988) study also reports the activities of *samāsira* (plural of samsār, broker) in the larger cities twenty-six years ago. There is little reason to think that they did not play a role before that too.

7. See Dresch (2012) on *aḥkām al-manʿ*, roughly "laws of protection," which deal with escort, refuge, and hospitality among Yemen's tribes.

8. Chant (1991) similarly found that Mexican women's entrance into the labor force was followed by the aggregation of new household members—often mothers, who move in to help with housework and childcare. Pasternak et al. (1976) use cross-cultural data to argue that extended-family households often develop when a woman's work outside the home makes housework and childcare difficult. Yanagisako replied that we might just as easily conclude that extended-family households encourage women to work outside the home as the other way around (1979, 173). Nevertheless, when a shortage of labor is felt, asking additional kinswomen to coreside seems a likely option.

9. Planel (2008) discusses day laborers in a Yemeni town. Blaauw, Louw, and Schenck (2006) and Harmse, Blaauw, and Schenck (2009) provide South African examples. Ordonez

(2012) studied Latino immigrant day laborers on street corners in California. See Valenzuela (2003) for a review of the day labor literature.

10. The French literature gives the impression every Moroccan domestic was called Fatima. In Algeria, *une Zohra* was the term for a maid. There are parallels with Irish Bridgets who came to work in England.

11. Cf. Salahdine (1988, 123–24) on the Moroccan mūqef for domestic workers and Ossman (1994, ill. 13) on a plumbers' mūqef in Casablanca.

12. Workers at other labor markets explained that they did not frequent l-Jarda because of its reputation. They quoted proverbs warning against spending time in the wrong company: "Ḥota waḥeda katkhanniz sh-shawārī (one [bad] fish makes the basket go off)"; "Maʿa min shuftik maʿa min shabbahatik (the one I've seen you with is the one who is like you)."

13. Couscous takes around three hours to prepare in the proper way.

14. Women at the Agdal mūqef, however, reported being taken by the police during the international music festival to a "charity" where they were fed bread and lentils—"as though we are in prison"—and locked in until evening: "They cleared us up so they could say we don't exist. . . . They don't write on our papers that we are workers. They write that we are beggars. All we want is to work for our children."

15. The need to be seen by potential employers is taken to an extreme by women in Agdal, who stand in the middle of the road. The l'Océan workers content themselves with sitting on the pavement but complain loudly if people park cars directly in front of them, thus blocking them from view.

16. The word *wasīṭa* does not have the negative connotations of *samsāra*.

17. Fouzia's office was in the same building as her family's home but on a different floor.

18. The flier is in French, but "nurses" is oddly in English and may refer to care workers.

19. Aicha, the *directrice* of Safmar agency in Rabat, interviewed by Amrani (2006), similarly said she made trips to several rural regions to establish a network.

20. The worker, even if adult, may be called a *bint* (girl), unless married.

21. Fees seemed to vary from 200dh to 600dh. Malika believed that samāsira adjusted their fees according to the distance they were sending the worker: from Fes to Rabat the employer has to pay 400dh, from Fes to Casablanca 500dh, within Fes 200 to 300dh.

22. On samāsira, see also Human Rights Watch (2005, 13–15) and Moujoud and Pourette (2005).

23. To do otherwise appears simply antisocial. I came to "know" people on both the supply and demand sides but this was thanks to other Moroccans who had introduced me to them. I thus found myself caught up in relationships of give and return where refusing to make introductions was withholding from people the very thing I asked of them.

24. On the commodification of social relations, see Smith, G. (1990).

25. Cf. Heuzé, writing about Dhanbad (India) on the pressure exerted by job seekers on wage earners from the same village to help secure employment. He observes that recommendations always emphasize connections with the guarantor (1996, 96).

26. McBride (1976, 75), writing on service in England and France between 1820 and 1920, notes bakers, grocers, and butchers were similar channels for the recruitment of domestics.

27. Several of the workers I knew had brothers working in construction. One brother earned 3,000dh a month, compared with his sister's 1,000dh—a difference that is only partly explained by her receiving board and lodging also.

28. The Deutsche Gesellschaft für Internationale Zusammenarbeit and the Moroccan Ministère de l'emploi et de la formation professionnelle interviewed workers in Bani Mellal, Fes, Tangier and Rabat.

29. Cf. Rivière (1984, 81–83) on Guiana, who argues trade with outsiders is simply necessary to maintain contact between settlements, even when the incoming goods are also available locally, so their scarcity is artificially created.

30. Ray and Qayum, writing on Indian domestics, found that, as with the Sebbari building, within one apartment building in Kolkata two different time and labor regimes existed: both family retainers strongly tied to one employer and part-timers who may work for four or five different households. They argue that "the coexistence of these dual regimes means that servants are aware of the gains and losses from each form of labor. While all agree that part-time work—freelancing—is preferable, they are keenly aware of the costs of autonomy" (2009, 91). As a day-laboring painter in Delhi expressed it, "The ideal job . . . has the perfect balance of kamai [pay] and azadi [freedom]. . . . The maalik owns our work. He does not own us" (Sethi 2012, 19).

PART II

DOMESTIC WORKERS IN THE WIDER WORLD

5

DOMESTIC WORKERS IN THE CITY

WAGE IN HAND, "NOMADIC" WORKERS EMBODY THE FREE, rational, individual actor choosing what's best for herself and appear to lose nothing in the short term by leaving one employer for another. But workers forfeit the long-term stability of being rooted in one place and the promise of a marriage arranged by their patron—a marriage that, in theory, signals the end of working as a domestic and the beginning of life as a full adult. The psychological toll of this rootless albeit independent life surfaces often: homesickness, tiredness, aggression, and an almost frantic search for a husband with whom to make a home. Passing a tree in l'Océan with a hefty root structure exposed aboveground, Rouqia, who had moved from one house to another numerous times throughout her working life, exclaimed, "Look at this beautiful tree! Look at the roots it's got. God willing, I'll be like that. You know, put roots down, have a family and children." Rouqia had taken the job of finding a husband into her own hands. Her increased mobility, knowledge of the city, and ability to deal with strangers went some way toward equipping her for this while her day off provided her with the freedom to look around.

This chapter takes as its subject the activities of workers on their days off, reflecting aspects of domestics' identity as lone female migrants from the countryside and particularly as individuals who have intimate and reproductive aspirations.[1] As Mahdavi (2016) argues, this is overlooked by much of the literature on migration, which tends to posit primarily economic forces as explanations for the mobility or immobility of women. I highlight a change for rural Moroccan women from socializing solely with people known to their families and whose families they also know to socializing with people who are unknown. This mirrors the shift, outlined earlier, from working for known employers to working for unknown ones.

Life Cycle Service, Freedom, and Marriage

As was the case for the majority of servants in medieval and early modern Europe (Laslett 1965, 1977) and up to the early twentieth century (McBride 1976, 84), for many Moroccan domestic workers, service is a transitory stage of the life cycle and ideally not to be pursued after marriage. A study of two hundred domestics, carried out by GIZ and the Ministry of Employment, states that 41 percent of workers interviewed in cities around Morocco were single, although this category broadens to 74 percent when widows (16 percent), single mothers (8 percent) and divorcées (9 percent) are included (Royaume du Maroc 2011, 19). Ages of workers also reflect that domestic service is, to a large extent, a life cycle occupation. The GIZ and Ministry of Employment study maintains that 30 percent of domestic workers interviewed were aged between eighteen and twenty-five years, 25 percent between twenty-six and thirty-three years, 22 percent between thirty-four and forty years, 15 percent between forty-one and forty-nine years, and only 8 percent fifty years and above (19). This was explained by employers' preference for the adaptability of younger workers who are willing to live in the employers' home and who lack other responsibilities (mainly children of their own), allowing them to dedicate themselves more fully to the work of the employers' household (8, 19, 23). To reverse the perspective, the same concern for the undivided commitment of domestic staff was voiced in *The Remains of the Day* by Ishiguro's (1989) butler protagonist, Stevens, whose overzealous "professionalism" prevented him from recognizing the love he felt for the housekeeper.

Not only does a person's marital status have an impact on their employability or availability for domestic service, but historical demographers have shown that service has an impact on marriage patterns. The correlation between the circulation of servants and "delayed first marriage" in northern Europe has been established by Hajnal (1982, 1983).[2] Others have pointed to the effect of rural-urban migration on the matrimonial market in Europe (Fauve-Chamoux and Sogner 1994; Mullins and Griffiths 1986, 12). In seventeenth-century Europe, while "being a servant was ... an opportunity to amass wages and marry at a higher social level ... the transitory stage of domestic service with its moral dangers, lasted far longer than expected, often beyond the limits of the normal age at marriage, and could become a permanent occupation" (Fauve-Chamoux 2004, 5).[3] My own experience of Moroccan domestics showed their situation to be similar, with many worrying that people would say of them, "sherfāt [she's grown old]," implying they are too old for marriage.

The difference in status between unmarried "girls" and married "women" in Morocco (Cheikh 2011a, 42) has made spinsterhood a particularly unattractive option so that often, as Lucy states in Surtees's *Facey Romford*, "a bad husband was a deal better than none" [(1865) 2006, 39]. Newcomb highlights the protective function of having a husband, even just on paper. One maid in Fes, abandoned by her husband when he took a second wife twenty years previously, had not pressed for her right to divorce and explains, "If I were divorced, it would not be easy. People take advantage of divorced women. A wife is protected" (Newcomb 2009, 75). Many of my domestic-worker friends looked forward to marriage as a way of establishing a family in which they would be central adult members instead of marginal "girls," for, to quote Lucy again, "there's nothing so bad as dependence" ([1865] 2006, 409). It has, however, been argued that marriage is generally the third situation of domination that servants experience. Davidoff argues for Victorian Britain that "the majority of girls moved from paternal control in their parents' home, into service and then into their husband's home—thus experiencing a lifetime of personal subordination in private homes" (1995, 21). Workers were not only carrying the stigma of their occupation but also that of their *état civil*, which did not accord them status as "full persons."[4] Crawford observes, "The shanty towns stew with men and women unable to form households, unable, in other words, to become full members of Moroccan society, where producing children is a cultural ideal—even in the city, where bearing young workers is not an economic incentive" (2008, 15). Morocco is said to be experiencing a "crisis of the matrimonial sector" (Cheikh 2011a, 36), marked by decreasing marriage rates and a rise in the average age at first marriage.[5] With fewer people able to afford marriage, men are increasingly looking for wives who earn enough to contribute significantly to household finances (Ossman 1994, 47; Ali 2010). In this climate of shortage, freedom to meet potential husbands becomes pressing, as it was in Britain post–World War I.

Fremlin's study of domestics in interwar London dedicated ten pages to the difficulties domestics faced in finding marriage partners. A certain employer could not understand domestics' demands for leisure time: "But Mrs. X is forgetting that what they want time off for is not amusement, but a hard and exacting job; the job of securing a husband in the face of savage competition from the other million superfluous women in this country"

(1940, 132). Writing on early twentieth-century northern Britain, Roberts underlined workers' desire for "freedom—above all, freedom to meet men easily" (1973, 222) as an explanation for the decline in residential service. This is understated in much literature, which treats time off as a chance for undiluted "agency" (being able to do what one wants, whether this is eating ice cream or going to the fair) when the question is, rather, is there space in which workers can become full persons?

Some workers in Rabat, like Malika at Nadia's in the Sebbari building, rarely had time off. This was not due to employers expecting domestics to work all the time but rather to employers wanting their domestics to be always *available* for work. Many employers pointed to the fact that they do not prevent their workers from watching television between tasks, or, as one person said, "The worker might not work at all the whole day, and then just at night they might ask her to do something." When it was suggested that although a worker may not be busy around the clock, neither was she free to go elsewhere, the employer responded that she had never thought of this. Fremlin (1940) describes similar blindness among well-meaning British employers in the 1930s.

What was missing in many cases was an understanding that a worker may need or desire time away from the workplace, not just periods of inactivity. This is tied up with notions of her role as "one of the family." In Dār Sebbari, this attitude was reinforced by the women Latifa had brought up, who witnessed on visits the "demands" of current waged domestics: "She has to go and see her sister every single week?" exclaimed Najat, a former "daughter of the house," following an announcement by Huriya (Nadia's live-in at the time) that she would be spending the night with her sister in Salé. Najat, an orphan, had never had any *congé*.[6] Where would she have gone? Time off takes on significance only when work becomes the reason for someone's presence in the house, rather than her fosterage being paramount and her work a by-product. Moroccan women do not usually take time off from their own families. Domestics taking time to go out for leisure is therefore seen as a new phenomenon, often interpreted by employers as workers' getting above their station because they have developed a taste for more than the daily bread the employing family provides. A Moroccan woman who had employed the same worker for six years told an agent on the phone that she wanted to replace the girl, as she had become "full up from bread." The shopkeeper who related this explained, "She had saved money and become beautiful. She wants to go out and see things. And that's normal. So she should. But they want her to always be the shy, hungry country girl."

<u>Sha</u>ʿbī (ordinary) employers who pride themselves on treating their workers "like daughters" often pointed out to me that they took their workers with them on outings on the weekend. This was seen as an act of kindness, extending to the domestic worker the conservative principle of not allowing daughters out unaccompanied: it signified that she too was cherished and merited protection, and that employers cared for her moral reputation (and its reflection on theirs), as they did for that of their own daughter. At age eighteen, Nadia's daughter Zahra did not go out without being accompanied by her mother, her father, her brother, or one of the women whom Latifa had brought up, such as Rachida. This explained the difference where congé was concerned between the lot of Malika and Huriya, who were both employed by Nadia. Having a married sister in neighboring Salé provided a legitimate reason for Huriya to leave the workplace whereas Malika had never asked for a day off, assuming that, with no one to visit, her request would be received as one to shamelessly wander the streets alone.

Most <u>sha</u>ʿbī households followed this pattern so that, as was common in eighteenth-century England, "servants were either the beneficiaries of a condescending patronage or the accessories of their masters' pleasure" (Hecht 1956, 127). Those employers who were less <u>sha</u>ʿbī gave more time off for the workers to spend independently, which meant they could develop social lives of their own. The Souissi security guard's comment—"There's no 'my son,' 'my daughter' here"—accords with having little desire to take their workers on family outings. This did not mean they did not interfere where workers' morality was concerned. My friends who worked in the affluent Hay Riad area told their employers that they met up with me on their days off, and one even took me to the bank where her employer worked as manager to introduce me, as a way of countering accusations that she went out to meet men. On the rare occasions workers stayed the night at my apartment, they would insist I speak to their employers on the phone—a reassuringly female voice. Many workers in Rabat had sisters or aunts living in Salé who also provided moral cover for workers' time off. And even if workers did not visit them regularly, the proximity of these family members also lent morality to workers' presence in the city from the point of view of their home community.

Most workers in non-<u>sha</u>ʿbī households were allowed one day off a week, usually Sunday, although sometimes it was a weekday at the employers' convenience, preventing the worker from being able to meet her friends. Days off were often cut short, thanks to the cell phones that allowed employers to keep their workers on short leashes. Having been disturbed by an ill and fractious employer on a previous occasion, Nawar, for instance, turned off her cell phone when we went to spend a day off at her aunt's house in Salé: "It's best if I say that I forgot to take the phone charger with me. That way she won't disturb me!" This Sunday connectivity had two faces, however, and workers usually wanted to have their phones switched on so they could meet up with friends old and new.

Birds of a Feather

The domestic workers I knew did not gather with others in any formal way. I came across no migrant village associations such as have been documented for workers in various sectors elsewhere.[7] Writing on South Africa, Jacklyn Cock noticed the absence in the domestic worker's social world of circles of friends or kin from home who had also migrated to the city (1980, 62, 72). Hirabayashi (1986) discusses reasons why some migrants form associations while others do not and argues that politicization is the single most important development leading to the formation of migrant village associations in Latin America. He also points to studies that show that for associations to form, "migrants to the city must be far enough from their point of origin that frequent visits home are impossible or inconvenient" (Hirabayashi 1986, 10, citing Fischer 1976; Skeldon 1980). Moroccan domestic workers in Rabat were rarely so far from home and even less likely to be politicized, but I suspect the lack of village associations is due more to domestics frequently moving from one city to another, with only small numbers from each village in any one city at a time. Added to this are the structural constraints of their work, which allow them little flexibility in the times they can leave the employers' house. As one unusually perceptive employer suggested, "The problem is that domestics don't all have the same time off. Some have Saturday and some have Sunday and some don't have any time at all. And even if they did have the same day off, Rabat is big. One is in Hay Riad, another in Salé, another in Temara. They'd have to spend a lot of money just to meet. So they don't."

Get-togethers between domestics were therefore limited to those demanding minimum organization: one or two telephone calls to fix a place and time. In fact, there was often a marked absence of contact in the city between women from the same village. On trips home with workers at the ʿīd (a feast day), I was often surprised to hear the daughters of neighbors in a village discover they had been in the same city without realizing it. News about other people's daughters could be garnered from phoning one's mother in the village, but then a daughter's location was not the kind of thing people shouted about: Where's your daughter? Oh, yes, mine's working in houses in Rabat too. How shameful for us both! Crawford (2008, 167) notes that the women in the Atlas village where he did fieldwork did not talk about their work in the city.

Not only do workers telephone women from their home village whom they know to be in the same city, arranging to meet up in the city center, but they also look out for others "like them" to be new friends. Ilham explains, "You meet them in the street, in the bus. You're sitting there, and a girl comes up to you: 'Can I sit with you?' You talk, and you exchange phone numbers, and then you go out together another time." One of the first questions women ask one another is, "Where are you from?" Most women who wander the center of Rabat alone are from somewhere else; "proper" local girls like Zahra are always accompanied, and less proper girls would at least have friends with whom to go out. Ilham often spotted people from her own region, the Gharb, and would congratulate herself: "When I saw you, I knew you were *gharbawīya* [from the Gharb]. It's obvious!" The idea of migrant workers seeking out those from the same region echoes accounts of Welsh workers who gathered on their days off at the "Welsh corner" in Hyde Park during the 1920s and '30s (Scadden 2013, 128–29). Stereotypes about Welsh workers among early twentieth-century Londoners probably paralleled those about women from the Gharb region during my fieldwork: conscious of their perception as country bumpkins, pigeons not eagles (to use the terms of l'Océan's graffiti artist), it is not surprising they "flocked together."

Although shared regional origins facilitated connections between *bnāt l-blād* (girls of the home-country), it was not a vital component of friendships. Ilham had made friends in Rabat with women from all over Morocco. Equivalence of social status was a more decisive factor, as she explained when I asked, "Do you have friends who aren't from another place? Do you have Ribāṭī friends?"

> "Wear clothes that fit you."[8] Go with people who are like you. If you see someone dressed like you, then they will want to talk to you. They will be like you. They will be happy that you talked to them, and you will enjoy talking to them.

There will be understanding, because you are the same. If you see someone who is just looking up, and she's dressed nicely and wearing heels and has her hair all done and sunglasses and is all made up, then don't talk to her. She would think, *Why are you talking to me?* She won't be interested in you because she will only look at the outside [of a person].

I was often surprised at friends' ability to spot their "equals" from a distance, using indicators such as hairstyle and clothing and whether the woman was accompanied. As Ossman notes,

> [The street] is the only truly communal space in which people of all conditions meet; consequently, it is one of the places in which it is important not simply to *be* something but to demonstrate that identity through one's appearance. Cars, clothes, and companions add to one's physical 'look'. . . . The color and texture of hair, the shade of skin and eyes, the elegance of mannerisms, the style and price of clothing and jewelry, the brand of cigarette—all of these details indicate origin, social class, and even level of education. The speed and accuracy with which people can judge one another concerning family origin, educational background, and current wealth is remarkable (1994, 40).

Such "skilled vision" (Elliot 2016, 495) allowed workers to identify other domestics, with whom talk would quickly turn to a comparison of their working conditions and salaries. The following conversation between Ilham and Wafa, a woman we met for the first time in the park outside Bab Chellah, is an example. Wafa, having told us she only did the cooking while another worker did the cleaning, asked Ilham about her job:

ILHAM: I do everything.

WAFA: Everything? Alone? The cleaning and the cooking and the children?

ILHAM: No, they don't have children. It's just the man and his wife. But the daughter comes and spends time at the house with her children.

WAFA: And how much do they pay?

ILHAM: 32,000 [1,600dh].

WAFA: Are you crazy? You work alone for that price? And it's a villa?

ILHAM: Yes, but the wife helps me. She and I do the cooking together.

WAFA: Even if she helps you, you still do the cooking. You do salads and *rūmī* [foreign cuisine] and *bildī* [traditional Moroccan cuisine] and *brīwāt* [pastries]?

ILHAM: Yes, I made brīwāt yesterday and the day before. Two days, and I've been folding them. I did ones with meat and ones with chicken. And pizza.

WAFA: Pizza? Big ones or small ones?

ILHAM: That big [Ilham drew a somewhat spiral shaped circle with her finger in the air, so it wasn't too clear how big the pizzas were].

WAFA: Well, you are crazy to work for that money. I'm sorry, but no villa in Hay Riad has just one worker to do everything. And no one does the cooking for less than 40,000. Some work for 50,000 now. And she gives you your day [off] and congé?

ILHAM: I get Saturday and Sunday off, and I've just been to the blād for ten days.

WAFA: And she didn't take it out of your pay?

ILHAM: Yes, she did. She won't pay me for those days.

There followed a discussion about paid holiday as a "right." Without a legal code on which to base assessments of their lot, and with unionization unheard of, workers use personal experience to generate rules that, when put together by women talking among themselves, form numerous "industry standards." These vary across networks, depending on who has talked to whom, which explains why Ilham evaluated her position differently from Wafa. While Wafa was incredulous of Ilham's complacency, Ilham considered her conditions far better than those of many of her friends, who were indeed paid less and seemed to do more work. These comparisons and the catchphrase "l-khedma mujūda [work is available]!"—something like "plenty more fish in the sea!"—encourage workers to ask for a pay rise or more time off, or to quit in the hope of a better job elsewhere.

Workers who meet by chance like this will often exchange phone numbers promising to telephone next time they come into the city center on a day off, though they might never actually renew the connection. Individuals do not usually have a large group of friends but will telephone to meet up with just one or two women by preference. The other numbers saved in their phones or noted on scraps of paper in their handbags act as standbys for days when their usual companions have no time off or have gone back to the countryside or to another city.[9]

Sons of You Don't Know Whom

Watching and assessing others in public space has another dimension: domestic workers are aware they might be watched by a potential husband. I often spent Sunday "going out" with Rouqia and Ilham, who were both from a community in the Gharb, and one or two of their friends—all single women. While the verb *khorij*, to go out, is used for any outing for enjoyment, day or night, it can also have connotations of going out explicitly to meet men. Cheikh argues that "'*sortir*' (to go out) . . . encompasses all acts contrary to good female behavior (to go out in the street, to go out for fun, to go out with a boy)" (2013, 270). Khorij, as opposed to just going outside, is marked by changing from "pajamas" into "street clothes" (one might go to the local shop or run an errand in the neighborhood in house clothes) and generally a significant amount of time being spent on hair (or head covering) and makeup. The importance of this is vividly portrayed by Elliot, writing about young rural women studying at university in the Moroccan town of Zafiah: "the meticulous preparation of the self they undertake before leaving their student rooms and walking to the town's old medina—populated by a wealth of potential husbands—is one of the many actions Zineb and her friends perform in view of their predestined futures" (2016, 489). My domestic worker friends were no less concerned with looking their best about town, often with relatively scarce resources. Clothing, shoes, and accessories, if of cheap quality, were always spotless and color coordinated and makeup modestly applied. I felt shabby by comparison and learned to check that my shoes were at least passably clean before meeting up.

When tired of weaving through the medīna's markets, Ilham, Rouqia, and I might head for the Nouzhat Hassan Park, the *place du seize novembre*, or the *corniche* by the Bou Regreg River. These, like the parks of Georgian London (Horn 2004, 229) were ideal places for domestics to strike up acquaintances. Writing about Casablanca, Ossman identifies these kinds of space as a "public *vitrine*" (1994, 45) in which one is on display. She describes how teenagers promenade around the Arab League Park hoping to attract potential dates. This is not unlike the "Sunday best" promenading of European tradition.[10] The people who see these young Moroccans are not "known" people, like neighbors, relatives, or the local shopkeeper, who might report back to family. Rather, "a certain anonymity allows for open flirting and invitations to ice-cream parlors or cafés" (45), which contrasts with norms for interaction between men and women in smaller towns and rural areas (Ossman 1994, 208; Mernissi 1975; Davis and Davis 1989). Ossman's point is about Casablancans from different city neighborhoods mingling, but the rural domestic workers of my study, who are not from the city at all, are even less likely to be seen by people they know. This accords them a freedom to talk to men in a way that they would not in their own village. Cheikh similarly notes that, for women sharing apartments in Casablanca and Tangier, "the distance of their families means these women are no longer constrained to rules regarding women in public places (going out frequently, without a precise goal and at night is not tolerated, even forbidden)" (2009, 5). This is not to say that women do not talk to men in their own village. Hoffman (2008, 59–61, 149–55) gives an account of courtship and mixed group gatherings in an Anti-Atlas community. But these interactions are with known men, and certain rules for behavior are followed, at least in the presence of others.

Although they are away from family, the degree of freedom accorded live-in domestics in Rabat nonetheless fell short when compared with other blue-collar jobs such as factory or shop work, making these a more attractive option for some, as they were in Britain a century ago: "The most important advantage of factory life was freedom. Factory girls did not have to endure the daily petty humiliations of being at the beck and call of a condescending mistress; of having no set hours to call their own, of having pitifully few opportunities to meet men (or even other women)" (Lethbridge 2013, 94).

In Morocco factory girls could at least enjoy some freedom on the walk to and from work (Cairoli 2012). Comparisons are often made between the freedom enjoyed by "city girls" and by their country sisters. Generally speaking, migration for service increases the number of potential marriage partners (Wall 2004, 20), and this is reflected in the way those left behind in the countryside tease returnees from the city who are "*still* not married," insinuating, "despite all those men you must have met!" The GIZ and Ministry of Employment study maintains that single women from the countryside sometimes justified their decision to work as domestics in cities in order to "gain in freedom and mobility when they leave their village. Paradoxically, it should be noted that living with employers has a major impact on the freedom sought by workers" (Royaume du Maroc 2011, 23). Indeed, a Moroccan woman explaining why "it's hard to employ someone you trust these days" pointed to a change in the level of freedom allowed women in the countryside—it had potentially overtaken that of domestics in the city, leading to a decline in the appeal of live-in employment: "People don't want to work as domestics these days. Where we live in Azzrou, women will do hard agricultural work in the fields but not work in houses.... They want to go out. Women used to just stay in the house.... Now they've started to have a bit of freedom, to go to the market or to town. They don't want to give this up by going to work in a house where they won't be allowed out.... Things are changing."

Women's purpose in spending time out and about is often verbalized among themselves: "Debberū linā kāmlīn [find (husbands) for us all]! Find four of them and let me know," a worker commissioned us as she left our group in the Nouzhat Hassan Park to return to her employers' house a little early one Sunday. "Let the work continue in my absence." On one level it was a joke, but the two other women who remained with me nodded in agreement: "O Lord, bring me *shī* weld n-nās maʿqūl [a serious, literally reasonable, son of the people)." *Weld n-nās* (son of the people), used widely in profiles on Moroccan dating websites, is code for "an ideal husband," even an ideal son-in-law. The ideal husband is someone's *son*. That Moroccans translating the term into French render it as *fils de bonne famille* suggests that *nās* involves the idea of respectability. This is more evident in *bint n-nās*, whose foil is *bint s-sūq* or *bint z-zinqa* (girl of the market or of the street)—i.e., a prostitute.

That the search was for a *son* to marry was clear from the outset. One of the first times I "went out" in Rabat with Ilham, aged thirty or more, and Rouqia, in her midtwenties, we were sitting on a bench in the park at place du seize novembre. Rouqia's phone rang. She jumped up, answered it, and walked away from us to talk, then returned, saying, "I'm going to go and meet him. He told me to tell you I'm going to run an errand!" She laughed—no need to lie to her best friend, Ilham. She left us, and Ilham and I continued talking. Soon a man approached and sat on our bench. He greeted us both, then spoke to Ilham in a low voice and passed her a piece of paper on which he had written a phone number. I could not hear what he said, but the response was clear: "No, I'm with my friend, I only see her on Sundays. We'll speak on the phone." The man went away, and Ilham explained that he wanted to take her for coffee and that he had followed her all the way from Bab Chellah, where, an hour before, she had gotten off the bus. I expressed what had been rooted in me since childhood: "Don't talk to strangers!" But Ilham responded, "Look! How else are we going to marry? If we were in the village, *weld shī ḥed* [the son of someone], or someone whose family we know, would come to the house, and the families would arrange the engagement. But we are here, and we don't know anyone."

This sense of exclusion from circles of known people who would provide a fiancé may well have been more trenchant when frequent communication between the city and the blād was more difficult. In the past, family members sometimes visited the daughters they placed with richer city folk only once a year. This was the case with Ḥajja Jamila's former domestic, who became mentally ill when she passed the age at which she would have married had she remained in the blād. Ḥajja Jamila's daughter remembered,

"We took her to the doctor, and he said, 'There's nothing wrong with her. She just wants to get married.' We took her back to her village, and we found all the people of her age had already married."

Like weld n-nās, the hypothetical fiancé in the countryside is weld s̲h̲ī ḥed. That a husband is first and foremost somebody's son is equally apparent in Hoffman's ethnography of Sous valley and Anti-Atlas Berbers, in which one married woman explains, "My father and my husband's father are friends, and they proposed we marry, and so I said okay" (Hoffman 2008, 149). Such marriages, arranged by elder family members, serve more to strengthen ties between families than to satisfy the needs of their sons and daughters as individuals.[11] That a woman worked in the city did not prevent a man from going, during her absence, to her family in the countryside to ask for her hand in marriage, but once workers had lived in the city, most did not *want* to marry someone in the countryside. Hanane, who worked for Nadia at Dār Sebbari before my arrival on the scene, had to leave because her family engaged her to a man in the blād. According to Nadia's daughter Zahra, Hanane had not wanted to marry and had attempted to run away from her family and return to Dār Sebbari before the marriage took place: "She was used to being with me." Salahdine argues that exposure to the comfortable life of wealthy urban employers means domestic workers are less likely to be content with marriage to a man who can offer them only the bare necessities (1988, 102).[12] This is quite a widespread motif. Bourdieu (1962) and Jenkins (2010, chap. 6) describe discontented peasant bachelors in rural Southern France due to local women preferring to marry urbanites. The following are typical of Gharb workers' responses when asked in the village about their hopes for the future:

> I want to marry in the city. Here, life is hard. If you don't have this [she flexed her arm and patted her biceps with her hand], you don't live.
>
> I don't want to live here. *Kaytaqarfsū* [they suffer] here.
>
> I want to get married so I can stop doing this work. I want [to live in] the city. I wouldn't mind working if my husband worked too. We'd both help out [with household finances].
>
> When I think about marriage, it will be in the city. I live in the city now, and I see things. I dream about them. Am I going to marry in the country? To suffer in the mud? No, I've worked hard; I've suffered. When I marry, it's to have a good life. . . . I don't want to have children myself. I have had enough of looking after them. I'm bored with these problems. . . . I have never lived a white day, I've lived only black days. I want to change my life.

In a similar vein, Huriya, who worked for Nadia in the Sebbari building, told me how a rural man who knew her family had asked to marry her while she was in the city: "They engaged me to him, but I told them, 'No, I don't want to. I've got used to the city.' And *anā maʿarifa maʿa* [I'm getting to know] a man from Tunis, only by phone. He sends me phone credit." By the time I left the field, Huriya had never met face to face with this Tunisian (she had been a willing victim of random dialing on the man's part) but was looking forward to his visiting Rabat and expected he might ask to marry her.[13]

Huriya's story shows a divergence between old and new marital strategies. Ethnographic literature suggests that companionate ideals evolve with the rise of individuality—"the idea that one particular person would be a more satisfying and pleasurable partner than any other because of his or her specific characteristics" (Hirsch and Wardlow 2006, 5). Domestic workers' migrant status, separation from their families, and reliance on their own labor reinforce their sense of individuality (Abu-Lughod, L. 2002, 124). Wage labor generally—because it allows women to be less financially dependent on their families or potential husbands (Ahearn 2001; Collier 1997)—and commodity consumption (Illouz 1997) have been argued to be key elements of the shift toward "companionate" ideals elsewhere, though how far the ideals are actualized is seldom clear.

It is not incidental that cell phones loom large. For Ilham, Rouqia, and Huriya, their phones played a vital role in facilitating access to and ongoing acquaintance with "a new world" of strange men. The significance of cell phones for social mingling between men and women is not unique to Morocco. Writing generally, Ferraro and Andreatta state that "cell phones and text messaging now permit both men and women to circumvent the traditional prohibitions against premarital social interaction" (2012, 218).[14] It has also been argued that the independence of space of a cell phone is part of a process of individualization (Garcia-Montes, Caballero-Munoz, and Pérez-Alvarez 2006, 69), and Cheikh notes the women of her Casablanca study spent a large portion of their income on telephone cards; topping up phone credit was the first thing women did when money came in, and sometimes they passed whole nights on the phone with men (2011b, 183n). Domestic workers I knew often asked employers for advances on their monthly wages in order to purchase phone credit, although this was used for talking to family back home as well as to men. Most owned bottom-of-the-range cell phones costing around 200dh, or about four days' wages for a typical live-in. When network providers had promotional deals, workers could purchase cards that allowed them an hour's talk-time for 20dh—just under half a day's wage. Ilham juggled three cell phones so that she could have a different SIM card in each and make the most of the promotions of one network provider after another.

Talking on the phone allows men and women to get to know one another at a distance. Even when men approach them physically while out and about, women like Ilham prefer to pursue relationships over the phone at first. This way she can ascertain the man's intentions without compromising her reputation. Ilham disapproved of going to cafés with men, as her friend Rouqia did—it was "shameful." For Ilham the ideal would be that a man state straightaway that he would like to marry her. This had happened to her several times, as she explained: "They come up to me and say, 'Excuse me, my sister.[15] Can I talk to you?' 'Yes, go ahead.' He says, 'I saw you and I liked you. Can I marry you?' I tell him, 'Give me your telephone number, and we'll talk.'" The direct link between "seeing" and wanting to marry is also documented by Ossman, whose friend Bouchra told her, "'I always try to look nice. What if a nice guy sees me out with my friends? You never know when he might come along.' Bouchra expects that once this suitor's gaze has been captivated by her beauty and good taste in clothes, he will hope to marry her" (1994, 46). But such encounters had not yet ended in a marriage for Ilham. The following Sunday, she and I met in the usual park, and she recounted the next part of the story regarding the man who had sat on our bench and slipped her his phone number:

> "I telephoned him and he said to me, 'If you just want to have fun, then no, if you want to marry me, then yes.' I said to him, 'That's what I want too, marriage.' [Pause] They all say the same thing! It's just lies."

"How do you know he wasn't telling the truth?" I asked.

"Because he hasn't called again!"

Ilham felt that because her response to this man's statement confirmed that she would not engage in "fun" (premarital sex) with him, he was uninterested in pursuing the relationship.[16] As for Rouqia, she would leave us more and more often, almost every Sunday, to have coffee with men who signaled to her from some way off or telephoned her after a prior meeting. When Ilham began to criticize her, I came to Rouqia's defense: "She's only trying to find a husband." But Ilham corrected me: "No, I'm sorry, but the men you meet here, they are *never* going to marry you." After several disappointments, Ilham was starting to doubt the effectiveness of meeting men who *kayṣīdū* (literally hunt or fish) in the squares and parks of Rabat. She said, "It's not like that that you find a husband. God brings you your husband." Both Ilham and Rouqia professed a trust that "everything was in God's hands" (as the prayer "O Lord, bring me s̲h̲ī weld n-nās maʿqūl" indicated) and at the same time implied that they had a decisive role to play, as the verb *debber* (to find, to [manage] to get hold of) (Haloui and Bowman 2011) indicates (Debberū linā kāmlīn [find (husbands) for us all]!). One worker's response to my own singleness was also telling: "It's because you don't put yourself in situations which allow you to get to know men." It was my own fault. This coexistence of destiny and agency in shaping the "conjugal futures" of Moroccan women is discussed by Elliot: "Women know that using lipstick, caring for their bodies, and applying foundation cream will attract the attention of men about town and thus precipitate encounters with possible husbands. While they do not know whether marriage, and marriage to a migrant man, has been written for them by God, they do know what actions are required in the human world to precipitate such a future, *were this future written for them*" (2016, 493). In light of this analysis, earlier literature that emphasizes the passive role of Moroccan women in securing husbands seems to offer a rather one-sided perspective.[17]

Ilham continued, "If he is serious, he will follow you to the blād." A serious suitor would ask directions to one's family. If a man "sees" someone he would like to marry in the anonymity of public space, the ideal is still to seek approval in the private realm of the family, for, as Ossman notes, "the world of the open street and that of the home and the family remain radically separate" (1994, 49). The vastness of the city, where people are not necessarily "seen" near their homes or among groups of kin with whom enquiries can be made, means a man who wants to marry a certain woman must approach her directly. When one of Mahmood's interlocutors, a mosque volunteer, is approached by a colleague who asks for her hand in marriage, the advice given by a pious friend is "to tell this man to approach her parents formally to ask for her hand in marriage, and allow her parents to investigate the man's background in order to ascertain whether he was a suitable match for her" (Mahmood 2001, 218). When Mahmood questioned the "correctness" of this approach, as I had done with Ilham, she was told, "But there is nothing wrong in a man approaching a woman for her hand in marriage directly as long as his intent is serious and he is not playing with her. This occurred many times even at the time of the Prophet" (219).

The length of time that passes before family approval is sought varies, and a delay sometimes calls into question the intentions of the woman or the man. Hafida, a divorced worker in her thirties, complained that she could not trust men who wanted a period of *taʿarruf* (acquaintance) before seeking family approval. She and I often chatted while watching a series like *Ḥubb fī mahab ar-rīḥ* (*Love in the Wind*), a Turkish soap opera dubbed into Arabic, in which the daughter of a rich family falls in love with the domestic worker's son but is forced instead into an engagement with a wealthy man who turns out to be a criminal. Some Moroccans vehemently criticize the broadcasting of these Turkish soaps, which "do not even correspond to Moroccan society." The impact of television on ideas about love and marriage is well documented, and for domestic workers who watch several hours of television every day, the importance of media must outweigh that of coeducation.[18] In the advertisement breaks, Hafida would talk about her own unrequited loves.

When a man "from the Sahara" approached her in Rabat and talked of marriage, Hafida was unsure how she felt: "My heart did not go with him." She eventually decided to broach the matter with her family to gauge their opinion. Rather than introducing the suitor in person (this would be too public and would commit her to him in the eyes of her entire village), she asked him for a photo to show her family. It was significant that they could accept or reject the man on the basis of his appearance; the suitor had dark skin compared with Hafida's family, who were fair. The time for her next visit to the village came, but the suitor did not provide the photo—an indication, in Hafida's eyes, that he was not serious.

Next, the teacher of the free literacy classes that Hafida attended in a local mosque two evenings a week told her, "*Aʿjbtīnī* [I like you]. I'd like to get to know you." Simply going out to attend the classes had evidently boosted Hafida's self-esteem: "Dressed up and carrying my folder in the street, you'd say, 'There's a student going to university.'"[19] She went for coffee with the teacher a couple of times, and he told her on the phone, "I miss you. I wouldn't mind hearing your voice every day." Hafida's response was, "Well, let's talk about marriage, then." He had agreed, "Yes, that's what I'd like, *in shaʾ allāh* [God willing]." "*In shaʾ allāh*," repeated Hafida bitterly. "I don't like it to be *ʿalāqa* [a 'relationship,' in contradistinction to marriage] like that. He says, 'Not yet, not yet. I need to get to know you better.' But I don't trust them when they say that."

The city men who flirt with domestic workers and whose families are unknown contrast with the ideal of the *weld l-blād* (son of the home country) who "can be trusted." Miriam, another unmarried domestic in the city, was going out with a man from a village near her own, although she had not known him in the countryside. He, like most of his friends, worked in construction. Her sister, Safae, on the other hand, often talked and exchanged phone numbers with strangers she met in the street. Miriam underlined the difference, pointing to a group of young men, among whom was her boyfriend: "These are *awlād l-blād* [sons of my home country]. They are trustworthy, not like those my sister goes out with, *lī mā katʿarfīsh awlād min hadūl* [whom you don't know *whose* sons they are]." Similarly, in Collier's study of courtship in the Spanish village of Los Olivos, people contrasted "local boys who knew the girls' families" with "boys from other towns" who "might regard any Los Olivos woman as fair game" (Collier 1997, 92). The same logic, applied to the context of crime, causes the Botswanan heroine of McCall Smith's detective stories to reflect, "Life was far better, thought Mma Ramotswe, if we knew who we were. In the days when she was a schoolgirl in Mochudi, the village in which she had been born, everybody had known exactly who you were, and they often knew exactly who your parents, and your parents' parents, had been" (McCall Smith 2005, 3).

Being known means actions have long-term consequences, so people adhere locally to norms for morality in a way they do not among strangers in larger towns further afield. Knowing people in an ideal sense is expressed in Morocco in terms of filiality: those "whom you don't know whose sons they are" stand in opposition not only to the trustworthy awlād l-blād but also to the weld shī hed who is out of reach for Ilham in the city and the weld n-nās whom the women in the park prayed God would bring them. Trust is implicit in someone whose relatedness to others is known, since the other people referenced by the use of the term *weld* act as a safety net: a son has a father, a mother, and, by extension, a wider family. These people could be called upon if the bride's family had cause for complaint.[20] The same logic makes cousins the safest marriage partners, as they are sons of one's own kin. Knowing someone in this way is binary: one either knows whose sons they are, or one does not. It contrasts with a different kind of knowing, the *anā maʿarifa maʿa* (literally I am knowing with) of Huriya. Her use of *maʿarifa*, the active participle, implies a process of increasing acquaintance that starts from nothing. Her friend is simply "a man." His parents do not feature at all; rather, the individual, disassociated from his family, is foregrounded.

Despite the fact that all the single workers I interviewed stated that they wanted to marry in the city, the younger married workers or ex-workers I knew had married relatives or "sons of the country" who approached their families at home before a period, brief if it happened at all, of *ta'arruf* (acquaintance). Cousin marriages are common in North Africa and the Middle East (Tapper and Tapper 1992–93; Tillion 1983; Holy 1989). Among my interlocutors, spouses could be a cross cousin or parallel cousin, paternal or maternal. This was an option for Malika, whose father's brother's son proposed to her, but she refused him and soon after accepted an offer from an acquaintance. Shortly before leaving the field, I attended their wedding in her family's newly built home next to their former shantytown. The house had been built partly with Malika's earnings, but she was not to live in it. Malika's husband, who worked as a gardener and swimming pool maintenance man, had an apartment in a sha'bī quarter of Fes. His circumstances, though modest, were a step above Malika's, and although he was himself well aware that she had worked as a domestic, his family was not to be told.

Others married men with whom they had worked and so had regular contact over an extended period. From opposite ends of the country, Loubna (a *jiblīya*, or "mountain girl," from near Ouezzane), who worked a month for the Sebbaris to earn money for her wedding, and her husband (from Tiznit in the south) met working in a café in Rabat. Ikram developed a friendship with a man with whom she had worked planting onions on a farm near her home. He asked her to marry him but later withdrew the proposal, having heard that one of Ikram's sisters smoked in public. Being "known" was not always to one's advantage. As discussed in chapter 2, workers of an older generation who stayed with the same family for a long period, like Rachida, were married off by their employer-guardians. Marriage with an urban stranger was not a common occurrence among my circle of domestic-worker friends.[21]

Many of the domestic workers I knew were past the usual age for marriage (early twenties) and seemed to be stuck between, on the one hand, a desire for a love match, which the presence of men who "hunted" in Rabat's parks made seem possible, and on the other hand a preference for the known, safe son of a family friend who, however, provided only the country life that workers have left behind. The latter would be hard to settle for as long as hope for the former renewed itself in the park each Sunday. And yet the former was unlikely to come to anything, seeing as these apparently kinless men could take advantage of rural women for as long as they wanted to avoid the cost and responsibility of marriage, without any wider circle of acquaintances calling them to account as *sons*. Ossman argues that these new interactions between strangers in public places are not yet governed by a "socially validated script"; thus even mature women giggle nervously when men approach (1994, 47). Writing about women in Fes, Newcomb maintains similarly that "while 'rules' for women's behavior in new spaces are not always clear, women themselves navigate among competing ideologies to occupy those spaces according to their own standards" (2009, 147). Although women knew they could choose partners, they were unsure how to go about it.

When I returned three years after my main period of fieldwork, both Ilham and Rouqia had married rural men. Ilham, who looked more tired and tanned than she had in Rabat, told me that Rouqia was "having problems" in her marriage. Hafida married a Berber-speaking construction worker in a small town on the Mediterranean coast where she had moved to work in a café. The family from whom she rented a room, seeing she was a decent woman, had introduced her to an acquaintance. He was fair skinned like her, and Hafida's family had approved. Hafida moved into her husband's windowless one-room hut and although romantic (it has a sea view if you prop the door open), she felt it was hardly an ideal place to raise the child they were expecting. Hafida asked me for news of her old friend Miriam. Miriam had moved on from her weld l-blād boyfriend and met a metalworker in Casablanca through her employer's neighbor. They had married after one month. "The wedding day is the only day that is nice," she commented bitterly. Miriam's husband was abusive, and she was desperately unhappy living with her in-laws, but she had a son, and at the time of writing she had opted to remain with her husband for the child's sake. Her sister Safae was still working as a domestic and juggling relationships, largely over the phone, with men she was convinced were lying to her. In any case she was not in a hurry to marry, since she had seen her sister suffer, and with Miriam married and not working, Safae alone was able to financially support their ailing single mother in the village. Marriage was certainly not the end of a domestic worker's struggles.

Identity, Consumption, and Leisure

Walking around the city, domestic workers were keen to point out anyone they thought was a domestic with her employing family. Comments were usually accompanied by the epithet *miskīna* (poor thing), more because the woman in question was unable to hide her identity (a skin color darker than that of her companions or a different style of dress gave her away) than because she was doing this work in the first place. In the anonymity of modern urban life, domestic workers who are allowed out alone have the opportunity to appear as someone different. Zhor, a domestic worker interviewed by Mernissi, would spend summer Sundays at the beach and maintained that "when you're in a swimming suit, it's difficult to tell if you're the daughter of a millionaire or of a bird and cage seller" (1982, 18).[22] Zhor claimed that none of her friends knew she worked as a domestic and was shocked at Mernissi's suggestion that a boyfriend might telephone her at an employer's house: "My God! At my employer's place! So that he'll know that I'm working as a maid? ... You know that in our country, to be a maid is the lowest of jobs; nobody respects you. Nobody wants to go out with a maid or have a friendship with her. Moroccans despise maids and ridicule them" (16–17). The person Zhor revealed in public was "a facade. It's not possible for them to know the true Zhor" (17).[23] The men she met on the beach sometimes expressed an interest in marrying her, but Zhor felt she could never marry a wealthy man because the relationship would be based on inequality, and she would not be respected: "The first time I do something wrong or have a difference of opinion with him or his mother or his sister, they would say, 'You should talk, you, whose father threw you out into the street. You, a maid, who washes people's dishes and toilets'" (19).

Because so much can usually be judged by appearance, those whose physiological features do not link them to a certain background are able to manipulate through dress the impression they give to others. Some workers, like Malika's younger sister Ikram, have a talent for this. On her day off, Ikram wanted to go to a telesales office to enquire about a face cream she had seen advertised that she thought might get rid of scars a childhood accident had left on her forehead. The cream started at 700dh, almost half her monthly wage (1,500dh), but, wearing a pastel pink trench coat over figure-hugging jeans, and with her hair in curls around her shoulders, Ikram looked like someone who might spend that much on face cream. I noticed there were a couple of staples in the hem of her coat from the dry cleaner's label, indicating the effort she had gone to. I felt sorry for her and for the salesman who was wasting his time. Ikram declined his offer to deliver the cream the following day but was asked for her contact details and address. Having missed large parts of her schooling, Ikram could hardly write and did not know her employers' address in full. But rather than explain this, and the fact that she did not want to be contacted at her employers' house, she simply said, "Well, you've got my telephone number. I'll come back next

Sunday." The whole episode was about playing a part, not letting on that she did not have her own address, that she was not from the city and that she could not afford the cream anyway.[24] Going to the office and enquiring was the closest she would get to obtaining this product and realizing her dream of a scar-free face.

I had similar experiences with other domestic workers who felt they had to play a part even to ask cosmetics sellers about products they had seen their employers use. The imitation of employers' styles greatly concerned colonial social scientists who saw this as a sign of declining morals but also a threat to the boundary between the local and European populations. Montagne, for example, wrote that "others, more brazen, sometimes wear a European dress and shoes, borrowed or received as presents, use their employer's lipstick, and take a chance on mixing with the western crowd in the street for a few hours" (1952, 240). Ilham had noticed her employer's daughter's skin grow fairer over time and had one day seen her apply a cream. She had asked the daughter where she bought it and decided to save up to buy the same herself. Rather than enquire directly about a cream she was unlikely to be able to afford, Ilham tried to make it look as though I were interested. When she discovered the price (35dh), she looked at me pointedly, asking, "Are you sure that's the one?" Confused, and thinking Ilham was indirectly asking me to lend her the money, I handed 35dh to the shopkeeper. Once away from the shop, Ilham explained that, since the cream was too expensive, she had wanted me simply to say, "No, that's not the one." She nonetheless took the cream and repaid me 35dh the following week.

It has been argued that consumer practices such as these go hand in hand with a process of individualization (Appadurai 1996, 7; Bauman 2000, 105). Writing on postsocialist Poland, Dunn argues that "consumption is heightened when people believe they are the aggregate of potentially divisible qualities that they can act upon by purchasing specific goods (i.e., a young woman's attractiveness can be improved by face cream)" (2001, 277). In this respect, domestic workers like Ikram and Ilham were "choice-making 'entrepreneurs'" (277) who, Dunn argues, must also be owners of all their properties, including their labor. Ideals of a more individual personhood and the commoditization of labor with its potentially short-term contracts are, however, complicated by ongoing practices such as the worker's family appropriating her wage to tile their courtyard in the village or insisting she marry instead of continuing in paid work. Moreover, the purchase of face cream and clothing seemed part of aspirations for marriage, with workers' ultimate goal in the city, as Crawford notes for both male and female migrants, being "not to own commodities but to establish a household" (2008, 185). Until they formed their own, most workers supported their natal households. Either way, workers ultimately spent their money in support of the ideal of households rather than atomized individuals.

Not for consumerism as much as the space in which it occurs, markets and shopping arcades are nonetheless domestic workers' pleasure grounds; the workers can look, touch, turn over, try on, and imagine owning items, without having to buy. And unlike the parks and squares where anyone idling is presumed available, or the cafés and patisseries where only paying customers can relax, everyone is welcome to spend time here. Picking through stalls lends a purposeful air to women who have nothing better to do and nowhere else to go than back to their employers' houses. In Rabat's medīna, Hafida and Sukaina, friends from the same village, would stand over piles of secondhand clothing, pulling out garments at random and holding them up only to throw them back on the pile, but all the while exchanging stories about what their employers had said and done. It was here, in the hustle and bustle, rather than in the apparent tranquility of the park, that women could talk in peace.

Although there are some covered arcades, markets are usually set up in the open air. Indoor leisure beyond the home being the preserve of men (who can acceptably spend hours in cheap cafés) and wealthy women (who can afford refreshments in expensive women-friendly patisseries, clubs, and hotel spas), workers do not usually leave the employers' house if the weather is very bad. Still, I spent hours wandering the city in the cold wind or oppressive sun with domestics who had nowhere to shelter. In her *Book of Household Management*, Mrs. Beeton suggested servants should be "given opportunities for welcoming respectable friends in their employer's house, and need not be forced by absence of such a provision for their comfort to spend their spare time out of doors, often in driving rain, possibly in bad company" ([1861] 1907, 15). Because the house is their job, Moroccan workers are effectively homeless on days off, unless they choose to stay at their workplaces. Many do not have their own rooms but sleep in the living room or share bedrooms with children or other family members, so staying at home will not guarantee any private space, even if it offers the right to rest. Exceptions are those who have sisters or aunts living in nearby Salé, where they can spend the day. Chen, borrowing Woolf's idea of *A Room of One's Own* (1929), argues that an alternative "space" is required for a "self of one's own" (2005, 336). She describes how Taiwanese immigrant women, as converts to Buddhism and Christianity, use these religions as spaces to construct a sense of self, distinct from their employing families. Faith-based activities, such as the pilgrimages organized for domestics by evangelical churches in Israel, also help domestics carve out an identity (Liebelt 2011, 248). Ueno (2010), studying strategies that Indonesian and Filipino domestics use in "identity management," describes how workers in Singapore seek to gain additional roles through volunteering or church activities in order to define themselves as "more than just a maid." I was not aware of any such alternative spaces accessed by domestics in Morocco, with the exception of literacy classes and attending prayers at a mosque. Leisure and relaxation, therefore, had to happen in public—either the smaller public of the employing family or the greater public of the outside world.[25] In this respect, the situation of Moroccan domestics is paralleled by that of domestics globally: Filipina workers in Hong Kong congregate in public places, including the steps of the national bank, where they perform "private" rituals such as painting their nails and cutting hair (Constable 1997, 540). In Tel Aviv, Filipina domestics socialize at the Central Bus Station (Liebelt 2011, 145–55); in Singapore at the Lucky Plaza Mall (Huang and Yeoh 1998, 593); and in Rome at the Termini train station (Parreñas 2001, 202–4).[26]

Added to this difficulty of exposure (to the public eye as much as to the elements) is the fact that workers rarely eat properly on days off. Some bolster themselves with large breakfasts before leaving their employers' houses while others, desperate to leave, skip food entirely. Few employers give workers money specifically to buy lunch (the main meal of the day in Morocco), but some set a portion of the family meal aside for them to have on their return. Ilham often packed snacks (leftovers, fruit) in her bag, which she shared with others. Rouqia, on the other hand, never planned what she would eat but readily accepted invitations to cafés, where men presumably paid the bill. Miriam, who spent her day off strolling with her sister, her boyfriend, and other awlād l-blād could afford to buy a tuna baguette for lunch but restrained herself when with the group, knowing that her boyfriend would feel embarrassed; he could barely pay for his own lunch, let alone hers as well.

The amount of money domestic workers spent on these days off varied according to their stages in life, how many others were contributing to family income, and, often, the progress of the construction of their family's new house in the countryside. Ilham explained, "I don't buy [anything] because we haven't painted our house yet." She would, however, buy things for a special occasion like a trip home for ʿīd, which required a new outfit. Rouqia, on the other hand, had that very day bought a faux-leather jacket and some fancy underwear. Ilham explained that Rouqia "has now started to buy things, but there was a time when she didn't. Her house is now finished, and she is not the only one in her family working either. I am the only one in my family who works."

Conclusion

Days off for domestics amount to a small fraction of their total time in the city, but these days reveal a disproportionate amount about their conditions, identities, and desires. Not only is the day off a time when work, so often conducted alone, can be discussed and compared with others, out of earshot of employers, but it also provides an anonymous space in which women are free to be someone other than subordinates.[27] Being consumers is a large part of this; being girlfriends or potential wives is another. In contrast to the daily grind (in the words of one domestic, "what you do today, you do tomorrow"), days off are about futures, toward which workers move on individual projects of self-improvement.

While workers join up with others to help achieve these goals, there is always a sense of the fragility of the links that bind them, made evident every time Rouqia dropped us for one of those men in the park or whenever someone left Rabat for a job elsewhere. Workers are individuals and move as such. At the end of the day, everyone goes home to her own employer. Getting someone's phone number is important only because one cannot be with them always. The ongoing societal shifts that have allowed workers to get to know the cities as well as the houses where they work, to meet unknown employers and unfamiliar men, are facilitated by and epitomized in the object of the cell phone. Every worker has her own and takes it wherever she goes, a fixed accessory in the flux of modern life. In the next chapter, I describe my experience of accompanying workers to visit their homes in the blād. This is not a world of atomized individuals but of families and neighbors, among whom everyone is known as someone's son or daughter, and where cell phones are abandoned on windowsills, drain of power, and blink out.

Notes

1. Liebelt (2011), Ueno (2010), Huang and Yeoh (1998), and others have written about Filipina and Indonesian workers on their days off in various cities.
2. This concerned farm servants rather than strictly domestic servants.
3. Cf. M. Smith (1973) on the possibility of social mobility for domestic workers in Lima.
4. Having recorded life stories of domestic servants in Cairo, Lila Abu-Lughod observes that "it is always a rupture to the ideal of women's embeddedness in family and marriage that accounts for their positions doing work that is both hard and not respectable, and for their not being, in a sense, full persons" (2002, 125). The social discrimination against single women in Cairo is also emphasized by Mahmood (2001, 219), who describes relatives constantly asking why women are not married.
5. Cheikh categorizes the women of her study who engage in monetized sexual exchanges as "the unemployed of the matrimonial sector" (2011a, 39): "They suffer indeed from a lack of opportunities for marriage and, as a consequence, of their incapacity to conform to that which, for girls without qualifications, remains the ideal of female realization *par excellence*" (41). The average age of girls at their first marriage rose from seventeen to twenty-seven years between 1960 and 1999 (Rachik 2005, 14), although since the reform of the Moroccan Family Code the number of marriages of girls who are minors has increased in certain rural areas (Zvan Elliott 2009, 219).
6. Moroccans use the French word *congé* for both a regular day off (*jour de repos*) and longer periods of leave.
7. See, for example, J. Abu-Lughod (1970) for Cairo.
8. This is a Moroccan proverb: *Lbes ʿalā qddik iwātik*.
9. Illiteracy is often a problem in noting down names and numbers; some workers can write numbers with pen and paper but not navigate phone menus or type names on a keypad.
10. Collier records that in the Andalusian village of her study during the 1960s, "on Sunday afternoons the girls dress up and walk out along the paved road that leads from town to the main highway. The boys also walk then, and the two sexes get a chance to look each other over" (1997, 77). Davis and Davis (1989, 118–19) similarly describe the walk to school in the small Moroccan town of their study as a time in which boys and girls flirt with each other. In this case there is less emphasis on display. Coeducation, which rose in prominence in Morocco from the 1980s and is often cited as the harbinger of courtship and companionate marriage, is of little importance for domestic workers, most of whom left school at a young age if they attended at all.
11. On arranged marriages in the context of a small Moroccan town during the 1980s, see Davis and Davis (1989, 105–07). They stress that "the main concern is the girl's reputation. If she is a relative, her behaviour and personal qualities are well known. When spouses are related the larger family provides an interested support group in times of marital stress" (106).
12. See also Hoffman (2008, 60, 71) on women's hopes to marry out of the Moroccan countryside.
13. I was surprised at the frequency of "wrong number" calls I received until I realized many Moroccans dialed at random in the hope of being able to engage someone in romantic

conversation (cf. Kriem 2009; Cheikh 2011b, 179n; Carey 2012). My host sister would often play along with this technique, even arranging rendez-vous she had no intention of keeping, as a safe way of having some fun with men.

14. The same is true of online chatting, although few domestics engage in this due to low levels of literacy. See Newcomb on mixed-gender conversations in cyberspace in which "women control to whom they will speak and what they will reveal, and whether to arrange physical meetings or limit their encounters to the printed word" (2009, 146). Cf. Boutieri (2016, chap. 6). For another Muslim society, see Bano (2012, 139) on Pakistan.

15. When approaching unknown people, the use of kinship terms such as "my brother" and "my sister" is polite and unthreatening but also implies equality and hints at an obligation to help the speaker. Writing on Berber-speaking Moroccans, Carey explains, "The ideological foundation of a (horizontal) relationship is equivalence or at least similarity. For instance, if one wants to compliment or merely be nice to the anthropologist, one calls him 'son of [our shared] natal village' (*ou tamazirt*— . . . 'son of the soil'), and if one wants to establish closeness to a girl, one can refer to her as sister (*ultama*)" (2012, 198).

16. On the social productivity of lies and opacity in Moroccan relationships, including flirtation, seduction, and rupture, see Carey (2012).

17. For example, Davis and Davis (1989, 105). See Mahmood (2001) on Egyptian women.

18. On these shifts in Morocco, see Davis and Davis (1989, 115), and in Pakistan, Bano (2012, 139). For Egypt, Lila Abu-Lughod argues that "emotions in Egyptian melodrama might provide a model for a new kind of individuated subject" (2002, 117), thus shaping the personhood of viewers. See also Abu-Lughod, L. (2005).

19. Hafida's employer suggested she attend the classes but gave her less time off on the weekend to compensate.

20. Writing on the arranged marriages and love marriages of poor women in Delhi, Grover argues that in the latter, "the couple's respective families may have no contact and communication with each other, and may therefore be unable to mediate during times of marital distress and conflict" (2009, 3–4).

21. See Zontini (2010, 114–23, 174–84) on marriage strategies of Moroccan women working in Bologna and Barcelona, some of whom find partners on return visits to the blād, while others marry men they meet through friends or strangers they encounter in public places.

22. On young maids in Kolkata who dressed to "pass" as middle-class women, see Ray and Qayum (2009, 156–58), and on carers who pretended they were residents rather than workers in an exclusive resort-style care home in Israel, see Liebelt (2011, 99).

23. A nod toward Goffman (1971) seems appropriate. Goffman argues that we have onstage and offstage personas to manage other people's perceptions of us. Differences in Moroccan dress for the home and for the street vividly mark the boundary between onstage and offstage.

24. Ikram probably gave herself away by failing to be familiar with various landmarks the salesman gave her when directing her to the office; she had to keep phoning to ask for more help finding her way. It was clear that Ikram did not know the city well, nor did she know how to navigate unknown places.

25. Parreñas, writing on Filipina domestics in Rome and Los Angeles, saw domestics choosing to eat alone when employers gave them the option of eating with the family as "an act of reclaiming their own space away from that of the employer where their identity is that of a perpetual domestic worker. Confining themselves to their own space within the workplace is possibly a creative act of retreat—a break—from their role as a worker" (2001, 166).

26. See also Gill (1994, chap. 5) on the lives "away from the workplace" of Bolivian servants in La Paz.

27. Talib's ethnography of stone-quarry workers outside Delhi highlights the importance of workers' sharing stories together in leisure time to make sense of their work experience as part of "symbolic worldbuilding" (Talib 2010, 237). Cf. Khosravi (2008, chap. 4) on the self-fashioning of Iranian youths "idling" in a Tehrani shopping mall.

6

DOMESTIC WORKERS AT HOME

THE HOME LIFE FROM WHICH WORKERS MIGRATE IS something that studies of transnational domestic workers often overlook. By home life I do not mean a region of origin but a familial space in which the worker grew up. When the domestic contexts of employer and worker are separated by thousands of air miles, the study of households at both the supply and demand end is scarcely feasible: the point in time and space where employer and worker meet (the employer's home) becomes the locus of study, without reference to the way households at the other end organize housework and hierarchy. If domestic life is of more than economic value, however, we should consider the extent to which the worker retains her position within her natal household once she has spent time away. Moroccan domestic service, to take just this case, is an element in the much wider context of domestic labor, waged and unwaged.

Literature on domestic work makes a theoretical distinction between someone who cleans a floor to earn a wage and someone who does it for other reasons—e.g., because she is the youngest capable household member. I suggest, however, that we can gain a better understanding of the "persons" made through housework by treating those who perform domestic tasks—both paid and unpaid—as of the same kind, in contradistinction to those who do not perform those tasks. The waged domestic work that has been our focus so far is at the far end of a scale where labor is exchanged for money in a short time frame. At the near end of the scale is family, where who extracts value from whom, through which tasks, is subject to flexible hierarchies, and "people are not paid money for their time but are instead provided with food, shelter, love and security" (Crawford 2008, 50). Here, as Crawford argues, the time frame of give and return tends to be longer: duties mean rights but not straightaway.

Homecoming

"Be careful of thieves. And don't wash your clothes there. Bring all your dirty laundry home. You'll see, they don't know anything there; it's just the countryside." Such was the advice my host mother gave me as I left her house in l'Océan to accompany Hafida to her home village in the Gharb for ʿīd l-kabīr (the great feast).[1] I didn't tell her that I hardly knew Hafida and, at the time, had met her only once. It was thanks to another worker, Miriam, that I was making this trip. Miriam worked on the Sebbaris' street, a couple of buildings up from them, and had answered the door while I was attempting a survey of the street. Her employer had been out, and we had talked with the door six inches ajar. Miriam later told me, "I didn't trust you at first," but she had taken my phone number. Days later she phoned to ask if I knew the way to a quarter of Rabat where her friend Hafida was working, and we went together. Miriam did not stay more than a month with this employer, but when she left, she invited me to the *blād* (country) for ʿīd and suggested that I make the journey with Hafida, from the village next to hers. I accepted, despite my host mother's concerns for my laundry, and met Hafida at the train station at 7:00 a.m. on the day before the ʿīd.

It was the end of October. Hafida had not been home since July, when she had stayed six days, and she had chosen not to return at all for ʿīd ṣ-ṣaghīr at the end of Ramadan so that she could stay a full ten days this time. As is not uncommon for workers returning home, she had slept badly and been sick in the night. The stress of preparing to travel, packing, buying gifts, completing the extra work employers demand so they have less to do in the worker's absence, and sometimes dealing with disputes over leave and pay, combined with excitement over and anticipation of seeing family again, often prevented workers from eating or sleeping well. Once on their way, they expressed peace and relief (*rāḥa*) and commented on the contrast between these homeward journeys and their return to the city. Hafida told me, "I'm so happy to be going home. I miss them so much. I'm always happy to go to our *dār*. But then when I'm coming back the other way, *kanḥ ess b ḍīq* [I feel a tightness, constraint, hardship]." The train was so full of people going home for the feast that Hafida and I had to push our way on to join crowds standing in the corridors, and at Sidi Kacem, where we got off, we followed hundreds of wheeling suitcases up the road to the "grand taxi" station, where people squeezed themselves, two to a seat, into the old Mercedes that shuttle between towns. The drivers doubled the fare for the festive season. "We are people too, just trying to get home," complained

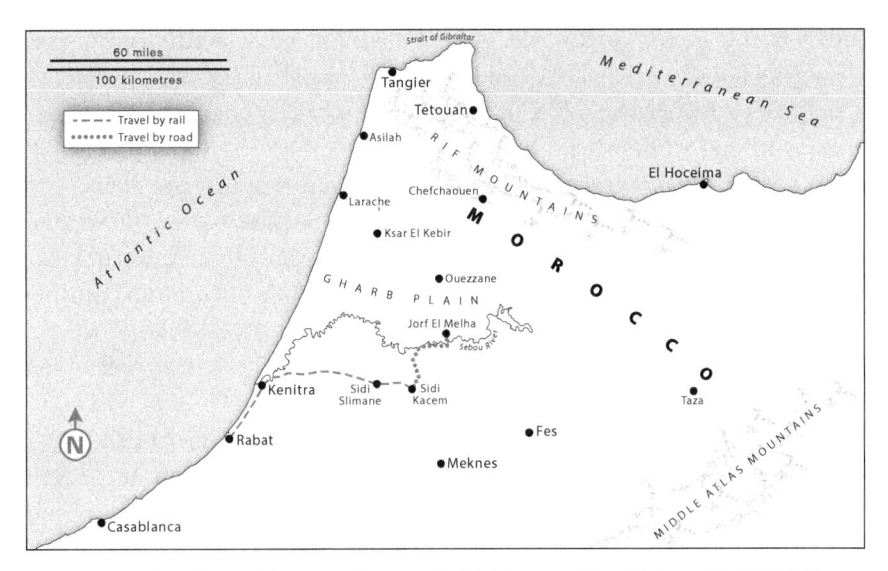

Fig. 6.1 Map of northwest Morocco, showing Hafida's journey from Rabat to Jorf El Melḥa. Cartography by Martin Lubikowski.

Hafida, and at 30dh each, together with the 45dh train ticket, her journey's cost was pushed up to two days' wages. Figure 6.1 shows our journey from Rabat to Jorf El Melḥa.

It was raining heavily by the time we got to Jorf El Melḥa (literally cliff of salt), so called because of salt deposits in a cave nearby. Located on a rise in the Gharb plain that stretches from Meknes to Ouezzane, it is often referred to simply as Jorf or, among those who live in smaller settlements just beyond it, *l-fīlāj*, from French *le village*, but by European standards it is more a town. With around twenty thousand inhabitants, Jorf is central to the lives of people in the region: this is where nearly all their marketing is done and where they visit the doctor or, more often, the pharmacist and go to secondary school.[2] Hafida's father, a retired butcher from a family of butchers, used to work here daily. We left our luggage with him while Hafida made some purchases. As I watched her buy two kilos of apples and bananas and another two kilos of chicken, and then spend 100dh (more than two days' wage) at a general store on fourteen pots of yoghurt, ten packets of biscuits, twenty-four cheese triangles, five liters of milk, and a large tub of margarine, I began to feel my own gifts would be inadequate. This pattern of buying was repeated on every trip I made with a domestic worker to her family. Sometimes the timing of the visit was even planned to coincide with the weekly market, where better quality and value made provisioning more worthwhile. Added to these homecoming purchases were gifts bought in the city. Food is much cheaper in the countryside, so apart from some *ḥelwa* (sweets) and *ghayf* (pancakes) one employer "sent" home with her worker (who helped to make them), these were rarely food items but rather toys and clothing for the children of family members.[3]

The short ride in another shared taxi to our final destination (not shown in fig. 6.1) cost us a further 5dh each. We were dropped off at the top of Hafida's village, Douar Ba Karim, where she sent a couple of children running down the muddy path to alert her family to our arrival while we waited by a pile of luggage and shopping bags. Everyone who passed welcomed her warmly—"'alā salāmtik [Praise God for your safety]!"—and offered to help carry something, bringing home to me the context of rural Moroccans' complaints about the failure of city neighbors to greet one another in the street. By the time Hafida's sisters appeared, wearing headscarves and brightly colored pajamas, some with gingham aprons around their waists for modesty as well as to keep their clothing clean, there was little left to carry. Hafida stood out from the others; she had gone to a salon to have her hair blow-dried the previous day and was dressed in fitted black jeans and a checked shirt. Her high-heeled shoes with pointy toes were not faring well in the mud. The other women wore plastic sandals.

Hafida's family's *khayma* (literally camp), a stone's throw from the Sebou river, was a large walled compound, roughly triangular in shape owing to part of the original space being sliced off to make a separate compound for another branch of the family. The rooms (*biyūt*, singular *bīt*) and veranda were arranged around three sides of the courtyard with a separate bīt for Hafida's father where his meals were brought to him. Hafida's house and courtyard were larger and had more biyūt than many others in Douar Ba Karim. With the exception of recently built dwellings, the roofs in the village were thatched or of corrugated iron; the walls were whitewashed adobe, with stripes of blue, yellow, pink, or turquoise around the bottom and sometimes the top. Hafida's had pink and yellow stripes and flowers on the walls too—all done, surprisingly, by Hafida's brother's young wife, Dawiya.

There were probably a little over a hundred *khiyām* (camps) in each of Hafida's and Miriam's villages. Government statistics are not available, and the time frame of my stays, and my hosts' concern that I not venture out alone, allowed me to gather information only from people I was introduced to. Miriam's sister, Safae, named twenty-three women in their village, Awlad

Ahmed, who worked as domestics in cities, including Rabat, Tangier, and Casablanca. In Douar Ba Karim, Hafida's village, six young women and girls were identified as working in city houses, and three others had recently stopped working to get married. I felt there were probably more. I was told that the next village (further away from Jorf) has a greater proportion of women working in agriculture and almost no one working in city houses, but I wondered if this was a function of facts being hidden from outsiders.[4] I gathered from the Ba Karim women that numbers of girls and women who went to the cities for domestic work had dropped in the last two decades. While there used to be "three or four in each khayma who worked in cities," one of Hafida's neighbors explained, "Now men go to work instead of girls. Girls don't go to work anymore. [Those who do are] few. They used to marry late—thirty, thirty-five. Now they marry early, fifteen, sixteen, seventeen, eighteen, so they don't have to work." Notions of appropriate life stages for work varied from one household to another. Hafida's father had taken his girls out of school when they were young because he did not want them to walk there alone but had not allowed them to work until they were older: "It's better that we live on what God has written rather than laboring to get more," he had said. The men from Douar Ba Karim and Awlad Ahmed migrated to the cities for work in construction or cafés. Those who stayed behind worked in Jorf as butchers (like Hafida's father), shopkeepers, painters, builders, or mat makers. Some sold goods such as clothing, sandals, or vegetables in the regional markets, going to a different one on each day of the week.

Others were farmers (arable and pastoral) or laborers in the fields, orange groves and orchards that spread out from the village along the banks of the Sebou. Agricultural work was also open to women. Safae took me to an orchard near Awlad Ahmed and pointed out the different trees, telling me the season of each one's fruit. There were apples, oranges, lemons, figs, peaches, quinces, and pomegranates. She had never worked in fruit picking, although her sister and mother had: "It's hard work. But to tell the truth, though it's hard, it doesn't have problems like work in houses. Everyone tells you work in houses has problems, right?"

Working for the House

On the second day of the ʿid, Hafida and I hitched a lift back toward Awlad Ahmed and went to Miriam's house. Miriam (twenty-one) and her younger sister Safae (twenty) lived with their mother, Lamia; the girls had been born to a Moroccan whom the mother met in France but who had abandoned the family when Miriam and Safae were small. Lamia and the girls had returned to live in her natal k͟hayma. In the last few years, Miriam and Safae had persuaded their mother to use the money from their earnings to build a new breezeblock and concrete house on the site of their former adobe home in the corner of their grandfather's k͟hayma. Rebuilding was widespread in Awlad Ahmed, new dwellings almost outnumbering adobe ones; less so in Ba Karim, where people still worked hard to maintain the adobe walls, thatched roofing, and wood and bamboo ceilings that are easily damaged by rain. When Yousra showed me the site where her family was building a new house, she pointed to some breezeblocks piled up, saying, "This is better than our other house—it stays clean. The other has to be redone and redone." Home improvements financed through remittances are a visible outcome of migration everywhere. In the Kabyle village of Scheele's ethnography, for example, patriarchs built large houses to which they hoped (pretty much in vain) their sons would return with their own children (2009, 118).

Miriam's house was almost complete by the time of my visit. A metal door led into the courtyard, which, in contrast to Hafida's, where the heavy rains had made a muddy pool, was of smooth concrete with a drain to let the water out. "It's the best thing you've done, this courtyard," commented Hafida. "If you saw the mud at ours!" On one side of Miriam's courtyard, steps led up to the roof terrace; on the other side was a small kitchen where a waist-high counter, used more as a shelf, reflected urban designs for cooking spaces. Washing dishes at Miriam's was, however, still done in a bucket by the tap in the courtyard, and cooking was done on a small gas burner placed on the floor.

The main part of the house comprised a living room with mattresses on the floor facing the television, a guest room with raised couches and a table, and a small dressing room where clothes, blankets, and valuables were stored in locked cupboards. All but the courtyard was tiled and could thus be cleaned in exactly the same way Malika cleaned Nadia's floor in the Sebbari building, described in chapter 1. At Hafida's k͟hayma, by contrast, the floors were adobe and were cleaned by sweeping with a short broom made from twigs. In summer these traditional floors need to be sprinkled with water before sweeping to keep the dust at bay and are resurfaced yearly. While the skills for building and maintaining an adobe house could be found within the familial group, these new homes were built with materials and labor (local workmen) purchased on the market, thus reinforcing integration with the cash economy. Miriam explained that they would save their wages for three or so months, then come home and put the money toward work on the house: "If we give Mother money every month, she just spends it on this and that." As well as paying for the house, the workers I knew saved up for gold jewelry to put by for themselves as a secure form of investment.

While there was a general feeling that keeping earnings back for oneself was shameful, especially when one's family was still "building," workers did so to varying degrees. One of Malika's older cousins who, together with a sister, had worked in carpet making, explained, "We didn't even touch the money we brought home. What I earned I would bring home to my mother without a *riyāl* [a twentieth of a Moroccan Dirham] missing from it. *Ḥashmnā* [we were too ashamed, respectful] to ask her to give us [money] to buy something for ourselves. But mother never deprived us of anything. Praise God, I won't complain, but I'll just say that it's not the same story with our husbands. *Ṣabr ū ṣāfī* [patience, that's all]."

Crawford wrote that the young in the Berber village of his study worked for their fathers' households but "have ways of resisting by siphoning off a portion of their earnings for themselves or by avoiding labor that their fathers expect of them. Ultimately, the young resist by abandoning the village altogether, along with their responsibilities to their natal households" (Crawford 2008, 172). Cheikh's young female interlocutors in Casablanca kept for themselves a large part of their income (derived from multiple sources, including men with whom they had sexual relationships), and Cheikh suggests this was made possible by the fact that "they live far from their families and can therefore better control information about their income" (2011a, 41). Having supported her family for a year and a half, one of Cheikh's interlocutors "progressively diminishes the amount of money she gives to her mother and thus forces her sister to help her" (41). Rouqia, also from Awlad Ahmed, explained similarly, "I used to give half to my parents and keep half back for me. But that half wasn't enough for me to buy clothes and things for myself, so I stopped giving my parents anything." A friend commented that this was acceptable because Rouqia's family had completed their new house.

Some domestic workers, particularly those whose families had also finished building, made no bones about saying, as Zineb did, "I work for myself." She had worked for so long that when she went to her family in the blād, she did so as a visitor rather than a member of the household. As such, she brought gifts rather than contributing her wage. Hafida did the same, putting her earnings into a post office savings account. As a divorced woman, if she were to return to live permanently in her natal home, she would need to contribute in some way, but by living and working in the city, Hafida maintained her independence from her own family, though not from others. In some respects, this gave these workers a position above that of their families, even senior members, who were recipients of gifts or loans to meet specific needs. Zontini argues similarly for Moroccan domestics in Europe: "in spite of the ideal of the male breadwinner, many Moroccan women have found themselves as the economic pillar of their families—a role that gives them both new prestige and further burdens" (2010, 164). This was true of Zineb, who, on one trip home, asked her father to return 400dh she had lent him. There was something cheerless in seeing an aging man dig into his pockets to pay debts to his own daughter. The country and city economies are hardly more separable than in the nineteenth century.

Comparisons: Here and There

While an idealized view of the countryside is that everyone is neighborly and helps others, another perspective dictates how much time migrant workers are prepared to spend there. Ilham had not left Rabat to go home for several months when Rouqia asked her:

"Don't you miss the blād?"

"No, what would I miss about it? I'd only be washing the dishes there."

"And us, don't we wash dishes here [in the city]?"

"There you're washing them in cold water."

These negative associations of the countryside contradict the feelings of rāḥa expressed by homeward-bound workers. In his ethnography of an Atlas mountain community, Crawford argued, "It is not surprising that for young village women the city almost always looks desirable. They dream of indoor plumbing, a gas stove as opposed to a wood oven, indoor rather than outdoor work, a cement roof and a room with furniture rather than a leaky mud roof in a room bare except for some old carpets to sit on" (2008, 15).

My friends in Rabat made comparisons between their family's home and that of their employers. While workers usually looked forward to going home, they often complained once they were there. Boredom had a lot to do with it. On my second day at her family's house, Zineb said, "I'm fed up. We'll leave tomorrow." She had watched enough television. Women in the countryside passed their time predominantly by doing work, sometimes dragging out what might have been a quick task over several hours—why hurry? Workers' feelings of boredom were thus exacerbated by their understandable unwillingness to pitch in with domestic tasks, saying they had come to rest, not work. But they often began to sound like their employers, telling family members how things ought to be done, in another echo of the "civilizing mission" discussed in chapter 3. Stay-at-home sisters who felt they were doing all the work without thanks or compliment had to listen to their city-based counterparts, who, in their idle state, scrutinized the minor details of domestic life. When Hafida, for example, sat down to rest on the mattresses placed on the floor around the edge of the room, she sighed, "I'm used to high couches. These are really low. I don't like them."

If workers did housework on visits home, it was mostly confined to cooking. Staying with Zineb and her family, I noticed that she took over the kitchen, making comments like, "*n-nās l-kebār* [important people] in Rabat like my food. Doctors eat *my* food." In order to feel superior to her sisters, Zineb aligned herself with her employer's status, as had many domestics who worked for the French in Algeria (Jansen 1987, 204) and as those who identified themselves in court as "gentleman's servant" had done in seventeenth- and eighteenth-century London (Meldrum 2000, 132). In Moroccan cities, cooking was a cut above other paid domestic jobs, and cooks earned a higher wage than workers employed to clean, so it was natural that women emphasized this part of their role. In the countryside, however, cooking was more on a par with other jobs. Hafida tried to explain urban cooking to an aunt who was surprised to hear of the pay difference: "But in the city, cooking is complicated. You have to do several dishes and salads and put out forks and spoons." Even when showing off was not in the worker's nature, family members expected to be given a taste of "city" dishes. This was the case for Rachida, the Sebbaris' former domestic, who returned extremely tired from a visit to her mother in the blād. I assumed her fatigue was from travelling such a distance, but Rachida added:

"Also from the work there. I didn't stop. They wanted me to cook roast chicken."

"Didn't they have anyone who could cook?"

"They don't know how to cook that stuff. They don't have that in the blād."

The recipes and methods that workers learned in the city often involved ingredients or appliances they did not have in the blād, and differences in available or affordable produce caused further tension. During a meal of sheep's trotters and chickpeas with her family, Hafida remarked:

"It's nice, but something is missing."
"What?" the others asked.
"Salad."

Salad is not generally considered a vital part of meals in the countryside, but workers are usually asked to make salads in the city and grow accustomed to the more varied diet.

A similar problem occurred when Malika—who took over the cooking at her home, mobilizing the labor of all three younger siblings to get done what she wanted—made *harīra*, the spicy tomato soup with which Moroccans of all classes break the fast in Ramadan. Her mother's kitchen was not as well stocked as that of her employers. The soup wanted meat, of which there was none, and *smen* (fermented butter), but there was none of that either. Malika's thirteen-year-old brother commented dryly that Malika was "doing things the way *nās l-kebār* [grand, important people] do things, *nās lā bās ʿalīhum* [well-off people]." Indeed, on arrival in Fes after leaving Nadia's, Malika had gone to the market and purchased a secondhand food processor, a frying pan for making the crêpes that Nadia's daughter had taught her to do, and a cheese grater (see fig. 6.2) exactly the same as Nadia's.

The list of missing items seemed inexhaustible. Malika later complained that there was no ladle of the right size, which meant the pancakes did not come out quite right. On another day she bought a flan dish for quiche (something else she had learned to make at Nadia's) and a stand for a roll of paper towels, like the one on Nadia's table. These purchases reflected a desire to reproduce the dining table of her former employers, for whom, if we recall from chapter 2, Malika did not have much respect, asserting that "they don't know how to live!" The problem was inversed at the city end— one worker recalled putting clean plates away in the refrigerator on her first job, never having seen one before and thinking it was a cupboard.

Comparisons about dress and appearance were also prevalent, and because stay-at-home girls could see the imprint of "city life" on the physical appearance of their returned sisters, they too made comparisons between city and countryside. Writing on domestic service in the British Shires

Fig. 6.2 A new cheese grater hangs in pride of place on the wall of Malika's family's half-finished kitchen. A sink for washing dishes at waist height is also a novelty. Photograph by author.

after World War I, Mullins and Griffiths note that "for most girls, holidays meant an annual week or two at home with mother and a chance to show off acquired finery and fashions to her peers . . . Mother used to like to hear everything; dinner parties, 'Oh fancy all that food', she used to say. [Housemaid from south Wales, London 1920s]" (Mullins and Griffiths 1986, 17).

City life inspired some Moroccan country folk with a similar awe. When Hafida and I arrived in Ba Karim, a woman greeted us and, indicating our clothing, said, "Allāh ʿalā l-medīna," which would translate as something like "wow—the city!" Inside the khayma, Hafida and I wore "pajamas" like the other women, but when we went out to visit among neighbors and kin, which the others did in pajamas also, Hafida's mother would tell us to change into our "street clothes"—namely, jeans and a long-sleeved tunic. She seemed keen to broadcast the urban identity of her guests. Sara, Hafida's younger but married sister, told me that her family thought the clothes Hafida (and presumably I) wore were ḥashūma (shameful), but that they let her do what she wanted, as she had been living in the city. "People here know that, so it's okay for her to dress this way." Another worker, however, in a knee-length skirt and wedge sandals, went too far, in Sara's opinion: "Does she think she's in Casa[blanca]? *Tak, tak, tak.* [Sara imitated her mincing along in high heels]. Did she go out like that in front of her mother? Next time she comes I'll tell her, if you want to visit us again, dress *mstūra* [modestly, literally covered]. If you dress mstūra, you're welcome; if not, don't come to our <u>kh</u>ayma!"

Having "nice" clothes is widely seen as a mark of living in the city (see fig. 6.3). One of Abu-Lughod's Egyptian interlocutors "wanted to go to Cairo because she saw her sisters, who had gone there to find work, coming home dressed well and wearing gold" (Abu-Lughod, L. 2002, 23). Having fairer, younger-looking skin is another marker for which city-based workers seem universally envied. One woman commented about the newly arrived bride of a neighbor's son, "She doesn't look like *bint l-ʿarūbīya* [a country girl]. She doesn't look like she has lived in the countryside. She has the whiteness of the city. Maybe she worked in the city. She looks like she has been working there several years. There are so many girls who work in the city, and when you see them you say, she is *medīnawīya* [of the medīna, city], not *ʿarūbīya.*"

Hafida, for her part, looked young for her thirty-one years when compared with her twenty-six- and twenty-four-year-old sisters. When, on returning from a visit to Hafida's family without her (Hafida could not get leave), I showed her a photo I had taken of her married sister, she lamented, "My poor sister. It's the countryside and the work that's done that to her."

Workers' hands, described by Lethbridge as "a painful badge of their profession" (2013, 71), were a particular focus for comparison in the village. Although cracked hands are taken by Moroccan brokers and employers as proof of work experience (M. Montgomery 2019), the use of washing machines and other appliances in cities means women living there probably spend less time with their hands in contact with water or heat than their stay-at-home sisters. Yousra, who lived in the village, showed me her hands, all red and cracked from working in cold water, and said, "You see Nawar [Yousra's sister, who worked in Rabat], she's white and beautiful, working in the medīna. You wouldn't say she's from here." Another Ba Karim woman, whose hands were temporarily dyed red from repainting the ceiling of her family's traditional adobe house, joked that I should send her a pair of rubber gloves to use next time. I never saw a Moroccan woman using gloves for domestic work, in city or country, and this is possibly due to a notion that the work was easier or more effective without them. Emily Keene, the self-styled "Shareefa of Wazan," relates her experience of teaching a Moroccan servant to black a grate: "Naturally, I wore gloves in demonstration, and the next time the operation had to be performed I thought I would give a peep, when I found my blacky had religiously donned my gloves, and, though hard at work, was much encumbered by the same. I recovered them, and suggested she should work without them" (1912, 157).

Rural women were particularly skilled at using their hands, without utensils, for cooking and other domestic tasks. With a mesmerizing range of movements far better adapted to need than rigid spoons or thick pot-holders, mixing bowls were scraped out, water directed in a single stream or sprinkled, hot pans lifted off the gas, and their scalding contents tasted, stirred, or flipped. While these skills were learned through watching and imitating others, and agility and resistance built up over time, employers often expressed notions of innate insensitivity, toughness, and the naturalness of hard work for rural women.

Besides what country girls could infer about life in the city from the physical appearance of returned migrants, there were verbal accounts. Revelations about the nature of work in the city varied according to different audiences and whether workers were trying to incite pity or impress. Zineb, for example, often complained about her employer, Hayat, especially her deficient hospitality and culinary skills: "A sandwich she made—what a state it was! And her couscous—*tasteless*! She cooked it with meat and then removed nearly all the meat and put in cold chicken from the day before. Who does that?" But these negative comments were expressed only to her sisters; to her friends, Zineb made domestic work sound like a barrel of laughs, encouraging them to join her in the city: "You work in the day, and then you finish and the evening and weekend is yours. We go out, to the sea. Ask Mary—we've been to the beach a couple of times [in fact, we had been just once and very briefly], we have picnics in the forest [this again was a one-off and the occasion of the sorry sandwich mentioned above], we go to the medīna. And you make friends and go out with them. And you get your 50dh a day, so you can buy clothes and things." One of Zineb's rural friends responded, "God, that's better [than here]. Here the work never finishes." That migrants on visits home depict to villagers the "splendour of the city" (Majumdar and Majumdar 1978, 116) to add to their own prestige has become commonplace in the literature.

To more distant acquaintances in the village, however, the true nature of Zineb's work remained hidden. When one woman asked after Zineb's

Fig. 6.3 In her best clothes, a worker walks from Kenitra station toward the stand for shared taxis to her family's village. She carries gifts including a blanket for her sister's newborn child. Photograph by author.

Fig. 6.4 A woman in "pajamas" and apron washes laundry by the Sebou River at Ba Karim. Her posture, bending from the hip, is typical for rural domestic tasks, which are based predominantly at ground level, and contrasts with the upright position required for working at waist-high counters and sinks in urban homes. Photograph by author.

sister, Sharifa (who was at the time working as a domestic), Zineb replied, "She's fine, praise God. She's working in a *sharīka* ["company," implying a factory]—the same one I'm working in." This was not an uncommon tale. Cheikh (2011a, 39) discusses the importance of "lies and the unsaid" for her female interlocutors in their home settings. The true nature of their source of income, monetized sexual encounters, was not usually talked about, although family members often knew and kept quiet. The domestic workers I knew steered clear of this kind of woman, electing to live in their employers' homes rather than share rented accommodation with "café girls," waitresses and others whose morality was questionable, but in the eyes of villagers, those who worked in houses were also potentially immoral. Zineb claimed that people would laugh at them and speak ill of them if they knew they worked in houses, but I wondered why she had told her friends and not this woman. Zineb explained, "I know them well; it's normal for them, it's fine. But this woman wouldn't understand. And she's a bit of a gossip."

Writing on the Moroccan city of Oujda, Bourqia remarks that, although about 5 percent of the families she interviewed were sending their daughters to work in wealthy households, "out of pride many families do not admit it to neighbors and strangers" (1996, 32). The low status of domestic work meant it was kept private from some people but partially revealed to others, for, as Dresch argues, "The social everywhere involves selective privacy, and privacy is always layered" (2000, 112). The advantage of the distance between the village and the city is that the nature of a daughter's urban existence can be glossed over at home. It would be a very different thing for the family's honor if their daughter cleaned the house next door for a living.

Going Out

In chapter 5 I described workers going out in the city and mentioned that living in the countryside no longer meant young women could not go out. Most rural ways of socializing were interwoven with daily tasks; women snatched time to talk while they were getting water or on their way somewhere else. For Awlad Ahmed women, at least those whose khayma did not have its own well, the spring above the village was a place they could gather and talk while waiting their turn to fill containers. Men stood on a nearby hillock, presumably not exactly minding their own business, though they were too far off to be party to any conversation. There was a sense that this was women's space, but it was plainly watched by men.

The women of Ba Karim, by contrast, drew water from the Sebou River, where I never saw anyone linger (there was no excuse, the river being big enough for everyone's use at once), or at a shared tap if potable water was required, but the tap was too central to the village to be a place women could talk out of male earshot. There was, however, a small plot of land between two "camps" on which nothing was being grown. Ba Karim women often stepped into this space so they could talk away from the main thoroughfare. The empty plot also formed a section of the route out to the main road if one wanted to avoid going past the *qahwa* (café), the social hub of the village as far as men were concerned. Men lingered outside the café, where it was rumored alcohol was served, so that for a woman to walk past required a certain presence of mind; or, as one woman put it, "you just have to be *mhānīya f rāsk* [confident in yourself]. If you go past giggling and scared, then it's going to make the men look at you." The women joked about the fallow plot of land as "l-qahwa diyāl l-bnāt [the girls' café]."

A more plainly pleasure-bent activity was going for a trip into Jorf or for a walk outside the village. As in the city, this kind of "going out" involved a long period spent getting ready. The following account is typical.

Miriam put on jeans and a fitted jacket and brushed her long hair out down her back. Her sister Safae wore a short black dress over leggings and spent a long time on her makeup. Earlier she had washed the mud from everyone's shoes, but they were dirty again as soon as we stepped out the front door. Hafida was with us too, and all three seemed to know various men on the road, stopping to talk to them. Hafida made a phone call to a friend who drove a taxi, asking him to come back from Jorf "empty" to pick us up. Meanwhile we walked on toward the town with the daylight fading, stopping by a puddle where Miriam suggested we wash our shoes (again), "so as not to go to Jorf muddy."

The friend with the taxi appeared, picked us up, and returned to Jorf, where he dropped Safae, Miriam, and me off in the square. Hafida took a turn with him in the car while we walked about under the streetlights and looked in shop windows. Safae wanted to take photos on her mobile phone, but it was too dark. A boy, barely a man, tried to chat her up from a distance while Safae shouted insults back at him and complained to me that people did not respect her. Eventually Hafida and the taxi man picked us up, and we rode back to Awlad Ahmed.

Such excursions could be undertaken only if one had finished all one's chores. This became clear when Hafida's mother, fearing I was getting bored in the khayma, and not being able to spare any of her own women from the work she wanted done, asked her brother's family to allow one of their daughters, Hala, to take me for a walk on the ridge behind the village (I was never allowed out alone).[5] We were gone, together with a friend of Hala's, for an hour and a half. "Oh dear," said Hala on our return, "the work will be waiting for me! They only gave me half an hour." The next evening, one of Hafida's sisters "took me out" (I felt like a pet dog), and we knocked for Hala's friend, and then for Hala, to ask if they could join us. While we waited at the khayma gate for someone to answer, Hala's friend joked, "Hala was with us *b sawā'ir* [by the hour] yesterday." The phrase *b sawā'ir* refers to payment on an hourly basis rather than for a day, week, or month of service. It is unheard of for domestic work but common in factories. The joke that Hala was allowed out "by the hour" pointed to an organization of work that was strict to a degree that seemed out of place in her own home. Though an extreme case, it demonstrates the extent to which regimes of work for family members can be as inflexible as those of waged labor and sheds light on the life of domestic workers in the city who sometimes have more freedom than girls like Hala. City and country are both idealized by those in the other, but while in the city one can usually seek a better situation, the options open in the countryside are more limited; there is nowhere to go.

Domestic Hierarchies

Ethnographic literature on North Africa points to a gendered division of labor from early childhood: "From about age four onwards, [girls] look after younger siblings, fetch and carry, clean and run errands" (Maher 1984, 73). Davis and Davis describe the daily routine of Hakima, a fourteen-year-old girl in a small Moroccan town northeast of Rabat (1989, 17–22). Between her shifts at school, Hakima's household tasks included folding away bedding, collecting water, washing dishes, and cleaning the floor. The description of her male peer's routine provides a striking contrast, his only remotely domestic task being to make coffee for himself before he left for school in the morning (24).[6] When asked, "What's better here in Morocco, to be a girl or to be a boy?" girls in Davis and Davis's study often mentioned having fewer household responsibilities as an advantage to being a boy.

Gender is not the only factor involved when dividing up labor; age is also important. Crawford (2008, 49) writes that "patriarchs rarely have much to say about women's labor, so in practice the eldest woman (often the wife, sometimes the mother of the patriarch) manages the feminine labor of the household. Thus there are parallel lines of age-based authority, one among women and one among men, with each person dominating the next youngest, but these lines converge in the patriarch."

Age alone is a simplistic criterion. Van Dusen argues that "age, or perhaps more accurately, life-cycle status, is an important factor in separating women of the Middle East into social groups with well-defined duties and prerogatives, as well as a fairly clear pecking order" (1976, 5).[7] Belghiti (1971, 304) observes the assignment of noble and less noble tasks to different people in her study of female relations in rural families:

> Generally, everything that is cleaning—sweeping, collecting up rubbish, removing animal dung, washing the dishes—is not popular work: one leaves it for little girls and newly married women who do not know how to cook. Making the stew, the bread, the couscous or pancakes is already a nobler task and reserved for the lady of the house. As for milking and making butter, it's the

oldest woman, the person who has been longest in the household, or the most highly regarded, who does this. Young brides do not have the right to raise poultry; they sometimes have to wait until they have children.

Maher, in another rural study, notes a similar "domestic hierarchy" in which members of the household can lay claim to status through the work they perform: "there is usually a graduation from older to younger women down from the performance of tasks involving skill and responsibility for resources towards those which merely involve expenditure of energy and the removal of dirt" (1974, 122). Domestic skills are transferred from older women as they delegate certain tasks to younger women and supervise their performance: "It is this constant attendance of girls on older women and the involvement in their tasks which characterizes women's lives. . . . A girl always experiences herself in a vertical relation of obedience and command" (Maher 1984, 73). This contrasts with boys, who relate horizontally, playing outside with age-mates (74).

Women in the rural households I knew organized work between themselves according to this principle of life-cycle status. The wife of the household head was in charge, telling daughters and daughters-in-law what to do. Older sisters took on a role as junior mothers toward younger sisters. With all the sisters I got to know, birth order mattered greatly. When in the city, this was made plain by the older sister acting as an intermediary, finding the younger one work, telling her to quit or stay and to do this or that with her wage. In their homes in the blād, the sisters fell into adjacent rungs of the domestic hierarchy. The older could boss the younger around, tell her to bring a glass of water, tidy the living room, attend to a child, wash the dishes, and so on.

Breakfast times in the village often functioned as household meetings in which women talked about the work that needed to be done that day, and those who were in a position to do so told others what to do. Who will knead the bread? Who will do the dishes from the evening before? Who will wash the clothes? During one breakfast at Hafida's, Dawiya, the daughter-in-law, was lamenting how much laundry she had to do: "The washtub is full!" At this point, Dawiya's eighteen-month-old daughter, Iman, waggled her tongue and gargled joyfully. Everyone laughed: "*Katzagher* [she's ululating]! The washtub's full, and you're ululating!" In Morocco, ululation expresses celebration, but there was nothing to be joyful about, just a day of scrubbing clothes in the river. This kind of humor could be used by women who thought they had been given more than their fair share of work and to reprove those who did not pull their weight. On another occasion Hafida's sister Aziza was still in bed at breakfast time; she claimed she was ill from having done too much laundry the day before. Another sister took breakfast to her in bed, more to laugh at her than out of concern, and her mother mocked Aziza from the courtyard where the rest of us were eating: "Did you wake up a bride?" In the run-up to her wedding, a bride is the only woman who can legitimately contribute nothing to the housework, preserving her health and beauty by resting and staying clean. In the female world, this is an exceptional state of being that does not last.

Whether from older sisters or mothers, reprimands about laziness with housework were nearly always implicitly about the intersection of gender and class. One comment that served to put people in their place was "where have you been *lalla akhaytī* [lady my little sister]?" *Lalla*, or lady, is, almost by definition, someone who need not work; a little sister (note the diminutive) is someone who ought to. Similarly, when Miriam asked Safae to do something, Safae responded with "yes, *madame*," implying that Miriam was taking herself for one of Safae's middle-class employers. Miriam was in fact a year older than Safae and so, according to custom, had a legitimate claim on her younger sister's labor. At Malika's home, Ikram was lying on the couch when her mother said, "Call yourself a woman? Well, get up!" Ikram's mother also mocked what she perceived as Ikram's fancy urban ways: she imitated her mincing around the house, twisting her hips and talking in a silly, high-pitched voice. If Ikram, the second youngest of five sisters and niece to six aunts, thought she had become someone through living in the city, her mother was trying to assure her she had not.

It shocked me somewhat that Ikram and Malika took little notice of their mother or shouted and answered back, sometimes telling her to be quiet, while the sisters who had remained at home had a more respectful attitude. Their mother, for her part, complained that "her word no longer passed in the house." This is not surprising considering Malika and Ikram spent so much time away and in submission to another authority, compared with whom their mother, according to certain urban criteria (education, knowledge of cuisine, dress, and manners), fell short. After a physically violent fight between Malika and her younger sister Ikram, Malika stormed out of the house, commenting that the neighbors would overhear and laugh at her mother. "You're not my mother," Malika had screamed. She was suggesting that the fight reflected a mother's inability to maintain order in her household.

A link between the duty to provide for and the right to discipline a child is made by one of Zontini's Moroccan interlocutors doing domestic work in Barcelona. Selwa, a divorced mother, considered remarrying but worried a new husband would not treat her child well: "But can I tell him not to touch the child because he's not his son if I don't work and he is the one who works? When I'll ask him for money to buy something for the child he can reply, 'If I can't beat him, if I can't shout at him, I also can't buy him anything, he's not my son'" (Zontini 2010, 180). By sending Malika and Ikram out to work, their mother lost her status as authority figure as well as caregiver. The daughters no longer needed her (in fact she needed them, or their wages at least, to finish building the house), so nor would they obey her.

Malika emphasized that she opted for work in cities like Rabat and Casablanca, far away from her family in Fes, "to stay away from the troubles with my family." It has been observed elsewhere that what is ostensibly labor migration is rarely motivated by economic reasons alone (Mahdavi 2016). Alpa Shah notes for migration to brick kilns in India, "how often it was also perceived in terms of the temporary need to be in a space away from the village and from the constraints and obligations of kinship, from domestic disputes and a narrow-minded and oppressive village environment" (2006, 106).[8] A study of service in the English shires in the nineteenth and twentieth centuries records domestics' keenness to get away from family demands (Mullins and Griffiths 1986, 4). In both this and the Moroccan context, workers left home in the hope of greater autonomy, not only from family but from larger hierarchical structures—a fact early rural migrants to the city summarized by saying, "We have come here to be 'our own *qāi'ds* [headsmen]'" (Montagne 1952, 251).[9] But just as the "liberation" of middle-class women from the drudgery of housework was dependent on the exploitation of working-class women, the relative "freedom" of older sisters in the city was effectively bought by younger sisters who stayed in the village to look after the house and care for parents.

If younger sisters had a hard time, granddaughters had it worse, owing labor to grandparents, parents, and older siblings as well as potentially to aunts and cousins. Hafida's five-year-old niece, Fatima-Zohra, had begun to fetch and carry for her mother, her grandmother, and everyone in between and, by the time I left the field, was given notably more tasks than the first time I visited the village eight months previously. Fatima-Zohra seemed to undertake these tasks joyfully. She was happy to be included, noticed, named—to exist. She was rarely thanked but was sometimes told, "You're a good girl." Similarly, a little girl often came and hung around Miriam and Safae's house. They would send her on various errands and explained, "Her father died, and her mother is alone looking after a boy and this girl. No one thinks of her." Their sending her on errands was a way of "thinking of her," and the girl seemed to take real pleasure in performing these small tasks.

That household hierarchies are organized along two axes—the young submitting to the old, and women submitting to men—is perhaps most evident in the person of the daughter-in-law, who must submit to both her husband and her mother-in-law, her *ḥamā*. Moroccan kinship units are traditionally patrilocal: the bride moves to live with her husband's family. This move is particularly momentous in rural contexts if marriage partners are sought from another village, as Hoffman found: "Marriage in rural Morocco was more about this change of residence than about romance. The common Tashelhit way of saying 'She is going to marry a boy from the Tililit [village]' was *tra Tililit*, literally 'She wants Tililit' and meaning 'She is going to Tililit'" (2008, 119–20).

This displacement allows for the treatment of the bride as a stranger (Belghiti 1971, 322). Added to this is the fact that, historically, girls were married very young, in the words of one of Belghiti's interlocutors, "so that she'll obey her husband and not be too worldly wise" (313). Rassam, studying families in Fes and Meknes in the 1970s, observes that "the extreme emphasis on the youthfulness of the bride means that she will be both helpless and dependent" (1980, 174). The closer the bride can live to her natal family, the more chance she has of being defended by her own family against that of her husband. The age of brides is, however, rising—reforms have included a minimum marriage age of fifteen for women (Keddie 2007, 145).

Traditionally, then, the bride's triply subordinate identity as a young, female outsider places her at the very bottom of the pecking order within her husband's household. Maher (1984, 79) describes the life of the rural daughter-in-law as characterized by hard work, service to her husband and his male kin, subordination to female affines, and inadequate provision of food, clothing, and other goods. Dwyer records the words of one woman on the topic of her daughter-in-law: "But a bride is there to cook, sweep, and launder, not to be liked by her husband" (1978, 3; cf. Davis 1983, 131). Kapchan's study, *Gender on the Market*, emphasizes the status of the daughter-in-law as a "'good' from the marketplace," the property "not only of the husband but his entire family, and most particularly of his mother" (1996, 212). She records the story of Khadouj in rural northeast Morocco in the 1920s, who, still prepubescent, was tattooed on her wrists, ankles, and chin by her soon-to-be mother-in-law to mark her as a "promised article of exchange" between the two families (212).[10]

As a low-status stranger from the market, the daughter-in-law's position is, I suggest, structurally similar to that of a migrant domestic worker. Kasriel, writing on Aït Haddidou women of the High Atlas, suggests that "the main wealth of a woman is her labor force" (1989, 62–3). The equation of bride with maid is explicit in discourse recorded by fieldworkers. One of the women in Munson's (1984) *Oral History of a Moroccan Family* is approached for marriage by a wealthy and esteemed sociology lecturer, but she refuses his offer, saying that what he and his mother want is the free labor of a maid. Similarly, one of Newcomb's Fassi interlocutors had married a widower and felt that "the primary reason he had wanted to remarry was to gain a caretaker and a maid" (Newcomb 2009, 54).[11] As when a woman takes on a maid, gaining a daughter-in-law marks a significant change in the daily life of the Maghrebi mother-in-law. Lacoste-Dujardin's account of the addition of a new bride to the Lâali family, Algerians living in Paris, illustrates this: "She served docilely in the house of her parents-in-law, did the housework and the cooking, while her brothers- and sisters-in-law were at school or college, under the orders of a triumphant Madame Lâali who could now be more available for shopping, knitting or crochet, visiting her friends. *Tesaâ tislit*, in Kabyle: 'She has a daughter-in-law', I was starting to understand what that meant: a household servant" (1985, 57).

In Rassam's study of "domestic power," she found, somewhat surprisingly, that many girls were relatively untrained in domestic skills. Furthermore, the norm demanded that those who were trained feign ignorance: "A daughter-in-law who openly displays her expertise in cooking is thought to be exhibitionistic and immodest—and her action is interpreted as a direct challenge to the mother-in-law. Passivity, submission, and ignorance, feigned or real, are the ideal traits of a bride" (Rassam 1980, 174). Davis (1983, 37) also stresses the importance on the part of the bride of what Hochschild (1983) would call "emotional labor." Just as domestic workers are often expected to act out the part of an inferior and "*appear* grateful," as discussed in chapter 3, a daughter-in-law must manage her emotions to display deference towards her affines.

A woman's status changes dramatically when she becomes a mother. One of Belghiti's (1971) interlocutors recollects that her mother-in-law stopped locking the store cupboard with a key when she became pregnant.

A woman earns particular status as the mother of sons because this assures the continuation of the patriline; her status will change again when she becomes a mother-in-law, and, with this rise to power, she can finally take "her revenge on her daughter-in-law" (Belghiti 1971, 328). Dwyer (1978), Rassam (1980) and Davis (1983) also note the cyclical nature of this power relation. Davis characterizes the life experience of Moroccan women as one of "patience and power": "The daughter-in-law is expected to endure everything patiently, attempting to do the best she can to prove her worth to the household" (1983, 131), so that one day she in turn will be mulat d-dār.

While much of this literature is outdated, especially where the city is concerned, as relatively few young couples reside with parents, it seemed to ring true in Hafida's home. Hafida's mother would sit in the kitchen with a pottery dish for mixing dough for ḥelwa on the floor in front of her and, just as Latifa did with her domestic at Dār Sebbari, ask her daughter-in-law Dawiya to pass her things, pull up the sleeves of her tunic, retie her headscarf, sift flour, fill bowls with oil, zest a lemon, or rinse the eggs. The mother-in-law was the cook; Dawiya was assisting, not making the ḥelwa herself. I thought Dawiya might have joined in rolling and shaping the sweets, but she waited by the side. Every now and then she would be told to bring more flour, sometimes to be quicker. Dawiya was mostly respectful but sometimes answered, saying something like, "You want *more* flour?"

Hafida commented to me, "Here, marriage is hard. You don't take a husband; you take his mother. It's like you are kheddāma 'andhā [her worker or servant]." Hafida herself had been home on a break when a man came to the village, saw her, liked her, and asked her family to give her in marriage. Hafida said, "I didn't want to marry, but they wanted me to and made me, and I married and went to live with him in another town." When Hafida's husband returned to work in Libya, Hafida was left with her mother-in-law: "She would just sit there, and I would bring in the food and clear it away and wash up, and when we went to the ḥammām [public bath] it was I who scrubbed her." Although the husband made arrangements for Hafida to join him in Libya, his mother would not allow it.[12] Hafida complained to both her father and his and finally got a divorce, but in the meantime she remained in his mother's house and felt powerless: "My father was ill, and my mother was ill, and I couldn't work for them to help them. Because back home [i.e., in the countryside as opposed to Rabat], you can't work unless you are divorced." What Hafida meant is that one cannot undertake paid work to help support one's natal family if one is married.

Conclusion

Spending time with workers in their family homes put their lives in Rabat into perspective. Generally, the way domestic service in the city was presented in the country meant stay-at-home sisters envied their city-based counterparts more than the other way around. Working in the city not only gave workers a different physical appearance, particularly thanks to indoor work out of the sun and appliances such as washing machines, which saved their hands, but also access to and a taste for fashions uncommon in the countryside. Added to this was the knowledge of urban domesticity and cuisine; prestige reflected from the status of their employers as "important," "well-off" people; and the nature of Rabat as the "capital" and a place for leisure (picnics, trips to the beach), which had currency within the rural household and as far beyond it as gossip based on the shame of domestic service was not feared. Workers who had taken control of their earnings rather than contributing them to the household appeared particularly powerful, their gifts or loans of money to parents and sisters only adding to this appearance. The altered person of the worker did not always fit back into existing hierarchies at home, her presence frequently causing tension. Mothers felt undermined, and the pecking order among female kin was sometimes upset.

The hierarchy in which domestics worked under employers was a simpler version of the complex, multilateral power relations in the extended families from which workers were sometimes glad to distance themselves. Ikram, for example, left her employer, where she served a couple and their two children, to come home and be bossed around by a mother and father, three older sisters, six aunts, and numerous cousins. Views on the treatment of daughters-in-law in particular shed light on workers who were prepared to forgo the trustworthiness of "sons of the blād" to seek husbands in apparently motherless urban strangers. Paid work, in the meantime, at least had the merit of being temporary, a new employer being more easily secured than a divorce. While workers complained that no one knew them in the city, making it difficult to get married, the intimacy of village life could be claustrophobic, evident in the problem of people "talking," something that was itself much talked about. In the village, women had to pass by men who had courted and then betrayed them, and everyone else knew about this. As Crawford wrote, for some of the young men who migrated from the village he studied, "alienation is preferable to the grinding domination of the local patriarchal order, anonymity and isolation are better than a world cloyingly suffused with memory, where every rock has a name, and everyone knows it. For some the city is attractive precisely *because* the market has no memory" (2008, 184).

While days at home were characterized by gossip, family hierarchy, poor-quality food, boredom, and, in the rainy season, mud, some workers missed the blād. A Ba Karim woman explained that migration for domestic service was seasonal: "In the winter the village gets muddy, and girls get fed up here and go and work in the city. In the summer, when it's beautiful here, they come back and stay. It's not necessary to work all year." Demand for agricultural labor peaked in the summer, so work was available at this time for both men and women locally. The conception at the supply end of domestic work as seasonal does not suit urban demands for year-round service, and workers' desire to be in the blād for the summer may partly explain the high turnover of urban domestic service. Workers cannot get leave for a summer break, so they simply quit and then seek a new employer before the arrival of the autumn rains.

Notes

1. Called ʿīd al-aḍḥā in standard Arabic, meaning the feast of the sacrifice. A sheep is slaughtered to commemorate Ibrahim's willingness to sacrifice his firstborn son.

2. The 5dh journey from the village to Jorf is, however, too expensive for many families, and the walk is considered too far and risky for a girl. Hafida's niece (eleven years old) therefore stays with family in another town, where the school is close to their house. Other girls rely on the compassion of the taxi drivers to count them as "half" a passenger or not charge them for every journey.

3. This pattern is reported by Cheikh elsewhere in Morocco: women returning home "load themselves up with presents for their sisters, brothers and parents but sometimes also for aunts and even neighbors, as though to compensate for and justify their absence honorably" (2011a, 38).

4. Zineb's village, also in the Gharb region but on the coast north of Kenitra, was presented like this. Women were occupied in family-based agriculture (bananas, strawberries, cows, goats, etc.) for sale and subsistence, and Zineb and Sharifa claimed to be the only ones from their village who worked as domestics.

5. "We're not finished!" was a phrase Hafida's mother said to outsiders of the khayma who made requests for labor or to whom she made a request, as though each day had an apportioned amount of domestic work.

6. For Algerian and Tunisian examples, see Lacoste-Dujardin (1985, 77) and Zamiti-Horchani (1983).

7. Cf. Mundy (1979) on women's life-cycle status and inheritance in Yemen.

8. Cf. Parry (2003) on motivations for seeking labor away from the village in India.

9. Migrants did not leave all such relationships of dominance behind. Montagne wrote that the prestige of *murābiṭ* (religious teachers) and *shurfa* (descendants of Mohammed) of rural origin did not disappear if they moved to the city. He cites a Berber domestic of maraboutic origin in Rabat who received visits and "offerings" from Soussi domestic workers every Friday (1952, 34).

10. Moroccan women were tattooed with a needle dipped in ashes to enhance their beauty but also as a marker of property (Kapchan 1996, 212). As Kapchan observes, this is rare in contemporary Morocco.

11. The subordination of new brides to their mothers-in-law is widespread; see, for example, Ray and Qayum (2009, 123) on the bride as domestic servant in Kolkata. Brahman brides in Nepal, sought for the labor they can provide as well as their fertility, are given heavy chores and criticized openly but receive better treatment with the birth of each child (Bennett 1983; Stone 2006, 96–112). See also Minturn on changing relations between women in-laws in Rajasthan (1993, chap. 6).

12. Perhaps to guard against this kind of situation, marriage contracts in Ottoman Egypt, particularly in port towns, were concerned with the husband's travel: "In a typical case from Dumyat, the husband agreed: 'If I [travel and] leave my said wife for a period exceeding six months . . . [then] she can be divorced "one divorce" with which she would own herself' (Dumyat sikillat 1005/1597, 28:n.p.–28)" (Abdal-Rehim 1996, 102).

7

DOMESTIC WORKERS AND THE LAW

STUDIES EVERYWHERE REVEAL A STORY OF DOMESTIC LABOR'S exclusion from the legal codes regulating workers and employers in other sectors. Domestic service has been considered something other than work, and not part of economics, or indeed of history: "Domestic servants were omitted from the writings of most of the central theorists, among them Adam Smith, Karl Marx and Edward Palmer Thompson, who concentrated so heavily on the manufacturing sector that they tended to disregard the significance of domestic work. This paved the way for leaving a very central and involved group of workers—domestic servants—outside the scope of theoretical thought about the labour market, its workers, and its laws" (Albin 2012, 233).[1]

The specificity of domestic service stems in part from its conceptualization as a woman's "natural" role, and this naturalizing is furthered by the "one of the family" rhetoric that, in the Moroccan context, originates in the institution of *trebbī* (bringing up). Here, a mother's love and a bellyful of warm pancakes is return for a service that helps to make the "mother" as much as the pancakes. Family is itself a code that appears to transcend Law with a capital *L*, a distinction expressed in medieval England in the alternative systems of love and law (Clanchy 2003).

In Europe, early regulation of the relationship between domestics and their employers was through family law in both civil- and common-law systems, because of "the special characteristics of their employment relationships: direct dependency on the head of house, paternalism, subordination ... and requirements of loyalty and trustworthiness" (Veneziani 1986, 45–46). For early modern and industrializing England, the role of the Poor Law in regulating employment has been emphasized: "settlement" (the right of a poor person to material relief from his or her parish) could be gained through a yearly hiring.[2] Steedman (2009, 18) writes about English domestic service that "as far as I can discover, the anonymous author of *Laws Concerning Master and Servants* of 1785 was the last *legal* voice to aver that 'Master and Servants are Relatives'" and underlines that service was a legal arrangement of contract. But the specificity of the location and nature of their labor has continued to set domestics apart from other workers. In nineteenth-century England, the nature of work in a household and the relationship between household members and their servants legitimized the exclusion of domestic servants from the protection of the Employers' Liability Act 1880: they were "persons whose personal relations in the household or retinue of their masters made it inconvenient that the disputes between them and their masters should be settled before magistrates" (*Pearce v Lansdowne*, cited in Albin 2012, 239). In Morocco, a similar logic explains reluctance to extend labor law to domestic workers.

A Special Law: Defining Domestic Work

Article 4 of the Moroccan *Code du travail* (June 2004) states that "the conditions of employment and work for household employees who are linked to the head of the house by a work relationship are fixed by a special law." All household employees, such as gardeners, chauffeurs, and domestic workers, were thus excluded from the general law and promised one of their own. But the "special law" (*Projet de loi n° 19-12*) has remained in draft since 2006, when the government began work on it. In October 2011, the draft was approved by the Conseil de gouvernement, and it was rapidly submitted to parliament, but the new government, to which Abdelilah Benkirane of the Islamist Parti de la justice et du dévelopment (PJD) was appointed head in January 2012, opted for a reexamination of the law by Interministerial Delegation (June 2012). The then minister of Employment and Professional Training, Abdelouahed Souhail of the Parti du progrès et du socialisme (PPS), stated in an interview that the law was a "priority" (Human Rights Watch 2012, 33) but no draft laws were reexamined that year. In May 2013, toward the end of my fieldwork, it was announced on national television that the law had been approved by the Conseil de gouvernement but with further amendments to be made. The law was again voted on by parliament in July 2016 and was to come into effect a year after its publication in the *Bulletin Officiel*, which, at the time of writing, has not happened. It will not have helped that Morocco was without a government for five months following the reappointment of Benkirane as prime minister after his party won elections in October 2016. To end the deadlock, in March 2017 the king replaced Benkirane with Saadeddine Othmani (PJD), who appointed Mohamed Yatim (also PJD) as minister of Employment and Professional Integration the following month. Although Yatim's photo now presides over the ministry's website, at the time of writing the last word on the draft law for domestic workers was posted sometime in 2016 by Yatim's predecessor, Abdeslam Seddiki (minister of Employment and Social Affairs) of the PPS. His remarks stress internal disagreement. For example, the PPS wanted to set the minimum age of work for domestic workers at eighteen, but this did not gain general approval in parliament. The minimum age originally suggested was fifteen, but Seddiki had insisted on sixteen years, with the consent of legal guardians for those aged between sixteen and eighteen (Royaume du Maroc 2016). Yatim may have other ideas. At any rate, the project does not seem enough of a priority for any one government to push it through before another takes over, makes changes to the draft law, and seeks reapproval in parliament, causing further delays. As people remark, the relevant ministry has gone by three different names since the draft first emerged.

The draft law that circulated in 2011[3] defines domestic workers as "any natural person who undertakes, on a permanent basis, for payment, tasks associated with the house" and the household head (*ṣāḥib al-bayt* in standard Arabic but understood to coincide with Moroccan Arabic's *mul d-dār*) as "any natural person who hires the labor of a worker to undertake work linked to the house which does not aim to make financial gain."[4] This echoes Smith's dichotomy of productive and unproductive labor: "A man grows rich by employing a multitude of manufacturers: he grows poor by maintaining a multitude of menial servants" (Smith, A. [1776] 1986, 430). This is the specificity of domestic workers everywhere and in part explains their exclusion from general labor regulation and national statistics—their work is not seen as contributing to the GDP. Such definitions make poor provision for the fact that the employer, in a practical sense, is not a sole person but a household or sometimes—thinking of Dār Sebbari, where a shout from the stairs sufficed to call a worker from one apartment to another—a group of households. The domestic worker's contract is defined as that "which binds with its governance the domestic worker to undertake specific work in the house," and the following jobs (article 2) are delimited:

> Cleaning
> Cooking
> Care of children or household members who, because of their age or condition, have special needs

Driving the car for household errands
Tending to the household garden
Guarding the house

Such enumeration of roles is a move away from an understanding that domestic workers can be asked to do any task that members of a household require. Many of these demands would fall under a rubric of companion or, historically in England, "lady's maid" and thus be excluded if work were strictly limited to roles in the above list.

Historical analysis of domestic service in Britain, where "what men did was definite, well-defined, limited. . . . What women did was everything else" (Prior 1985, 95, cited in Meldrum 2000, 132), suggests that the problem of an ill-defined role was particular to female workers. Women simply "went into service," but men were more specifically grooms, butlers, coachmen, and footmen (Meldrum 2000, 132). While this may be the appearance when the domestic world is viewed from a public standpoint, nineteenth-century English novels suggest that women domestics were ranked as strictly as men. While on the surface Moroccan women "worked in houses" or "did the work of houses," probably a function of the predominance of live-in arrangements for women, among themselves they might discuss whether they did *ménage* (housework—another broad category in which cleaning is only one element), cooking or childcare, or "everything," as in the conversation between Ilham and Wafa. Men, meanwhile, usually stated outright that they were chauffeurs, gardeners, or security guards or a specified combination.[5] While the Moroccan draft law leaves vague the definition of work to be performed, stating simply that "domestic workers undertake work requested by, in accordance with the wishes of, and under the supervision of the homeowner" (article 4), the legislation of some states stipulates that contracts must precisely define workers' tasks. The Moroccan Conseil national des droits de l'homme, who have produced a memorandum on the draft law, cite Irish and South African legislation, the latter even including a model contract with checkbox lists for employers to fill out (CNDH 2013, 9, 14).

As in the Moroccan labor code for general workers, the draft law for domestics requires a written contract that will comply with the Code des obligations et contrats (December 1913), with a copy for each party and a third sent to the work inspection office. The CNDH suggest that the contract include "the type of work to be done, remuneration, how it will be calculated and the frequency of payments, all payment in kind with its monetary value, pay-rate and compensation of overtime, normal working-hours, paid annual leave and daily and weekly rest-periods, provision of food and lodging, the probation period, if necessary, conditions of repatriation (in the case of a foreign worker), a description of lodgings provided, the method for recording overtime and on-call hours worked, and how the domestic worker will have access to this information" (CNDH 2013, 9). A written contract is, however, not a straightforward solution in contexts of limited literacy. For example, Nabila, whom we met in chapter 4, required the intermediary of Soumiya, the agency manager, to tell her what was in her contract and to sort out any discrepancies.[6]

A further step toward "formalizing" work, which, as I gathered from Soumiya's agency, seems to necessitate a decent number of pieces of paper, comes with the requirement that the domestic worker provide for the household head documents related to marital status, name, residential address, and date and place of birth as well as certificates of education and vocational training and a validated copy of her national identity card (article 4). A worker must also inform the employer of any change of residential address or marital status.

Much has been made of article 5, concerning the prohibition of employment of workers under the age of fifteen, which, in a more recent draft, Abdeslam Seddiki moved to sixteen, and requiring that permission is obtained from guardians for those under eighteen years. This is punishable with fines between 2,000 and 5,000dh on the first offense or a three-month prison sentence in the case of a repeated offense (article 15). The president of OMDH (Organisation Marocaine des droits humains), Mohamed Nechnach, commented that "these are derisory sanctions which will not have any dissuasive impact on the employer" (Benezha 2013). Representatives of GIZ and ODT (Organisation démocratique du travail) stressed to me that domestic work is unsuitable for anyone under eighteen, whether guardians agree to it or not, while others feel the minimum age should be raised to twenty years (Benezha 2013).

A Special Law: Rest, Remuneration, and *Raqāba*

Weekly rest days, annual leave, national and religious holidays and sick days are covered in part three of the draft law. In line with article 10 of ILO Convention 189, domestics in Morocco are to be given at least twenty-four continuous hours of rest per week, which can, if the worker and household head agree, be accumulated over two consecutive months (article 8). Paid annual leave, the length of which is not, however, stipulated in the draft, can be taken after six months of work and can also be accumulated over a period of two years (article 9). Religious and national holidays are paid rest days, although these can be used at a later date if both parties agree (article 10). One wonders how easily an agreement can be reached, since usually workers want to spend ʿīd (a feast day) with family but employers are reluctant to dispense with help at such peak times in the domestic calendar. It was precisely a disagreement over this that, in chapter 4, meant Miriam quit working for l-Ḥajja after one month and returned to Awlad Ahmed with half of Hafida's wage.

If disagreements about holidays are common, so are those about time off for family events, especially as employers are wary of the excuse of an ill mother. Article 11 lists a whole series of family events with the number of days paid leave the worker is allowed:

- The marriage of the domestic worker, 3 days.
- The marriage of one of the children of the domestic worker, 1 day.
- The death of the domestic worker's spouse, one of his children or one of his parents, 2 days.
- The death of a brother or sister of the worker, 1 day.
- A surgical operation of the spouse of the worker or one of his children, 1 day.

An employer who complains that her worker may take weeks visiting a sick relative and then be surprised to find her job filled by someone else would be glad to have a law like this, but the calculated measurement of human kindness, so many days off for this or that potentially traumatic or emotionally charged life event, seems an inferior substitute for the spontaneous compassion of employers. The fact that such a provision is necessary also reflects the possibility that days off on compassionate grounds may otherwise be denied. Here, at least, is recognition that the worker may be part of a family other than the employing household and may therefore have commitments elsewhere.

While stipulating periods of rest is important, it means little when the maximum working hours per day and week are not determined by law. Article 10 of ILO convention 189 calls for members to ensure that legislation for hours of work, overtime compensation, periods of rest, and paid leave for domestic workers is on a par with that of workers generally, but while the Moroccan Code du travail sets the working week at forty-four hours, the draft law remains silent on this issue and makes no provision for limiting or compensating overtime. Fatima, my Océani-based friend who worked as a daily domestic in Agdal, was one of many who complained about working hours, recognizing that live-ins—some of whom, like Malika, are effectively on call twenty-four hours a day, seven days a week—have it worse. Fatima described an exception: a French woman for whom she had once worked as a live-in had a chart on the wall where she recorded hours worked. She had explained to Fatima and her coworker that she noted down the finish time only once they had removed their aprons and she heard them close the door of their room: "Then I know you've finished your work." This was the only instance of working *b sawāʿir* (by the hour) that I came across in a domestic context (apart from jokingly at Hala's house in Ba Karim); Fatima saw this as a radical way of organizing work and wished her current Moroccan employer would do the same.

Domestics who work on the understanding that they are "one of the family" have commented that clock watching is at odds with this approach. Hafida's employer one day scolded her, "How long are you going to talk on the phone? This is time for work, not for the phone!" Later Hafida reflected, "She shouldn't say that. I'm not like a *worker*. I used to come down when I was working in the apartment above, and I would do the washing up and tidy things and then go on my way—for free! I was good to her; she should be good to me." Employers who count the minutes workers spend on the phone are no better than those who counted Danones. L-Ḥajja also put the clock forward by ten minutes in the living room where Hafida slept on a couch, supposedly to encourage her to get up earlier in the mornings. This manipulation of time could go both ways. I once heard Latifa ask Badia, her then paid worker, what time it was. The kitchen clock read 1:30 p.m., but Latifa was in the other room, and Badia answered from the kitchen that it was 2:00 p.m. Badia told me she wanted to serve lunch early, so she could get on with washing the dishes, finish her work, and leave to pick up her son from school on time. This is an age-old trick of the trade. A popular nineteenth-century manual, *The English Housekeeper* (1842), "advised keeping the kitchen clock under lock and key lest the cook alter it with a broom handle to suit her purposes" (Light 2007, 34).

The "difficulty" of counting a domestic's hours is often used as a basis for not doing so. In Bouharrou's (2014) analysis of the labor code's provision for working hours, in which he notes the exclusion of domestics as well as the absence of set hours in the Projet de loi, he explains that "domestic workers perform tasks inside houses which are distinctive workplaces. They do their work during an effective working time but are often at the disposal of their employers, the household heads. It is difficult to distinguish between working hours and their presence in the home, especially for those who are accommodated in their employers' home, and as a consequence to establish precise working hours."

The ILO deals with this problem by acknowledging the paradox of domestic work. The "work like any other" approach calls for legislation regarding overtime while the "work like no other" approach permits exceptions: "Judges expressed sympathy for the difficulty faced by employers in keeping track of domestic workers' routines" (Blackett 2011, 34). It has been argued that while Fordist practice reorganized the management of industrial work, domestic work has not been rationalized to the same extent because "the concept of productivity . . . makes no sense in cleaning or cooking, much less in caring" (Sarasúa 2004, 538). This has an effect on regulation: "In industrial undertakings, rationalisation has always gone hand in hand with a reduction in the working hours of labour, while in unrationalised undertakings—for instance, among artisans—the regulation of hours is also less effective" (Blackett 2011, 19).[7] Labor laws evolved in an industrializing society are ill equipped to cope with service: "to rethink labour regulation to include domestic workers meaningfully is necessarily to reimagine labour regulation beyond the industrial workplace model, while retaining from modern employment law, that which distinguished work from servitude" (20). ILO policy, which is heavily based on Blackett's research, states that "periods during which domestic workers are not free to dispose of their time as they please and remain at the disposal of the household in order to respond to possible calls shall be regarded as hours of work to the extent determined by national laws, regulations or collective agreements, or any other means consistent with national practice" (International Labour Office 2011, c. 189, article 10).

Perhaps the most contentious part of Morocco's draft law is article 12, which covers remuneration. The wage, to be agreed on by both parties, is to take "other material supplements and payment in kind" into account. The 2011 draft stipulates that the monetary portion of the wage must not be less than 50 percent of the minimum wage (SMIG, *salaire minimum interprofessionnel garanti*) for the industrial, commerce, and service sectors, but this has been increased under Seddiki's draft to 60 percent for live-in workers and 100 percent for those who live out.[8] During fieldwork, 60 percent of the SMIG would have meant 1,400dh monthly, while the average wage of thirty domestics who disclosed this information to me was 1,170dh monthly—more like 50 percent of the SMIG.

Asmae, a hospital nurse and activist who identified herself in chapter 1 as a *shaʻbī* (ordinary) employer ("We shaʻbī people, we can't count food"), surprised me by making a case for the injustice of the law: "It's the middle class who will suffer." Her complaint was that she and her friends and family had worked hard and educated themselves at a price. "Now uneducated women are to receive the same salary? . . . It's *thulm* [oppression] for the *muwazzafa* [public sector employee], this law." Asmae's public-sector employee is a female one, for this was not a battle of the sexes but one between women of different statuses. Asmae believes that paying 60 percent of the SMIG is too much, unless qualified workers like herself are suddenly going to be paid double the SMIG. Her own and her husband's monthly salaries combined do not exceed 4,000dh. Asmae's problem is not so much with her own wage but, like the laborers in the parabolic vineyard, with the difference between the value of her work and that of others. It is easier to enact the shaʻbī notion of largesse when it came to yogurt, it seems, than when it comes to still more symbolically loaded dirhams. The wage, as Kessler-Harris argues, is regulated by custom and tradition and is "simultaneously a set of ideas about how people can and should live and a marker of social status" (1990, 7). Sonencher (1989, 194) likewise argues that "the wage was a cipher in which a number of different assumptions were encoded" (cited in Meldrum 2000, 196). These ideas dictate to Asmae who should and should not be consuming what and where and provoke comments when people are seen to be out of place. On a walk around Mega Mall, Rabat's largest Western-style shopping center, Asmae remarked that most of the shops and cafés were too expensive for her own family, so why were there a number of Filipinas (assumedly domestic workers) sitting with friends in the food court? "They can't afford it!" Asmae exclaimed. While being able to identify as shaʻbī is not connected to income, being "middle class" is. For Asmae, the law presents a zero-sum game: by giving more to domestic workers, women of her own kind lose something. This has echoes in Moroccan legal reform more widely, particularly that which deals with relations within the family.

Writing on responses to the new Mudawwana, or Family Code (2004), Zvan Elliott contends that "for many people 'doing justice to women' implies injustice to men and, consequently, the family as the core of society, particularly in the absence of a system that would safeguard the rights of all, women and men alike" (2015, 139). She points out that the new Family Code claims to bring justice to women while preserving men's dignity (70), as though the former present a potential threat to the latter. Asmae too seems to want assurance that decent wages for domestic workers would not lower her own dignity and that of middle-class Moroccans more generally.

The question of wages for domestics is complicated by lawmakers arguing that having a domestic worker has become *ḍarūrī* (indispensable) for ordinary Moroccans. A representative of the Ministry of Employment explained, "The mother and father both work and need someone to take care of the house and children. It is not just well-off people, *nās kebār* [grand, important people], who have a domestic. And for someone who earns 3,000dh or 4,000dh or even 5 or 6,000dh, it is difficult for him to pay the domestic 2,000dh a month." In the past, the proportion of expenditure on employing a worker was significantly lower than this. Khelladi (1938) recorded the budgets of several low- and middle-ranking government employees recruited during the protectorate period (i.e., the kind of ordinary Moroccan who today earns 3,000-6,000dh/month). The monthly expenditure of an unmarried male schoolteacher near Casablanca was 895 francs (his salary was 1,200 francs) and included just 50 francs for a servant (Khelladi 1938, 265). A married teacher who had "three children of nine, seven and three years and a *petite bonne*" earned 1,650 francs a month and spent 1,535.50, of which the "*bonne* (with board and lodging)"—she slept in the kitchen—accounted for a mere 30 francs (266). Meanwhile, a "Europeanized" civil servant living with four children spent 2,125.55 francs monthly and allotted only 40 francs for the expense of keeping a servant (again, with board and lodgings). His noted expenditure for clothing did, however, include 200 francs for that of the bonne (276) while he spent 1,800 francs on clothing for the other four children combined. One wonders whether this civil servant claimed to treat the bonne "the same" as his own children. Perhaps part of what it meant to be "Europeanized" was a move away from such shaʿbī ideals.

For those who view a domestic as a necessity, affordability takes on the qualities of a citizen's right, especially where childcare is concerned. In eighteenth-century Britain, for example, Prime Minister Pitt's servant tax was supposed to tax luxury rather than necessity, so it was gentler on employers with children. If legislation made domestic help prohibitively expensive, then the government would appear to be actively withdrawing provision, despite the fact that they were not the ones doing the providing in the first place; instead they simply protected the "right" of the rich to exploit the poor by not regulating the relationship between the two. Lawmakers did not appear to consider the importance of supporting the development of care structures out of the home or promoting more flexible working hours for parents, which, argues Cox (2006, chap. 6), are crucial to diminishing reliance on domestic workers.

Although the latest draft of the Moroccan law for domestics limits the portion of remuneration to be paid in kind to live-in employees to 40 percent, this is still higher than in equivalent legislation elsewhere. Examples include South African law, which allows only a 10 percent reduction of salary for lodging; Spain limits payment in kind to 30 percent and Uruguay to 20 percent while Brazil forbids a reduction in salary for food, clothing, lodging, and hygiene facilities (CNDH 2013, 16). Calculating the monetary value of payment in kind is easier said than done. Danone yogurts stand out as being easily countable food because not much else is, considering Moroccan workers usually represent just one more hand dipping bread into the common pot. Assessing the value of clothing given to workers is more straightforward, but if push comes to shove and 60 percent of the SMIG must be paid in cash, the remaining in-kind payments will allow room for "tiny acts of domestic economy" (Steedman 2009, 152). Writing on eighteenth-century British service, Steedman suggests that "the tax may have meant that some employers paid for stay-mending less regularly, decided the girl could do without a new pair of shoes, that she didn't really need tea to her breakfast, and that reducing her dinner would do no harm" (152).

As part of the same effort to control the nonmonetary side of domestic arrangements, the ILO recommendations for accommodation seem overly prescriptive despite provisos for the local situation:

> When provided, accommodation and food should include, taking into account national conditions, the following:
> (a) a separate, private room that is suitably furnished, adequately ventilated and equipped with a lock, the key to which should be provided to the domestic worker;
> (b) access to suitable sanitary facilities, shared or private;
> (c) adequate lighting and, as appropriate, heating and air conditioning in keeping with prevailing conditions within the household; and
> (d) meals of good quality and sufficient quantity, adapted to the extent reasonable to the cultural and religious requirements, if any, of the domestic worker concerned (International Labour Office 2011, r. 201, paragraph 17).

The mere stipulation for a private room would exclude lower-middle-class employers such as my Océani friends, many of whom did not themselves sleep in a private room but rather on couches in the living room. Wealthier Moroccans might suggest that such people have no business employing a domestic, but the Moroccan draft law contains no description, even adapted to allow for such customs, of appropriate living conditions. CNDH recommend that this be rectified, citing the Swiss and South Africans, whose legal codes specify minimum requirements for domestic workers' lodging (CNDH 2013, 14).

The Moroccan draft law also comes under criticism for failing to address adequately the question of social security. Employers of other workers pay into a CNSS (Caisse Nationale de Securité Sociale) account on their behalf, and a 1971 *mrsūm* (decree, distinct from a *qanūn*, as it is not coercive) declared domestic workers eligible to benefit from the Caisse Nationale, but when I telephoned the CNSS information line to see how one would go about registering a domestic worker, the person on the other end hung up. I tried three times, explaining alternately in Arabic and French (no one else throughout fieldwork had struggled to understand me in either language), but each time the person hung up. I can only surmise they did not know the answer. A number of employers, particularly French or Moroccans who had lived in France, told me they had had every intention of "declaring" their domestic workers, but on inquiry they had discovered it was "nearly impossible" and so gave up.

Another widely discussed problem is that of *raqāba* (surveillance or inspection). The Projet de loi states that "a special body belonging to the governmental power responsible for work will undertake surveillance of the application of this law" (article 14). At the Ministry of Employment, I was told that raqāba was covered by two measures: first, the copy of the contract that has to be given to the *inspecteur du travail* (work inspector)—"when he sees the paper on his desk, he can read it and pick up on anything illegal, the wage, for example"; and second, the fact that when a worker complains, the inspecteur du travail will summon the employer. Yet, workers and others made comparisons with raqāba in workplaces such as factories or schools, arguing that someone needs to surveil what happens on the ground for domestic workers—i.e., inside the employer's home. "Who can guarantee for us that the law will be applied properly?" said one twenty-four-year-old domestic interviewed by a journalist (Touahri 2009). In the same vein, Fatima in l'Océan argued, "The gas man comes and knocks on the door, and the electricity man. They go in and check. But no one knocks on the door to check that the *kheddāma* (domestic worker) is given enough time off. There is no *taftīsh* [inspection], no raqāba. People say that now there are inspectors for the workers in factories, but not in houses."

Fatima also noted the possibility that employers might conceal illegal arrangements from an inspector and that a worker might, out of fear of the employer, state that she is treated according to the law even if she is not. I was reminded of comments made by Moroccans when, on arrival in the field, I explained I wanted to live with a family who employed a worker. I was repeatedly told, "You won't see anything. They'll be on their best behavior in front of you." Again, a precedent is found in eighteenth-century state surveillance of the employment of taxable servants, which "had a perceptible effect on how households were organized, from making sure that a servant in husbandry was never seen leading the horse out of the stable (for that would make him a 'stable boy'—a servant 'within the meaning of the act'), to judges of the King's Bench and Tax Office officials solemnly deliberating the question of 'Labourers or Husbandmen . . . Cleaning Boots'" (Steedman 2009, 133).

State Surveillance

Those people, including the representative of the Ministry of Employment, who claim that inspection of homes is practically impossible cite the *ḥurma* (sacredness or inviolability) of the house (which I discussed in the context of hospitality in chapter 4) and point to article 24 of the Constitution: "Every person has the right to the protection of his private life. The home is inviolable. Searches cannot be made except under conditions and in ways provided for by law." Moroccan law currently allows only the *parquet* (public prosecutor) access to the home. In a number of Latin American countries, conversely, "the constitutionally protected 'inviolability' of the home does not translate into a bar on inspections. The household becomes a workplace once a domestic worker is hired" (Blackett 2011, 39). Elsewhere, Blackett argues that "to remain a legally tolerated component of workplace relationships, a 'live-in' option should carry with it the understanding that the employer must cede a certain degree of domestic 'privacy' in recognition that the home had become both the workplace and dwelling of a particularly vulnerable category of worker" (2004, 263).

In earlier chapters I discussed the reluctance of sha'bī Moroccans to employ strangers. The representative of the Ministry of Employment saw this as a recent trend, commenting that "*already* some people are not employing because they do not want a stranger in their homes." Even Moroccans who do not consider themselves sha'bī, and who do without the personalized connection with workers that makes strangers so problematic, invoke the construct of the sacrosanct home to argue against inspection. The high walls and gates that enclose the villas in Mabella and Souissi are outward signs of this conceptualization of the home. Historically, one must admit, it was precisely the unique position of servants on the inside of the domestic fortresses of England ("a man's house is his castle") that made them particularly useful to the law. They could provide testimony in cases of adultery and divorce because "in the intimate worlds of household and community life few things escaped their notice or prying gaze" (Richardson 2010, 198). In a study of court records from early modern London, servants were found to make up 16 percent of witnesses who were summoned (Gowing 1996, 48, cited in Richardson 2010, 198).

A productive area of study for questioning the specificity of the home as a legal space is the largely feminist North American literature on domestic violence (Pleck 1987; Schneider 2002; Suk 2009), which argues that "concepts of privacy permit, encourage, and reinforce violence against women" (Schneider 2002, 87). Those who dominate the home space can, in the name of privacy, deny others legal protection from their power, whether they be a spouse, child, or domestic worker—although this literature does not mention the latter, a point made by Blackett (2011, 7) about Suk's work. Suk argues that while the home has historically been an exception to the reach of law and was protected instead by etiquette practices such as "calling," it is today "where the most basic questions about the relation between individuals and state power arise" (2009, 3), as legal practices narrow the difference between public and private spaces.[9] Analyzing US court proceedings regarding state intrusion in the home, Suk observes a gendered aspect to privacy—"to theorize privacy in the home is to imagine a woman" (130)— but she also identifies a class dimension: "privacy in the face of split consent (to enter) depends on whether one imagines the home and the woman in it as respectable and thus needing privacy, or alternatively, as disordered and thus needing police protection from privacy" (122–23). The same prejudices mean that while many British working-class families live in dread that social services may take away their children for the slightest mishap, parents whose homes are ostensibly middle class are less fearful of intervention. In Morocco, as elsewhere, employers and workers are both women in the home, but one is imagined as respectable, the other disordered; the claim of the former for privacy seems usually to override the claim of the latter for protection. Interestingly, the privacy of the worker is rarely problematized; if she is a live-in, an inspection of her workplace also means an inspection of her home.

The comments of the representative from the Ministry of Employment who agreed to an interview in June 2013 emphasized the symbolic rather than coercive role of this legislation. His version of the story involved the election of the new government as a "coincidence" postponing the progress of a law that would otherwise have come into force some time ago. Yet he did not appear to envisage enforcement of the law even once it has been approved, voted, signed, and announced, arguing instead for a gradual, progressive approach: "Of course this is a sector we need to protect, but progressively. . . . We need to go with the *rūḥ* [spirit] of the times. . . . You have to pick up the stick in the middle. If you pick it up at one end or the other, something else is going to be negatively impacted. . . . There will be difficulties if we demand [*exige*] too strongly that employers follow the law. It's delicate."[10]

Picking the stick up in the middle recalls Asmae's argument that the middle-class muwaẓẓafa ought to be the first to gain a pay raise. The "difficulties," which for the ministry representative centered on the minimum-wage stipulation, would fall on two sets of victims. First, if families stopped employing domestic workers because they could not afford to pay the legal wage, this would create "family problems" between the husband and wife of the employing family or dangers for the children.[11] Second, if a proportion of employers cease to employ, workers will "go out into the street."

That domestic work is the only thing that keeps swathes of uneducated women and girls out of prostitution is a widespread claim in Morocco and elsewhere. The "social theory—simple in the extreme—that had every dismissed maid-servant turn prostitute" (Steedman 2009, 141) was aired in Britain when Prime Minister William Pitt introduced a tax on female servants (1785) to help offset debt incurred from the American War of Independence.[12] There was little evidence for an increase in prostitution, or indeed a decrease in the employment of female servants as a result of the tax, although the numbers of returned, taxable female servants decreased as employers found "many ways through its labyrinthine system of exemptions of not paying it at all" (Steedman 2009, 157). As Steedman argues, "street-walking by dismissed maidservants was a cultural text, not a sociological observation" (149). At least public Moroccan comments seem free of the lewd jokes and sniggers that enlivened fiscal debates in eighteenth-century England and that were "part of the social comedy of denigrating maidservants" (149), but the feeling that "taking in" a woman to work as a domestic is effectively saving her from moral downfall plays into the notion of a charitable civilizing mission for which workers are expected to be grateful, as discussed in chapter 3. At the heart of these anxieties in Morocco is the negation of all things "street," as opposed to the house, where every respectable woman should be.[13]

The ministry representative blamed the bad treatment of domestic workers on "mentalities" that stem from "customs and traditions" in which domestic workers ranked low. He opposed contemporary attitudes with the justice of early Islamic ethics: "Mentalities have to change. People think, 'She's just a <u>kh</u>eddāma.' People need to realize that this is a human being. And [yet] the Prophet said to us, 'Give the worker his wage before his sweat dries.'" This ḥadīth, attributed to Ibn Mujah, is frequently cited by both employers and workers in the context of discussions about the mistreatment of workers. Significantly, the mistreatment in question is usually other than delayed payment, but the ḥadīth still serves as a plumb line. The government official went on to illustrate his vision of "progressive" correction with examples from Islamic culture:

> As with getting people to respect the space of the mosque ... if we tell people what to do they will say, "No, don't interfere." But if we say, "Peace be upon you, may God reward you with goodness, my brother. I have an observation [to make], if possible. I saw that when you pray you put your hands like that, but the Prophet, peace be upon him, told us, put your hands like this, because when you put your hands like that, it's like a dog sitting on the ground." That way, he'll say, "Ah, thank you. I didn't know."

He drew a second example from the "environment" of early Islam: "People drank wine a lot. And in the Qur'ān it says, 'Do not approach prayer when you are drunk' [Qur'ān 4:43]. He did not say, 'Do not drink wine.' Drink, but do not come to pray when you are drunk.[14] You see, we need to show people <u>sh</u>wīya b <u>sh</u>wīya [little by little]."

Reminiscent of the colonial *mission civilisatrice*, change would require "education" and "awareness campaigns," which approached the social problem in its entirety. Before the law was enforced, measures had to be taken to ensure the fifteen-year-olds who would be put out on the streets by newly criminalized employers would be taken care of. To act without the readiness of the Ministry of Youth and Sport, for example, would only make things worse: "There's no synergy," the government representative told me. The Ministry of Employment was not solely responsible for moving things forward; Morocco was simply not ready to follow such a law. For the moment, the role of the law was "to make people respect domestic workers."

My interlocutor did not seem worried that a law that the kingdom did not dare enforce may be detrimental not only to the respect of domestic workers but also to that of the judicial system. Significantly, the employment minister, speaking at a seminar in 2013 on "fundamental rights at work," concluded that the challenge would not only be to enrich and extend legislation for work but also to "make sure that it is applied and respected" (Salaheddine 2013). Debates surrounding the new Family Code were colored by a similar notion of gradualism. Moroccans told Zvan Elliott repeatedly that "the Mudawwana should be treated in a flexible way and that local traditions and customs overpower it" (Zvan Elliott 2015, 178). She argues that the oft-cited "ignorance" of the reformed law was not the reason for its lack of implementation but rather provided something at which politicians and activists could point their fingers in blame (139).

Some Moroccans were opposed to a domestic workers' law on principle, feeling that relations between workers and employers were best regulated by the moral rectitude of employers. Fatima Moustaghfir, lawyer and MP, points out that although several draft laws have been approved by the government, none have made it through parliament (Ali 2009). Moustaghfir would rather "relations between employers and domestic workers are approached from an ethical and moral point of view." Her own domestic worker, to whom she admits she owes the success of her career, has been with her since her days as a trainee lawyer. "She is not yet married, because she is very tied to our family. If she marries, she will live with me. I cannot envisage my life without her" (Ali 2009). Moustaghfir emphasizes the importance of mutual respect: "'These women work hard', she explains. 'The best salaries do not exceed 2000 dirhams, a sum that does not reflect the effort they make'. She asks all employers to 'thank them and encourage them' to keep up their good work" (Ali 2009). Reading between the lines, if we thank our domestics enough, maybe we can get away without passing legislation to allow them lives of their own.

A comment posted by "Soumia" (who claims to manage a domestic service agency) in response to an online news article (Touahri 2009) about the law (believed to be imminent at the time) reveals a reasoned if not evidence-based mistrust of state intervention: "Copying the west is not a good thing, for their laws create many more delinquents and thugs than there have been in our Arab and Muslim countries. The proof is there, all these former maids [in Morocco] are now cooks." Soumia's claim that leaving employers alone (90 percent of her clients are "truly *évolués* [cultivated] and . . . treat their household staff well" anyway) has resulted in domestics spontaneously up-skilling to become cooks is the converse of the fall into prostitution and delinquency that new legislation everywhere seems to threaten. The tone of Soumia's comment echoes that of colonial observers who envisaged the evolution of Morocco into a "modern" society, and the term *évolué* could have come from Lyautey.

The reflections of Soumia and Moustaghfir on domestic service go against the grain of a "women's human rights" frame, "in which transnational feminist activists have sought to make violence against women and other human rights issues a *state* problem that can be addressed legally and politically rather than a personal, private problem addressed within families" (Evrard 2014, 47). The Moroccan women's rights movement, Evrard argues, involved "translating transnational ideals of equality and women's human rights such that they are relevant to and resonant within the Moroccan context" (3). Perhaps precisely because domestic service is a women's issue, rather than an issue between women and men, domestic workers are largely lost in translation, but when the king promised the reform of the Family Code, one activist urged Moroccan women to "begin with ourselves . . . grow up, comport yourself like an adult. Don't accept being infantilized, even if it seems better to rely on someone else. . . . Don't replicate the same pattern of domination over less fortunate people, and here I refer in particular to household help" (Sakhri 2003, 4, cited in Evrard 2014, 2).

Organizing Domestic Workers

"Why does all other work have rights and not work in houses?" exclaimed Fatima in the context of a conversation about the ongoing protests against unemployment outside parliament. In chapter 5 I touched on possible reasons domestic workers do not form home village associations in Rabat: the high mobility of workers from one city to another and the structural constraints of work, which allow little flexibility in time off. The same applies to workers' associations. While many of the workers hope to settle in a city after marriage, they do not aspire to remain in domestic work. As Scadden wrote about Welsh domestics in London, "Young girls working well into the evening are not going to spend their precious free time going to meetings to better their conditions when they saw service as an interim part of their lives, a rite of passage between school and marriage" (2013, 127).

Writing on European domestic service, Sarasúa suggests that Marxist theories of value excluded domestics from such collective bargaining: "Since only workers producing surplus value were exploited, political activism and trade unionism made sense only among the truly exploited class. The same process that constructed factory workers (particularly male factory workers) as the real working class, constructed domestic workers (and female workers in general) as alien to it" (2004, 521). Sarasúa also suggests that proximity to the bourgeoisie and distance from the "real working class" prevented "nineteenth-century revolutionaries" and "twentieth-century trade unionists" from taking domestics into their fold (521). While the odds seem to be stacked against collective organization for domestics on many fronts, Blackett (2004, 266) identifies a point of strength: "Unlike the classic paradigm of the movement of most factors of production, employers of domestic workers are not footloose multinational enterprises who move across oceans in search of cheap labour pools. Rather, domestic workers' employers are very much tied to place. In other words, the work does not, indeed will not, go away."

The ILO recognizes that while protecting rights to collective bargaining and freedom of association is vital, these can be realized only if workers' and employers' organizations exist in the first place, to which "the isolation of the domestic worker and the usual absence of co-workers are practical challenges" (International Labour Office 2012, 26).[15] It recommends that member states should "give consideration to taking or supporting measures to strengthen the capacity of workers' and employers' organizations, organizations representing domestic workers and those of employers of domestic workers, to promote effectively the interests of their members, provided that at all times the independence and autonomy, within the law, of such organizations are protected" (International Labour Office 2011, r.201, paragraph 2).

Van Raaphorst describes domestics in the United States between 1870 and 1940 who, "against all odds," came together in both mainstream and independent workers' organizations.[16] Examples from Denver included an employment office card file for excluding "cross and undesirable mistresses" and setting down "how many children you have and how well or ill-trained they are" (1988, 191).[17] Van Raaphorst maintains, however, that rather than planned collective action, "far less dramatic but far more common was the individual practice of quitting. In other words high job turnover was a fundamental characteristic of domestic service and a way the worker sought to find improved working conditions. The high degree of domestic worker turnover may well have been a reflection of the many difficulties inherent in unionization. A much simpler and seemingly more successful tactic was simply to quit" (209–10).

This tactic of quitting equates with the way Moroccan domestics I knew coped with poor working conditions, as discussed in chapters 2 and 3. I suspect that once the draft law governing household workers comes into force, it will be put to use by employers against domestics who leave them in the lurch. Significantly, the majority of master-servant disputes discussed in Steedman's study of eighteenth-century England were brought to a local magistrate by employers complaining about servants leaving before time (Steedman 2009, 23; cf. Richardson 2010, 203). If the domestic worker contracts were legalized in Morocco, this could provide more reason to collectively bargain for better conditions, since the hitherto easy option of walking out would effectively be barred.

As far as I can tell, the closest thing to an organization of Moroccan domestic workers were the guilds for specialist workers of early twentieth-century Fes. Cooks, for example, were organized in a mixed corporation of largely former slaves, headed by a male *amīn* (secretary) (Le Tourneau 1949, 295, 562).[18] *Neggāfāt* (*marieuses*, or dressers of the bride), also predominantly freed slaves, were organized into companies (fifteen to forty women), each with a *patronne*, expert assistants, and apprentices, many of whom would never obtain a higher rank (527–8). When there was work, the neggāfāt earned enough to support themselves, but as most weddings took place in the summer, in the down season some would try to return to their old masters for a while, "on the condition that they take part in the housework, as previously"; others stayed a week with one client family, a week with another, and so on (529). Families readily obliged because this gave them favor with the powerful neggāfāt, who collectively were a force to reckon with. Domestic workers I knew hardly wielded this sort of power.

The Organisation démocratique du travail (ODT), a leftist Moroccan workers' union whose distinctive red and yellow placards often made it into front-page photos of protestors on Avenue Mohammed V, showed some concern for domestics' rights. They provided me with a leaflet produced by Organisation Yelli pour la protection de la fille, which called for a stop to the employment of child domestics, and were interested in discussing the matter with me. At the time of my fieldwork, there were, however, no Moroccan domestic workers among ODT's members, only a growing number of Filipina women who had joined and formed their own affiliated subgroup of the union, Filipino Migrant Workers in Morocco. Among other things, it aims to educate Filipinas about their rights and how to legalize their status in Morocco. They seem to be some way off from collective bargaining on issues like shorter working hours, for example. The formation of the group relied heavily on the passing of information through church-based social networks.[19] Many Filipinas shared apartments where they could rest and cook together on days off—something few live-in Moroccan domestics can afford.

Foreigners Welcome

The employment of Filipinas by wealthier Moroccans has become more common over the past decade, especially in Rabat and Casablanca (Lamlili 2008; Deback 2009). These workers, like Moroccan domestics, are not covered by the Code du travail, and most work without contracts, some outstaying their visas and remaining illegally. They are usually recruited by Moroccans living in the Persian Gulf area, agencies based in Jordan (Mounib 2012b, 21), or Filipinas living in Morocco. A Moroccan involved in the formation of the Filipino Migrant Workers in Morocco group introduced me to Maria, a Filipina who had lived in Morocco for fourteen years. As we drank expensive bottled water in the Western-style café where she worked, Maria explained how she recruited other Filipinas to come to Morocco as domestics:

> People see me here in [the café] because this is where the rich Moroccans come, and they ask me, please will you help me and bring me over a Filipina to work for me? And I do, but I don't ask for money. And even when they offer me a "gift," I do not take it, because if I take it, and something bad happens with the person, then I am responsible. But if I don't take it, then it's not my problem; it's their problem. I take their phone number, and I give the Filipina their phone number, and I tell them to call each other. Then it is between them and not me. . . . Even though my cousins are here, and my sisters and everyone, I have never had problems with them. [She knocks her hand on the table to "touch wood"]. I don't have problems with the employers, because I know them. If someone comes here all the time and I know them, then I know they are good. Or if I know they are bad, I do not send someone to them.

Although she kept clear of money, Maria was unwittingly reproducing the shaʿbī rhetoric of the *samsāra* (broker) who "knows" her clients.

A feature in the *Observateur du Maroc* (Mounib 2012a, 2012b) on the trend of employing Filipinas suggests that they are seen as a status symbol. In addition, they are valued by Moroccans for their English-language skills and reputation for working hard.[20] These ideas were echoed by employers I knew. Abdelouahed Souhail (minister of Employment at the time of my fieldwork) stated that he had heard Filipinas are "kind, gentle, receptive and professional" (Mounib 2012a, 24) while a mother of two who employs a Filipina as a nanny stated that "Filipina domestic workers generally excel in the area of discipline and are very professional. Their discretion, their care, and their habitually calm mood help children to concentrate. They are perfect" (20). This employer did not hide the fact that she preferred recruiting "a Filipina nanny rather than 'taking the risk' of hiring a Moroccan domestic" (20). This notion of the risky employment of Moroccans echoes that voiced by Océani residents about bringing strangers into the home. The logic of employing a Filipina is, however, the polar opposite of the sha'bī preference for locals. By hiring a complete foreigner, privacy becomes a nonissue: Maria, cited above, said a Moroccan had explained to her that Filipinas were preferable to Moroccan workers "because they cannot understand what is going on in the house, and they cannot tell a Moroccan. You know, for example, when the man . . ." Maria twisted her hands together, indicating she meant when the man has a lover. Filipinas as strangers are outside the moral, social, and linguistic community of Moroccans and therefore less threatening to employers' notions of privacy. A parallel can be drawn with Carsten's account of Malays working with Chinese outsiders in the fishing sphere so that commercial disputes are not divisive to relations between kinsmen and other more lasting local relationships (1989, 128).

Also at stake here is the level of experience and training undergone by the worker. Many Filipinas are mature women, often mothers themselves who have left children with parents and sisters back in the Philippines. Although some learn childcare on the job, many have undergone training and psychological aptitude tests. A family I knew in Rabat's wealthy Souissi district employed a Moroccan to do the housework, a Senegalese to cook, and a Filipina for childcare, a hierarchical international division of labor reflecting the qualifications of the workers. While the Moroccan had worked before, she was not educated; the Senegalese had done a course in massage (of questionable relevance for kitchen work); and the Filipina had completed two years' training: "Lydia learnt how to look after children, how to change a nappy, etc." explained a grown-up daughter of the employing family. She continued, "And she speaks English. The crazy thing is the Moroccan women ask to be paid the same price as these women who are trained, so of course you take trained women who speak English from other countries. So the Moroccan women work for other families maybe, who don't want to pay so much. . . . Soon the Moroccan women will be saying, 'These foreign women have taken our job!' Yes [shrugging her shoulders], that's globalization."

Much is made of the abuse of Filipina workers, although Mounib claims the majority she interviewed state, "without hesitation, that they find their Moroccan employers kinder than their Saudi, Kuwaiti or Jordanian counterparts" (2012b, 21). The first Filipina I met through the Organisation démocratique du travail had escaped via the balcony from the apartment where her employer had locked her in. Once ODT had gathered together a number of Filipina domestics who were prepared to speak about their experiences, they held a press conference on December 6, 2012, with speeches emphasizing that Malians and Senegalese face similar issues in Morocco, as do Moroccans who migrate for work as domestics in the Middle East. One Filipina testified to the fact that her employer, who appeared to mastermind a network bringing Filipina workers from the Middle East, had confiscated her passport, a well-used means of retaining foreign workers in the absence of a contract. Another claimed that her employer's husband, a retired general, had "used" her—interpreted by ODT as rape. The press printed the story as a rape case (see, for example, El-Massae 2012, 6), omitting the name of the general and his wife, who, as far as I know, were not charged.[21]

My friend Fatima, hearing about the alleged rape, cursed the general and commented characteristically that "foreigners can do that. They can say that this happened to me, that happened to me, my employer raped me. . . . But Moroccans cannot do that." Fatima's point is twofold—first that local conceptions of shame make it hard for victims of sexual violence to bring offenders to justice, and second, a point that the press conference failed to address: why all this fuss about the plight of Filipinas when, with the exception of child domestics, who frequently make headlines, Moroccan workers suffering similar abuses go relatively unnoticed?

Conclusion

The "servant problem" in postwar Britain, brought on by the availability and relative freedom of work for women in other sectors, was to be solved by enticing women back into a "profession": "its practitioners [would be] given a professional-sounding new title like domestic houseworker, and endowed with training, qualifications, diplomas and certificates" (Lethbridge 2013, 157). With this came a discourse of rights, but, as Light argues, "once women began to think of themselves as 'workers' with rights then much of the idea of service made little sense" (2007, 241). The same reasoning in Morocco means resistance on the part of employers to a law that seeks to bring "rights" to workers since it strips the arrangement of much that gave it meaning: the status-driven ethics of the mother-daughter relationship, charity, reward and gratitude, and, importantly for people like Asmae, status differentials. Take these away from sha‘bī employers and much of the attraction of having a live-in kheddāma is done away with while the possibility of being able to afford to legally employ and accommodate one is simultaneously diminished. Not only does the law make kheddāmāt into workers like other kinds of workers, but it also makes mulīn d-diyūr into employers like other employers—something the "one of the family" rhetoric seeks to avoid.[22]

Behind opinions on the draft law, whether its progress should be held back or hurried, lies a playoff between love and law: between Latifa Sebbari and the likes of Nigella Lawson. On the one hand, the sha‘bī view, based on the connectivity and inequality of ordinary Moroccans, recoils from the impersonal domesticity of the draft law. On the other hand, NGO workers and policymakers at both Moroccan and international levels see the personal as oppressive, to be remedied by "modern" state regulation ensuring the moral equality of atomized individuals. The two standpoints are inversions of each other, but neither is tenable. The stifling maternalism of the one and the cold courtroom of the other seem equally unsuitable places for domestic workers to end up. While adhering to a code of practice and checking boxes would work well for many things, there are certain kinds of jobs that cannot easily be reduced to sets of explicit rules.

Scott (1998, 310–11) makes this point using the example of "work-to-rule" action, where workers achieve the same disastrous effect on production of a walkout strike by following the workshop's rule book to the letter. Keeping things running smoothly, Scott argues, relies instead on local "mētis" or "practical knowledge," which state institutions generally fail to recognize. Practical knowledge of what? Common-sense or common-courtesy ways of relating to others are based not on "law" but on "love": "the strange human habit of kindness beyond the call of duty or the power of coercion, which, like the baby splashing happily in the bathwater, ought not to be thrown away" (Light 2007, 301). The call for explicit laws is based on the premise that some people are not kind, and this is not a new problem. What is new is the relationship of local communities to the state and the transparency that this requires in the name of "rights." Nonlegal forms of entitlement, meanwhile, slip quietly away so that people no longer feel they can greet neighbors in the street or legitimately ask to borrow an electric whisk. This is simply a rehearsal of Tönnies's [(1887) 2001] conceptual distinction between *Gemeinschaft* and *Gesellschaft*, imagined "community" against "society."[23] Those Moroccans who have no use for this sha'bī world have begun to free themselves from connections with neighbors and pseudo kin by employing Filipinas. What ordinary Moroccans will do, if not clean their own houses, remains to be seen.

Notes

1. Western feminists in the '60s and '70s attempted to change this conception by demanding "wages for housework" because they saw that the value of their domestic labor, essential to the reproduction of the labor force (Marx [1867] 1967), was being extracted by the owners of the factories where their husbands worked: James and Dalla Costa (1972); Seccombe (1974, 1975); Coulson, Magas, and Wainwright (1975); Federici (1975); Gardiner (1975); Smith, P. (1978); Kaluzynska (1980); Glazer (1984); Fortunati (1995).

2. On the Poor Law and labor generally, see Deakin and Wilkinson (2005); on its significance for domestic labor, see Steedman (2007, chap. 4; 2009, chap. 4) and Richardson (2010, chap. 9).

3. More recent drafts have not been made public. I cite my own translation from the Arabic text of this draft throughout.

4. Note that the household head is never called "the employer."

5. In the past Moroccan men did "work in houses" too, but this role has been entirely feminized in post-independence Morocco.

6. The ILO's guide to designing labor laws for domestic work suggests responsibility be placed on the employer for ensuring that the content of the contract is understood by the worker and observes that "a noteworthy feature of the legislation of both the United Republic of Tanzania and South Africa is that in both cases the employer must ensure that the terms are explained to the domestic worker in a manner that she or he understands. Such provisions may be an important corollary to the requirement for a contract in writing, as such a legal requirement is only of practical value if the worker, who may or may not be literate, fully understands the terms" (International Labour Office 2012, 18).

7. While perhaps true for the post-World War II economy, this is a shortsighted view of history since early rationalization largely ignored workers' needs.

8. The SMIG is fixed by governmental decree and applies to all sectors other than agricultural work. The slightly lower SMAG (*salaire minimum agricole garanti*, guaranteed minimum agricultural wage) applies to the agricultural sector and takes into account the lower cost of living in rural Morocco.

9. The boundary between the home and public space is marked by statements such as "the law will not invade the domestic forum or go behind the curtain" (State v. Black, 60 N.C. (Win.) 266, 267 (1864), cited in Suk 2009, 137), and "etiquette is a barrier which society draws around itself as a protection against offences the 'law' cannot touch" (Day 1844, cited in Suk 2009, 190).

10. The ministry representative code switched the French verb *exige* into his formal Arabic, which gave me the impression that he felt to make demands in an "unprogressive" way was a French thing to do, one that would be culturally insensitive.

11. It was unclear whether the ministry's representative envisaged danger in the shape of the children being left at home alone or being assigned the work the domestic worker would have done. Both are possible.

12. See Steedman (2009, chap. 5) and Brown, S. (2007, 17–18).

13. Cf. Graham (1988, 4) on domestics and slaves in nineteenth-century Rio de Janeiro for contrasting images of "*casa e rua*": "House signified a secure and stable domain. To house belonged the enduring relationships of family or blood kin. To street belonged uncertain or temporary alliances in which identity could not be assumed but had to be established. Street was suspect, unpredictable, a dirty or dangerous place."

14. Of course, a traditional scholar would be shocked by this interpretation.

15. See Convention No. 87 on Freedom of Association and Protection of the Right to Organize (1948) and Convention No. 98 on The Right to Organize and Collective Bargaining (1949).

16. The odds against these workers included "the individual nature of the work, the low economic and social status of the workers, the intense competition among them, their isolation from one another, their ethnic and racial origins, the low value placed on service occupations, the historic indifference of organized labor" (Van Raaphorst 1988, 187).

17. See also Salzinger (1991), Romero (1992), and May (2011) for collective action in the United States and Fremlin (1940, 161) on the Domestic Workers' Union founded in Britain in 1938. On the difficulties of organizing domestics in early twentieth-century Britain, see also Todd (2005, chap. 6); for the twenty-first century, see Cox (2006, 126–28).

18. Most corporations were all male, the only female corporations being the "*marieuses*" and "*chanteuses*," each led by a female amīn (Le Tourneau 1949, 295). Despite the large numbers of women spinners and embroiderers in the medīna and seamstresses and menders in the *mellāḥ* (Jewish quarter), they were not organized into corporations, probably because they worked at home (295). Cf. Massignon (1925) on Moroccan craft guilds and Snouck on late nineteenth-century Mekka ([1931] 1970, 23–31, 88).

19. See Liebelt (2011) on the importance of church groups for Filipina domestics and carers in Israel.

20. See Lan (2003) for a discussion of Filipinas who speak better English than their Taiwanese employers.

21. Later I was told the worker had resisted the general's advances until he offered money. Either way, the worker had suffered harassment.

22. In the contemporary British context, Cox found that "employers of domestic workers have much more complicated feelings about their position than employers in other situations and this tends to stop them wanting to take on that role in a straightforward way" (2006, 133).

23. Cf. Dresch and Scheele (2015).

CONCLUSION

While Filipinas are rarely described by Moroccans as "one of the family," many Moroccan workers are surprised when any other sort of role is offered them. In the case of Mui Latifa's "daughters," the "one of the family" rhetoric is bolstered by photographs, tales of milk teeth, and quantities of couscous, but more generally it has become "just words" and some token signs of care applied to a working relationship for the few weeks or months that it lasts. In either case, the repetition of "bintī [my daughter]" spins a cocoon around the exchange, a protective layer around a cozy world in which law has no place. These "daughters," for the most part, are no longer from the families of clients, neighbors, or friends but come rather from the "market" or even the "marketplace." The sha'bī ideal, illustrated by Dār Sebbari, is of a household that exchanges with others within the community (a community that preferably straddles city and countryside), but in a potentially alien or asocial space, like the new l'Océan that is being built, the household as a moral unit ceases to exchange externally, and communality with its attendant hierarchy exists only inside the house.

Hierarchy and Exchange

Writing on households in a Malay fishing community, Carsten (1989) posits a gendered opposition between the unity of the house and the division represented by economic exchange between houses. Outside the household, men fish and earn money in relations of exchange according to the business ethics of the Chinese, which assume individualism and competition. Their profits are symbolically transformed by women who, inside the household, cooperate in hierarchical relationships based on the morality of kinship. Both Malay and Moroccan households are organizations like firms, which operate somewhere along a continuum between "hierarchy" and "market" (Williamson 1975), doing some things internally and buying in others. Chapman and Buckley (1997) revisit Coase's (1937) question: "'Why do firms exist?' Why, are some transactions organised through a market (buying and selling between organisations or between individuals), and others organised through hierarchy (giving and taking orders, as in a company or university)? Why is it not feasible to have all transactions organised through a market? Or, conversely, why is the world not one big firm?" (Chapman and Buckley 1997, 225). Or, for that matter, one big family? The answer is that transaction costs mean there is a point at which it makes more sense to coordinate with those we know and trust, and whose work quality we can monitor, to get something done *within* the organization rather than to exchange with the outside world. Thus, "the boundary of every company is a specific solution . . . to transaction cost problems" (227). Decisions about this boundary are reasoned if not always rational, with considerations about, for example, the reliability of supply, often outweighing those of price.[1]

An ideal shaʿbī household gets things done by simply extending its boundaries to encompass and care for those who will do its work. But Moroccans who say "she's our daughter" of a domestic they hired through a samsāra, who herself may have met the worker only that day, are presenting as internal, that is moral, an outsourcing of labor that was arranged through market exchange rather than community. The fact that the worker may live in, more a consequence of the nature of her work than of her relationship to the household, masks the logic in operation. The "daughter" kind of domestic has the appearance of a low-status insider, like a member of staff in a firm, but, assuming she has no contract and may choose to leave after a month or two, is in effect as much an outsider, transacting with the household on an equal footing, as a new supplier of parts to that firm. Let us take Crawford's definition of Moroccan household membership: "Being *of a household* is to be economically obligated—you either work for and receive sustenance from a particular household or you do not. It is not an affective cultural category, or not just an affective category, but an economic one" (Crawford 2008, 51).[2] While paid domestic workers are expected to take on the affective role of daughter in the employing household, their economic obligations lie elsewhere. The value of their labor, their earnings, makes its way out of that household to another, usually the worker's natal home in the countryside.

The mūqef, on the other hand, represents a clear case of exchanging on the market rather than through internal hierarchy. Mūqef workers opt out of appearing as affective members of a hiring household. By remaining outsiders, just like suppliers to rather than employees of a firm, they can control their output and continue to exchange with others as it suits them. When I asked the workers at l'Océan mūqef if they were looking for "work by the month"—i.e., relatively permanent positions—all but a couple said that they preferred day labor. "I wouldn't work by the month if you paid me 60,000 dirham" was Nabila's response. Saida commented that employers for permanent positions had demanded too much of her: "Am I a *traks* [tracked excavator machine]?" Another explained, "We wouldn't work for someone *dīma* [always]. We are free. We can work hard one day and then sleep the next or go to some celebration."

The Sebbaris, like most households, engage in market exchange as well as hierarchy but keep the two distinct, as the following example involving Loubna's mother illustrates. Loubna had, like others we met in chapter 2, spent periods of time as a teenager living and working in Dār Sebbari and returned to work for them during my fieldwork but stayed barely a month. After that time, Loubna's mother, rarely finding work at the mūqef, would go to the Sebbaris' without their calling her. She complained that they paid her only 50dh, half the going rate for day labor. Loubna's mother saw the Sebbaris as patrons who should respond to her need: "My daughter stayed with them a lot. . . . They should take care of me." The Sebbaris' low pay showed they did not see her as a dependent. From the mulat d-dār's perspective, the convenience of mūqef workers lies in the fact that, as well as being easy to locate, as strangers rather than neighbors they can be hired with no strings attached. They do not take on a fictive kinship role. Risk is high, as these workers are an unknown quantity; but responsibility is low, and the relationship need last only a day. Loubna's mother was no stranger to the Sebbaris' and therefore not suitable for mūqef work there.

For people like the Sebbaris, exchange is also a possibility in community. This is evident in the reciprocal labor arrangements of both the sha'bī urban context (sometimes little more than a memory) and the Moroccan countryside, where the division of domestic labor within households, governed by hierarchies of mothers, daughters, sisters, and daughters-in-law, stands in opposition to that between households. Households exchanging with each other assumes at least moral equality between units. In the Atlas village of Crawford's study, while men work the fields on a rota system (one household assists another and is assisted in return later), women are responsible for preparing food for the work parties, and the assistance they draw from other households must also be reciprocated (Crawford 2008, 61). Women's cooperation for name-giving feasts in a village near Ceuta is described similarly by Rosander (1997, 117–18).[3] Maher, writing on rural Morocco, analyzes "action sets" formed by recruiting larger or smaller circles of cooperators (1974 121–23). The equality of participants in any given exchange network (whether kin-based or otherwise) has been noted in Tunis, where visits, gifts, and services must be reciprocated if relationships are to be maintained (Holmes-Eber 2003, 123). While women in one network might exchange labor such as a babysitting, a wealthier network might transact in imported goods (123).[4] Class difference between households therefore precludes the equal exchange of visits or services, much as Abu-Zahra argues for Tunisian peasant communities: if one brother is much poorer than the other, "the wife will refrain from visiting, because her friends and neighbors may think that she is helping her husband's brother's wife with the household chores in return for money or food" (1976, 163). We might apply to these North African contexts the terms of Bohannan's (1955) account of spheres of exchange among the Tiv (Nigeria), in which conversions between categories were morally charged—e.g., an exchange of brass rods (in the "prestige" category) for yams (in the "subsistence" category). While exchanging labor for labor is "neutral," the "conversion" of labor into something of a different order (access to work, education, or material goods) has implications for the status of those involved. It signals asymmetric relations of dependency.[5] Thus, in Tunisia, "A married sister may also receive support from her wealthier brothers if her husband is in need . . . [and] in return for these services she has to help her brothers' wives with the household chores. All this would weaken the position of the husband, as he would not have exclusive rights over his wife" (Abu-Zahra 1976, 166).

Crawford points out that exchanges of labor in rural Morocco operate "over time periods that extend from a few hours to multiple generations" (2008, 17). I did not spend nearly sufficient time in any of the villages I visited to gain an idea of the long-term rhythm of give and take, but I did take part in the sharing of tasks between households related by kinship in the run-up to festivities. Malika's wedding was one such occasion. Malika's mother had six aunts, all of whom were expected to help, together with their daughters. The mother of one of these girls found us hard at work and began arguing with one of her nieces and telling her daughter to come and do chores in her own home instead. For her part, she announced, "I'm going to *smāḥ fīhum* [let them down] in this wedding. No one helped me in my son's circumcision." Incidentally, domestics apply the same phrase (*smāḥ fīhum*) to the act of walking out on employers without notice. Later, other family members who caught wind of this attitude discussed how they had, in fact, all rallied around and helped for the circumcision party; the aunt owed them her labor in return at this wedding. The feeling was one of an overwhelming amount that needed to be done, and the challenge was how to get people to help without their having the impression they had been invited for that reason alone. There was a tension between guests' expectations to be on the receiving end of hospitality and the hosts' expectations of support from family (referred to as "us") in the hosting of *barānīyīn* (outsiders), namely the groom's family. Two of Malika's older cousins were assigned the task of cleaning and cutting up the offal from the cow that had been slaughtered. The eldest confided, "I didn't come to do *temmāra* [hard work] like this." She complained less loudly than some of the other relatives and did the work anyway, but she seemed to be expressing what everyone was feeling: that this wedding was hard work. For the wedding celebration itself, the women who were closest to the bride's mother barely showed and indeed did not hire a *tak<u>sh</u>iṭa* (traditional dress for dancing) like the other women but remained in "pajamas," as they were busy with the catering.

The distinction between us (who worked) and the barānīyīn (who were served, watched the spectacle, and had little idea how much work had gone on behind the scenes) was exacerbated by the poverty of Malika's family. They could afford to cater only for a select group, so the best food went to the barānīyīn, and while neighbors and children from the entire community had gathered to watch the procession of gifts from the groom driven on a donkey cart to the bride's house, only the groom's folk were invited in to take tea. There would not have been enough cakes and sweets to go around for everyone who had gathered in the street. Malika's people held back while members of the groom's family were present, eating freely only once they had gone. I had not known who was part of the family and who was not during the procession of gifts to the house and took photos of all and sundry who asked. But Malika, seeing the photos later, remarked, "They aren't family!"—reflecting, as in Mui Fatiha's and Jihane's albums, the use of the photographic frame for marking the boundary between "kin" and "non-kin." Unlike the Sebbaris, whose wealth meant they could afford to make others into insiders to do work for them in the <u>sh</u>aʿbī fashion, as well as giving out to those less well off in the neighborhood, Malika's was a <u>sh</u>aʿbī family who used their own people to get work done and whose openness was restricted to those outsiders they could afford to host. Malika's household was characterized by a tightfistedness in which people struggled to assert their positions: few felt they had enough or were respected enough, and nearly everyone felt too much work was asked of them. It was a difficult place to be, and I came away understanding Malika's preference for a position as a paid domestic far away in another household, until she was "saved" by a husband. While the Sebbaris ostensibly hired Malika, a daughter, to carry on being a daughter, implying an exchange between equal households, the outcome was anything but equal. Malika, who came somewhere near the bottom of the pecking order at home, found herself at the very bottom of the heap at Dār Sebbari, a fact for which her pay hardly accounted. It made sense to simply say, "They aren't family" and to move on. At home, meanwhile, her pay did count for something. The tensions inherent in such cases are less about a transition from hierarchy to market exchange than simply two visions of the same thing.

Households and Gender

The work of Carsten and Crawford is striking, not least because households have gone relatively unnoticed by ethnographers while kinship, albeit "transformed" through a shift to "new arenas of study and new conceptualisations" (Lamphere 2001, 21), is a staple of anthropological study. This is perhaps because fieldwork is largely done by young people without long-term constraints (Dresch 2000) and because anthropologists have struggled to define the household, as Yanagisako's (1979) review of the literature demonstrates. She observes that, although the terms *family* and *household* are often conflated, most researchers agree that family is about kinship (itself an odd-job term) whereas household is about propinquity, namely a shared living space. Although residence patterns can "provide a basic index of the boundaries of the internal structure of domestic groups" (Fortes 1958, 3), the criterion of coresidence cannot by itself define the household. Yanagisako (1979, 164) raises the question of whether to include servants, apprentices, boarders, and lodgers and why individuals living alone constitute "households" but institutions such as orphanages and army barracks do not.[6] These examples illustrate that a household is more than a group of individuals sharing a living space; "some set of activities" is also shared (165). Grouped loosely as "domestic" activities, these most often involve food production and consumption and social reproduction (childbearing and child-rearing). People who do not live together may, of course, also engage in these activities. Bender (1967) therefore argues for a conceptual separation of families, coresidential groups, and domestic functions that allows for a more precise understanding of what a particular social unit does, as well as the possibility of several types of coresidential groups coexisting at different levels within the same society: "An individual may simultaneously belong to two or more nested coresidential groups: for example, a nuclear family hut, in a patrilaterally extended family compound, within a patrilineal descent-based settlement" (Yanagisako 1979, 165).

Only by going beyond questions of definition are we able to analyze how households connect as units to make up society. Characterized in terms of repute and honor, as Bourdieu (1965, 1977) does, male exchanges between households, particularly among brothers and cousins, have been ready material for ethnographers. Relations among women, however, have been routinely dismissed as "gossip." Meneley's (1996) study of a Yemeni town is a rare example of a focus on female interhousehold exchange. Different houses are linked together by secrecy and prestige in what she terms "tournaments of value" played out through visiting and hospitality. But little has been written about relations within households—that is, female domesticity and hierarchy. The mother-daughter relationship, an elementary structure of kinship if ever there was one, hardly features at all. Mothers-in-law and daughters-in-law fare a little better; these, after all, are relationships that result from exchange with the outside, articulating Carsten's tension between unity within and division (enabling exchange) without—the very stuff of *parenté* in Lévi-Strauss.

Writing on Maghrebi kinship structures, Charrad also identifies these two contradictory principles: "a principle of unity, based on ties among men in the agnatic lineage, and a principle of division, introduced by the necessity to accept in the kin group a number of women from other lineages" (2001, 51). This is common to patrilineal systems. Stone (2006, chap. 3) uses ethnographic data on exogamous patrilines among the Nuer and Nepalese Brahmans to show that women as wives from outside are seen as divisive, a threat to the solidarity of males in the patriline, but vital to its continuity. The literature on patrilateral parallel cousin marriage in Arab societies also deals with this: FBD marriage keeps "the secret of family intimacy" safe, whereas marriage with a stranger "creates a breach in the protective barrier which surrounds the intimacy of the family" (Bourdieu 1965, 227–28).[7] By forming a conjugal unit that might break away, the daughter-in-law represents the potential for division in the agnatic kin group. This threat can be kept at bay by relegating the daughter-in-law to a low status position; assigning her the worst of the housework is a handy mechanism to do this. The mother-in-law, as mulat d-dār in charge of the domestic realm, is naturally the one who implements this subordination. Thus the young wife experiences her mother-in-law as *personally* dominating while she is in fact merely the domestic face of the agnatic group. Implementing this subordination, the mother-in-law is masculinized, as, Hammoudi (1997) argues, are all Moroccan power holders in relation to feminized power seekers. Belghiti notes that she takes on the identity of the men of the group: "The mother-in-law is a woman in spite of everything ... but one who detaches herself from the women's group and acquires certain privileges otherwise reserved for men, such as being able to go about freely, to go to the market. The mother-in-law in fact tends to play the role of intermediary between the female and male worlds. She is rid of all the prohibitions that weigh down on the other women and tends to side with male opinion" (1971, 327). Thus, while the older woman's desire for revenge might play a role, such psychological explanations do not satisfactorily account for the perpetuation of the typically servile position of the daughter-in-law. The key lies beyond relations between individuals, in the larger structure of the patrilineage. We have seen how the relationship between employer and worker is similarly embedded in a continuum of power relations: colonizer and colonized, state and citizen, man and woman, mother and daughter, older sister and younger sister. While our focus has been on relations between women, these are perhaps more fully understood as in part a reflection of relations between the genders.

Feminist research has long sought to uncover why housework nearly always falls to women, and this literature is associated with the positing of binaries such as nature:culture, outside:inside, and public:private (Ortner 1974; MacCormack and Strathern 1980). A central hypothesis suggests that women's bodies link them to the care of children, and they are therefore associated with reproductive rather than productive labor.[8] This correlates with a spatial division in which woman is linked to the domestic and man to the public space, which seems everywhere to mean women's subordination (Rosaldo 1974).[9] In her study of domestic work in Turkey, Ozyegin (2001) found that it was performed solely by women. She follows West and Zimmerman's (1987) notion of "doing gender" and Berk's (1985) view that the division of household labor facilitates the production not only of goods and services but also of gender itself. Thus "women make themselves accountably feminine by doing housework and men make themselves accountably masculine by avoiding it" (Ozyegin 2001, 172–73). Ethnographic literature on North Africa points to the importance of similar normative beliefs according to which *doing* certain activities constitutes *being* a man or a woman (Rugh 1985, 276). In Morocco, we find strictly gendered divisions of labor: men ideally never work in the house. Maher recounts how, when she asked women in Berber-speaking hamlets to describe their daily activities, she failed to elicit a response: "Perhaps the only feasible reply to my question would have been 'I have been being a woman all day'" (1984, 74). For both men and women in subsistence settings, little distinction is made between work and "being busy" (Crawford 2008, 31), but "money transactions tend to transform social roles by removing the activities attached to them from the sphere of rights and duties and giving them a quantitative aspect: so much work for so much pay" (Maher 1984, 75). And as soon as there is the opportunity for marketable work, this is usually taken first by men. Cooking in the home is done by women, in the restaurant by men. As if to necessitate a different value judgment of the work (Mead 1949), men and women may perform the same tasks using a different method. In large families, for example, young men may do their own washing and that of their male elders: "Men always pound the clothes with their feet, thus distinguishing their activity from that of women, who crouch over the lid of a petrol drum, rubbing the clothes with their hands" (Maher 1974, 110). By contrast, women's activities are defined as "not work" and are therefore seen as part of their lives as women.[10] Even when women marketed, this was outside the monetary sphere. Benet, for example, discusses women peddlers who visit the village when the men are away: "This uncommercial form of trade is undisputed women's prerogative; no money is used, barter is the governing principle" (1970, 182).

The association between women and the domestic realm in Morocco means the act of doing housework can serve as a metonym for the feminine. What happens, then, when men do housework? The idea is played with in Moroccan media. I once caught the end of a Moroccan sitcom in which a man wearing an apron and holding a duster was repeatedly offering, in a feminine voice, to make tea for his wife. At first the wife just looked embarrassed and declined, but she soon appeared to crack, begging him to remove the apron and leave her alone. My host family explained that earlier in the episode, she had put a spell on him so that he would serve her, "but in the end she didn't like it." The wife appeared deeply troubled by the usurpation of her own role and the emasculation of her husband. Moreover, the husband's hovering around in the domestic space is felt as an intrusion in the wife's domain—"a husband's place is not in the home" (Oakley

1974, 153).[11] In a similar vein, in 2011 Morocco's second national channel broadcast a reality TV show, *Madame M'safara* (literally *Madam Is Away*), that documented what happened when the wives in ten working-class families occupying the same Casablancan apartment block were taken on holiday to Marrakech. Goodbye scenes involved hasty lessons in how to cook and clean as, left behind with their children, husbands were forced to take on domestic responsibilities. The gendered division of labor was more reinforced than challenged as a result. Men were self-conscious about the "femininity" of the tasks they were performing, and their jokes reflected this: "*Anā kheddāma!* [I'm a servant!]" said one father to another as he peeled carrots, using the feminine form of the word when he could have used the masculine, *kheddām*. He felt not only servile but also feminine.

The image of a feminized man doing housework is not new. A well-known Sufi saint, Abou Ya'za (eleventh century), reportedly dressed in women's clothing to wait on a disciple and his wife [Tādilī (1229) 1984, 218–19]. In fact it was common for medieval mystical initiates to pass through a stage of "femininity" in the passage to masterhood: "The fuqarā living in Ilgh prepare the evening meal. Within a zāwiya this goes unnoticed; but for men of their cohort, apart from in exceptional circumstances (such as travel or work away from home), the act of cooking would reflect badly on their masculine identity.... Those under al Haj 'Ali's guidance also collected wood and used a handmill to grind grain—a most typically feminine task. When they are on the move... they must make the master's bed, have water ready for his ablutions, and, sometimes, wash his clothes" (Hammoudi 1997, 97). In this paradigm, the disciple "becomes a woman for a while" (148–49). The result of repeated master-disciple relationships over time is a "chain of men whose [symbolic] procreation does not involve women" (148–49). Hammoudi argues that this stylized inversion involving signs of femininity (submission and service) forms the basis of a specifically Moroccan authoritarianism present in all spheres of life, from the level of family to that of state.[12] Female power is systematically bypassed, and the structural tension inherent in Moroccan patriarchal society (that women are needed to maintain the agnatic line) is circumvented.

States and economics versus family and hierarchy are constantly being played out in male-female terms. One of the reasons Moroccan domestic service is so problematic is that these things threaten to collapse in on themselves. The economics of market exchange are being brought by women into the familial space of the home while the state, with its predominantly male lawmakers and inspectors, is imposing its own version of equality on local forms of hierarchical community. The institutions that differentiated ordinary Moroccan women from their hitherto social inferiors appear to be losing their sway, and, noticeably, men have little to say about it. This is a matter between women. For the moment, a woman can indeed "have it all" on the condition that other women do her housework.

Notes

1. A problem with this, of course, is that it sets up a false opposition between, on the one hand, trust and cooperation and on the other, rationality and selfish optimization. "Most inter-firm relationships, which might be expected to display market characteristics, have about them aspects of relationship, trust, consideration, friendship, loyalty, commitment and so on" (Chapman and Buckley 1997, 230).

2. Cf. Seddon's use of "budget unit" for rural Morocco: "a group of individuals sharing a common 'fund' and exchanging goods between each other without reckoning" (1976, 177–78).

3. For Amman in Jordan, Shami makes a distinction between "mutual-aid units"—households that reciprocate daily in housework, shopping, and childcare—and "special-purpose units," or those formed around a single task (1997, 94). Cf. Ghosh (1987) on reciprocal labor among *fellāḥīn* in northwestern Egypt and Lamphere's more general "proximity strategy" for recruiting help beyond the residence group (1974, 102).

4. On childcare arrangements between women in Amman's squatter settlements, see Shami and Taminian (1995).

5. Cf. Piot (1991) on relational spheres of exchange among the Kabre (Togo).

6. Laslett describes domestic groups in seventeenth-century England where "family" encompassed the household head, his wife, paid employees, apprentices, maidservants and children (1965, 1–3).

7. See further Ayoub (1959); Murphy and Kasdan (1959); Keyser (1974); Bourdieu (1977); Holy (1989).

8. For cross-cultural analyses of the gender division of labor, see Boserup (1970); Brown, J. (1970); Murdock and Provost (1973); Rosaldo (1974); Brudner and White (1977); Ember (1983); Afshar (1985). See also Toth (1991) on gendered labor in rural Egypt.

9. For critiques of the public/private dichotomy, see Mathieu (1973), Pateman (1983), Lamphere (1993), and, specific to the Middle East, Nelson (1974) and Shami (1997, 85–88). See also Shirley Ardener's ([1981] 1993) volume on women and space, which explores the intersection of social and spatial boundaries in different societies.

10. Sacks (1974) illustrates this with African examples, where a shift from production for immediate use to production for exchange causes the increased domestication of women. See Baron (1994) and Badran (1995) on the reinforcement of women's domestic roles in modernizing Egypt. Cf. White's (1994) Turkish study in which atelier owners paid pieceworkers a low rate, claiming that the women did not see it as "work."

11. Cf. the British cliché of the wife who complains that she married "for better or for worse, but not for lunch" (Hibourne 1999). In Morocco, lunchtime is in fact the only time a man may legitimately be found at home during daylight hours (Bourqia 1996, 25).

12. See also Combs-Schilling (1989); Bourqia and Miller (1999).

REFERENCES CITED

Books and Articles

Abdal-Rehim, Abdal-Rehim Abdal-Rahman. 1996. "The Family and Gender Laws in Egypt during the Ottoman Period." In *Women, the Family, and Divorce Laws in Islamic History*, edited by Amira Sonbol, 96–111. Syracuse, NY: Syracuse University Press.

Aboderin, Isabella. 2006. *Intergenerational Support and Old Age in Africa*. London: Transaction.

Abu-Lughod, Janet. 1970. "Migrant Adjustment to City Life." In *Readings in Arab Middle Eastern Societies and Cultures*, edited by Abdulla M. Lutfiyya, 664-78. The Hague: Mouton.

———. 1971. *Cairo: 1001 Years of the City Victorious*. Princeton, NJ: Princeton University Press.

———. 1980. *Rabat: Urban Apartheid in Morocco*. Princeton, NJ: Princeton University Press.

Abu-Lughod, Lila. 1986. *Veiled Sentiments: Honour and Poetry in Bedouin Society*. Berkeley: University of California Press.

———. 2002. "Egyptian Melodrama—Technology of the Modern Subject?" In *Media Worlds. Anthropology on New Terrain*, edited by Faye Ginsburg, Lila Abu-Lughod, and Brian Larkin, 115-33. Berkeley: University of California Press.

———. 2005. *Dramas of Nationhood: The Politics of Television in Egypt*. Chicago: University of Chicago Press.

Abu-Zahra, N. 1976. "The Family in a Tunisian Peasant Community." In *Mediterranean Family Structures*, edited by John G. Peristiany, 157-71. Cambridge: Cambridge University Press.

Adam, André. 1973. "Berber Migrants in Casablanca." In *Arabs and Berbers: From Tribe to Nation in North Africa*, edited by Ernest Gellner and Charles Antoine Micaud, 137–62. Lexington, MA: Lexington.

Afshar, Haleh, ed. 1985. *Women, Work and Ideology in the Third World*. London: Tavistock.

Ahearn, Laura. 2001. *Invitations to Love: Literacy, Love Letters, and Social Change in Nepal*. Ann Arbor: University of Michigan Press.

Alber, Erdmute. 2010. "No School without Foster Families in Northern Benin: A Social Historical Approach." In *Parenting after the Century of the Child: Travelling Ideals, Institutional Negotiations and Individual Responses*, edited by Haldis Haukanes and Tatjana Thelen, 57–78. Aldershot: Ashgate.

Alber, Erdmute, Sjaak van der Geest, and Susan Reynolds Whyte, eds. 2008. *Generations in Africa: Connections and Conflicts*. Berlin: Lit.

Albin, Einat. 2012. "From 'Domestic Servant' to 'Domestic Worker'." In *Challenging the Legal Boundaries of Work Regulation*, edited by Judy Fudge, Shae McCrystal and Kamala Sankaran, 231–39. Oxford: Hart.

Ali, Siham. 2009. "Les maîtresses de maison et les femmes de ménage font état de leurs doléances." *Magharebia*. Accessed September 26, 2014. http://magharebia.com/fr/articles/awi/reportage/2009/12/04/reportage-01 (site discontinued).

———. 2010. "Moroccan Bachelors Seek Wives Who Work." *Magharebia*. Accessed September 26, 2014. http://magharebia.com/en_GB/articles/awi/features/2010/08/09/feature-01 (site discontinued).

Amrani, Yousra. 2006. " Une femme de ménage? Passez par l'agence." *Magazine, Jeunes du Maroc*. Accessed August 13, 2012. http://www.jeunesdumaroc.com/+4734-Une-femme-de-menage-Passez-par-l+.html (site discontinued).

———. 2012. "Femmes du 'moukef': l'espoir renait chaque jour." *Le Matin*, August 7, 2012.

Andall, Jacqueline. 2000. *Gender, Migration and Domestic Service: The Politics of Black Women in Italy*. Aldershot: Ashgate.

Anderson, Bridget. 2000. *Doing the Dirty Work? The Global Politics of Domestic Labour*. London: Zed.

Anderson, Paul. 2011. "'The Piety of the Gift': Selfhood and Sociality in the Egyptian Mosque Movement." *Anthropological Theory* 11: 3–21.

Appadurai, Arjun. 1981. "Gastro-Politics in Hindu South Asia." *American Ethnologist* 8 (3): 494–511.

———. 1996. *Modernity at Large: Cultural Dimensions of Globalization*. Minneapolis: University of Minnesota Press.

Apt, Nana. 2005. *A Study of Child Domestic Work and Fosterage in Northern and Upper East Regions of Ghana*. Paris: UNICEF.

Ardener, Shirley. (1981) 1993. *Women and Space: Ground Rules and Social Maps*. Oxford: Berg.

Armbrust, Walter. 1996. *Mass Culture and Modernism in Egypt*. Cambridge: Cambridge University Press.

Atia, Mona. 2012. "'A Way to Paradise': Pious Neoliberalism, Islam, and Faith-Based Development." *Annals of the Association of American Geographers* 102:808–27.

Au fait. 2013. "Mort de la petite Fatima à Agadir: punir mais aussi réhabiliter les autres petites filles exploitées." Accessed September 25, 2014. http://www.aufait.ma/2013/09/23/punir-mais-aussi-rehabiliter-les-autres-petites-filles-exploitees_9256 (site discontinued).

Austen, Jane. (1814) 2003. *Mansfield Park*. London: Penguin.

Ayoub, M. 1959. "Parallel Cousin Marriage and Endogamy: A Study in Sociometry." *Southwestern Journal of Anthropology* 15: 266–75.

Azizi, Abdellatif, El. 2005. "Société. Bonne à torturer." *TelQuel*. Accessed April 24, 2012. http://www.telquel-online.com/archives/158/sujet4.shtml (site discontinued).

Badran, Margot. 1995. *Feminists, Islam, and Nation: Gender and the Making of Modern Egypt*. Princeton: Princeton University Press.

Bakan, Abigail, and Diava Stasiulis, eds. 1997. *Not One of the Family: Foreign Domestic Workers in Canada*. Toronto: University of Toronto Press.

Bano, Masooda. 2012. *The Rational Believer: Choices and Decisions in the Madrasas of Pakistan*. Ithaca, NY: Cornell University Press.

Bargach, Jamila. 2002. *Orphans of Islam: Family, Abandonment, and Secret Adoption in Morocco*. Oxford: Rowman & Littlefield.

Baron, Beth. 1994. *The Women's Awakening in Egypt: Culture, Society, and the Press*. New Haven, CT: Yale University Press.

Baron, Huot, and Paye Baron. 1936. "Condition économique et niveaux de vie des travailleurs indigènes au Douar Doum." *Bulletin économique du Maroc* 111 (13): 176–84.

Barraud, Emilie. 2011. "L'adoption au prisme du genre : l'exemple du Maghreb." *CLIO, Histoire, Femmes et Sociétés* 34: 153–65.

Bauman, Zygmunt. 2000. *Liquid Modernity*. Cambridge: Polity.
Beeton, Isabella. (1861) 1907. *Mrs Beeton's Book of Household Management*. New edition. Revised. Enlarged. Brought up to date. And fully illustrated. London: Ward, Lock.
Belarbi, Aicha. 1988. "Salariat féminine et division sexuelle du travail dans la famille: Cas de la femme fonctionnaire." In *Femmes Partagées: Famille-travail*, edited by Fatima Mernissi, 79–98. Casablanca: Le Fennec.
Belghiti, Malika. 1971. "Les relations féminines et le statut de la femme dans la famille rurale—dans trois villages de la Tessaout." In *Etudes sociologiques sur le Maroc*, edited by Abdelkebir Khatibi and Paul Pascon, 289–361. Rabat: Bulletin économique et social du Maroc.
Bender, Donald R. 1967. "A Refinement of the Concept of Household: Families, Co-residence, and Domestic Functions." *American Anthropologist* 69: 493–504.
Benet, Francisco. 1970. "Explosive Markets: The Berber Highlands." In *Peoples and Cultures of the Middle East, Vol I*, edited by Louise Sweet, 173–203. New York: Natural History.
Benezha, Hajar. 2013. "Travail domestique: Les mesurettes du projet de loi." *L'Economiste* no. 4025. Last modified July 5, 2013. http://www.leconomiste.com/article/906411-travail-domestiqueles-mesurettes-du-projet-de-loi.
Bennett, Lynn. 1983. *Dangerous Wives and Sacred Sisters: Social and Symbolic Roles of High-Caste Women in Nepal*. New York: Columbia University Press.
Benthall, Jonathan. 1999. "Financial Worship: The Quranic Injunction to Almsgiving." *Journal of the Royal Anthropological Institute* 5 (1): 27–42.
———. 2012. "Charity." In *A Companion to Moral Anthropology*, edited by Didier Fassin, 359–75. Oxford: Wiley-Blackwell.
Berk, Sarah Fenstermaker. 1985. *The Gender Factory*. New York: Plenum.
Bin Ashu, Khadija. 2013. "Qiṣa thlāth khādimāt fārqna alḥayat bisabab al-ʿunf al-mufrit li-mushaghlayhina." *Sahara al-Maghribiya*, May 27, 2013.
Blaauw, Phillip, Huma Louw, and Rinie Schenck. 2006. "The Employment History of Day Labourers in South Africa and the Income They Earn—a Case Study of Day Labourers in Pretoria." *South African Journal of Economic and Management Sciences* 9 (4): 458–71.
Blackett, Adelle. 2004. "Promoting Domestic Workers' Human Dignity through Specific Regulation." In *Domestic Service and the Formation of European Identity: Understanding the Globalization of Domestic Work, 16th–21st Centuries*, edited by Antoinette Fauve-Chamoux, 247–73. Bern: Peter Lang.
———. 2011. "Introduction: Regulating Decent Work for Domestic Workers." *Canadian Journal of Women and the Law* 23, Special Issue: Regulating Decent Work for Domestic Workers: 1–96.
Bloch, Maurice. 1973. "The Long Term and the Short Term: The Economic and Political Significance of the Morality of Kinship." In *The Character of Kinship*, edited by Jack Goody, 75–86. London: Cambridge University Press.
———. 1982. "Death, Women and Power." In *Death and the Regeneration of Life*, edited by Maurice Bloch and Jonathan Parry, 211–39. Cambridge: Cambridge University Press.
Bodenhorn, Barbara. 2000. "'He Used to Be My Relative': Exploring the Bases of Relatedness Among Iñupiat of Northern Alaska." In *Cultures of Relatedness: New Approaches to the Study of Kinship*, edited by Janet Carsten, 128–48. Cambridge: Cambridge University Press.
Bohannan, Paul. 1955. "Some Principles of Exchange and Investment among the Tiv." *American Anthropologist* 57 (1): 60–70.

Bonner, Michael, Mine Ener, and Amy Singer, eds. 2003. *Poverty and Charity in Middle Eastern Contexts*. Albany: State University of New York Press.
Bornstein, Erica. 2012. *Disquieting Gifts: Humanitarianism in New Delhi*. Palo Alto, CA: Stanford University Press.
Borrmans, M. 1955. "La femme de ménage musulmane en service dans les familles européennes." Diplôme d'Etudes Supérieures de Psychologie Sociale, Alger.
———. 1977. *Statut personnel et famille au Maghreb: De 1940 à nos jours*. Paris: Mouton.
Boserup, Ester. 1970. *Women's Role in Economic Development*. London: Allen & Unwin.
Bougdal, Lahsen. 2010. *La petite bonne de Casablanca*. Paris: L'Harmattan.
Boughali, Mohamed. 1974. *La représentation de l'espace chez le Marocain illettré, Mythes et Traditions Orales*. Paris: Éditions Anthropos.
Bouharrou, Ahmed. 2014. "La notion de temps de travail effectif dans le code du travail: Analyse." *Al Bayane*. Accessed September 26, 2014. http://www.albayane.press.ma /index.php?option=com_content&view=article&id=20306:la-notion-de-temps-de -travail-effectif-dans-le-code-du-travail&catid=54:special&Itemid=140 (site discontinued).
Bourdieu, Pierre. 1962. "Célibat et condition paysanne." *Etudes Rurales* 5–6:32–135.
———. 1965. "The Sentiment of Honour in Kabyle Society." In *Honour and Shame: the Values of Mediterranean Society*, edited by John G. Peristiany, 191–241. London: Weidenfeld & Nicolson.
———. 1977. *Outline of a Theory of Practice*. Translated by Richard Nice. Cambridge: Cambridge University Press.
Bourqia, Rahma. 1996. "Habitat, femmes et honneur: le cas de quelques quartiers populaires d'Oujda." In *Femmes, culture et société au Maghreb*, edited by Rahma Bourqia, Mounira Charrad, and Nancy Gallagher, 15–34. Casablanca: Afrique Orient.
Bourqia, Rahma, and Susan Gilson Miller, eds. 1999. *In the Shadow of the Sultan: Culture, Power, and Politics in Morocco*. Cambridge, MA: Distributed for the Center for Middle Eastern Studies of Harvard University by Harvard University Press.
Boutieri, Charis. 2016. *Learning in Morocco: Language Politics and the Abandoned Educational Dream*. Bloomington: Indiana University Press.
Brac de la Perrière, Caroline. 1987. *Derrière les héros . . . Les employées de maison musulmanes en service chez les Européens à Alger pendant la guerre d'Algérie (1954-1962)*. Paris: L'Harmattan.
Brady, Ivan. 1976. "Problems of Description and Explaination in the Study of Adoption." In *Transactions in Kinship: Adoption and Fosterage in Oceania*, edited by Ivan Brady, 3–27. Honolulu: University of Hawaii Press.
Brass, Tom. 1986. "The Elementary Strictures of Kinship: Unfree Relations and the Production of Commodities." *Social Analysis* 20: 56–68.
Brontë, Emily. (1847) 2003. *Wuthering Heights*. London: Penguin.
Brown, Judith. 1970. "A Note on the Division of Labor by Sex." *American Anthropologist* 72 (5): 1073–78.
Brown, Kenneth. 1976. *People of Salé: Tradition and Change in a Moroccan City, 1830–1930*. Manchester: Manchester University Press.
Brown, Susan. 2007. "Assessing Men and Maids: The Female Servant Tax and Meanings of Productive Labour in Late-Eighteenth-Century Britain." *Left History* 12 (2): 11–32.
Brudner, Lillian Burton, and Douglas White. 1977. "A Model of the Sexual Division of Labor." *American Ethnologist* 4 (2): 227–51.
Buitelaar, Marjo. 1993. *Fasting and Feasting in Morocco: Women's Participation in Ramadan*. Oxford: Berg.

Bujra, Janet. 2000. *Serving Class: Masculinity and the Feminisation of Domestic Service in Tanzania.* Edinburgh: Edinburgh University Press.

Búriková, Zuzana and Daniel Miller. 2010. *Au Pair.* Cambridge: Polity.

Caillé, Alain. 1994. *Don, intérêt et désintéressement. Bourdieu, Mauss, Platon et quelques autres.* Paris: La Découverte.

Cairoli, M. Laetitia. 2012. *Girls of the Factory: A Year with the Garment Workers of Morocco.* Gainesville: University Press of Florida.

Caplan, Lionel. 1971. "Cash and Kind: Two Media of 'Bribery' in Nepal." *Man* 6:266–78.

Carey, Matthew. 2012. "'The Rules' in Morocco? Pragmatic Approaches to Flirtation and Lying." *HAU* 2 (2): 188–204.

Carrier, James. 1997. *Meanings of the Market: The Free Market in Western Culture.* Oxford: Berg.

Carsten, Janet, 1989. "Cooking Money: Gender and the Symbolic Transformation of the Means of Exchange in a Malay Fishing Community." In *Money and the Morality of Exchange*, edited by Jonathan Parry and Maurice Bloch, 117–41. Cambridge: Cambridge University Press.

———. 2000. *Cultures of Relatedness: New Approaches to the Study of Kinship.* Cambridge: Cambridge University Press.

Carsten, Janet, and Stephen Hugh-Jones. 1995. Introduction to *About the House: Levi-Strauss and Beyond*, edited by Janet Carsten and Stephen Hugh-Jones, 1–46. Cambridge: Cambridge University Press.

Casinière, H. de la. 1924. *Les municipalités marocaines: leur développement, leur législation.* Casablanca: Vigie Marocaine.

Cather, Willa. (1918) 1994. *My Antonia.* Lincoln: University of Nebraska Press.

Celarié, Henriette. 1931. *Behind Moroccan Walls.* Translated and adapted by Constance Lily Morris. New York: Macmillan.

Chang, Grace. 2000. *Disposable Domestics: Immigrant Women Workers in the Global Economy.* Cambridge, MA: South End.

Channa, Aicha Ech-. 1996. *Miseria: Témoignages.* Casablanca: le Fennec.

Chant, Sylvia. 1991. *Women and Survival in Mexican Cities: Perspectives on Gender, Labour Markets and Low-Income Households.* Manchester: Manchester University Press.

Chapman, Malcolm, and Peter J. Buckley. 1997. "Markets, Transaction Costs, Economists and Social Anthropologists." In *Meanings of the Market*, edited by James G. Carrier, 225–50. Oxford: Berg.

Charrad, Mounira. 2001. *States and Women's Rights: The Making of Postcolonial Tunisia, Algeria, and Morocco.* Berkeley: University of California Press.

Cheikh, Mériam. 2009. "Echanges sexuels monétarisés, femmes et féminités au Maroc: une autonomie ambivalente." *Autrepart* 49:173–88.

———. 2011a. "Les filles qui sortent, les filles qui se font: attitudes transgressives pour conduites exemplaires." In *Marges, normes et éthique: Marges et marginalités au Maroc. Maghreb et sciences sociales 2011*, edited by Céline Aufauvre, Karine Bennafla and Montserrat Emperador-Badimon, 35–44. Tunis: Institut de Recherche sur le Maghreb Contemporain; Paris: L'Harmattan.

———. 2011b. "L'Urbain en détail et au féminin: portraits de colocataires femmes à Casablanca." In *Casablanca: Figures et scènes métropolitaines*, edited by Michel Peraldi and Mohamed Tozy, 167–96. Paris: Karthala.

———. 2013. "'Bnat lycée dayrin sexy': de l'amusement à la prostitution à Tanger (Maroc)." In *Jeunesses arabes, du Maroc au Yémen: loisirs, cultures et politiques*, edited by Laurent Bonnefoy and Myriam Catusse, 264–73. Paris: La Découverte.

Chekroun, Mohamed, and Mohamed Boudoudou. 1986. "Définition sociale de l'enfance et de l'enfant: conditions sociales de production de la légitimité sociale de la mise au travail des enfants au Maroc." *Bulletin économique et Social du Maroc* 157: 99–123.

Chen, Carolyn. 2005. "A Self of One's Own: Taiwan Immigrant Women and Religious Conversion." *Gender and Society* 19 (3): 336–57.

Cheng, Shu-Ju Ada. 2003. "Rethinking the Globalization of Domestic Service: Foreign Domestics, State Control, and the Politics of Identity in Taiwan." *Gender and Society* 17 (2): 166–86.

———. 2004. "When the Personal Meets the Global at Home: Filipina Domestics and Their Female Employers in Taiwan." *Frontiers: A Journal of Women Studies* 25 (2): 31–52.

Cherifi, Rachida. 1983. *Le Makhzen politique au Maroc: hier et aujourd'hui*. Casablanca: Afrique Orient.

Childress, Alice. 1956. *Like One of the Family: Conversations from a Domestic's Life*. New York: Independence.

Chin, Christine. 1998. *In Service and Servitude: Foreign Female Domestic Workers and the Malaysian "Modernity" Project*. New York: Columbia University Press.

Choukri, Mohamed. 1993. *For Bread Alone*. Translated by Paul Bowles. London: Saqi.

Churchill Home Insurers. 2011. "Upstairs, Downstairs Britain; One in Seven Brits Hire Domestic Help." Accessed September 26, 2014. http://www.churchill.com/press-office/releases/2011/01072011.

Clanchy, Michael. 2003. "Law and Love in the Middle Ages." In *Disputes and Settlements: Law and Human Relations in the West*, edited by John Bossy, 47–68. Cambridge: Cambridge University Press.

Clarke, Morgan. 2008. "New Kinship, Islam, and the Liberal Tradition: Sexual Morality and New Reproductive Technology in Lebanon." *Journal of the Royal Anthropological Institute* 14 (1): 153–69.

CNDH. 2013. *Les conditions d'emploi des travailleurs domestiques (Projet de loi No 12-19)*. Memorandum, November 2013. Rabat: Conseil National des Droits de l'Homme.

Coase, Ronald. 1937. "The Nature of the Firm." *Economica* 4 (16): 386–405.

Cock, Jacklyn. 1980. *Maids and Madams: A Study in the Politics of Exploitation*. Johannesburg: Raven.

Cohen, Mark. 2003. "The Foreign Jewish Poor in Medieval Egypt." In *Poverty and Charity in Middle Eastern Contexts*, edited by Michael Bonner, Mine Ener, and Amy Singer, 53–72. Albany: State University of New York Press.

Cohen, Shana. 2004. *Searching for a Different Future: The Rise of a Global Middle Class in Morocco*. Durham, NC: Duke University Press.

Colen, Shellee. 1989. "'Just a Little Respect': West Indian Domestic Workers in New York City." In *Muchachas No More: Household Workers in Latin America and the Caribbean*, edited by Elsa Chaney and Mary Castro, 171–94. Philadelphia: Temple University Press.

Collier, Jane. 1997. *From Duty to Desire: Remaking Families in a Spanish Village*. Princeton, NJ: Princeton University Press.

Combs-Schilling, Elaine. 1985. "Family and Friend in a Moroccan Boom Town: The Segmentary Debate Reconsidered." *American Ethnologist* 12 (4): 659–75.

———. 1989. *Sacred Performances: Islam, Sexuality, and Sacrifice*. New York: Columbia University Press.

———. 1999. "Performing Monarchy, Staging Nation." In *In the Shadow of the Sultan: Culture, Power, and Politics in Morocco*, edited by Rahma Bourqia and Susan Miller, 176–214. Cambridge, MA: Harvard University Press.

Conklin, Alice. 1997. *A Mission to Civilize: The Republican Idea of Empire in France and West Africa, 1895-1930*. Stanford, CA: Stanford University Press.
Constable, Nicole. 1997. "Sexuality and Discipline among Filipina Domestic Workers in Hong Kong." *American Ethnologist* 24 (3): 539–58.
———. 2003. "Filipina Workers in Hong Kong Homes: Household Rules and Relations." In *Global Woman: Nannies, Maids and Sex Workers in the New Economy*, edited by Barbara Ehrenreich and Arlie Hochschild, 115–41. London: Granta.
Costantini, Dino. 2008. *Mission civilisatrice: le role de l'histoire coloniale dans la construction de l'identité politique française*. Paris: La Découverte.
Coser, Lewis. 1973. "Servants: The Obsolescence of an Occupational Role." *Social Forces* 52 (1): 31–40.
Coulson, Margaret, Branka Magas, and Hilary Wainwright, eds. 1975. "The Housewife and Her Labour under Capitalism: A Critique." *New Left Review* 89:59–71.
Cowan, J. Milton, ed. 1994. *The Hans Wehr Dictionary of Modern Written Arabic*. Urbana, IL: Spoken Language Services.
Cox, Rosie. 2006. *The Servant Problem: Domestic Employment in a Global Economy*. London: I.B. Tauris.
Crawford, David. 2008. *Moroccan Households in the World Economy: Labour and Inequality in a Berber Village*. Baton Rouge: Louisiana State University Press.
———. 2010a. "Globalization Begins at Home: Children's Wage Labor and the High Atlas Household." In *Berbers and Others: Beyond Tribe and Nation in the Maghrib*, edited by Katherine E. Hoffman and Susan Gilson Miller, 127–49. Bloomington: Indiana University Press.
———. 2010b. "How Life Is Hard: Visceral Notes on Meaning, Order, and Morocco." In *Clifford Geertz in Morocco*, edited by Susan Slyomovics, 199–217. London: Routledge.
Crawford, David, and Katherine E. Hoffman. 2000. "Essentially Amazigh: Urban Berbers and the Global Village." In *The Arab-African and Islamic Worlds: Interdisciplinary Approaches*, edited by Robert K. Lacey and Ralph Coury, 117–33. New York: Peter Lang.
Davidoff, Leonore. 1995. *Worlds Between: Historical Perspectives on Gender and Class*. Cambridge: Polity.
Davis, Susan Schaefer. 1978. "Working Women in a Moroccan Village." In *Women in the Muslim World*, edited by Lois Beck and Nikki Keddie, 416–33. Cambridge, MA: Harvard University Press.
———. 1983. *Patience and Power: Women's Lives in a Moroccan Village*. Cambridge, MA: Schenkman.
Davis, Susan Schaefer, and Douglas A. Davis. 1989. *Adolescence in a Moroccan Town: Making Social Sense*. New Brunswick, NJ: Rutgers University Press.
Day, Charles William. 1844. *Hints on Etiquette and the Usages of Society; with a Glance at Bad Habits*. Boston: W. D. Ticknor.
Deakin, Simon, and Frank Wilkinson. 2005. *The Law of the Labour Market: Industrialization, Employment, and Legal Evolution*. Oxford: Oxford University Press.
Deback, Zoé. 2009. "Scandale. Bonnes philippines, mauvais employeurs." *TelQuel*. Accessed April 24, 2012. http://www.telquel-online.com/archives/364/mag1_364.shtml (site discontinued).
———. 2010. "Législation. Un espoir pour les petites bonnes?" *TelQuel*. Accessed April 24, 2012. http://www.telquel-online.com/archives/420/actu_maroc1_420.shtml (site discontinued).
Deeb, Lara. 2006. *An Enchanted Modern: Gender and Public Piety in Shi'i Lebanon*. Princeton, NJ: Princeton University Press.

Dill, Bonnie. 1994. *Across the Boundaries of Race and Class: An Exploration of Work and Family among Black Female Domestic Servants.* New York: Garland.

Dixon, Hayley. 2014. "Grillo Sisters Feel 'No Guilt' over Exposing Nigella Lawson's Drug Use." *The Telegraph.* Accessed September 26, 2014. http://www.telegraph.co.uk/news/celebritynews/10555358/Grillo-sisters-feel-no-guilt-over-exposing-Nigella-Lawsons-drug-use.html.

Doeringer, Peter B., Philip I. Moss, and David G. Terkla. 1986. "Capitalism and Kinship: Do Institutions Matter in the Labor Market?" *Industrial and Labor Relations Review* 40:48–60.

Donner, Henrike. 2013. "Of Untold Riches and Unruly Homes: Gender and Property in Neoliberal Middle-class Kolkata." November 1. Unpublished paper presented at Departmental Seminar, ISCA, University of Oxford.

Douglas, Mary. (1966) 2002. *Purity and Danger: An Analysis of Concepts of Pollution and Taboo.* London: Routledge.

Dresch, Paul. 1998. "Mutual Deception: Totality, Exchange, and Islam in the Middle East." In *Marcel Mauss: A Centenary Tribute*, edited by Wendy James and Nicholas Allen, 111–33. Oxford: Berghahn.

———. 2000. "Wilderness of Mirrors: Truth and Vulnerability in Middle Eastern Fieldwork." In *Anthropologists in a Wider World: Essays on Field Research*, edited by Paul Dresch, Wendy James, and David Parkin, 109–27. Oxford: Berghahn.

———. 2005. "Debates on Marriage and Nationality in the United Arab Emirates." In *Monarchies and Nations: Globalization and Identity in the Arab States of the Gulf*, edited by Paul Dresch and James Piscatori, 136–57. New York: I. B. Tauris.

———. 2006. "Foreign Matter: The Place of Strangers in Gulf Society." In *Globalization and the Gulf*, edited by John Fox et al., 200–22. London: Routledge.

———. 2012. "Aspects of Non-State Law: Early Yemen and Perpetual Peace." In *Legalism: Anthropology and History*, edited by Paul Dresch and Hannah Skoda, 145–72. Oxford: Oxford University Press.

Dresch, Paul, and Judith Scheele, eds. 2015. Introduction to *Legalism: Rules and Categories*, 1–28. Oxford: Oxford University Press.

Drummond, Lee. 1978. "The Transatlantic Nanny: Notes on a Comparative Semiotics of the Family in English-speaking Societies." *American Ethnologist* 5 (1): 30–43.

Dunn, Elizabeth. 2001. "Carrots, Class and Capitalism: Employee Management in a Post-Socialist Enterprise." In *Poland Beyond Communism: "Transition" in Critical Perspective*, edited by Michal Buchowski, 259–80. Fribourg, Switzerland: University Press.

Duxbury, Neil. 1996. "Do Markets Degrade?" *Modern Law Review* 59:331–48.

Dwyer, Daisy H. 1978. *Images and Self-Images: Male and Female in Morocco.* New York: Columbia University Press.

Early, Evelyn. 1993. "Getting It Together: Baladi Egyptian Business Women." In *Arab Women: Old boundaries, New Frontiers*, edited by Judith Tucker, 84–100. Bloomington: Indiana University Press.

The Economist. 2011. "The Servant Problem." December 17, Christmas Special Edition, 77–80.

Ehrenreich, Barbara. 2010. *Nickel and Dimed: Undercover in Low-Wage USA.* London: Granta.

Eickelman, Dale. 1974. "Is There an Islamic City? The Making of a Quarter in a Moroccan Town." *International Journal of Middle East Studies* 5 (3): 274–94.

———. (1981) 2002. *The Middle East and Central Asia: An Anthropological Approach.* Englewood Cliffs, NJ: Prentice Hall.
Elliot, Alice. 2016. "The Makeup of Destiny: Predestination and the Labor of Hope in a Moroccan Emigrant Town." *American Ethnologist* 43 (3): 488–99.
El-Massae. 2012. "Tafāṣīl muthīra hawal s̲h̲abakat at-titjār fī al-k̲h̲āddimāt al-filibīniyāt bi-al -mag̲h̲rib." December 7, 6.
Ember, Carol. 1983. "The Relative Decline in Women's Contribution to Agriculture with Intensification." *American Anthropologist* 85 (2): 285–304.
England, Paula. 1993. "The Separative Self: Androcentric Bias in Neoclassical Assumptions." In *Beyond Economic Man: Feminist Theory and Economics*, edited by Marianne A. Ferber and Julie A. Nelson, 37–53. Chicago: University of Chicago Press.
Ennaji, Moha, and Fatima Sadiqi. 2008. *Migration and Gender in Morocco: The Impact of Migration on the Women Left Behind.* Trenton, NJ: Red Sea.
Ennaji, Mohammed. 1999. *Serving the Master: Slavery and Society in Nineteenth-Century Morocco.* Translated by Seth Graebner. Basingstoke: Macmillan.
Ensel, Remco. 1999. *Saints and Servants in Southern Morocco.* Leiden: E. J. Brill.
Etienne, Jean d'. 1951. "La vie et les sentiments d'une famille marocaine à Casablanca." In *L'évolution sociale du Maroc* (Cahiers de l'Afrique et l'Asie, 1), edited by Jean d'Etienne, Louis Villème, and Stéphane Delisle, 5–51. Paris: Peyronnet.
Etienne, Mona. 1979. "Maternité sociale, rapports d'adoption et pouvoir des femmes chez les Baoulé (Côte-d'Ivoire)." *L'Homme* 19 (3–4): 63–107.
Evrard, Amy Young. 2014. *The Moroccan Women's Rights Movement.* Syracuse, NY: Syracuse University Press.
Farag, Eftetan. 1995. "Working Children in Cairo: Case Studies." In *Children in the Muslim Middle East*, edited by Elizabeth Fernea, 239–49. Austin: University of Texas Press.
Faris, Mohammed. 2016. *The Productive Muslim: Where Faith Meets Productivity.* Swansea: Awakening.
Fauve-Chamoux, Antoinette. 2004. Introduction to *Domestic Service and the Formation of European Identity: Understanding the Globalization of Domestic Work, 16th–21st Centuries*, edited by Antoinette Fauve-Chamoux, 1–18. Bern: Peter Lang.
Fauve-Chamoux, Antoinette, and Solvi Sogner, eds. 1994. *Socio-Economic Consequences of Sex-Ratios in Historical Perspective, 1500–1980.* Milan: Universita Boconi.
Federici, Silvia. 1975. *Wages against Housework.* London: Power of Women Collective and Falling Wall.
Fernea, Elizabeth. 1988. *A Street in Marrakech: A Personal View of Urban Women in Morocco.* Prospect Heights, IL: Waveland.
Ferraro, Gary, and Susan Andreatta. 2012. *Cultural Anthropology: An Applied Perspective.* 9th ed. Wadsworth: CENGAGE Learning.
Fischer, Claude. 1976. *The Urban Experience.* New York: Harcourt Brace Jovanovich.
Fihri, Nouzha Fassi. 2010. *Dada l'yakout.* Casablanca: Le Fennec.
Findlay, Allan, Anne Findlay, and Ronan Paddison. 1984. "Maintaining the Status Quo: An Analysis of Social Space in Post-Colonial Rabat." *Urban Studies* 21:41–51.
Foley, Winifred. (1974) 1991. *A Child in the Forest.* Cheltenham: Thornhill.
Forget, Nelly. 1962. "Attitudes towards Work by Women in Morocco." *International Social Science Journal* 14:105–12.
Fortes, Myer. 1958. Introduction to *The Developmental Cycle in Domestic Groups*, edited by Jack Goody, 2–9. Cambridge: Cambridge University Press.

———. (1969) 2004. *Kinship and the Social Order*. London: Routledge.

———. 1987. *Religion, Morality and the Person: Essays on Tallensi Religion*. Cambridge: Cambridge University Press.

Fortunati, Leopoldina. 1995. *The Arcane of Reproduction: Housework, Prostitution, Labor and Capital*. Translated by Hilary Creek. Brooklyn: Autonomedia.

Foster, George. 1965. "Peasant Society and the Image of Limited Good." *American Anthropologist* 55: 159–73.

———. 1972. "A Second Look at Limited Good." *Anthropological Quarterly* 45 (2): 57–64.

Fremlin, Celia. 1940. *The Seven Chars of Chelsea*. London: Methuen.

Gaitskell, Deborah, et al. 1984. "Class, Race and Gender: Domestic Workers in South Africa." *Review of African Political Economy* 27–28:86–108.

Garcia-Montes, José M., Domingo Caballero-Munoz, and Marino Pérez-Alvarez. 2006. "Changes in the Self Resulting from the use of Mobile Phones." *Media, Culture and Society* 28 (1): 67–82.

Gardiner, Jean. 1975. "Women's Domestic Labour." *New Left Review* 89:47–58.

Gaskell, Elizabeth. (1851) 1977. *Cranford*. Oxford: Oxford University Press.

"GCC: Kafala, UAE." 2012. *Migration News* 19 (1). https://migration.ucdavis.edu/mn/more.php?id=3740.

Geertz, Clifford, Hildred Geertz, and Lawrence Rosen, 1979. *Meaning and Order in Moroccan Society: Three Essays in Cultural Analysis*. Cambridge: Cambridge University Press.

Geertz, Hildred, 1979. "The Meanings of Family Ties." In *Meaning and Order in Moroccan Society: Three Essays in Cultural Analysis*, edited by Clifford Geertz, Hildred Geertz, and Lawrence Rosen, 315–91. Cambridge: Cambridge University Press.

Geremek, Bronislaw. 1994. *Poverty, a History*. Translated by Agnieszka Kolakowska. Oxford: Blackwell.

Ghosh, Amitav. 1987. "Categories of Labour and the Orientation of the Fellah Economy." In *The Diversity of the Muslim Community: Anthropological Essays in Memory of Peter Lienhardt*, edited by Ahmed al-Shahi, 115–38. London: Ithaca.

Gill, Lesley. 1994. *Precarious Dependencies. Gender, Class and Domestic Service in Bolivia*. New York: Colombia University Press.

Glazer, Nona. 1984. "Servants to Capital: Unpaid Domestic Labor and Paid Work." *Review of Radical Political Economics* 16 (1): 61–87.

Godbout, Jacques T. 2000a. *Le don, la dette et l'identité. Homo donator vs homo oeconomicus*. Collection Recherches. Paris: la Découverte.

———. 2000b. "Homo Donator versus Homo Oeconomicus." In *Gifts and Interests*, edited by Antoon Vandevelde, 23–46. Leuven: Peeters.

Goffman, Erving. 1971. "The Nature of Deference and Demeanor." *American Anthropologist* 58 (3): 473–502.

Goichon, Amélie Marie. 1929. *La femme de la moyenne bourgeoisie Fāsīya*. Paris: P. Geuthner.

Goody, Esther. 1982. *Parenthood and Social Reproduction—Fostering and Occupational Roles in West Africa*. Cambridge: Cambridge University Press.

Goody, Esther, and Jack Goody. 1967. "The Circulation of Women and Children in Northern Ghana." *Man* 2 (2): 226–248.

Goody, Jack. 1969. "Adoption in Cross-Cultural Perspective." *Comparative Studies in Society and History* 11 (1): 55–75.

Gowing, Laura. 1996. *Domestic Dangers: Women, Words, and Sex in Early Modern London*. Oxford: Clarendon.

Graeber, David, 2006. "Turning Modes of Production Inside Out: Or, Why Capitalism Is a Transformation of Slavery." *Critique of Anthropology* 26 (1): 61–85.
Graf, Katharina. 2016. "Beldi Matters: Negotiating Proper Food in Urban Moroccan Food Consumption and Preparation." In *Halal Matters: Islam, Politics and Markets in Global Perspective*, edited by Florence Bergeaud-Blackler, Johan Fisher and John Lever, 72–90. Abingdon; New York: Routledge.
Graham, Sandra Lauderdale. 1988. *House and Street: The Domestic World of Servants in Nineteenth-Century Rio de Janeiro*. Cambridge: Cambridge University Press.
Granger, Michel. 1987. "Agadir Avant. The Family and the Poor Cousins: Native-European Relations in Agadir under the Protectorate." *The Journal of Ethnic Studies* 14 (4): 127–33.
Grotti, Laetitia. 2004. "Société : Halte au travail des 'petites bonnes.'" *TelQuel*. Accessed April 24, 2012. http://www.telquel-online.com/archives/132/sujet3.shtml (site discontinued).
Grover, Shalini. 2009. "Lived Experiences: Marriage, Notions of Love, and Kinship Support amongst Poor Women in Delhi." *Contributions to Indian Sociology* 43 (1): 1–33.
Gudeman, Stephen. 2001. *The Anthropology of Economy*. Oxford: Blackwell.
Guerraoui, Driss. 1996. "Famille et développement à Fès." In *Femmes, culture et société au Maghreb, Vol. 1: Culture, femmes et famille*, edited by Rahma Bourquia, Mounira Charrad, and Nancy Elizabeth Gallagher, 157–78. Casablanca: Afrique-Orient.
Hajnal, John. 1982. "Household Formation Patterns in Historical Perspective." *Population and Development Review* 8 (3): 449–494.
———. 1983. "Two Kinds of Pre-industrial Household Formation System." In *Family Forms in Historic Europe*, edited by Richard Wall, Jean Robin, Peter Laslett, and Jacek Kochanowicz, 79–90. Cambridge: Cambridge University Press.
Haloui, Abdennebi El-, and Steve Bowman. 2011. *Moroccan Arabic Verb Dictionary. English-Moroccan Arabic*. 2nd ed. Mount Joy, PA: Artisanal Treasures.
Hamel, Chouki El-. 2013. *Black Morocco: A History of Slavery, Race and Islam*. Cambridge: Cambridge University Press.
Hamid, Abdul Ali. 2003. *Moral Teachings of Islam: Prophetic Teachings from Al-Adab Al-Mufrad by Imam al-Bukhari*. Walnut Creek, CA: Altamira.
Hammoudi, Abdellah. 1997. *Master and Disciple: The Cultural Foundations of Moroccan Authoritarianism*. Chicago: University of Chicago Press.
Hansen, Karen. 1986. "Household Work as a Man's Job: Sex and Gender in Domestic Service in Zambia." *Anthropology Today* 2 (3): 18–23.
Harmse, Alet, Phillip F. Blaauw, and Rinie Schenck. 2009. "Day Labourers, Unemployment and Socio-Economic Development in South Africa." *Urban Forum* 20 (4): 363–77.
Harris, Olivia. 1982. "Households as Natural Units." In *Of Marriage and the Market: Women's Subordination in International Perspective*, edited by Kate Young, Carol Walkowitz, and Roslyn McCullagh, 49–68. London: CSE.
Hart, Ursula Kingsmill. 1994. *Behind the Courtyard Door: The Daily Life of Tribeswomen in Northern Morocco*. Ipswich, MA: Ipswich.
Hatem, Mervat. 1987. "Towards the Study of the Psychodynamics of Mothering and Gender in Egyptian Families." *International Journal of Middle Eastern Studies* 19: 287–306.
———. 1999. "The Microdynamics of Patriarchal Change in Egypt." In *Intimate Selving in Arab Families: Gender, Self, and Identity*, edited by Suad Joseph, 191–210. Syracuse, NY: Syracuse University Press.
Haywood, Eliza. 1743. *Present for a Servant-Maid: Or, the Sure Means of Gaining Love and Esteem*. London: T. Gardner.

Hecht, J. Jean. 1956. *The Domestic Servant in Eighteenth-Century England*. London: Routledge and Kegan Paul.

Heuzé, Gérard. 1996. *Workers of Another World: Miners, the Countryside and Coalfields in Dhanbad*. Delhi: Oxford University Press.

Hibourne, Marion. 1999. "Living Together Full-Time? Middle-Class Couples Approaching Retirement." *Ageing and Society* 19 (2): 161–83.

Hill, Bridget. 1996. *Servants: English Domestics in the Eighteenth Century*. Oxford: Clarendon.

Hirabayashi, Lane Ryo. 1986. "The Migrant Village Association in Latin America: A Comparative Analysis." *Latin American Research Review* 21 (3): 7–29.

Hirsch, Jennifer, and Holly Wardlow. 2006. *Modern Loves: The Anthropology of Romantic Courtship and Companionate Marriage*. Ann Arbor, MI: University of Michigan Press.

Hirschkind, Charles. 2006. *The Ethical Soundscape: Cassette Sermons and Islamic Counterpublics*. New York: Columbia University Press.

Hirschon, Renée. 1978. "Open Body/Closed Space: The Transformation of Female Sexuality." In *Defining Females: The Nature of Women in Society*, edited by Shirley Ardener, 66–88. London: Croom Helm.

Hochschild, Arlie. 1983. *The Managed Heart: Commercialization of Human Feeling*. Berkeley: University of California Press.

Hoexter, Miriam. 2003. "Charity, the Poor, and Distribution of Alms in Ottoman Algiers." In *Poverty and Charity in Middle Eastern Contexts*, edited by Michael Bonner, Mine Ener, and Amy Singer, 145–64. Albany, NY: State University of New York Press.

Hoffman, Katherine E. 2008. *We Share Walls: Language, Land, and Gender in Berber Morocco*. Malden, MA; Oxford: Blackwell.

Hoffman, Katherine E., and Susan Gilson Miller. 2010. *Berbers and Others: Beyond Tribe and Nation in the Maghrib*. Bloomington: Indiana University Press.

Holmes-Eber, Paula. 2003. *Daughters of Tunis: Women, Family, and Networks in a Muslim City*. Boulder, CO; Oxford: Westview.

Holy, Ladislav. 1989. *Kinship, Honour and Solidarity: Cousin Marriage in the Middle East*. Manchester: Manchester University Press.

Hondagneu-Sotelo, Pierrette. 2003. "Blowups and Other Unhappy Endings." In *Global Woman: Nannies, Maids and Sex Workers in the New Economy*, edited by Barbara Ehrenreich and Arlie Hochschild, 55–69. London: Granta.

———. 2007. *Doméstica: Immigrant Workers Cleaning and Caring in the Shadows of Affluence*. Berkeley: University of California Press.

Horn, Pamela. 2004. *Flunkeys and Scullions: Life below Stairs in Georgian England*. Stroud: Sutton.

Howell, Signe. 2003. "Kinning: The Creation of Life Trajectories in Transnational Adoptive Families." *Journal of the Royal Anthropological Institute* 9 (3): 465–84.

Huang, Shirlena, and Brenda Yeoh. 1998. "Negotiating Public Space: Strategies and Styles of Migrant Female Domestic Workers in Singapore." *Urban Studies* 35 (3): 583–602.

———, eds. 2000. "'Home' and 'Away': Foreign Domestic Workers and Negotiations of Diasporic Identity in Singapore." *Women's Studies International Forum* 23 (4): 413–29.

Human Rights Watch. 2005. *Inside the Home, Outside the Law: Abuse of Child Domestic Workers in Morocco*. New York: HRW.

———. 2012. *Lonely Servitude, Child Domestic Labour in Morocco*. New York: HRW.

Hunt, Abigail, and Fortunate Machingura. 2016. "A Good Gig? The Rise of On-Demand Domestic Work." Working Paper 7, Overseas Development Institute. Accessed October 25, 2017. https://www.odi.org/sites/odi.org.uk/files/resource-documents/11155.pdf.

Illouz, Eva. 1997. *Consuming the Romantic Utopia: Love and the Cultural Contradictions of Capitalism.* Berkeley: University of California Press.

Ingold, Tim. 2004. "Culture on the Ground: The World Perceived Through the Feet." *Journal of Material Culture* 9 (3): 315–40.

International Labour Office. 2011. *Decent Work for Domestic Workers. Convention no. 189 and Recommendation no. 201.* Geneva: ILO.

———. 2012. *Effective Protection for Domestic Workers: A Guide to Designing Labour Laws.* Geneva: ILO.

Ishiguro, Kazuo. 1989. *The Remains of the Day.* London: Faber.

Jacquemin, Mélanie. 2002. "Travail domestique et travail des enfants : le cas d'Abidjan (Cote d'Ivoire)." *Revue Tiers Monde* 43 (170): 307–26.

James, Selma and Mariarosa Dalla Costa. 1972. *The Power of Women and the Subversion of the Community.* Bristol: Falling Wall.

Jansen, Willy. 1987. *Women without Men: Gender and Marginality in an Algerian Town.* Leiden: E. J. Brill.

———. 2004. "The Economy of Religious Merit: Women and Ajr in Algeria." *Journal of North African Studies* 9 (4): 1–17.

Jelin, Elizabeth. 1977. "Migration and Labor Force Participation of Latin American Women: The Domestic Servants in the Cities." *Signs* 3 (1): 129–41.

Jenkins, Timothy. 2010. *The Life of Property: House, Family and Inheritance in Béarn, South-West France.* New York: Berghahn.

Joseph, Suad, ed. 1999. *Intimate Selving in Arab Families: Gender, Self, and Identity.* Syracuse, NY: Syracuse University Press.

Jutte, Robert. 1994. *Poverty and Deviance in Early Modern Europe.* Cambridge: Cambridge University Press.

Kaluzynska, Eva. 1980. "Wiping the Floor with Theory: A Survey of Writings on Housework." *Feminist Review* 6:27–54.

Kapchan, Deborah. 1996. *Gender on the Market: Moroccan Women and the Revoicing of Tradition.* Philadelphia: University of Pennsylvania Press.

Kasriel, Michèle. 1989. *Libres femmes du Haut-Atlas?* Paris: L'Harmattan.

Katz, Jonathan G. 2001. "The 1907 Mauchamp Affair and the French Civilising Mission in Morocco." In *North Africa, Islam and the Mediterranean World: From the Almoravids to the Algerian War,* edited by Julia Clancy-Smith, 143–66. London: Frank Cass.

Katzman, David. 1978. *Seven Days a Week: Women and Domestic Service in Industrializing America.* New York: Oxford University Press.

Keddie, Nikki R. 2007. *Women in the Middle East: Past and Present.* Princeton, NJ: Princeton University Press.

Keene, Emily. 1912. *My Life Story, by Emily, Shareefa of Wazan.* London: Edward Arnold.

Kessler-Harris, Alice. 1990. *A Woman's Wage: Historical Meanings and Social Consequences.* Lexington, KY: University Press of Kentucky.

Keyser, James. 1974. "The Middle Eastern Case: Is There a Marriage Rule?" *Ethnology* 13 (3): 293–309.

Khan, Afzar. 2014. "Why It's Time to End *Kafala*." *The Guardian,* February 26, 2014.

Khatib-Chahidi, Jane. 1981. "Sexual Prohibitions, Shared Space and Fictive Marriages in Shi'ite Iran." In *Women and Social Space: Ground Rules and Social Maps*, edited by Shirley Ardener, 112–35. London: Croom Helm.

Khelladi, A. 1938. "Les budgets des petits et moyens fonctionnaires musulmanes recrutés après l'établissement du protectorat français au Maroc." *Bulletin Economique du Maroc* 5 (22): 265–68.

Khosravi, Shahram. 2008. *Young and Defiant in Tehran*. Philadelphia: University of Pennsylvania Press.

Kriem, Maya S. 2009. "Mobile Telephony in Morocco: A Changing Sociality." *Media, Culture & Society* 31 (4): 617–32.

Ksikes, Driss. 2004. "Rapport: Le drame des petites bonnes." *TelQuel*. Accessed April 24, 2012. http://www.telquel-online.com/archives/207/maroc6_207.shtml (site discontinued).

Kuuwirti, Rachid, El-. 2013. "'Wusiṭa' yajūbūn alaswāq alusbūʻīya biTaounat liltanqīb ʻan khāddimāt almanāzil." *Ṣaḥara' al-maghribīya*. "Milf: khāddimāt al-biyūt." Monday, May 27, 8.

Kuran, Timur. 2003. "Islamic Redistribution through *Zakat*: Historical Record and Modern Realities." In *Poverty and Charity in Middle Eastern Contexts*, edited by Michael Bonner, Mine Ener, and Amy Singer, 275–94. Albany, NY: State University of New York Press.

Lacoste-Dujardin, Camille. 1985. *Des mères contre les femmes: Maternité et patriarcat au Maghreb*. Paris: Éditions de la Découverte.

Lahlou, Mehdi. n.d. " Child Labour in Morocco: The Socioeconomic Background of the 'Little Maids' Phenomenon." Accessed May 7, 2012. http://www.abhatoo.net.ma/content/download/10404/166851/version/1/file/Child_Labour_in_Morocco.pdf.

Laidlaw, James. 2000. "A Free Gift Makes No Friends." *Journal of the Royal Anthropological Institute* 6 (4): 617–34.

Lallemand, Suzanne. 1988. "Adoption, Fosterage et Alliance." *Anthropologie et Sociétés* 12 (2): 25–40.

———. 1993. *La circulation des enfants en société traditionnelle. Prêt, don, échange*. Paris: L'Harmattan.

Lambek, Michael. 2010. *Ordinary Ethics: Anthropology, Language, and Action*. New York: Fordham University Press.

———. 2011. "Kinship as Gift and Theft: Acts of Succession in Mayotte and Ancient Israel." *American Ethnologist* 38 (1): 2–16.

Lamlili, Nadia. 2008. "Société. Chouette, ma 'bonne' parle anglais!" *TelQuel*. Accessed April 24, 2012. http://www.telquel-online.com/archives/311/maroc5_311.shtml (site discontinued).

Lamphere, Louise. 1974. "Strategies, Cooperation, and Conflict among Women in Domestic Groups." In *Woman, Culture and Society*, edited by Michelle Z. Rosaldo and Louise Lamphere, 97–112. Stanford, CA: Stanford University Press.

———. 1993. "The Domestic Sphere of Women and the Public World of Men: The Strengths and Limitations of an Anthropological Dichotomy." In *Gender in Cross Cultural Perspective*, edited by Caroline Brettell and Carolyn Sargent, 67–77. Englewood Cliffs, NJ: Prentice Hall.

———. 2001. "Whatever Happened to Kinship Studies? Reflections from Feminist Anthropology." In *New Directions in Kinship Studies*, edited by Linda Stone, 21–47. Lanham; Oxford: Rowman and Littlefield.

Lan, Pei-Chia. 2003. "They Have More Money but I Speak Better English: Transnational Encounters between Filipina Domestics and Taiwanese Employers." *Identities: Global Studies in Culture and Power* 10 (2): 132–61.

———. 2006. *Global Cinderellas: Migrant Domestics and Newly Rich Employers in Taiwan.* Durham, NC: Duke University Press.

Laslett, Peter. 1965. *World We Have Lost.* London: Methuen.

———. 1977. "Characteristics of the Western Family Considered over Time." In *Family Life and Illicit Love in Earlier Generations: Essays in Historical Sociology*, edited by Peter Laslett, 12–49. Cambridge: Cambridge University Press.

Le Parisien. 2011. "Maroc : une petite bonne de 11 ans battue à mort." Accessed December 7, 2011. http://www.leparisien.fr/international/maroc-une-petite-bonne-de-11-ans-battue-a-mort-20-09-2011-1617312.php.

Le Tourneau, Roger. 1949. *Fès avant le Protectorat: étude économique et sociale d'une ville de l'Occident musulman.* Casablanca: Institut des hautes études marocaines.

Lem, Winnie. 1991. "Gender, Ideology, and Petty Commodity Production: Social Reproduction in Languedoc, France." In *Marxist Approaches in Economic Anthropology*, edited by Alice Littlefield and Hill Gates, 103–17. Lanham, MD: University Press of America.

Lethbridge, Lucy. 2013. *Servants: A Downstairs View of 20th-Century Britain.* London: Bloomsbury.

Lévi-Strauss, Claude. 1983. *The Way of Masks.* Translated by Sylvia Modelski. London: Jonathan Cape.

Liebelt, Claudia. 2011. *Caring for the 'Holy Land': Filipina Domestic Workers in Israel.* New York; Oxford: Berghahn.

Light, Alison. 2007. *Mrs Woolf and the Servants.* London: Penguin.

Lyautey, Hubert. 1927. *Paroles d'action: Madagascar, Sud-Oranais, Oran, Maroc (1900-1926).* Paris: Armand Colin.

Lyautey, Pierre, ed. 1953. *Lyautey l'africain: textes et lettres de Lyautey.* 4 vols. Paris: E Plon.

Macauley, Stewart. 1963. "Non-Contractual Relations in Business: A Preliminary Study." *American Sociological Review* 28 (1): 55–67.

MacCormack, Carol, and Marilyn Strathern. 1980. *Nature, Culture and Gender.* Cambridge: Cambridge University Press.

Mahdavi, Pardis. 2016. *Crossing the Gulf: Love and Family in Migrant Lives.* Stanford, CA: Stanford University Press.

Maher, Vanessa. 1974. *Women and Property in Morocco: Their Changing Relation to the Process of Social Stratification in the Middle Atlas.* London: Cambridge University Press.

———. 1976. "Kin, Clients and Accomplices: Relationships among Women in Morocco." In *Sexual Divisions and Society: Process and Change*, edited by Diana. L. Barker and Sheila Allen, 52–75. London: Tavistock.

———. 1984. "Work, Consumption and Authority within the Household: a Moroccan Case." In *Of Marriage and the Market*, 2nd ed., edited by K. Young, C. Wolkowitz, and R. McCullagh, 69–87. London: CSE.

Mahmood, Saba. 2001. "Feminist Theory, Embodiment, and the Docile Agent: Some Reflections on the Egyptian Islamic Revival." *Cultural Anthropology* 16 (2): 202–36.

———. 2005. *Politics of Piety: The Islamic Revival and the Feminist Subject.* Princeton, NJ: Princeton University Press.

Majumdar, Prasanta S., and Ila Majumdar. 1978. *Rural Migrants in an Urban Setting: A Study of Two Shanty Colonies in the Capital City of India.* Delhi: Hindustan.

Malik, Muhammad Farooq-i-Azam, 2013. *English Translation of the Meaning of Al-Qur'an: The Guidance for Mankind*. Houston, TX: Institute of Islamic Knowledge.
Makdisi, Jean Said. 1999. "Teta, Mother, and I." In *Intimate Selving in Arab Families: Gender, Self, and Identity*, edited by Suad Joseph, 1–24. Syracuse, NY: Syracuse University Press.
Mandeville, Bernard. (1732) 1988. *The Fable of the Bees or Private Vices, Publick Benefits*. 2 vols. With a commentary by Frederick B. Kaye. Indianapolis: Liberty Fund.
Marx, Karl. (1867) 1967. *Capital*. 3 vols. New York: New World.
Massignon, Louis. 1925. *Enquête sur les corporations musulmanes d'artisans et de commerçants au Maroc*. Paris: Ernest Leroux.
Mathieu, Nicole-Claude. 1973. "Homme-culture et femme-nature?" *L'Homme* 13 (3): 101–13.
Mattson, Ingrid. 2003. "Status-Based Definitions of Need in Early Islamic *Zakat* and Maintenance Laws." In *Poverty and Charity in Middle Eastern Contexts*, edited by Michael Bonner, Mine Ener, and Amy Singer, 31–52. Albany: State University of New York Press.
Mauss, Marcel. 1925. "Essai sur le Don: Forme et Raison de l'Échange dans les Sociétés Archaïques." *Année Sociologique* 1 (2): 30–186.
May, Vanessa. 2011. *Unprotected Labor: Household Workers, Politics, and Middle-Class Reform in New York, 1870-1940*. Chapel Hill: University of North Carolina Press.
Mayhew, Graham. 1991. "Life-Cycle Service and the Family Unit in Early Modern Rye." *Continuity and Change* 6 (2): 201–26.
McBride, Theresa. 1976. *The Domestic Revolution. The Modernisation of Domestic Service in England and France, 1820-1920*. London: Croom Helm.
McCall Smith, Alexander. 2005. *In the Company of Cheerful Ladies*. Edinburgh: Abacus.
McDonald, Tom. 2011. "From the Soil: Relations between Floors and Persons in the Chinese Home." October 28. Unpublished paper presented at the Ethnicity and Identity Seminar, ISCA, University of Oxford.
McMurray, David. 2013. "Thinking about Class and Status in Morocco." In *Encountering Morocco: Fieldwork and Cultural Understanding*, edited by David Crawford and Rachel Newcomb, 56–76. Bloomington: Indiana University Press.
Mead, Margaret. 1949. *Male and Female: A Study of the Sexes in a Changing World*. London: Victor Gollancz.
Meillassoux, Claude. 1975. *Femmes, greniers et capitaux*. Paris: Maspero.
Meldrum, Tim. 2000. *Domestic Service and Gender 1660-1750: Life and Work in the London Household*. Harlow: Pearson.
Meneley, Anne. 1996. *Tournaments of Value: Sociability and Hierarchy in a Yemeni Town*. Toronto: University of Toronto Press.
Mernissi, Fatima. 1975. *Beyond the Veil: Male-Female Dynamics in Muslim Society*. Cambridge, MA: Schenkman.
———. 1982. "Zhor's World: A Moroccan Domestic Worker Speaks Out." *Feminist Issues* 2 (1): 3–31.
Messiri, Sawsan. 1978. *Ibn Al-balad: A Concept of Egyptian Identity*. Leiden: Brill.
Miers, Suzanne, and Igor Kopytoff. 1977. *Slavery in Africa*. Madison: University of Wisconsin Press.
Minturn, Leigh. 1993. *Sita's Daughters: Coming out of Purdah: The Rajput Women of Khalapur Revisited*. New York; Oxford: Oxford University Press.
Mittermaier, Amira. 2013. "Trading with God: Islam, Calculation, Excess." In *A Companion to the Anthropology of Religion*, edited by Janice Boddy and Michael Lambek, 274–93. Chichester: Wiley Blackwell.

Moghadam, Valentine. 1993. *Modernizing Women: Gender and Social Change in the Middle East*. Boulder, CO; Lynne Rienner.
Montagne, Robert. 1952. *Naissance du prolétariat marocain. Enquête collective 1948–1950*. Cahiers de l'Afrique et l'Asie. Paris: Peyronnet & Gie.
Montgomery, Lucy Maud. (1908) 1994. *Anne of Green Gables*. London: Penguin.
Montgomery, Mary. 2019. "The Place of Strangers in Moroccan Domesticity: Nostalgia, Secrets and the Continuity of Scandal." In *The Scandal of Continuity in Middle East Anthropology: Form, Duration, Difference*, edited by Judith Scheele and Andrew Shryock. Bloomington: Indiana University Press.
Moujoud, Nasima, and Dolorès Pourette. 2005. "'Traite' de femmes migrantes, domesticité et prostitution. À propos de migrations interne et externe." *Cahiers d'Etudes Africaines* 45 (179–80): 1093–121.
Mounib, Noura. 2012a. "C'est honteux de savoir qu'au 21ème siècle, la violence et l'exploitation existent encore!" Entretien: Abdelouahed Souhail, *L'Observateur*, May 15–June 21.
———. 2012b. "Les nounous venues des Philippines." *L'Observateur*, May 15–June 21.
Msḥat, Abdderraḥman. 2013. "Tawwasiṭ al-ʿishrīn khādima muqābil 1000 dirham tdfaʿhā al-ʿāʾilāt al-mushaghila." *Ṣaḥara' al-maghribīya*. "Milf: khāddimāt al-biyūt." May 27, 2013: 8.
Mundy, Martha. 1979. "Women's Inheritance of Land in Highland Yemen." *Arabian Studies* 5: 161–87.
Mullins, Samuel, and Gareth Griffiths. 1986. *Cap and Apron: An Oral History of Domestic Service in the Shires, 1880-1950*. The Harborough Series, No. 2. Leicester: Leicestershire Museums, Art Galleries and Records Service.
Munson, Henry, Jr. 1984. *The House of Si Abd Allah: The Oral History of a Moroccan Family*. New Haven, CT: Yale University Press.
Murdock, George and Caterina Provost. 1973. "Factors in the Division of Labor by Sex: A Cross-Cultural Analysis." *Ethnology* 12 (2): 203–25.
Murphy, Robert, and Leonard Kasdan. 1959. "The Structure of Parallel Cousin Marriage." *American Anthropologist* 61 (1): 17–29.
Nagata, Mary Louise. 2004. "Domestic Service and the Law in Early Modern Japan." In *Domestic Service and the Formation of European Identity: Understanding the Globalization of Domestic Work, 16th–21st Centuries*, edited by Antoinette Fauve-Chamoux, 211–33. Bern: Peter Lang.
Nahum-Claudel, Chloe. 2017. "Pyrotechnical Mastery: Lévi-Strauss's Materialism and Amazonian Cuisine, Care and Craft." Unpublished paper presented at the Research Seminar on Anthropological Theory, London School of Economics, April 28.
Nelson, Cynthia. 1974. "Public and Private Politics: Women in the Middle Eastern World." *American Ethnologist* 1 (3): 551–63.
Nett, Emily. 1966. "The Servant Class in a Developing Country: Ecuador." *Journal of Inter-American Studies* 8 (3): 437–52.
Newcomb, Rachel. 2009. *Women of Fes: Ambiguities of Urban Life in Morocco*. Philadelphia: University of Pennsylvania Press.
Nieuwkerk, Karin van. 1995. *"A Trade Like Any Other": Female Singers and Dancers in Egypt*. Austin: University of Texas Press.
———. 2005. "Credits for the Hereafter: Changing Ways to Collect Religious Merit, Ajr, among Moroccan Immigrant Women in the Netherlands." In *The Dutch and their Gods: Secularization and Transformation of Religion in the Netherlands since 1950*, edited by Erik Sengers, 125–42. Hilversum: Uitgeverij Verloren.

Nouvel, Jacques. 1938. "Petits métiers indigènes, Taches accessoires pratiquées par les enfants indigènes." *Bulletin Economique du Maroc* V(22), October 1938: 269–71.
Oakley, Ann. 1974. *The Sociology of Housework*. New York: Pantheon.
Ordonez, Juan Thomas. 2012. "'Boots for my Sancho': Structural Vulnerability among Latin American Day Labourers in Berkeley, California." *Culture, Health & Sexuality: An International Journal for Research, Intervention and Care* 14 (6): 691–703.
Ortner, Sherry. 1974. "Is Female to Male as Nature Is to Culture?" In *Woman, Culture and Society*, edited by Michelle Z. Rosaldo and Louise Lamphere, 67–87. Stanford, CA: Stanford University Press.
Ossman, Susan. 1994. *Picturing Casablanca: Portraits of Power in a Modern City*. Berkeley: University of California Press.
Ozyegin, Gul. 2001. *Untidy Gender: Domestic Service in Turkey*. Philadelphia: Temple University Press.
Palmer, Phyllis 1989. *Domesticity and Dirt: Housewives and Domestic Servants in the United States, 1920-1945*. Philadelphia: Temple University Press.
Parreñas, Rhacel. 2001. *Servants of Globalization: Women, Migration and Domestic Work*. Stanford, CA: Stanford University Press.
———. 2008. *The Force of Domesticity: Filipina Migrants and Globalization*. New York: New York University Press.
Parry, Jonathan. 1986. "The Gift, the Indian Gift and the 'Indian Gift.'" *Journal of the Royal Anthropological Institute* 21 (3): 453–74.
———. 2003. "Nehru's Dream and the Village 'Waiting Room': Long-distance Labour Migrants to a Central Indian Steel Town." *Contributions to Indian Sociology* 37:217–49.
Parry, Jonathan, and Maurice Bloch. 1989. "Introduction: Money and the Morality of Exchange." In *Money and the Morality of Exchange*, edited by Jonathan Parry and Maurice Bloch, 1–32. Cambridge: Cambridge University Press.
Pasternak, Bernard, Carol Ember, and Melvin Ember. 1976. "On the Conditions Favoring Extended Family Households." *Journal of Anthropological Research* 32: 109–23.
Pateman, Carol. 1983. "Feminist Critiques of the Public/Private Dichotomy." In *Public and Private in Social Life*, edited by Stanley I. Benn and Gerald F. Gaus, 281–303. London: Croom Helm.
Peets, Leonora. (1983) 1988. *Women of Marrakech: Record of a Secret Sharer 1930-1970*. London: Hurst.
Pelham, Nick. 2000. "Street Life." BBC World Service report. Accessed September 26, 2014. http://www.bbc.co.uk/worldservice/people/highlights/streetlife.shtml.
Piamenta, Moshe. 1983. *The Muslim Conception of God and Human Welfare as Reflected in Everyday Arabic Speech*. Leiden: Brill.
Piot, Charles. 1991. "Of Persons and Things: Some Reflections on African Spheres of Exchange." *Journal of the Royal Anthropological Institute* 26 (3): 405–24.
Pitt-Rivers, Julian. 1977. "The Law of Hospitality." In *The Fate of Shechem or The Politics of Sex: Essays in the Anthropology of the Mediterranean*, edited by Julian Pitt-Rivers, 94–112. Cambridge: Cambridge University Press.
Planel, Vincent. 2008. "Les hommes de peine dans le paysage urbain. Spécialisations régionales et ordre social à Taez." *Revue des mondes musulmans et de la Méditerranée* 121: 145–61.
Plattner, Stuart, ed. 1989. *Economic Anthropology*. Stanford, CA: Stanford University Press.
Pleck, Elizabeth. 1987. *Domestic Tyranny: The Making of Social Policy against Family Violence from Colonial Times to the Present*. Oxford: Oxford University Press.

Polanyi, Karl. 1957. *The Great Transformation*. Boston: Beacon.
Prior, Mary. 1985. *Women in English Society 1500–1800*. London: Methuen.
Proust, Marcel. (1922) 1973. *Swann's Way*. Translated by C.K. Scott Moncrieff. London: Chatto & Windus.
Qureshi, Kaveri. 2013. "Sabar: Body Politics among Middle-aged Migrant Pakistani Women." *Journal of the Royal Anthropological Institute* 19 (1): 120–37.
Rachik, Hassan. 2005. "Jeunesse et changement sociale." In *50 ans de développement humain et perspective 2025*. Accessed September 26, 2014. http://www.kenitra.ma/document/fr/Developpement%20humain%20et%20perspectives%20pour%202025.pdf (site discontinued).
Rassam, Amal. 1980. "Women and Domestic Power in Morocco." *International Journal of Middle Eastern Studies* 12:171–79.
Ray, Raka, and Seemin Qayum. 2009. *Cultures of Servitude: Modernity, Domesticity, and Class in India*. Stanford, CA: Stanford University Press.
Rees, Albert. 1966. "Labor Economics: Effects of More Knowledge. Information Networks in Labor Markets." *American Economic Review* 56 (1–2): 559–66.
Richardson, Roger C. 2010. *Household Servants in Early Modern England*. Manchester: Manchester University Press.
Rivet, Daniel. 1999. *Le Maroc de Lyautey à Mohammed V. Le double visage du Protectorat*. Paris: Denoel.
Rivière, Peter. 1984. *Individual and Society in Guiana: A Comparative Study of Amerindian Social Organization*. Cambridge: University Press.
Roberts, Robert. 1973. *The Classic Slum: Salford Life in the First Quarter of the Century*. Hardmondsworth: Penguin.
Rodary, Meryem. 2002. "Argent des femmes et honneur des hommes au Maroc: un quartier de Marrakech." In *Dissemblances. Jeux et enjeux du genre*, edited by Rose-Marie LAgra, Agathe Gestin, Eléonore Lépinard, and Geneviève Pruvost, 117–30. Paris: L'Harmattan.
Rollins, Judith. 1985. *Between Women: Domestics and Their Employers*. Philadelphia: Temple University Press.
Romero, Mary. 1992. *Maid in the USA*. New York: Routledge.
Rorty, Richard. 1998. "Justice as a Larger Loyalty." In *Cosmopolitics: Thinking and Feeling beyond the Nation*, edited by Pheng Cheah and Bruce Robbins, 45–58. Minneapolis: University of Minnesota Press.
Rosaldo, Michelle Z. 1974. "Women, Culture, and Society: A Theoretical Overview." In *Woman, Culture and Society*, edited by Michelle Z. Rosaldo and Louise Lamphere, 1–42. Stanford, CA: Stanford University Press.
Rosander, Eva Evers. 1997. "Women in Groups in Africa: Female Associational Patterns in Senegal and Morocco." In *Organizing Women: Formal and Informal Women's Groups in the Middle East*, edited by Dawn Chatty and Annika Rabo, 101–23. Oxford: Berg.
Rosen, Lawrence, 1984. *Bargaining for Reality: The Construction of Social Relations in a Muslim Community*. Chicago: University of Chicago Press.
Royaume du Maroc (Ministère de l'Emploi et de la formation professionnelle) and GIZ (Deutsche Gesellschaft für Internationale Zusammenarbeit). 2011. *Réalités socio-économiques des Travailleuses de maison et leurs conditions de travail*. Rabat: Royaume du Maroc.
Royaume du Maroc (Ministère de l'Emploi et des affaires sociales). 2016. "Remarques sur le projet de Loi sur les travailleurs domestiques au Maroc." Accessed April 27, 2017.

http://www.emploi.gov.ma/index.php/fr/presse/actualites/597-remarques-sur-le-projet-de-loi-sur-les-travailleurs-domestiques-au-maroc.html.

Rubbo, Anna, and Michael Taussig. 1983. "Up off Their Knees: Servanthood in Southwest Colombia." *Latin American Perspectives* 10 (4): 5–23.

Rugh, Andrea. 1985. "Women and Work: Strategies and Choices in a Lower-Class Quarter of Cairo." In *Women and the Family in the Middle East*, edited by Elizabeth Fernea, 273–88. Austin: University of Texas Press.

Saaf, Abdallah. 1999. *Carnets de bus: essai sur le quotidien des quartiers Sud-Ouest de Rabat*. Casablanca: EDDIF.

Sacks, Karen. 1974. "Engels Revisited: Women, the Organization of Production, and Private Property." In *Woman, Culture and Society*, edited by Michelle Z. Rosaldo and Louise Lamphere, 207–22. Stanford, CA: Stanford University Press.

Sakhri, Aïchi Zaïmi. 2003. "Editorial: L'émancipation, c'est aussi l'idée que nous nous faisons de nous-mêmes." *Femmes du Maroc* 85:4.

Salahdine, Mohamed. 1988. *Les petits métiers clandestins: "Le business populaire"*. Casablanca: EDDIF.

Salaheddine, Ahmed. 2013. "L'OIT juge le droit du travail au Maroc: un séminaire à Rabat chapeauté par l'Organisation international du travail." *Aujourd'hui Le Maroc*. Accessed September 26, 2014. http://www.aujourdhui.ma/maroc/societe/l-oit-juge-le-droit-du-travail-au-maroc-100559#.U-NYF-NdUrU.

Salzinger, Leslie. 1991. "A Maid by Any Other Name: The Transformation of 'Dirty Work' by Central American Immigrants." In *Ethnography Unbound: Power and Resistance in the Modern Metropolis*, edited by Michael Burawoy, 139–60. Berkeley: University of California Press.

Sandel, Michael. 2012. *The Moral Limits of Markets: What Money Can't Buy*. New York: Farrar, Straus and Giroux.

Sarasúa, Carmen. 2004. "Were Servants Paid According to their Productivity?" In *Domestic Service and the Formation of European Identity: Understanding the Globalization of Domestic Work, 16th–21st Centuries*, edited by Antoinette Fauve-Chamoux, 379–408. Bern: Peter Lang.

Sartre, Jean-Paul. 1982. Introduction to *The Maids and Deathwatch*, by Jean Genet. Translated by Bernard Frechtman. New York: Grove.

Scadden, Rosemary. 2013. *No Job for a Little Girl*. Llandysul: Gomer.

Schacht, J. 2012. "Aladjr." In *The Encyclopedia of Islam (Second Edition) Online*, edited by P. Bearman et al. Leiden: Brill.

Scheele, Judith. 2009. *Village Matters: Knowledge, Politics and Community in Kabylia, Algeria*. Woodbridge, UK: James Currey.

Schielke, Samuli. 2009. "Being Good in Ramadan: Ambivalences, Fragmentation, and the Moral Self in the Lives of Young Egyptians." *Journal of the Royal Anthropological Institute (N.S.)* 15: S24–S40.

Schneider, Elizabeth. 2002. *Battered Women and Feminist Lawmaking*. New Haven, CT: Yale University Press.

Scott, James. 1998. *Seeing Like a State: How Certain Schemes to Improve the Human Condition Have Failed*. New Haven, CT: Yale University Press.

Seccombe, Wally. 1974. "The Housewife and her Labour under Capitalism." *New Left Review* 83: 3–21.

———. 1975. "Domestic Labour—Reply to Critics." *New Left Review* 94:85–96.
Seddon, David. 1976. "Aspects of Kinship and Family Structure among the Ulad Stut of Zaio Rural Commune, Nador Province, Morocco." In *Mediterranean Family Structures*, edited by John G. Peristiany, 173–94. Cambridge, England: Cambridge University Press.
Sethi, Aman. 2012. *A Free Man: A True Story of Life and Death in Delhi*. London: Jonathan Cape.
Shah, Alpa. 2006. "The Labour of Love: Seasonal Migration from Jharkhand to the Brick Kilns of Other States in India." *Contributions to Indian Sociology* 40 (1): 91–118.
Shah, Saubhagya. 2000. "Service or Servitude? The Domestication of Household Labour in Nepal." In *Home and Hegemony: Domestic Service and Identity Politics in South and Southeast Asia*, edited by Sarah Dickey and Kathleen Adams, 87–118. Ann Arbor: University of Michigan Press.
Shami, Seteney. 1997. "Domesticity Reconfigured: Women in Squatter Areas of Amman." In *Organizing Women: Formal and Informal Women's Groups in the Middle East*, edited by Dawn Chatty and Annika Rabo, 81–100. Oxford; New York: Berg.
Shami, Seteney, and Lucine Taminian. 1995. "Children of Amman: Childhood and Child Care in Squatter Areas of Amman, Jordan." In *Children in the Muslim Middle East*, edited by Elizabeth Fernea, 68–76. Austin: University of Texas Press.
Shaw, Bernard. (1903) 2004. *Man and Superman: A Comedy and a Philosophy*. London: Penguin.
Shryock, Andrew. 2004. "The New Jordanian Hospitality: House, Host, and Guest in the Culture of Public Display." *Comparative Studies in Society and History* 46 (1): 35–62.
Silber, Ilana. 2000. "Beyond Purity and Danger: Gift-giving in Monotheistic Religions." In *Gifts and Interests*, edited by Antoon Vandevelde, 115–33. Leuven: Peeters.
Simmel, Georg. (1908) 1965. "The Poor." Translated by Claire Jacobson. *Social Problems* 13 (2): 118–40.
———. (1908) 1971. "The Stranger." In *Georg Simmel: On Individuality and Social Forms* edited by Donald Levine, 143–50. Chicago: University of Chicago Press.
Sinemillioğlu, Nora. 2007. "Le mendiant 'à l'orientale': relecture critique d'une activité marginale." Unpublished master's thesis, Université de Provence, Aix-Marseille.
———. 2009. "Donner et mendier dans les rues de Damas: une enquête sur la pratique de la mendicité et de ses modalités dans le cadre urbain." Unpublished master's thesis, Université de Provence, Aix-Marseille.
Singerman, Diane. 1995. *Avenues of Participation. Family, Politics and Networks in Urban Quarters of Cairo*. Princeton, NJ: Princeton University Press.
Skeldon, Ronald. 1980. "Regional Associations among Urban Migrants in Papua New Guinea." *Oceania* 50: 248-372.
Smith, Adam. (1776) 1986. *The Wealth of Nations*. Books 1–3. London: Penguin.
Smith, Andrew. 2002. "Sedq in Morocco: On Communicability, Patronage, and Partial Truth." *Cultural Critique* 51 (2): 101–42.
Smith, Gavin. 1990. "Negotiating Neighbours: Livelihood and Domestic Politics in Central Peru and the Pais Valenciano, Spain." In *Work without Wages*, edited by Jane Collins and Martha. E. Gimenez, 50–69. Albany: State University of New York.
Smith, Margo. 1973. "Domestic Service as a Channel of Upward Mobility for the Lower-Class Woman: the Lima Case." In *Female and Male in Latin America: Essays*, edited by Ann Pescatello, 191–208. Pittsburgh: University of Pittsburgh Press.

Smith, Paul. 1978. "Domestic Labour and Marx's Theory of Value." In *Feminism and Materialism: Women and Modes of Production*, Annette Kuhn and Annmarie Wolpe, 198–219. London: Routledge and Kegan Paul.
Snouck, C. Hurgronje. (1931) 1970. *Mekka in the Latter Part of the Nineteenth Century*. Leiden: E. J. Brill.
Sommerfelt, Tone, ed. 2001. *Domestic Child Labour in Morocco*. Oslo: FAFO Institute for Applied Social Science.
Sonbol, Amira. 1995. "Adoption in Islamic Society: A Historical Survey." In *Children in the Muslim Middle East*, edited by Elizabeth Fernea, 45–67. Austin: University of Texas Press.
Sonencher, Michael. 1989. *Work and Wages: Natural Law, Politics and the Eighteenth Century French Trades*. Cambridge: Cambridge University Press.
Stark, Freya. (1948) 2013. *Perseus in the Wind*. London: Tauris Parke.
Steedman, Carolyn. 2007. *Master and Servant: Love and Labour in the English Industrial Age*. Cambridge: Cambridge University Press.
———. 2009. *Labours Lost: Domestic Service and the Making of Modern England*. Cambridge: Cambridge University Press.
Stockett, Kathryn. 2010. *The Help*. London: Fig Tree.
Stone, Linda. 2006. *Kinship and Gender: An Introduction*, 3rd edition. Boulder, CO: Westview.
Storey, Neil, and Molly Housego. 2011. *Women in the First World War*. Oxford: Shire.
Stringham, Edward Peter. 2011. "Embracing Morals in Economics: The Role of Internal Moral Constraints in a Market Economy." *Journal of Economic Behaviour and Organization* 78 (1–2): 98–109.
Studer, Heide. 2014. "Constituting Urban Space in the Moroccan Context." *Urban Studies Journal*. Published online May 6. https://doi.org/10.1177/0042098014531629.
Styles, John. 1983. "Embezzlement, Industry, and the Law in England 1500–1800." In *Manufacture in Town and Country before the Factory*, edited by Maxine Berg, Pat Hudson, and Michael Sonenscher, 173–210. Cambridge: Cambridge University Press.
———. 2007. *The Dress of the People: Everyday Fashion in Eighteenth-Century England*. New Haven, CT: Yale University Press.
Suk, Jeannie. 2009. *At Home in the Law: How the Domestic Violence Revolution is Transforming Privacy*. New Haven, CT: Yale University Press.
Surtees, Robert Smith. (1853) 1981. *Mr Sponge's Sporting Tour*. London: Bradbury, Agnew.
———. (1865) 2006. *Mr Facey Romford's Hounds*. Stroud: Nonsuch.
Sutherland, Kathryn. 2003. Introduction to *Mansfield Park*, by Jane Austen, xi–xl. London: Penguin.
Tādilī, A. at-. (1229) 1984. *At-Tashawwuf ilā rijāl at-taṣawwuf*, ed. Aḥmad at-Tawfīq. Rabat: Kulliyat al-Ādāb wa-al-ʿUlūm al-Insānīya.
Talib, Mohammad. 2010. *Writing Labour: Stone Quarry Workers in Delhi*. New Delhi: Oxford University Press.
Tapper, Richard, and Nancy Tapper. 1992–93. "Marriage, Honour and Responsibility: Islamic and Local Models in the Mediterranean and the Middle East." *Cambridge Anthropology* 16 (2): 3–21.
Tellis-Nayak, V. 1983. "Power and Solidarity: Clientage in Domestic Service." *Current Anthropology* 24 (1): 67–79.
Terrasse, Henri. 1952. *Histoire du Maroc*. Casablanca: Atlantides.

Thompson, Edward P. 1971. "The Moral Economy of the English Crowd in the Eighteenth Century." *Past and Present* 50: 76–136.

———. 1974. "Patrician Society, Plebeian Culture." *Journal of Social History* 7 (4): 382–405.

Tillion, Germaine. 1983. *The Republic of Cousins: Women's Oppression in Mediterranean Society*. London: El Saqi.

Todd, Selina. 2005. *Young Women, Work, and Family in England 1918–1950*. Oxford: Oxford University Press.

———. 2009. "Domestic Service and Class Relations in Britain 1900–1950." *Past and Present* 203:181–204.

Tönnies, Ferdinand. (1887) 2001. *Community and Civil Society*. Translated and edited by Jose Harris and Margaret Hollis. Cambridge: Cambridge University Press.

Toth, James. 1991. "Pride, Purdah and Paychecks." *International Journal of Middle East Studies* 23:213–36.

Touahri, Sarah. 2009. "Une nouvelle loi régissant le travail domestique verra bientôt le jour au Maroc." *Magharebia*. Accessed September 26, 2014. http://magharebia.com/fr/articles/awi/features/2009/03/13/feature-03 (site discontinued).

Troeltsch, Ernst. 1931. *The Social Teachings of the Christian Churches*. London: George Allen & Unwin.

Tsikata, Dzodzi. 2011. "Employment Agencies and the Regulation of Domestic Workers in Ghana: Institutionalizing Informality?" *Canadian Journal of Women and the Law* 23 (1): 213–33.

Ueno, Kayoko. 2010. "Identity Management among Indonesian and Filipina Migrant Domestic Workers in Singapore." *International Journal of Japanese Sociology* 19 (1): 82–97.

United Kingdom Government. 2014. "Employing Someone to Work in Your Home." Accessed September 26, 2014. https://www.gov.uk/au-pairs-employment-law.

Valenzuela, Abel J. 2003. "Day Labor Work." *Annual Review of Sociology* 29:307–33.

Van Dusen, Roxann. 1976. "The Study of Women in the Middle East. Some Thoughts." *Middle East Studies Association Bulletin* 10 (2): 1–19.

Van Raaphorst, Donna. 1988. *Union Maids Not Wanted: Organizing Domestic Workers, 1870–1940*. New York; London: Praeger.

Vaughan, Megan. 1991. *Curing Their Ills: Colonial Power and African Illness*. Palo Alto: Stanford University Press.

Veneziani, Bruno. 1986. "The Evolution of the Contract of Employment." In *The Making of Labour Law in Europe*, edited by Bob Hepple, 31–72. London: Mansell.

Villème, Louis. 1952. "L'Evolution de la vie citadine au Maroc." In *Cahiers de l'Afrique et l'Asie 2*, edited by Jean d'Etienne, Louis Villème, and Stéphane Delisle, 53–107. Paris: Peyronnet.

Wall, Richard. 2004. "The Social and Economic Significance of Servant Migration." In *Domestic Service and the Formation of European Identity: Understanding the Globalization of Domestic Work, 16th–21st Centuries*, edited by Antoinette Fauve-Chamoux, 19–42. Bern: Peter Lang.

Waltner, Ann. 1990. *Getting an Heir: Adoption and the Construction of Kinship in Late Imperial China*. Honolulu: University of Hawaii Press.

Weir, T. H. 2012. "Ṣadaḳa." In *The Encyclopedia of Islam (Second Edition) Online*, edited by P. Bearman et al. Leiden: Brill.

West, Candace, and Don H. Zimmerman. 1987. "Doing Gender." *Gender and Society* 1 (2): 125–51.

Westermarck, Edward. 1926. *Ritual and Belief in Morocco*. London: Macmillan.
Whisson, Michael, and William Weil. 1971. *Domestic Servants: A Microcosm of "The Race Problem."* Johannesburg: South African Institute of Race Relations.
White, Jenny. 1994. *Money Makes Us Relatives: Women's Labor in Urban Turkey*. Austin: University of Texas.
Williamson, Oliver. 1975. *Markets and Hierarchies: Analysis and Antitrust Implications*. New York: Macmillan.
Woolf, Virginia. 1929. *A Room of One's Own*. London: Hogarth.
Yan, Hairong. 2008. *New Masters, New Servants: Migration, Development, and Women Workers in China*. Durham, NC: Duke University Press.
Yanagisako, Sylvia. J. 1979. "Family and Household: The Analysis of Domestic Groups." *Annual Review of Anthropology* 8:161–205.
Zamiti-Horchani, Malika. 1983. "Les Tunisiennes, leurs droits et l'idée qu'on s'en fait." In "Femmes de la Méditerranée," *Peuples Méditerranéens*, 22–23.
Zerrour, Laila. 2011. "Affaire de la petite Khadija tuée à El Jadida: l'audience reportée au mercredi 5 octobre." *Aujourd'hui Le Maroc*. Accessed September 26, 2014. http://aujourdhui.ma/societe/affaire-de-la-petite-khadija-tuee-a-el-jadida-laudience-reportee-au-mercredi-5-octobre-79340.
Zontini, Elisabetta. 2010. *Transnational Families, Migration and Gender: Moroccan and Filipino Women in Bologna and Barcelona*. New Directions in Anthropology, 30. New York; Oxford: Berghahn.
Zvan Elliott, Katja. 2009. "Reforming the Moroccan Personal Status Code: A Revolution for Whom?" *Mediterranean Politics*, 14 (2): 213–27.
———. 2015. *Modernizing Patriarchy: The Politics of Women's Rights in Morocco*. Austin: University of Texas Press.

Websites

Banque Populaire. n.d. "Campagnes." Accessed September 30, 2014. http://www.gbp.ma/EspaceCommunication/Pages/Campagnes.aspx.
Maroc Telecom. n.d. Accessed October 3, 2014. http://www.iam.ma.
The Productive Muslim Company. n.d. Accessed September 26, 2014. http://productivemuslim.com/.
VIP Blog. n.d. Accessed September 26, 2014. http://www.vip-blog.com/vip/articles/5116620.html (site discontinued).
Ya Biladi. n.d. "Forums: Relations familiales et sociales." Accessed September 26, 2014. http://www.yabiladi.com/forum/aidez-orphelins-70-5475945.html.

Audio-Visual Sources

Tahiri, Zakia and Ahmad Boushala. 2011. *Madame M'safara*. Made in Morocco Films. Broadcast on 2M channel, December 2011.

INDEX

Abu-Lughod, Janet, 31n15
Abu-Lughod, Lila, 34, 146n4, 147n18, 160
abuse: of children, xvii; of workers, 55, 56, 57n16, 198
Abu-Zahra, N., 205
adoption, xvi, 36–38, 41, 56, 57n10, 58n27
affection, 59, 82, 85
Africa, 36, 57n5; North Africa, 5, 13, 23, 67, 88n19, 95, 139, 166, 209; sub-Saharan, 9. *See also* South Africa
Agdal, 5, 10, 12, 22, 96–97, 116n15, 181
agriculture, 6, 97, 131, 174n4; agricultural labor, 131, 153, 174, 200n8
ajr (religious merit), 59–60, 70–73, 74, 75, 76–77, 79, 81, 86, 98, 100, 110
Algeria, 6, 8, 33, 49, 71, 96, 116n10, 157, Algerians, 40, 61, 171
Almohads, 6, 31n6
Anderson, Bridget, 67
Andreatta, Susan, 134
anthropology, xxiv, 56, 66, 72, 75, 207; anthropologists, 30n1, 32n22, 47, 147n15, 207
apprenticeship, 40, 57n14, 195, 207, 212n6
Arabic language, xvi, 31n4, 70, 79, 91, 96, 137, 178, 187, 201n10
Armbrust, Walter, 19
Asmae, 20, 184, 190, 199
Atia, Mona, 88n20
autonomy, xviii, 85, 113, 117n30, 169, 194
Aziza, 110, 168

Bargach, Jamila, 37, 41
Barraud, Emilie, 37
Belarbi, Aicha, xix
Belghiti, Malika, 166, 170, 171, 209
Bender, Donald R., 207
Benet, Francisco, 210
Benkirane, Abdelilah, 177–78
Berbers, xviii, 14, 31n13, 77, 133, 155, 175n9; Berber language, 115n2, 140, 147n15, 210

Berk, Sarah Fenstermaker, 209
bidonvilles (shantytowns), 6, 96
Blackett, Adelle, 183, 188, 189, 194
Bloch, Maurice, 36, 57n7, 66
Blum, Léon, 67
Bohannan, Paul, 205
boredom, 30n1, 34, 157, 174
Borrmans, M., 49, 58n32, 61, 96
Bouchra, 64, 81, 135
Boudoudou, Mohamed, 17
Bouharrou, Ahmed, 182
boundaries, 46, 207, 212n9; and domestic workers, 30, 49, 51, 56, 58n26, 64, 203; of the family, 46, 206
Bourdieu, Pierre, 133
Bourqia, Rahma, 164
Brady, Ivan, 37
Brass, Tom, 80
brides, 45, 138, 160, 167, 168, 170–71, 175n11, 195, 206
Brown, Kenneth, 16
Buckley, Peter J., 202
Buddhism, 75, 144
Buitelaar, Marjo, 71
Bujra, Janet, 34

Caillé, Alain, 63
Caplan, Lionel, 36
care: and domestic workers, 35, 48, 54, 55, 56, 65, 79, 92, 93, 115, 185, 203, 204; familial, 55, 57n5, 65, 72, 169; pious, xxiv, 60; of poor, 64; signs of, xvi, 59, 60, 61, 65, 86, 202. *See also* childcare; *dadas*; motherhood, maternal care
Carey, Matthew, 147n15
Carrier, James, 86, 108
Carsten, Janet, 197, 202, 207, 208
Casablanca, 3, 7, 11, 31n14, 54, 58n26, 70, 130, 134, 140, 151, 153, 155, 169, 185, 196, 211
cell phones, 126, 134–35, 145
Chant, Sylvia, 115n8

237

Chapman, Malcolm, 202
charity, xvii, 38, 60, 62, 85, 88n13, 116n14; and domestic workers, 59, 61, 62, 64, 65–66, 68, 76, 79, 80–81, 85, 86, 100, 199
Charrad, Mounira, 208
Cheikh, Mériam, 58n26, 61, 130, 134, 146n5, 155, 163, 174n3
Chekroun, Mohamed, 17
Chen, Carolyn, 143
childcare, 115n8, 179, 185, 197, 212n3. *See also* dadas
Christianity, 144; Christians, 78
civilizing mission, xvii, 59, 68, 69, 86, 157, 191
Clanchy, Michael, 82
Clarke, Morgan, 37
class, xv, xx, 11, 12, 33, 80, 115n1, 128, 158, 168, 189; class divisions, xix, 13, 34, 42, 44, 74, 94, 113, 114, 205; employing, 8, 94, 99; lower, 6, 34; lower-middle, xix, 4, 186; middle, xx, 9–10, 13, 17, 18, 31n17, 68, 96, 168, 169, 184, 185, 189, 190; serving, xx; upper, 13, 17, 19, 20, 22, 42, 68; working, xxiii, 7, 8, 9–10, 13, 18, 22, 25, 31n14, 94, 169, 189, 194, 211
cleaning, xvii, xxi, 4, 11, 24, 25, 41, 42–43, 76, 97, 103, 105, 128, 149, 157, 164, 166, 178, 179, 183, 206, 211; of carpets, 43, 46, 56, 97; of floors, xxii, 26, 27, 34, 52, 92, 111, 149, 154, 166; *l-ʿawāshīr* (thorough cleaning before feast days), 45, 98; spring cleaning, 22, 97–98; of stairs, 10, 12, 25. *See also* housework
clothing, 35, 40, 60, 61, 65, 66, 70, 80–81, 87n4, 99, 103, 128, 130, 135, 143, 153, 155, 159, 160, 161, 162, 167, 170, 185–86; as gifts, 60–61, 67, 70, 152; house clothes, 130; pajamas, 66–67, 81, 130, 152, 159, 163, 206; as payment, 61–62, 86; street clothes, 66, 130, 159; used, 69, 101, 109, 143; washing of, 48, 91, 167, 210, 211
Cock, Jacklyn, 33, 126
Code des obligations et contrats (December 1913), 179
Code du travail, 177, 182, 196
Cohen, Mark, 64
Collier, Jane, 138, 146n10
colonization, 59, 209

Combs-Schilling, Elaine, 57n7
community, xvii, xxiv, 17, 21, 31n16, 62, 189, 197, 200, 202, 203, 204, 212
companionate ideals, 134
concierges, 10, 112–13, 114
Conseil national des droits de l'homme (CNDH), 179, 187
cooking, 15, 24, 28, 41, 43, 105, 107, 128–29, 154, 157–58, 161, 170, 171, 178, 179, 183, 196, 210, 211; cooks, 14, 103, 105, 157, 182, 192–93, 195, 197; learning, 23, 42, 166, 211. *See also* housework
Coser, Lewis, xv
Cox, Rosie, 186, 201n22
Crawford, David, xviii, 15, 77, 123, 127, 143, 149, 155, 156, 166, 173, 203, 204, 205, 207

dadas (female slaves assigned to the care of children), 23, 32n20. *See also* childcare
"daughters of the house" (*bint d-dār*), xv, xvi, 41, 47, 50, 81, 124
daughters-in-law, 24, 46, 58n28, 167, 170–72, 173, 204, 208–9. *See also* mothers-in-law
Davidoff, Leonore, 123
Davis, Douglas A., 146nn10–11, 166
Davis, Susan, xxiv n6, 39, 91, 146nn10–11, 166, 171–72
Dawiya, 152, 167, 172
debt, 80, 86, 156, 190
dignity, 91, 184–85
divorce, 7, 24, 39, 123, 156, 172, 173, 175n12, 189; divorce rate, 53; divorcées, 92, 122
Douglas, Mary, 52
Dresch, Paul, 17, 88n14, 164
Dunn, Elizabeth, 142
Dwyer, Daisy H., 170, 172

Early, Evelyn, 19
economy: cash, 155; domestic, 186; French-run, 31n9; gig, xxi; global, xviii; moral, xvii, 62, 79, 109, 113; patriarchal, 35. *See also* market, market economy
education, xvi, xxiv n2, 10, 11, 69, 128, 168, 191, 205; of women, xix, xx, 47, 72, 137, 146n10, 180
Ehrenreich, Barbara, xxii
Eickelman, Dale, 17, 21

Elliot, Alice, 130, 136
Employers' Liability Act (England), 177
employment agencies, 22, 34, 39, 102–3, 104–5, 106, 107, 108, 109, 112, 113, 114, 116n19, 180, 192, 196. *See also* employment brokers
employment brokers, (*samāsira*), xvii, xviii, 24, 54, 65, 90, 93, 102, 104, 105–6, 108, 109, 114, 115n6, 116n21, 160. *See also* employment agencies
Ennaji, Mohammed, xv, 38
Ensel, Remco, 71
Europe, xxi, 31n3, 44, 62, 63, 88, 122, 130, 156, 176, 185; European communities, 5–6, 105, 151; European domestic service, xxi, 193; European quarters, 7, 95; Europeans, 7, 8, 22, 31n9, 95–96, 114, 142
exchanges, 80, 81, 110, 113, 114, 149, 171, 202–3, 208, 212n10; exchange networks, 205; of labor, 205; long-term, 35, 36; of material goods, 92; nonmonetary, 14; peer-to-peer, xxi; reciprocal, 13, 35, 109; short-term, xvii, 35–36; spheres of, xvi, 205. *See also* market, market exchange
exploitation, 38, 89n27, 185, 193–94; of children, xvii; of domestic workers, 51, 54, 56, 59, 74, 85, 169

Family Code, 146n5, 184, 192, 193
family law, 37, 176
famine, 6, 31n7, 38, 72
Farag, Eftetan, 57n14
Fatiha, 44, 45
Fatima, 13, 14, 18, 21, 51, 73, 76–77, 79, 81, 85, 88n21, 182, 188, 193, 198
femininity, 60, 210–11
feminism, xviii, xix, xx, 189, 193, 200n1, 209
Fernea, Elizabeth, 16
Ferraro, Gary, 134
Fes, 3, 5, 11, 15, 40, 49, 50, 52, 54, 72, 78, 116n21, 116n28, 123, 139, 140, 151, 158, 169, 170, 195
Filipinas, xv, xx, 105, 144, 147n25, 184, 195–98, 200, 202. *See also* Filipino Migrant Workers in Morocco
Filipino Migrant Workers in Morocco, 195, 196. *See also* Filipinas

Findlay, Allan, 8, 93
Findlay, Anne, 8, 93
Foley, Winifred, 79, 80
Forget, Nelly, xix, xxiv n6
forgiveness, 60, 76, 78–79, 85
Fortes, Myer, 24
fosterage, xxiii, 23, 34, 36–40, 43, 44, 47–48, 49, 57n9, 57nn11–12, 57n16, 57n21, 60, 72, 73–74, 85, 124
Fouzia, 102, 103, 104, 108, 116n17
France, 4, 6, 67, 68, 69, 97, 105, 116n26, 133, 154, 187, 201n10; French administrators, 6, 7, 8, 31n9, 95; French language, 31n4, 57n18, 72, 91, 187; French people, 8, 40, 68, 115n4, 157, 187
Fremlin, Celia, 94, 123, 124

Geertz, Hildred, 14, 47
gender, xix, xx, xxiv, 58n23, 168, 189, 202, 209. *See also* inequality, gendered; labor, division of
generosity, 20, 71, 75, 85, 88n13; of family members, 14, 34; of employers, 67, 69, 77
Gharb people, 127, 133; Gharb region, xviii, xxii, 21, 55, 92, 93, 113, 127, 129, 150, 151, 174n4
gifts, xvi, 35, 56, 63, 70–71, 75, 77, 81, 92, 100, 109, 150, 151–52, *162*, 173, 205, 206; as payment, 33, 60–61, 62, 63, 65–67, 68, 69–70, 79, 82, 86, 109, 156, 196
Gill, Lesley, 87n1
God, 21–22, 38, 48, 70, 71–72, 73, 74, 76–79, 85, 86, 88n23, 95, 100, 136, 138, 153, 191; blessings from, 20, 25, 65. *See also* ajr
Godbout, Jacques T., 86
Goffman, Erving, 147n23
Goichon, Amélie Marie, 40–41, 48, 72
gold jewelry, 57n16, 60, 87n2, 155, 160
Goody, Jack, 37
Graeber, David, 66
gratitude, 59, 65–66, 69, 73, 79–80, 85, 86, 171, 191, 199; ingratitude, xvii, 65, 68, 79, 85
Great Britain, xviii, xx, xxi, 34, 48, 62, 64, 67, 77, 82, 91, 94, 104, 123–24, 131, 179, 185, 190, 198, 201n17
Grover, Shalini, 147n20
guarantors, 108, 115n5, 116n25
Gudeman, Stephen, xvii, 92, 109

ḥadīth, 37, 191
Hafida, xviii, 21, 47–48, 55, 83–84, 110–12, 137, 140, 143, 147n19, 150–53, 154, 156, 157, 158, 159, 160, 165, 167–68, 169, 172, 174n2, 174n5, 181, 182
Hajnal, John, 122
Hakima, 99, 166
Hala, 165–66
Hammoudi, Abdellah, 209, 211
Hanane, 49–50, 133
Hassan, 10, 16
Hassan district, 5, 10, 22, 96, 115n4
Hayat, xxiii, 47, 55, 65, 68–69, 73, 74, 80, 84, 91, 110, 161
Haywood, Eliza, 68, 88n12
hierarchy, 13, 55, 169, 203, 207, 211–12; familial, 34, 150, 173, 174, 204; household, xix, xx, 28, 30, 43, 85, 150, 167, 170, 173, 197, 202, 204, 208
Hill, Bridget, 87n8
Hinde, 43, 53
Hinduism, 71, 75
Hirabayashi, Lane Ryo, 126
Hirschkind, Charles, 72
Hochschild, Arlie, 171
Hoffman, Katherine E., 131, 133, 170
holidays, xxi, 50, 102, 104, 129, 159, 180, 211. *See also* ʿīd
Holmes-Eber, Paula, 23, 91
Hondagneu-Sotelo, Pierrette, 83
Hong Kong, 87n9, 144
hospitality, 3, 15, 71, 92, 94–95, 161, 206, 208
households, xvii–xviii, xix, xxi, xxiv, xxivn6, 4, 10, 17, 23–25, 27, 28, 29, 32n20, 34, 38, 40, 41, 51–52, 53, 54, 55, 57n8, 57n12, 58n23, 58n28, 62, 72, 89n27, 91, 93, 117n30, 122, 123, 143, 149, 153, 166–67, 168, 178, 181, 183, 186, 188, 189, 202–3, 207–8, 209; exchange between households, xx, 204–5, 207, 208, 212n3; household heads, xvi, 31n18, 87n2, 95, 178, 180, 182, 200n4, 212n6; household members, 56, 82, 115n8, 149, 156, 177, 178–79, 203, 207; natal, 143, 149, 155; rural, 13, 167, 173; wealthy, xv, 33, 38, 57n22, 164. *See also* hierarchy, household; *shaʿbī*, households
housework, 19, 22, 23, 25, 28, 30, 30n1, 34, 36, 41, 43, 58n24, 85, 91, 115n8, 149, 157, 168,
169, 171, 179, 200n1, 208, 209, 210–11, 212n3; by domestic workers, xxiii, 33, 39, 40, 50, 60, 80, 92, 113, 195, 197, 198, 212. *See also* cleaning; cooking
Howell, Signe, 56
human rights, xvii, xix, 38, 193; Human Rights Watch, 105
Huriya, 73–74, 124, 125, 134, 138
hurma (sacredness or inviolability), 94–95

ʿīd, 48, 69, 73, 81, 98, 111, 127, 145, 153, 181; ʿīd l-kabīr, 150; ʿīd ṣ-ṣaghīr, 60, 87n4, 150
identity, 24, 63, 128, 170, 201n13, 209, 211; of domestic workers, 56, 67, 121, 140, 144, 147n25; Egyptian, 19; modern, xix; Moroccan, xix. *See also shaʿbī*, identification as
Ikram, 53, 54, 66, 70, 78, 83, 139, 141, 142, 147n24, 168–69, 173
Ilham, 58n33, 76, 93, 110, 127, 128–29, 130, 132, 134–36, 138, 140, 142, 144, 145, 156, 179
inequality, xix, 20, 89n27, 90, 141, 199; of domestic workers, 56, 59, 62, 74, 85; gendered, xvi
inferiority, of domestic workers, 40, 53, 59, 66, 67, 68, 69, 171, 212
Ingold, Tim, 32n22
inheritance, 14, 36, 46
intermediaries, xviii, 65, 90, 102, 106, 109, 110, 113, 115, 167, 180, 209. *See also* employment brokers
International Labour Office, xvii, 180, 181, 183, 186, 194
Islam, 37, 71, 72, 73, 75, 88n14, 88n20; Islamic ethics, xvii, 76, 191. *See also* Muslims; mosques; Qurʾān
Italy, xx, 4

Jacquemin, Mélanie, 57n19
Jamila, 23, 24–25, 28, 29, 50, 54–55, 60, 132
Jansen, Willy, 33, 40, 71, 96
Jenkins, Timothy, 133
Jews, 8, 64, 68, 201n18
Jihane, 29, 42–43, 45, 60, 206
Jorf El Melḥa, 151, 153, 165, 174n2
Joseph, Suad, 46
justice, 79, 81, 87n7, 184, 191; divine, 78
Jutte, Robert, 63

Kapchan, Deborah, 87n2, 170, 175n10
Kasriel, Michèle, 171
Katz, Jonathan G., 68
Katzman, David, 65
Keene, Emily, 26, 91, 160
Kessler-Harris, Alice, 184
Khadija, 41–42, 43, 45, 53
khayr (goodness, blessing), 20, 59, 60, 70, 73, 80, 86, 110
kheddāmāt (servants), xvi, 90, 199
kinship, xv, xvi, xxiii, xxiv, 14, 21, 30, 33, 34, 36, 37, 38–39, 46, 47, 56, 58n23, 62, 80, 86, 90, 91, 94, 126, 136, 138, 159, 170, 173, 201n13, 202, 205, 206, 207, 208; dekinning, 56; fictive, 9, 33, 47, 204; idiomatic, 33; networks, 23, 205; obligations, 77, 169; pseudo, 200; terms, 33, 34, 36, 147n15; uterine, 38
Kuran, Timur, 63

labor, 3–4, 6, 28, 30n1, 35, 37, 57n14, 67, 71, 77, 83, 115n8, 117n30, 155, 158, 168, 169, 174n5, 175n11, 178, 201n16, 203, 206, 209; bonded, 80; commoditized, xxiv, 62, 143; "cousin," 92, 93; day, 78, 96, 204; demand for, 3, 13, 46, 97, 100; division of, 166, 197, 210, 211; domestic, xvii, xviii, 13, 25, 38, 43, 83, 91, 114, 149, 176–77, 200n1, 204; factory, xix, 58n27, 131, 163, 194; labor law, 62, 104, 177, 179, 182, 183, 200n6; monthly, 35, 54, 86, 105, 134, 141, 183, 184; unpaid, xv, 33, 46, 171; wage, 15, 33, 93, 134, 149, 166. *See also* agriculture, agricultural labor; exchanges, of labor; market, labor; payment
Lacoste-Dujardin, Camille, 171
Lallemand, Suzanne, 57n9
Lambek, Michael, 74
Latifa, 22–25, 27, 28–30, 41–46, 49, 51, 60, 70, 73–74, 78, 79, 81, 101, 124, 125, 172, 182, 199, 202
Latin America, xx, 126, 188
Lebanon, xix, 37, 71
leisure, xxi, 123, 124, 143, 144, 148n27, 173
Lethbridge, Lucy, 34, 160
Lévi-Strauss, Claude, 33, 208
Light, Alison, 44, 64, 198
literacy, 137, 144, 147n14, 180; illiteracy, 146n9

l'Océan, xxiii, 4, 5, 7, 8–9, 12–13, 14, 16–17, 19, 20–21, 23, 25, 26, 27, 30, 32n20, 35, 37, 39, 41, 42, 45, 50, 70, 84, 87, 92, 94, 95, 96, 100, 112, 122, 127, 150, 181, 187, 202; architecture, 7, 8–9, 16; Océanis, 4, 9–10, 11, 14, 15, 18, 21, 22, 43, 82, 85, 90, 94, 97, 99, 101, 186, 197, 203
Loubna, 51, 139, 204
loyalty, xviii, xxiii, 34, 86, 87n7, 176, 212n1
Lyautey, Maréchal, 5–6, 16, 193

Mahdavi, Pardis, 121
Maher, Vanessa, 13, 39, 71, 115n2, 167, 170, 204, 210
Mahmood, Saba, 72, 136, 146n4
Makdisi, Jean Said, xix
Malika, 25–28, 49–50, 52, 53–54, 69–70, 76, 78, 81, 116n21, 124, 125, 139, 141, 154, 155, 158, 159, 168–69, 182, 205–7
Mandeville, Bernard, 62
maʿrūf (known), *maʿrūfa* (f.), *maʿrūfīn* (pl.), 64, 86, 93, 97, 106, 108, 113, 114
market, 33, 59, 86, 87, 100, 108, 109, 202–203, 210, 212n1; labor, xix, xx, xxiii, 74, 78, 86, 92, 95, 96, 98, 110, 113, 114–15, 116n12, 176; market economy, 35; market exchange, xxiv, 36, 109, 203, 204, 207, 211
Marrakech, 3, 11, 21, 34, 55, 68, 211
marriage, xvi, 57n9, 131, 135, 136–37, 139, 146n5, 170, 171, 172; arranged, 40, 73–74, 121–23, 133, 147n20; companionate, 146n10; contracts, 175n12; to cousins, 138–39, 208; and domestic workers, xv, xviii–xix, xxi, xxiv, 40, 58n28, 83, 133, 140, 143, 146n4, 181, 193; love, 147n20; marriage rates, 123. *See also* brides; divorce
Marx, Karl, 176; Marxism, 10, 193
Mauss, Marcel, 66
McBride, Theresa, 116n26
McDonald, Tom, 32n22
medīna (old, walled city), 4, 5, 6, 7, 8, 16–17, 22, 23, 44, 72, 90–91, 93, 95, 130, 143, 160, 161, 201n18
Mehdi, 39, 97, 104
Meillassoux, Claude, 36
Meknes, 11, 151, 170
Meneley, Anne, 208
Mernissi, Fatima, 33, 141

Messiri, Sawsan, 19, 20, 31n15
migrants, xviii, xx, 7, 9, 11, 105, 106, 127, 134, 136, 156, 161, 174f, 175n9; female, xx, 122, 143, 171; rural-urban, xx, 122, 153, 161, 169; transnational, xv. *See also* migration
migration, xviii, xxiv, 6, 7, 8, 121, 126, 131, 150, 154, 169, 174, 198. *See also* migrants
Ministry of Employment, 79, 114, 122, 131, 185, 187, 188, 190, 191
Miriam, 66, 111, 138, 140, 144, 150, 152, 153–55, 165, 168, 170, 181
modernity, xvi, xix, 3, 6, 19, 31n15, 66, 102, 141, 145, 193; modernization, 62, 69
Montagne, Robert, 142, 175n9
morality, 36, 60, 74, 82, 139, 202; of women, 125, 163
mosques, 72, 87n4, 98, 136, 137, 144, 191
motherhood, 31n17, 115n8, 171–72, 173, 197, 204; maternal care, xvii, 17, 23, 38, 65, 86, 176; maternalism, xvi, 65, 69, 199; mother-daughter relationship, xviii, 35, 38, 45, 46, 47, 48, 54, 82, 83, 167, 168, 199, 208, 209
mothers-in-law, 23, 46, 77, 170–71, 175n11, 208–9
Mounib, Noura, 198
Moustaghfir, Fatima, 192, 193
Munson, Henry, Jr., 171
Muslims, 6, 21, 49, 58n28, 63, 70, 73, 76, 81, 88n14, 95; Muslim communities, 16, 37, 192. *See also* Islam; mosques

Nabila, 101, 105, 180, 204
Nadia, 23, 24–28, 29, 45, 49–50, 51–53, 54, 69, 70, 76, 81, 124, 125, 133, 134, 154, 158
Nafisa, 99–100
Naima, 102–5, 108
Najat, 73–74, 124
Nawar, 76, 78, 126, 160
Nechnach, Mohamed, 180
neighborliness, 14, 16, 17, 20–21, 63, 90, 156; neighbors, xv, xxii, 9, 11, 13, 14, 15–16, 17, 18, 21, 23, 25, 30, 31n16, 59, 63, 64, 65, 82, 87n4, 90–91, 96, 100, 107, 110, 112, 130, 145, 152, 159, 164, 168, 174n3, 200, 202, 204, 205, 206
Nejlae, 112–13
Newcomb, Rachel, xix, 14, 123, 140, 171
Nieuwkerk, Karin van, 71

nostalgia, 17, 95
Nouvel, Jacques, 7

obligation, xvi, xviii, 62, 77, 80, 110, 112, 147n15, 169, 203
Organisation démocratique du travail (ODT), 180, 195, 198
Ossman, Susan, 11, 31n14, 128, 130, 135, 136, 139
Oudaya Kasbah, 5, 6, 31n6
Ozyegin, Gul, 209

Paddison, Ronan, 8, 92
Paris, 11, 12, 42, 171
parliament, 177–78, 192, 193
Parreñas, Rhacel, 147n25
Parry, Jonathan, 36, 70, 88n14
Parti de la justice et du dévelopment (PJD), 177, 178
Parti du progrès et du socialisme (PPS), 177, 178
passports, 44, 198
Pasternak, Bernard, 115n8
patriarchy, 15, 46, 80, 154, 166, 174, 211. *See also* economy, patriarchal
patrilineage, 14, 172, 208, 209
patronage, 33, 35, 38, 46, 47, 57n12, 80, 86, 92, 110, 115, 121, 125, 204; patron-client relationship, 13–14, 53
payment, 36, 62, 70, 82, 86, 99, 109, 165, 178, 179, 191; in-kind, xvi, 61–62, 179, 183, 186
Persian Gulf, xx, 17, 31n16, 37, 196
Pitt, William, 185, 190
Poor Law (England), 176
poverty, xvii, xix, 37, 39, 63, 106; relativity of, 67, 68, 75
prestige, 17, 82, 156, 161, 173, 175n9, 205, 208
privacy, 17, 21, 164, 188, 189, 197
productivity, 36, 110, 178, 183, 209
Prost, Henri, 6
prostitution, 96, 108, 132, 190, 193
protectorate period, xvi, 4, 5, 6, 8, 95, 114, 185

Qayum, Seemin, 33, 117n30
Qurʾān, 37, 38, 62, 71, 76, 77, 191. *See also* Islam; Muslims
Qureshi, Kaveri, 77

Rabat, xv, xxii, xxv, 3, 5, 6, 7, 8, 9–10, 11, 12, 16, 21, 22, 24, 25, 30n1, 31n6, 71, 79, 92, 93, 96, 103, 106, 114, 116n21, 116n28, 126, 127, 132, 134, 136, 137, 140, 143, 150, 151, 156, 157, 166, 169, 172, 175n9, 184, 193, 196, 197; Rabat workers, 11, 105, 112, 115n6, 124, 125, 126, 127, 131, 139, 145, 153, 160, 173
Rachida, 38, 42, 43–46, 48, 49, 53, 58n24, 73, 125, 139, 157
Rahma, 80, 84
Ramadan, 50, 53, 60, 71, 72, 73, 84, 111, 150, 158
Rassam, Amal, 171–72
Ray, Raka, 33, 117n30
reciprocity, 15, 38, 66, 70, 79–80, 85, 86, 88n14, 109, 204–5. *See also* exchanges, reciprocal
relaxation, xix, 143, 144
remittances, xviii, 154
Rivière, Peter, 30n1
Roberts, Robert, 124
Rollins, Judith, 67
Rosander, Eva Evers, 204
Rouqia, 50–51, 110, 121, 129, 130, 132, 134, 135–36, 140, 144–45, 155, 156

Sacks, Karen, 212n10
ṣadaqa (voluntary alms), 63, 74, 88n19
Safae, 20, 48, 61, 78, 83, 113, 138, 140, 152–53, 154, 165, 168, 170
Salahdine, Mohamed, 40, 115n6, 133
salaire minimum agricole garanti (SMAG, guaranteed minimum agricultural wage), 200n8
salaire minimum interprofessionnel garanti (SMIG, minimum wage for the industrial, commerce, and service sectors), 183–84, 186, 200n8
Salé, 5, 8, 11, 16, 25, 39, 96, 97, 102, 124, 125–26, 143
Salima, 66–67, 70, 78
Salma, 14, 84, 112
samāsira. *See* employment brokers
Sartre, Jean-Paul, 67
Scadden, Rosemary, 193
Schielke, Samuli, 72
Scott, James, 199

Sebbari family, xxii–xxiii, 4, 22, 24, 28, 30, 42, 44, 45, 46, 50, 52, 60, 101, 105, 139, 150, 157, 204, 206–7; *Dār Sebbari*, 24, 25, 29, 38, 41, 43–44, 45, 47, 49, 52–53, 58n24, 60, 69, 101, 105, 124, 133, 172, 178, 202, 204, 207; Sebbari building, 23–24, 70, 117n30, 124, 134, 154. *See also* Jamila; Jihane; Latifa; Nadia; Salima; Zahra
Seddiki, Abdeslam, 178, 180, 183
Selwa, 21, 169
sexuality: marital, 58; monetized, 146n5, 155, 163; premarital sex, 135
shaʿbī, xv, xxi, 31n15, 87n4, 200, 204; behavior, 20–21, 22, 29, 42, 48, 108, 206; communities, 13, 14, 38, 56n3, 92, 139; definition of, 17–19, 20; employers, 20, 55, 105, 125, 184, 197, 199; households, xxiii, 30, 43, 95, 125, 203; ideal, xviii, 18, 20, 92, 100, 105, 114, 185, 202; identification as, 20, 24, 26, 30, 43, 55–56, 90, 92, 101, 105, 109, 184, 188, 196
Shah, Alpa, 169
Shah, Saubhagya, 57n12, 110
shame, 21, 24, 40, 80, 84, 97, 100, 101, 113, 125, 127, 135, 155, 159, 173, 198
Shami, Seteney, 212n3
Sharifa, 104, 163, 174n4
Shryock, Andrew, 94
Silber, Ilana, 75
Simmel, Georg, 67, 75, 114
Singapore, xx, 87n9, 144
sisterhood, 15, 17, 49, 54, 83, 84, 110, 168, 169, 173, 204, 205, 209
skin color, 42, 43, 128, 137, 140, 142, 160
slavery, xv–xvi, 115n3; slaves, 14, 23, 26, 27, 38, 40, 41, 42, 61, 67, 72, 195
Smith, Adam, 176, 178
social parenting, 37, 38, 72
social security, 37; *Caisse Nationale de Securité Sociale* (CNSS), 187
Sonbol, Amira, 37
Sonencher, Michael, 184
Soraya, 52, 60, 81
Souhail, Abdelouahed, 177, 196
Soumiya, 103, 104–5, 180
South Africa, xx, 33, 115n9, 126, 179, 186, 187, 200n6

Spain, 62, 138, 186; Spanish buildings, 4–5, 8, 99; Spanish people, 5, 8–9, 11
Stark, Freya, 75
Steedman, Carolyn, 49, 176, 186, 190, 195
Stone, Linda, 208
Styles, John, 82
Suk, Jeannie, 189
Sukaina, 61, 143
Surtees, Robert Smith, 20, 123

Taiwan, xx, 144
Talib, Mohammad, 148n27
Tanzania, xxiv n8, 34, 200n6
theft, 51, 60, 78, 80, 81–82, 85, 115n5, 150
Thompson, Edward Palmer, 176
Todd, Selina, 48
Tönnies, Ferdinand, 200
Touria, 10, 14, 15, 48, 84, 112
trust, and domestic workers, 65, 85, 90, 94, 101, 114, 115, 132, 176, 203; and suitors, 137–38, 173
Tunisia, 37, 91, 134, 205
turnover, job, 24, 25, 53, 174, 194

Ueno, Kayoko, 87n9, 144
unemployment, 14, 146n5, 193
unions, 129, 194, 195. *See also* Filipino Migrant Workers in Morocco
United States, xx, 69, 83, 194

Van Dusen, Roxann, 166
Van Raaphorst, Donna, 194
village associations, 126, 193
visiting, xxii, 3, 15, 37, 40, 87n4, 92, 94, 125, 132, 159, 171, 175n9, 181, 205, 208; workers visiting former employers, 30, 32n20, 46, 79, 107, 124; workers visiting home, xxii, 11, 21, 112, 126, 137, 145, 147n21, 150, 156, 157, 161

wages, xv, xvi, 20, 25, 33, 40, 49, 61, 63, 70, 71, 76, 86, 107, 121, 122, 134–35, 155, 167, 169, 183, 184–85, 187, 191, 200n1; high, 55, 104, 157; low, xviii, xxii, 54, 61, 86, 104; minimum, xix, 62, 183, 190, 200n8. *See also* labor, wage; payment
Waltner, Ann, 57n10
Warda, 106–9
wealth, xv, 3, 7, 8, 20, 30, 31n9, 33, 37, 38, 39, 57n22, 58n28, 59, 60, 63, 66, 74, 75, 85, 88n13, 96, 105, 128, 133, 137, 141, 143, 164, 171, 187, 196, 197, 205, 206. *See also* households, wealthy
West, Candace, 209
Westermarck, Edward, 71
widows, 7, 34, 91, 122
World War I, 123, 159, 200n7

Yacoub El Mansour, 25, 31n6
Yanagisako, Sylvia, 115n8, 207
Yatim, Mohamed, 178
Yousra, 111, 154, 160

Zahra, 24, 25, 27, 28, 29, 49–50, 76, 125, 127, 133
zakāt (yearly tax), 63, 64, 88n13
Zambia, xxiv n8, 57n8
Zimmerman, Don H., 209
Zineb, xxiii, 65, 68–69, 80, 84–85, 92, 108, 130, 155, 156–57, 161, 163, 174n4
Zontini, Elisabetta, 156, 169
Zvan Elliott, Katja, 184, 192

MARY MONTGOMERY gained her doctorate in social anthropology from the University of Oxford in 2015. She went on to hold a fellowship at the London School of Economics before becoming a teacher of modern foreign languages.

CPSIA information can be obtained
at www.ICGtesting.com
Printed in the USA
BVHW040914170319
542890BV00021B/433/P

9 780253 041012